The Lutheran Confessions

The Lutheran Confessions

History and Theology of The Book of Concord

Charles P. Arand, James A. Nestingen, and Robert Kolb

Fortress Press

Minneapolis

THE LUTHERAN CONFESSIONS
History and Theology of The Book of Concord

Library of Congress Cataloging-in-Publication Data
Arand, Charles P.
The Lutheran Confessions : history and theology of The Book of Concord / Charles P. Arand, James A. Nestingen, and Robert Kolb.
        p. cm.
Includes bibliographical references and index.
ISBN 978-0-8006-2741-6 (alk. paper)
1. Konkordienbuch. 2. Lutheran Church—Creeds—History and criticism.
I. Nestingen, James Arne. II. Kolb, Robert, 1941- III. Title.
BX8068.A82 2012
238'.41—dc232011042067

The paper used in this publication meets the minimum requirements of American National Standard for Information Sciences—Permanence of Paper for Printed Library Materials, ANSI Z329.48-1984.
Manufactured in the U.S.A.

16 15 14 13 12   1 2 3 4 5 6 7 8 9 10

Contents

Preface

Twenty years ago Timothy J. Wengert, James A. Nestingen, and Robert Kolb embarked on what was planned as a three-volume project, embracing a new translation of the documents in the Book of Concord; a volume that provides texts of other documents from the sixteenth century that either served as sources for one or another of the Lutheran confessions or illuminate the context in which they arose; and a historical introduction to the development and content of these documents. Specific tasks were divided among the three and work began. The translation appeared in 2000,[1] *Sources and Contexts of the Lutheran Confessions* a year later,[2] but for a variety of reasons the third volume was delayed. In the process a third author, Charles P. Arand, came to aid the two of us who set out to compose the historical introduction at the beginning. The delay, we believe, will bring more of recent scholarship to the reader's attention.

The volume contains three essays on three sections of the Book of Concord—the ancient Creeds, the six treatises authored by Martin Luther and Philip Melanchthon that came to be regarded as confessional standards; and the Formula of Concord, the work of students of Luther and Melanchthon reflecting the development of Wittenberg thinking a generation later. These three sections each were composed by one of us, with input from the others. Readers will notice that the authors represent different points of view on certain issues of historical interpretation. We have attempted to reflect the ongoing debates within the scholarly community without confusing readers. We hope that this is a useful intellectual challenge, not a discouraging dissonance.

Our initial resolve not to let the historical background of the Formula of Concord remain so large in relationship to the contexts of the other confessional documents—a tendency in such historical introductions—fell by the wayside to a great extent. That is due in large part to our sense that contemporary students bring less knowledge of the context to that document than to the others.

The authors intend through these essays to provide students of the Lutheran confessional writings throughout the world with historical orientation for their own task of confessing Jesus Christ in the twenty-first century. This will not be the last word on any of the subjects treated. We do hope that it will encourage many readers to do as we have done—to experience the joy of delving into the life and death stories of the sixteenth-century confessors. They placed much, including their lives, on the line to bring the gospel of Jesus Christ to his church and their society. In this they provide a model for Christian life and witness in our time as well.

Abbreviations

Ap   Apology of the Augsburg Confession
[+ *following the number designates readings from the second, octavo, edition, found in BC*]

ARG   *Archiv für Reformationsgeschichte*

BC   *The Book of Concord*, ed. Robert Kolb and Timothy J. Wengert, Minneapolis, Fortress, 2000.

BSLK   *Die Bekenntnisschriften der evangelisch-lutherischen Kirche.* Göttingen: Vandenhoeck & Ruprecht, 1930, 1991.

CCath   Corpus Catholicorum

CR   Corpus Reformatorum. Vols. 1–28: Ph. Melanthonis opera, C. G. Bretschneider and H. E. Bindseil, eds. Halle/Braunschweig: Schwetschke, 1834–1860. Vols. 29-87. Ioannis Calvini opera, eds. Wilhelm Baum et al., Braunschweig: Schwetschke, 1863-1880. Vols. 88–101. Huldreich Zwinglis Sämtliche Werke. Leipzig: Heinsius, 1908–1959.

Ep   Epitome of the Formula of Concord

FC   Formula of Concord

LC   Large Catechism

LQ   *Lutheran Quarterly*

LuJ   Lutherjahrbuch

LW   Luther's Works, American Edition. Saint Louis: Concordia, and Philadelphia: Fortress Press, 1955–1986.

MBW   *Melanchthons Briefwechsel,* ed. Heinz Scheible (Stuttgart-Bad Cannstatt: Fromann-Holzbog, 1977–); R = *Register* volumes

MSG   Jacques Paul Migne, *Patrologiae cursus completes…scriptorium… Graecorum…* Paris, 1857–1866.

SA   Smalcald Articles

SC   Small Catechism

SD   Solid Declaration of the Formula of Concord

SCJ   *The Sixteenth Century Journal*

StA   *Melanchthons Werke in Auswahl* (Studien Ausgabe) 7 vols., ed. Robert Stupperich et al. Gütersloh: Bertelsmann, 1951–1975.

TPPP   Treatise on the Power and Primacy of the Pope

TRE   *Theologische Realenzyklopädie*. Gerhard Krause and Gerhard Müller, eds., Berlin: de Gruyter, 1977–2005.

WA   D. Martin Luthers Werke. Kritische Gesamtausgabe. 61 vols. Weimar: Böhlau, 1883–1993.

WABr   D. Martin Luthers Werke. Briefwechsel. 18 Vols. Weimar: Böhlau, 1930–.

WADB   D. Martin Luthers Werke. Deutsche Bible. 12 Vols. Weimar: Böhlau, 1906–1961.

WATr   D. Martin Luthers Werke. Tischreden. 6 Vols. Weimar: Böhlau, 1912–1921.

ZKG   *Zeitschrift für Kirchengeschichte*

Series Abbreviations

AGTL   Arbeiten zur Geschichte und Theologie des Luthertums

AKThG   Arbeiten zur Kirchen- und Theologiegeschichte

APTh   Arbeiten zur Pastoraltheologie

BHTh   Beträge zur historischen Theologie

BLUWiG   Beiträge zur Leipziger Universitäts- und Wissenschaftsgeschichte

FKDG   Forschungen zur Kirchen- und Dogmengeschichte

FSÖTh   Forschungen zur systematischen und ökumenischen Theologie

LStRLO   Leucorea Studien zur Reformation und Lutherischen Orthodoxie

MSSB   Melanchthon-Schriften der Stadt Bretten

QFRG   Quellen und Forschungen zur Reformationsgeschichte

RST   Reformationsgeschichtliche Studien und Texte

SHCT   Studies in the History of Christian Thought

SMHR   Spätmittelalter, Humanismus, Reformation

SuRNR   Spätmittelalter und Reformation Neue Reihe

SVRG   Schriften des Vereins für Reformationgeschichte

VIEG   Veröffentlichungen des Instituts für Europäische Geschichte

Introduction
The Book of Concord, a Confessing of the Faith

This volume describes a phenomenon more peculiar than most readers will initially recognize. That phenomenon is the public confession of what a person believes to be the truth, the fundamental description of reality. The universal experience of placing humanity within the larger scheme of things—we call it "religion"—usually attempts in various ways to express a sense of awe and reverence before some Ultimate and Absolute, variously defined by human devices. Such expressions bind life together for adherents of each system. Many base their religion on some other element of what Christians often call a "belief system," and therefore they do not regard public confession of what they believe important. Unlike most, Lutherans are among those who define their way of life through the public confession of their faith in Jesus Christ.

Historians of religion suggest that all systems for describing ultimate reality and directing human beings to live successfully within that reality share basic elements. Ninian Smart has listed six: (1) doctrine or teaching, (2) narrative, (3) ritual, (4) ethics, (5) community, and (6) the personal faith or sense of awe and reverence that binds the first five together.[1] While every ideological system has some form of each, each religion combines them in different ways, choosing to orient the entire procedure for describing reality from specific starting points. All Christians practice their faith embracing all six elements, but different Christian traditions give different elements differing values and places in their entire practice of the faith. The central point for the orientation of life and for defining the nature and purpose of the church—the form that exercises organizing authority over the other elements—differs from group to group.

Liturgical ritual determines the shape of piety for Eastern Orthodox believers. And for Anglicans *The Book of Common Prayer* has formed the life of the church most decisively. Both the Orthodox and the Anglican faithful also count on their bishops to hold the church together. Roman Catholics are also united by common liturgy and doctrine, to be sure, but the polity based on the bishop of Rome's vicariate, governing the church militant in Christ's stead, is the factor upon which being truly Christ's church stands or falls. Among other English Protestants, forms of community also played a significant role, as churches claimed to be Presbyterian or Congregational in contrast to the Anglican establishment's "episcopal" form.

1

Baptists highlight their identity through one specific doctrine and related practices. Reformed and Lutheran believers have defined themselves by a broader focus on Christian teaching and interpretation of the biblical narrative. In the century following 1530, they composed documents they labeled "confessions of the faith" to do so.

In 1530 Emperor Charles V demanded an explanation of their religious policies from the governments of German principalities and towns that were introducing reforms proposed by Martin Luther and his Wittenberg colleagues. Charles wanted to know why their dissent from the Roman obedience was not illegal. Philip Melanchthon led the theologians on the diplomatic team put together by these Evangelical[2] rulers. Because the Wittenberg theologians regarded God as a God of conversation and community, Melanchthon insisted that Holy Scripture alone, as God's Word in authoritative form, served as the ultimate authority for the life of the church, the ultimate definer of its teaching, which was central for that life. But he also recognized that the church had always had secondary authorities to guide and mediate the delivery of the biblical message to the people of God. By the end of the second century, theologians spoke of a rule of faith (*analogia fidei*) that summarized biblical teaching. The writings of the ancient Fathers and decisions of councils and bishops had served as such authorities throughout the Middle Ages.

After 1530 Lutherans gradually came to accept the Augsburg Confession as an interpretation of the ancient creeds, along with several other documents regarded as "repetitions of the Augsburg Confession," finally gathered into the Book of Concord in 1580, as their secondary authorities. From the mid-seventeenth century on, Lutherans have called these confessional documents *norma normata* ("a normed norm," a standard set by something else, in this case by Scripture, the *norma normans*, or "norming norm"). At Augsburg Melanchthon and his colleagues established the nature of the Lutheran church as a church that defines itself by its ability to convey God's Word to the world in its confession of faith. This took place as Melanchthon explained to the emperor and the assembled representatives of the German empire what Luther's reform meant for the church. He entitled his explanation a "confession."

If the question, "What does it mean to be a Lutheran?" were posed, most people would probably answer with some mention of Martin Luther, the sixteenth-century reformer whose message spread across Germany and beyond with lightning speed in 1517–1518 and the subsequent years. Somewhat by accident he encountered the invention of Johannes Gutenberg—more than a half-century old at that point but with its potential still unrealized. The ability to print with moveable type contributed mightily to the spread of the Wittenberg call for reform. Indeed, this medium shaped in part the way in which Luther and his colleagues formulated and conveyed their message, the way in which they put their thinking to work.

As important as Luther was and remains for Lutheran identity, however, Lutheran churches have formally defined themselves through documents they label "confessions of faith." Some of these churches—in the Czech Republic, Poland,

and Slovakia, for example—even call themselves "the Evangelical Church of the Augsburg Confession," the key statement that has defined Lutheran belief, teaching, and confessing for almost five hundred years.

Melanchthon went to the imperial diet that the emperor, Charles V, had summoned to Augsburg in the spring of 1530 in order to serve his princes and other governments that were introducing reform in the Wittenberg manner.[3] Melanchthon expected that the explanation would be delivered orally by Christian Beyer, the vice-chancellor of the government of electoral Saxony, the leader of the Evangelical princes and municipalities. But Melanchthon did not entitle the speech he was composing for Beyer an "Explanation." In fact, he originally proposed to describe it as an "apology," that is, a "defense."[4] Melanchthon eventually realized that propaganda from the Roman Catholic side changed the situation in which he was writing. Johann Eck, professor in Ingolstadt and perhaps the leading theological opponent of Luther and his colleagues, attempted to demonstrate that the Wittenberg theologians were heretics and therefore had to be excluded from the Christian church and eliminated from Christian society. He did so by publishing a challenge to the Lutherans to enter into a formal disputation that he entitled *Four Hundred Four Articles*—short thetic statements combining quotations from the Wittenberg theologians that fairly presented their views, with inaccurate quotations or quotations out of context attributed to them and with citations of others with whom Luther and Melanchthon disagreed: "Sacramentarians," "Anabaptists," and other such groups.[5] This jumble of truth and falsehood portrayed the Wittenberg Reformation in the worst possible light. Its accusations had to be met. More was needed than a defense of Lutheran reforms. Melanchthon needed to show that Wittenberg teaching was anchored in Scripture and repeated the teaching of the catholic tradition since the time of the ancient church. Melanchthon reshaped his text for Beyer and retitled it "Confession."

Never before in the church's history had this term, as a noun, been used to designate a summary of the church's teaching. The Latin of the Middle Ages designated as *confessores* the monks and priests who heard confession in the sacrament of penance and used the words *confessio* and *confiteri* for the confession of sins or confessions of praise. The recital of the creed could constitute an act of confessing, as could dying for the faith.[6] But before 1530 the noun "confession" had not served as the technical term for or title of an official statement defining the church or its public teaching and practice. Heinrich Denzinger's collection of such official statements of Christian belief shows that the most frequently used labels for such statements were *symbola, canones, decreta,* and *constitutiones*. Popes often issued their formal pronouncements as *epistolae*. However, Denzinger and the editors who have continued his project have reflected the usage that stems from Melanchthon's choice of titles in 1530 and call such documents "confessions of faith," in German, *Glaubensbekenntnisse*.[7] The same usage is not reflected in the English-language equivalent of Denzinger.[8]

That is not to say that the concept of "confessing the faith" had not designated what bishops and councils did in issuing public statements of official teaching. The words for "believe"—*credo/credimus/πιστεύω*—were more frequently employed, but the Iberian regional synods of Toledo in 676 and 693 began their statements of doctrine with the phrase *confitemur et credimus* (or *credimus et confitemur*), equating believing with confessing (and thus implicitly "creed" with "confession").[9] Pope Leo II's epistle confirming decisions of Third Council of Constantinople (681) had affirmed its doctrines with the phrase "[this synod]...confessed in complete agreement with us."[10] This verb "confess," or its synonym "profess," occurs very occasionally in subsequent centuries in similar statements of public teaching.[11] So *confiteri* did serve as a word to describe the action involved in an official dogmatic decree but not as its title or formal designation. Melanchthon's way or habit of thinking of God and human creatures—in terms of what God has said to his people and the ways in which they respond in the conversation he has initiated—led him to fashion a new Christian literary genre, a new label for the definition of public teaching and therefore of the church itself.[12]

According to Peter Fraenkel, Melanchthon employed words such as *doctrina*, *traditio*, and *ministerium* as verbal nouns, nouns that have substance in their content but cannot exist without being put into action. *Confessio* reflected this principle. Melanchthon believed that the content of what he wrote in his Augsburg Confession was of vital, life-giving importance because it was God's tool for forgiving sins and restoring sinners to their humanity as children of God. But he also believed that this content demanded the act of confessing it in public.[13] Its content has a verbal impulse that explodes rather than lets itself be shut up on a page. That view of language came naturally to Luther with his background in Ockhamistic thinking. That view of printed texts came naturally to Melanchthon, whose use of the printed page often reflected the rules for oral communication that he wrote into the textbooks he composed on dialectic and rhetoric.[14]

The Augsburg "Confession" followed by one year a similar act of publicly stating beliefs by the Evangelical princes and municipalities. They had defended their reforms at the time at the diet conducted in Speyer and had labeled it a *protestatio*.[15] *Protestare* served as legal terminology for the act of stating one's position formally and publicly, not so much a protest but rather a testimony or public affirmation of belief or action, an explanation or rationale for a decision or course of action.[16] At Augsburg these public officials were to justify their policy that had already earned imperial condemnation.

Vice-chancellor Beyer read the text of the confession that Melanchthon had prepared in German to the assembled princes and municipal representatives, along with the emperor, who then received it in both Latin and German. Charles V had prohibited all Evangelical preaching in the city during the diet, but Luther thought that Beyer had more than made up for that: "our confession and defense were presented in most glorious fashion.... For the Word of God was placed in evidence against the opinions of emperor, pope, and the Epicureans. They wanted to smother it, but it arose and strode forth."[17] But Melanchthon's words resounded well beyond Augsburg's streets and markets. According to Luther,

> the effectiveness and power of God's Word is such that the more it is perse-
> cuted, the more it flourishes and grows. Just think of the diet of Augsburg,
> where truly the last trumpet before the Last Day was sounded. How the
> whole world was raging against the Word. We had to pray that Christ himself
> in heaven would be safe from the papists. But our teaching and our faith went
> out into the light through confession, so that in a very brief time by imperial
> mandate it was sent to all kings and princes. There were many minds of lead-
> ing men in these courts whom this teaching took captive, like a spark and
> then a roaring fire. Our confession and defense was brought before the world
> in a wondrous fashion while their confutation wasted away in the darkness.[18]

(He probably was referring to the fact that the emperor refused permission to publish the confutation of the Augsburg Confession or to share a manuscript copy with
the Evangelicals, whereas the Augsburg Confession appeared the next year in print.)
Without specific mention of the Confession itself, Luther reminded the Wittenberg
congregation in 1531 that God had triumphed through the Lutherans' weakness at
Augsburg.[19] Indeed, Luther's friend Georg Spalatin called the Augsburg Confession
"the most significant event that has ever taken place on earth,"[20] an opinion voiced
by several of Luther's and Melanchthon's students.[21]

After Augsburg in 1530 Anglicans and Reformed believers joined Lutherans
in defining the church by confessional document.[22] Within days of the presentation of Melanchthon's work, four cities in south Germany had presented their own
"confession" to the emperor, the *Confessio Tetrapolitana*.[23] Within a few years others working for the reform of the church had produced confessions, for example,
that of the city of Basel in 1534 and that of a group of Swiss churches, the "First
Helvetic Confession" of 1536, composed to present the teaching of these churches at
the papally called council.[24] By the twentieth century, a modern representative of the
Anabaptist movement changed the title of the "Schleitheim Articles" of 1528, one
of the earliest statements of Anabaptist belief, into the "Schleitheim Confession."[25]
In the wake of the recognition of adherence to the Augsburg Confession as a legal,
if inferior, political status in the Religious Peace of Augsburg in 1555, the German
term for the distinct churches became *Konfessionen* within the German empire in
the nineteenth century. Even Roman Catholics designated the papal church as a
Konfession, although documents bearing the title *Confessio* never came to replace
"canons" and "decrees" in defining the Roman church, its teaching, and its practice.[26]

The earliest reports on the diet in Augsburg from Lutheran pens regarded the
"Augsburg Confession" as the entire effort of presenting their understanding of the
faith, an activity that extended over the several months during which Melanchthon

and others were working on the text and explaining their confession to Roman Catholic theologians and secular counselors in extended negotiations. Then they came to speak of this "confession" as specifically the act of reading the document as the public confession of seven princes and two city councils before the assembled diet. Finally, gradually, in the 1540s and certainly by the second half of the sixteenth century, the term "Augsburg Confession" began to refer primarily and then exclusively to the document itself.[27]

The Wittenberg team could not have known how issuing a public confession to define the church would make its stamp on the life of their churches. For within a decade the document assumed the function that bishops and councils had performed as the agency by which ecclesiastical teaching and life were formulated and evaluated. Melanchthon and his colleagues at Augsburg intended simply to defend, explain, and justify Lutheran teaching in the Confession's first twenty-one articles and its plans for church life in its last seven. His test for proper practice arose from Scripture and from proper pastoral care.

Within the following decade the Augsburg Confession became recognized as a secondary authority, a "Binding Summary, Basis, Rule, and Guiding Principle," and an explanation of "how all teaching is to be judged in accord with God's Word and how the errors that have arisen are to be explained and decided in Christian fashion" (to use the description of the authors of the Formula of Concord for the function of that document in 1577).[28] One proof for that is that the document's text was not regarded as definitive text, a completed project, but rather as a working manuscript that could be altered to further the purpose for which it was written, justifying the existence of the Lutheran churches in the empire. When his prince, Elector Johann Friedrich the Elder, asked Melanchthon to reshape the text for further negotiation with Roman Catholics as the emperor called for a religious colloquy at the end of the 1530s, Melanchthon presumed that the Confession, as a policy statement of the princes and not his own work, could be changed to serve the purposes for which it was written at the behest of those princes and city council members who had risked their lives in 1530 by claiming the Confession as their own.

The later attempt of Calvinists to use the "Variata" of the Confession for their own political purposes lay beyond the imagination of anyone in the Wittenberg circle in 1540.[29] Melanchthon's right and obligation to revise the text were taken for granted, for the confession belonged neither to him nor to anyone else apart from the princes and municipal governments, those responsible for placing it in the legal record of the imperial diet. They wanted an improved "mission statement" with which to confess the faith in the dialogue with the Roman Catholics. Luther and the others in the Wittenberg circle used the revised text: one always uses the "improved"— the revised—text of a document. In the 1530s the "Augsburg Confession" was still regarded not only as a document but as an ongoing process. Circumstances and exigencies were different by the 1560s, when the debate over the proper text of the Augsburg Confession was sparked by Calvinist appeal to the text of the Variata.

Indeed, the Confession took on other purposes during the late 1530s and 1540s as well. Pastors and princes alike needed a common synopsis of how they were to teach and administer the church. They needed a clear, uniform, and simple standard for the formulation of public teaching, a summary of biblical content that provided a binding rule and norm for defining what the church was about. The Augsburg Confession quickly became that public definition chosen by most German territorial churches, as well as a *symbolon*, that is, a "mission statement," for the church and a public confession of what was to be proclaimed. Irenaeus had applied the term "the rule of faith" to such a standard, using a secondary authority to encapsulate the essence of Scripture for guiding the public proclamation of the gospel. In the early 1530s the Wittenberg theologians began calling such an *analogia fidei* a "body of doctrine" (*corpus doctrinae*). The Augsburg Confession and then its Apology and other documents, such as Luther's Smalcald Articles, began serving as the embodiment of this body of biblical teaching within the following decades in at least some Lutheran lands.[30]

The Religious Peace of Augsburg of 1555 extended the function of the Augsburg Confession.[31] It became a defining element of imperial law, a vital part of the constitution of the Holy Roman Empire of the German Nation. It became the public—governmental—standard for assessing the qualifications for ministry and public office, an official tool for the evaluation of what was being taught and confessed in the church.

The Augsburg Confession is a brief document. As new situations arose, the Confession required commentary, or as those who wrote such commentaries said later in the sixteenth century, "repetitions." The first of these commentaries came from the author's own pen in 1531, in Melanchthon's *Apology*[32]; the second in 1550 with the *Magdeburg Confession*; then with several more such "repetitions" in various parts of the empire and beyond in the subsequent two decades[33]; and finally—and once again officially for many Lutheran churches—in 1577 with the Formula of Concord.[34] By that time a number of churches had also accepted the Smalcald Articles along with the *Treatise on the Power and Primacy of the Pope* and Luther's catechisms, as similar standards for public teaching. They were being bound together in documents often labeled *corpora doctrinae*, as the overarching definition of the church in specific lands and of the adherents of the Augsburg Confession throughout the entire German Empire and beyond.

Not all followers of Luther have accepted the gathering of all these documents—the Book of Concord—as their definition of the church's teaching. Some, such as the churches in the kingdom of Denmark at that time (Denmark, Norway, Iceland) have used only the Augsburg Confession itself and Luther's Small Catechism. But however they have related to the documents gathered in the Book of Concord, Lutherans have continued to confess their faith. They have taken the confessional documents of the ancient church and the sixteenth century as hermeneutical keys to their formulation of God's Word for their own times and places. They have striven to deliver the content of Scripture as they have heard it passed on to them in the Lutheran Confessions to their own contemporaries. They have recognized that they are part of a community that has its origins in the Holy Spirit's guidance of the church over two millennia, with special foundations laid by the Spirit's leading the church to the gospel of Jesus Christ through Luther's proclamation. They have sensed that they are part of an ecclesiastical culture with roots and memories that help define and determine how they announce the salvation won by Christ's death and resurrection in new and fresh ways to meet the needs of the people God has called them to serve.

However, nowhere in the world are Lutherans experiencing "business as usual" at the beginning of a new century and a new millennium. The Lutheran confession of faith has lost numerical strength in the homelands of the Lutheran churches in central and northern Europe, in Germany and the Nordic lands. The often persecuted minority Lutheran churches in other parts of Europe, decimated by brutal oppression in the era of the Counter-Reformation, are rebuilding after the most recent dark night of persecution under National Socialist and Communist regimes in the twentieth century. Immigrants from Europe built strong churches in the Americas, Australia, and South Africa, and these churches continue to struggle with their own identity in cultures where Lutherans have often been allied with the "Christian" establishment in the past but never in charge of it. Mission churches, mostly in the Global South or Majority World, are in many respects the most dynamic among the Lutheran communities of the twenty-first century. They, too, however, struggle with questions relating to the proper use of the Lutheran confession of the faith in their situations. In these situations God calls Lutherans to repeat the special insights of the Augsburg Confession for the benefit of the whole church in our day.

Therefore, the question of how these confessions can still benefit the church looms ever larger for Lutherans in every part of the world today. It is a question with implications not only for Lutheran churches but for all other churches that might benefit from the ecumenical witness of Lutherans. The remnants of establishment and its supports are all but gone where they did exist. In the marketplace of religious ideas, Lutheran confessing of the faith is being challenged to express its message afresh and anew. This cannot be done apart from a firm sense of why Lutherans have been Lutherans, apart from the cultural heritage of the Europe of another time. And yet Lutherans cannot determine who they are to be in the twenty-first century as children of God apart from the memory of who they have been in the past. Such witness is our obligation and calling as those to whom God has given responsibility for sharing our heritage and its treasures with the whole household of faith. The memory bank of the Augsburg Confession and the documents designed to echo and reiterate its message gathered into the Book of Concord guide our understanding of the entire framework of biblical teaching as we are called to deliver it to the twenty-first-century world.

Confessing in the Wittenberg manner, following the example of those who composed the documents found in the Book of Concord, means (1) confessing the evangel of Jesus Christ at the center of proclamation and theological reflection, and doing so with (2) eschatological sensitivity, (3) ecumenical commitment, (4) evangelistic passion, and (5) the desire to edify God's people for the comfort of their consciences and for the further confession of their faith in word and deed.

1. One demonstration of the fact that the restoration of human righteousness in God's sight formed the center and governing principle of Melanchthon's confessions lies in two formal "paraphrases" of the Augsburg Confession, which Melanchthon wrote within the next six years. He composed them for the use of the German Evangelical princes in their diplomatic approaches to monarchs outside the German empire. They called upon Melanchthon to formulate a negotiating document that presented their confession of the faith in two critical instances. His proposal for reform in France for King Francis I, the *Consilium ad Gallos* of 1534, and a document of the same sort prepared for King Henry VIII of England, the "Wittenberg Articles" of 1536, did not insist on all the practical reform measures that the Wittenberg reformers had demanded for their own churches. Nonetheless, on the subject of justification by faith in Christ, Melanchthon found little room for maneuvering. That teaching constituted the foundation of his proposals for reform.[35]

A reading of the text confirms this. Although Wilhelm Maurer, focusing on the practical politics surrounding the Confession, argues that its organizing principle lies in its policy toward the medieval episcopal system, Timothy Wengert is correct in saying that Melanchthon regarded articles I through XXI as the heart and heartbeat of the document.[36] At the heart of those articles, quite clearly, is Melanchthon's understanding of the restoration of human righteousness through God's act of justification, accomplished through Christ's death and resurrection and through the Holy Spirit's creation of faith in Christ through the means of grace. The Lutheran Confessions promote the desire to foster the life of repentance that leads to the forgiveness of sins, salvation, and genuine human life—as a result of our trust in God's restoration of our righteousness through Christ—to the practice of righteous living in relationship to God's creation. The Book of Concord calls for the confession of the faith that changes our orientation to God's reality completely by placing him at its center. With that change of orientation for life, all aspects of life become different. We trust that we are God's children and live like it.

2. This means that we recognize that the task of confessing the faith is fundamentally eschatological. Believers always are conscious that their witness of Christ's love to other believers and those outside the faith takes place in presence of and though the power of the Holy Spirit. Thus, they confront God directly in the consciousness of their own limits and their own end, of God's ultimate and unconditional concern for them and his desire that they be his own and live under his rule.

They recognize the eschatological nature of their confession also because they realize that the struggle between God's truth and Satan's lie continues to the end of time (John 8:44). It never ends because new forms of the lie always are arising to challenge God's truth. The confessional documents continually sharpen the sword of the Spirit (Eph. 6:17) for combat with those lies. Luther repeatedly made it clear—for instance, in *On the Councils and the Church*—that God's people stand under attack from false alternatives to the gospel of Christ at every turn.[37] The Holy Spirit combats Satan's scams and schemes through the various forms of God's Word, which he uses as his sword. The Augsburg Confession made its positions clear and its place in the tradition of the church unambiguous by condemning ancient diversions from biblical truth. Other confessions followed this practice.

3. The confessors of the sixteenth century confessed for the sake of other believers. Melanchthon's task at Augsburg concentrated his attention on the ecumenical audience. He entered into intense, open, honest negotiations and exchange of insights with Roman Catholic theologians there. That remains the task of his heirs to this day, as they listen to fellow believers of other traditions with gentleness and respect and as they confess with clarity and boldness. Melanchthon recognized that the true unity of the church is found in proper and faithful use of God's Word, as conveyed to his people in oral, written, and sacramental forms. That means that we confess with ecumenical honesty: what Dominican theologian Richard Schenk called an ecumenical strategy with "a dual programmatic of affirmation and admonition."[38] For such conversations within Christendom seek above all clear confession of the faith and effective pastoral care, and only then organizational benefits.

4. Luther and Melanchthon, and their students as well, seldom met an unbaptized person. They had little opportunity for witnessing to their faith to those outside that faith, though the Wittenberg colleagues and at least some of their students exhibited the realization that this was indeed part of God's assignment in this world when it is possible.[39] In addition, they did recognize the challenge of bringing baptized people who were living apart from Christ to repentance. God's assignment in the twenty-first century to Lutherans in every corner of the globe involves drawing into the faith those who do not know the only name given among his human creatures by which sinners may be restored to the fullness of their humanity (Acts 4:12). For Luther's and Melanchthon's heirs cannot avoid the conviction that, re-created in the image of God, all the baptized are reborn to speak of the wonders of their Savior's love for all.

5. Although it was secondary in Melanchthon's task in 1530, edification of those who are making the confession of faith also flows from the act of confessing the faith and from our use of the documents we regard as our symbols and public declarations of what we teach and believe. Especially Luther's catechisms serve as instruments for the church's confession of the faith to itself and to its own. Like those outside the faith, those who trust in Jesus Christ as their Lord and Savior

daily need the call to repentance and the bestowal of the forgiveness of sins that arise out of the confession of the tradition and teaching of those who have gone before. In the Small Catechism, Luther confessed his faith before the children of German-speaking lands and continues to do so around the world today. In the Large Catechism, he issued his confession for those who teach the infants of God's family. In all confessional documents, the church finds texts that serve to build up the faith and life of God's chosen people as they provide a basis for access to Scripture and to the faith as it has been delivered to the saints. Although not primarily intended as textbooks for pastoral care or preaching, these documents reflect the spirit of the Wittenberg theologians as they guide those responsible for conveying the faith—parents, pastors, teachers, Christian friends—in the tasks involved in echoing God's saving Word and his plan for human living.[40]

Lutherans live now on every continent in a wide variety of situations. In the twenty-first century, the Lutheran Confessions do not have the strength of governmental reinforcement behind them, and no Lutheran church uses them to serve as a legal instrument for supporting the public definition of reality in their societies. Now more than ever, the confessional documents still have important functions in our world, as they define what Lutherans mean when they speak of Christ's church and its teaching, as they form the framework and foundation for confessing the Christian faith in the twenty-first century.

This volume intends to be an aid in jogging and vivifying the memory of the documents' origins and original purposes and goals. It follows in the tracks of a long train of historical interpretations of the situations from which the texts of these confessional documents arose and the meaning of the texts themselves. That tradition of historical interpretation goes back to the sixteenth century and debates over the Unaltered and Altered Augsburg Confession. Calvinist interpretations of the Augsburg Confession, its origins and its significance, had to be met by Lutheran critique.[41] In the seventeenth century, Lutheran students of theology used the confessional texts in their instruction.[42] The grand tradition of German theological scholarship produced the extensive and authoritative commentary on the Formula of Concord by Erlangen professor Fr. H. R. Frank.[43] In the United States the studies of Henry Eyster Jacobs,[44] James W. Richards,[45] Theodore E. Schmauk and C. T. Benze,[46] George Fritschl,[47] J. L. Neve,[48] and Friedrich Bente[49] accompanied students through much of the twentieth century. Eric Gritsch and Robert Jenson wrote a similar historical introduction.[50] Edmund Schlink's topical survey of the theology of the Lutheran confessional writings remains useful.[51] A twenty-first-century version of his work remains a desideratum. Most recently, Gunther Gassmann and Scott Hendrix have authored a basic introduction to the Lutheran Confessions,[52] and Gunther Wenz has synthesized current scholarship on these documents in thorough detail.[53]

In this same tradition of scholarship, this volume is intended to serve an international readership, putting the newer research of the past third of a century at the disposal of English-language readers. Luther's view of history demands that the church's testimony to Jesus Christ be understood in its historical context, for he believed that God works within the ever-changing human scene as he delivers his unchanging Word that conveys and effects his judging and saving will. This volume offers its readers, students of Scripture in general and of the Lutheran tradition in particular, the historical raw materials with which to glean from the past insights for the twenty-first century.

Part I
The Ecumenical Creeds

1

A History of the Ancient Creedal Texts

Apostles, Nicene, and Athanasian

Once taken for granted in a world that was largely Christian, the so-called ecumenical Creeds—the Apostles, Nicene, and Athanasian—today find themselves pushed increasingly into the foreground of a postmodern world for at least two reasons. First, they have become increasingly important because of the need to define the boundaries of historical Christianity in the face of numerous attempts to redefine Christianity in the light of ancient Gnosticism and revisionist versions of Christianity. However some may wish to revise the picture of early Christianity, the creeds define historically the faith as Christians have confessed it from its earliest centuries on. They embody the constituent components of the church's confession of Christ. Second, in a world of thirty thousand Christian denominations, the creeds set forth what all Christians have held in common throughout history. While each denomination or church body arose in a particular era and thus was shaped by it, they all arose out of a common history in the early church and lay claim to it.[1] In a pluralistic age, it has become increasingly important to stress what it means to be Christian as well as Lutheran. The ecumenical creeds fit the bill well.

The Lutheran church places the three ecumenical creeds first in its collection of confessional statements. Historically, the Apostles and Athanasian Creeds belong properly to the church's tradition in the West. Of the three, the Nicene Creed is the truly ecumenical creed acknowledged by the Eastern and Western church alike. But in the sixteenth century, all three were considered ecumenical in the West. The Lutheran Confessions themselves demonstrate that they give more than lip service to them. From the outset, in Article I, the Augsburg Confession grounds its confession of catholicity in its adherence to the faith of Nicaea. The Creeds also shape the contours of the faith set forth in the Lutheran Confessions. Augsburg Confession Article III uses the wording of the Apostles Creed, from which it draws out the soteriological implications for believers. Likewise, in part 1 of the Smalcald articles, Luther also draws on the Apostles Creed. Both of his catechisms expound this Creed. The first article of the Formula of Concord—on original sin—uses it as the rule by which it rejects Flacius' conclusions. The confessions also draw on language of the Athanasian Creed when speaking of the Trinity in Augsburg Confession Article I and Smalcald Articles, part I. Finally, the "Binding Summary" of the Formula points to the creeds as the pattern that they themselves wish to emulate when resolving the controversies of their own day.

15

Lutherans employ both a historical and a canonical interpretation of the Creeds.[2] They need to be read as documents that stand on their own within a particular historical context. Thus, for example, when considering the Nicene Creed attention must be given to the ecumenical councils in which the Christology of Nicaea was expounded and expanded. These councils provide something of the church's interpretation of the Nicene Creed and show its theological trajectory. At the same time, as documents that are gathered into a collection of other confessional writings such as the Book of Concord, they are seen to stand alongside and cohere with the church's subsequent theological confessions.

The Wittenberg Reformers found in the creedal tradition of the Western medieval church a foundational form for the confession of the message of Scripture. In their formal identification of who and what they understood their churches to be, the princes who sponsored the publication of the Book of Concord wished only to repeat and apply to their own time the teaching of Scripture as "briefly summarized in the time-honored ancient Symbols; teaching that was recognized as that ancient, united consensus believed in by the universal, orthodox churches of Christ and fought for and reaffirmed against many heresies and errors."[3] Their theologians affirmed as they set forth their "binding summary, basis, rule and guiding principle" for judging all teaching according to God's Word that their confession in the Formula of Concord only repeated "the true Christian teaching as it was correctly and soundly understood [and] summarized on the basis of God's Word in short articles or chief parts" formulated in the Apostles, Nicene and Athanasian, "the three ecumenical creeds."[4] Indeed, the authors of the Formula were only following the example of Philip Melanchthon, who had based the Augsburg Confession upon the Nicene faith[5] and placed lectures on the Nicene Creed into the Wittenberg curriculum in 1545/1546.[6] When Caspar Cruciger died while lecturing on the Creed, Melanchthon assumed the task. His lectures on the second and third articles, published a quarter century later, in 1574, began with the topic *De gratia et de iustificatione* (on "who for us human creatures and for our salvation descended from heaven"). In addition to the wide-ranging comments on faith and the good works that flow from it, Melanchthon treated the church and the sacraments in detail under the third article of the Creed.[7] The Creed provided him with a firm basis for the exposition of the heart of biblical teaching.

Luther offered commentary on the Apostles Creed in his catechisms and also in his treatise of 1538 on the Apostles and Athanasian Creeds and the *Te Deum Laudamus*, apparently assuming the Nicene Creed, which is printed at the end of the treatise, as the basis for the others.[8] Those who composed catechisms or catechetical sermons followed in his path, with often extensive proclamation of the creedal faith.[9] Two Wittenberg disciples composed devotional treatises on the Creed or parts of it.[10] Two of their fellow students issued series of sermons specifically on the Creed.[11] Amidst the sacramental and Christological controversies of the 1570s, Nikolaus Selnecker found the texts of all three ecumenical creeds as a suitable basis for a cultivation of careful consideration of the points under dispute. This effort grew out of his instruction of young people in Luther's catechism, he told his readers.[12] A decade later Johann Freder, rector of the University of Rostock and a student of David Chytraeus, used Chytraeus's lectures to defend the Christology of the Formula of Concord in the form of an exposition of the second article of the Apostles Creed.[13] The ancient creeds were thus deeply embedded in the thinking of Luther, Melanchthon, and all who taught and confessed the ancient, biblical Christian faith in their train.

The three creeds reflect very different historical developments that coincide with their respective purposes. The Apostles Creed developed as a baptismal creed for teaching the faith to catechumens and for liturgical use in the baptismal rite. The Nicene Creed represents a conciliar creed (though based on a baptismal creed and subsequently used as one). It was formulated in order to define the faith over and against the Arian heresy. The Athanasian Creed's history is shrouded in more mystery but appears to have served primarily as a summary of the faith for teaching purposes.

[Handwritten margin note, left: "proceeding from a Council"]

[Handwritten margin note, right: "Arian – look up John 14:28"]

The Apostles Creed

To this day the Apostles Creed remains the baptismal and catechetical creed used in most Lutheran congregations, in large part due to the continued use and importance of Luther's Small Catechism.[14] It is thus one of the first pieces of Christian literature that a child or newly converted adult learns. Apart from the Lord's Prayer, there is perhaps no set of words that the church uses more frequently. For most Lutheran churches it is also used on a regular basis in non-communion services and in catechetical services. As such, it provides perhaps one of the most important summaries of the faith for many Christians.

The Apostles Creed is at one and the same time the church's oldest creed and newest creed.[15] What we today refer to as the Apostles Creed was formulated over a period of five centuries (between the third and eighth centuries). We can point to a definitive and relatively fixed text only from the ninth century to the present. Its history can be divided roughly into two periods. The first involves the formulation of early forms of the Apostles Creed that are represented by the baptismal creed of the Roman church (referred to as the Old Roman Creed) and its variants that appear from the third to the eighth centuries. The second period of its history extends from the ninth century forward, a time when scholars can speak of a definitive and fixed text of this Creed (scholars usually refer to this as the *textus receptus*, the "received text") that came to be used widely within the Western church.

The Old Roman Creed

The Apostles Creed can trace its genesis back to the era of the New Testament. Already there we see the impulse for Christians to confess their faith. Simple and concise confessions of Jesus can be found on the pages of the New Testament. They often took the form of what scholars call Christological acclamations. The most common of these are easily recognizable: "Jesus is Lord," "Jesus is the Christ," and "Jesus is the Son of God."[16] Some think that they took the form of personal confessions of the faith by which one announced his or her allegiance to Christ. As acclamations they also offered him praise and adoration.

Alongside these personal confessions of faith and Christological acclamations, slightly longer confessional formulaic statements—sometimes called "Christological sequences" or Christological "catch-phrases"—arose at the beginning of the second century. These were summaries of Christ's life and often were formulated to address errors regarding the identity and story of Jesus. One such example is provided by Ignatius of Antioch: "For our God Jesus Christ was conceived by Mary according to God's plan, of the seed of David and of the Holy Spirit; who was born and was baptized that by his passion He might cleanse water."[17] In general, these recounted key moments in the life of Jesus.[18] In some cases they were composed to address Docetist[19] errors that brought into question the reality of Jesus' human existence. This appears to have been the case with Ignatius' formula. Already at the end of the first century, the Apostle John provided a few statements to be used as something of a litmus test. "Whoever says that Jesus has not come in the flesh is not from us" (1 John 4:2-3).

Jesus had no human body and his sufferings + death were apparent rather than real

Also in the second century, another form of confessional statement began to grow in popularity, namely, the "rule of faith" (Irenaeus) or the "canon of truth" (Tertullian).[20] In form, rules of faith utilized the Christological formulas or stereotypical narratives but adapted them with details of different events to refute gnostic teachings. These Christological formulas were at times combined with statements that included a confession of God as the creator. While the specific wording may vary, the underlying pattern remained fairly constant. It confesses Christ by mentioning some of the key events in his biography, notably his birth, death, resurrection, ascension, and second coming. Consider a rule of faith quoted by Irenaeus (d. ca. 200) as an example. He notes that Christians believe in:

> one God, the maker of heaven and earth and of all the things that are in
> them, through Christ Jesus the Son of God,
> who because of his outstanding love towards his creation
> endured the birth from the Virgin, uniting in Himself man to God,
> and suffered under Pontius Pilate,
> and rose again,
> and was taken up in splendour,
> and will come again in glory,
> the savior of those who are saved
> and the judge of those who are judged. (Adv. haer. 3, 4, 2)

With statements like these, Irenaeus argued that the Gnostics misread the Scriptures and assembled them in the wrong way.[21] Despite differences in wording between the various rules of faith, the church fathers maintained that they set forth one and the same faith across the church. By the fourth century synodal and conciliar creeds took over the function that the *regula fidei* ("rule of faith") served as touchstones of orthodoxy (that is, the Nicene Creed).

Sometime between 150 and 250 in Rome, Christological sequences were inserted into the trinitarian formula used for Christian baptisms, thus giving rise to the Apostles Creed (in the form of the Old Roman Creed). Liuwe Westra suggests that such a fusion of these two elements marks the birth of the Apostles Creed even though the precise wording of that first formula cannot be determined. A set of baptismal questions found in the *collectio Veronensis*, later Western forms of the Creed, and manuscripts containing the Old Roman Creed all point to an original form of the Creed that could be designated proto-R (Roman Creed), which appeared sometime around 250.[22] Because the Christological sequence was inserted into the trinitarian baptismal formula, Westra argues that the "Apostles Creed as we meet it in Rome and the rest of the Western church" bears the character of a liturgical text.[23] This text comes down to us both in the form of questions and answers (the interrogatory creed) and in the form of a straightforward statement of the faith (the declaratory creed).[24]

The interrogatory form of the Creed was used within the baptismal rite itself.[25] There the person being baptized was asked questions, beginning with, "do you believe in God the Father almighty, maker of heaven and earth?" To each question, the baptizand responded, "Yes, I believe," at which point he or she was submerged under the water.[26] In the early twentieth century, a set of baptismal questions resembling the Old Roman Creed and found in the *collectio Veronensis* came to be associated with the Roman presbyter Hippolytus (175–235) and the so-called "Apostolic Tradition" (*traditio apostolica*), which was thought to be his. Today, Hippolytan scholars question the authenticity of the so-called *traditio apostolica* within this collection and are less certain about both its date and its origin. More likely, the baptismal questions found in the *collectio Veronensis* belong to the fifth century and may represent material that goes back to the last quarter of the fourth century.[27] The wording of those baptismal questions reads as follows:

> Do you believe in God the Father almighty?
> Do you believe in Christ Jesus, the Son of God,
> who was born by the Holy Spirit from the Virgin Mary,
> who was crucified under Pontius Pilate, died, and was buried
> and rose again on the third day living from the dead,
> and ascended into the heavens,
> and sits on the right hand of the Father,
> and will come to judge the living and the dead?
> Do you believe in the Holy Spirit,
> in the holy Church,
> and the resurrection of the flesh?

This set of baptismal questions comes close to the text of the Old Roman Creed itself.[28] In fact, Westra sees the text of these questions as a sister to the Old Roman Creed although the wording of the questions comes very close to that of the declaratory form of the Old Roman Creed. There are minor differences, for example, the questions do not mention "only" (as "his only Son") or the "remission of sins" (third article).

The declaratory form of the creed became most frequently associated with the instruction of catechumens. It came to be used as part of a rite known as the *traditio symboli* (literally, "handing down of the symbol," the creed) and *redditio symboli* ("repetition of the symbol") late in the Lenten season just prior to Easter. These two rites usually culminated three years of instruction for catechumens in the catechumenate and prepared them for baptism. The *traditio* took place when the bishop spoke the Creed to the catechumens. He accompanied this with an exhortation for the catechumen to learn it by heart. The catechumens in turn were expected to recite it during the *redditio*. In this way those to be baptized gave public testimony to their faith in Christ and the teachings of the gospel. On these occasions a sermon on the Creed was delivered with an explanation of several of its articles.[29]

The existence of this declaratory creed that scholars call the Old Roman Creed is "vouchsafed by Rufinus (somewhat Ambrose and Augustine) in its outline and content, by several anonymous manuscripts in its wording, and a fourth-century date by Marcellus of Ancyra."[30] The Old Roman Creed reads as follows:[31]

> I believe in God the Father almighty;
> and in Christ Jesus His only Son, our Lord,
> who was born from the Holy Spirit and the Virgin Mary,
> who under Pontius Pilate was crucified, and buried,
> on the third day rose again from the dead,
> ascended to the heaven,
> sits at the right hand of the Father,
> whence he will come to judge the living and the dead;
> and in the Holy Spirit,
> the holy Church,
> the remission of sins,
> the resurrection of the flesh.[32]

As can be seen, the Old Roman Creed closely resembles the creedal questions of the "apostolic tradition." Because of their different purposes the two texts take on different forms, most notably, in their opening. All the forms of Old Roman Creed begin with "Credo" ("I believe"), whereas the interrogatory form begins with "Credis" ("do you believe?").

Scholars have debated whether the interrogatory form of the creed or the declaratory form of the creed came first and thus which should be regarded as original.[33] The issue of which came first depends in part upon whether or not the fusion of the trinitarian and Christological formulae that gave rise to the Apostles Creed took place before or after the *traditio* and *redditio symboli* became an established practice.[34] Kelly viewed them as interchangeable manifestations of the same phenomenon but generally saw the questions coming first.[35] Westra acknowledges that the questions probably came first, since baptisms go back to the days of the New Testament. Yet he suggests that the wording of the questions themselves seemed to "follow the fluctuations in wording" of declaratory creeds. Westra holds that, rather than trying to identify which came first, it might be best "to maintain that the Apostles Creed may be found both as a declarative creed and in the guise of baptismal questions."[36]

Augustine, Ambrose, and Rufinus all testify that the Apostles Creed—whether in its interrogatory or declaratory form—arose in Rome. Thus, the Apostles Creed and the Eastern baptismal creeds should be considered two different traditions. More importantly, the church fathers believed that the Creed itself traced its origin back to the apostles themselves. Ambrose of Milan (340–397) appears to be the first to ascribe the Creed's authorship to the apostles toward the end of the fourth century.[37] The most famous account of its authorship and its composition is given by Rufinus, a priest in Aquileia. In a commentary on the Apostles Creed in 404, he stated that upon Christ's resurrection each apostle took turns in contributing a phrase to the creed.[38] Accordingly, in the West the Creed came to be divided into twelve articles corresponding to the twelve apostles.

The Apostles Creed (the Old Roman Creed and its variants) spread throughout the Western church in the third and fourth centuries. Most scholars point out that this does not mean that there yet existed a standard or fixed text of the creed that was used universally throughout the church. Instead, a number of texts continue to show some variety in both wording and content.

Marcellus of Ancyra quotes the text of a Greek creed from 340 that resembles the Old Roman Creed. Marcellus was an ardent advocate of the Nicene faith who sometimes overstated his position in such a way that his opponents could accuse him of Sabellianism, or modalism. In order to defend himself, Marcellus wrote to Pope Julius I in Rome and offered a creed to which he adhered as evidence of his orthodoxy. In his commentary on the Apostles Creed, Rufinus referred to the Creed used in the Aquileian church and pointed out where it differed slightly from the Creed used in the church at Rome in both wording and content. Augustine of Hippo also quoted two different forms of the Creed. One appears to be from the *redditio symboli* that was used at Milan when he was baptized, whereas the other appears to be the creed that he used for the *traditio symboli* at Hippo after becoming bishop there.[39]

As the Creed spread across the Western church, it developed a number of regional types or variants from the fourth through the eighth centuries: "no two forms of the Creed from this period are exactly identical."[40] These regional forms of the Apostles Creed reveal slight differences in both content and wording. Some

[handwritten margin note: 3 modes" instead of 3 persons in the godhead]

changes were confined to certain regions while other changes migrated from one region to another. Westra hypothesizes that more substantial changes tended to find their way across different regions whereas minor changes were confined to a locale. While that generally proved to be true, he discovered that those minor changes that were Roman in origin tended to find their way into the rest of the church.[41]

Reactions to changes in the Creed took three forms. First, some expressed strong disapproval to making any changes. When Ambrose delivered the creed to catechumens in the rite of the *traditio symboli*, he exhorted them to memorize it word for word and not change a single word. Second, some defended the changes as necessary for dogmatic and pastoral reasons, or liturgical purposes (for example, Latin style that varied from place to place). Third, others remained silent on the matter. For example, Augustine seems more oblivious to the differences in wording of the Creed in his day and hardly ever mentioned them. His attitude tended to be characteristic of the early church at large.[42] Despite the variants the general assumption seems to be that they embody one and the same confession of the faith.

After the fourth century the Nicene Creed supplanted the Old Roman Creed in Rome as the baptismal creed of choice. But the latter continued to be used as the baptismal creed in some areas of the Western church and within the monasteries of western Europe for meditation and instruction within the daily offices of prayer. The Apostles Creed appeared in the eighth century in the form that we now use, and by the ninth and tenth centuries it again returned to its place within the baptismal liturgy at Rome.

The Textus Receptus of the Apostles Creed

The final form of the Apostles Creed shifts attention from Rome to Western Europe. By the ninth century many changes had taken place throughout the world. The Islamic empire had expanded considerably. Under Mohammed it had encompassed nearly the entire Saudi Arabian peninsula (612–632). It then expanded westward through the Middle East, Egypt, and Libya under the Rightly Guided Caliphate (635–661). Finally, it pushed across the rest of northern Africa and into the Iberian peninsula (Portugal and Spain) under the leadership of the Umayyad Caliphate (661–750). By 711 the Islamic Moors conquered the Visigoths in Spain and brought the Iberian peninsula under Islamic rule. They moved across the Pyrenees Mountains but were defeated by the Franks under Charles Martel in 732 at the Battle of Poitiers.

One of those affected by the Islamic push eastward into Europe was Pirminius, a Benedictine monk. In 718 the Saracens, under El-Hurr, pushed across the Pyrenees Mountains and took Narbonne in 720.[43] They especially targeted the churches ("with their furnishings and treasure") and their clergy. Pirminius might have been one of those forced to flee for his life from Gaul and to begin a new life in southern Germany. There he established and became the first abbot of the monastery at Reichenau. From there Christian missionary activity spread throughout southwest Germany, where Pirminius helped to establish numerous monasteries.[44]

Sometime between 710 and 724, the *De Singulis Libris Canonicis Scarapsus* (*Excerpt from Individual Canonical Books*) attributed to Pirminius appeared,[45] containing excerpts from the Scriptures and church fathers. It was intended to serve as a manual of preaching for the missionary monks. The *Excerpt* provides a text of the Apostles Creed that is virtually identical with the one that came to be used universally within the Western church to the present day. The treatise quoted the Apostles Creed on three separate occasions within the work. The first chapter retold the story of how the apostles composed the Creed (the story that goes back to Rufinus). The second chapter reminded the monks of their baptisms, the events that included their renunciation of the devil, and their confession of the faith. This wording has come to be known as the *textus receptus* of the Creed, and "Pirminius" is the "first literary witness" to its existence.[46]

Kelly argues that this text should not be regarded as of Roman origin or redaction. He argues that the author probably did not take this creed from Rome but "used the form of creed with which he had grown up in his native land" somewhere in the Visigothic region of France (Septimania) around the region of Narbonne. Other creeds virtually identical with the *textus receptus* began to appear in southern Gaul from the fifth century forward. Perhaps most importantly, a creed very similar to the *textus receptus* is found in the writings of Caesarius of Arles (542).[47] Kelly suggests that the Creed probably attained its present shape sometime in the seventh century. As a result, he argues that the present text of the Apostles Creed (the *textus receptus*) should be regarded as a Gallican and not a Roman redaction.

Scholars have paid significant attention to the question of how the *textus receptus* of the Apostles Creed came to replace the Nicene Creed as the standard baptismal text within the West in general and in Rome in particular. It appears to have occurred in two stages. First it became used almost exclusively in baptism throughout France and Germany. From there it eventually worked its way back to Rome.

The first period or stage occurred with the effort to promote Roman liturgical practices among the French and German churches after Pippin, king of the Franks (and Charlemagne's father), and Pope Stephen II agreed in 754 to bring liturgical uniformity into their realms. When Charlemagne became king of the Franks in 768 (and then king of the Romans in 800), he continued the program begun under Pippin of cultural, liturgical, and educational reform. It had centered on the celebration of the mass and the administration of the sacraments. As part of that program of reform, Charlemagne worked from 811 to 813 to establish uniformity in the baptismal service and foster the use of the baptismal creed as the instrument for instruction of catechumens as part of his education program. In a letter to all the metropolitans in his realm, he asked for information regarding what was being taught to priests and people through the texts of the baptismal rite, the scrutiny, and the creed. The results must have revealed a great deal of diversity in liturgical practices, prompting Charlemagne in 813 to insist that the Roman rite become the standard throughout the church.[48]

Charlemagne's reform program apparently did not directly impact the use of the Creed. There was no attempt to replace the *textus receptus* of the Apostles Creed with the Nicene Creed that was currently used in the Roman rite of the *traditio* and *redditio*. This is not to say Charlemagne was not concerned about the baptismal creed.[49] He insisted that the same creed be used by all the clergy within his realm.[50] The choice of creed fell upon the *textus receptus* of the Apostles Creed, which was "a native to Septimania in S.W. France, was in current use at Arles," and had been adopted in many of the German lands. The push for uniformity in the baptismal rite and the use of this creed as an educational instrument probably hastened its adoption throughout the West, since it "had already achieved a wide measure of diffusion and popularity." By the ninth century the *textus receptus* "began to enjoy practical monopoly in Western Europe."[51]

This leads to the question of the replacement by the Apostles Creed of the Nicene Creed for the *traditio* rite in Rome, in use there since at least the sixth century.[52] During a period that extended from the restoration of the empire under Otto I the Great in 962 to the beginning of the reign of Pope Gregory VII (1073), the church in Rome was characterized by corruption among the clergy and decay in its liturgical practices. When Otto I (912–973) became emperor of the Holy Roman Empire in 962, he set out to restore ecclesiastical standards for clergy within the church and so arranged for many German ecclesiastics to help with the process of reform in Rome. They brought with them the liturgical reforms that had been taking place in Western Europe since the days of Charlemagne. Thus, their Franco-German influence brought about a "Gallicanization" of the Roman liturgy, including the replacement of the Nicene Creed with the Apostles Creed.[53]

A further step in the direction of Rome's eventual adoption of the *textus receptus* of the Apostles Creed occurred when the great grandson of Otto I, Pope Gregory V (972–999), became the first German pope in 996. He quickly granted special privileges to the abbey of Reichenau (in 998) and requested that the liturgical works of Reichenau be sent to Rome periodically (usually with the ordination of new abbots). "The baptismal orders which travelled south to the papal palace from their scriptorium certainly contained the creed T [*textus receptus*] which had descended to them from their refugee founder."[54] At some point—the process is somewhat obscure—the *textus receptus* came to be considered the official form of the Apostles Creed within the Roman rite itself.[55] The Franco-German church gave back to Rome the rule of faith that it had first produced.[56]

Summary

The Apostles Creed conveys the essentials of the Christian faith in a straightforward, down-to-earth manner that is at once simple, concise, and easy to grasp. It does so with the language of the Scriptures themselves. It is perhaps not surprising then that the Apostles Creed has served so well as the creed of choice both for teaching new Christians the basics of the faith and for use in the baptismal rite when new Christians personally confess their faith in the Jesus of Scripture. Its stature for these purposes becomes enhanced with Luther's classic expositions of the Creed in the Small and Large Catechisms.

The Nicene Creed

Most who recite the Nicene Creed every Sunday may not realize either how important it is or how revolutionary it was for the confession of Jesus Christ within the Christian church. The theological controversy sparked by the Alexandrian presbyter Arius brought to a head nearly three centuries of theological debates and controversies over the confession of Christ. The Nicene Creed had to come to terms with what to many appeared to be two conflicting principles, namely, a monotheistic principle (there is only one God) and a Christological principle (the Son is fully God in the same way that the Father is fully God).[57]

From the beginning, Christians adhered to the monotheistic faith they had inherited from Israel. As Christians moved out into the Greco-Roman world, they found it necessary to defend their monotheistic faith when the wider culture pointed out what seemed to be contradictions between their confession and their practice. Pliny, Roman governor of Bithynia, reported that when Christians met on a fixed day at dawn, they gathered to "recite a hymn to Christ as to a god."[58] This raised the question of why Christians would not worship the traditional gods when they themselves venerated Jesus as a god. Rome, after all, had no difficulty in incorporating foreign gods into its pantheon alongside the native gods.[59] How did Christians reconcile these two theological convictions?

Prior to Nicaea, the monotheistic principle was taken for granted as being non-negotiable. The one God was most often identified in the New Testament with the Father of Jesus (1 Cor. 8:6). But as the church took its confession of one God into a Hellenistic culture, it had to contend with the filtering of the biblical confession of one God through philosophical understandings of the nature of God. For example, what does it mean to say that God is "one"? That God is a monad? A singularity? Similarly, it was virtually axiomatic for everyone that God does not suffer. God is perfect and hence immutable. Change in God would imply either movement toward perfection or away from perfection. Suffering would be a form of change. And yet Christ suffered and died. How can he be God in the way that the Father is?

In the attempt to defend their monotheistic confession, various church fathers articulated the Son's relation to the Father in a way that (at least to later generations) seemed to compromise either the full deity of the Son or the personhood of the Son. The Apologists (Justin Martyr, Athenagoras, and Theophilus, bishop of Antioch) in the second century argued that the Logos ("thought" or "reason") within God became the Son when the Father sent him forth "in creative speech" according to Genesis.[60] The Adoptionists (Theodotus, Paul of Samasota) in the late second and early third centuries, contended that the Spirit descended on the man Jesus and adopted or empowered him as Son of God.[61] The Subordinationists (Tertullian and

Origen) in the third century tended to affirm that the Son always existed with the Father but in a way that implied a derived and hence subordinate deity of the Son (as the spring from which a stream flows).[62] The Modalists (Praxeas, Sabellius) in the third century contended that one God played three different roles in the three-act play of salvation. All of this culminated with the controversy sparked by Arius. He argued that the Son was a creature, indeed the first and most powerful of all God's creatures, but still a creature.

Nicaea marks the critical turning point in the discussion. The bishops at Nicaea refused to compromise the Christological principle, that is, the full deity of the Son of God. If that means that one must redefine what it means to be monotheistic, then so be it. The church subsequently needed to interpret the oneness of God so as to embrace plurality in a biblical way.[63] No longer was the confession of God's oneness understood to mean that God is a monad or mathematical singularity. Hilary of Poitiers put it well, "Though he is one, he is not solitary."[64] As a result of the Nicene confession, the two other monotheistic religions, Judaism and Islam, do not regard Christians as monotheists. Instead, they see Christians as having a society or association of gods.

The tensions between the monotheistic and Christological principles can be illustrated by the challenge of interpreting and reconciling two statements of Jesus from the Gospel of John: "The Father is greater than I" (14:28) and "The Father and I are one" (10:30). Should we consider the first as the clear and non-negotiable passage, how might we interpret the second in light of it? One possibility is, "The Father and I are one in will and purpose." But if we consider the passage, "the Father and I are one" the clearer—understanding it to affirm the equality of the Father and the Son in deity—then how does one interpret the other passage, "the Father is greater than I"? The orthodox answer referred it to his human nature. The Nicene Creed points in that direction. Thus, the Athanasian Creed later confessed that the Son is "equal to the Father with respect to his deity; less than the Father with respect to his humanity."

The Controversy Erupts

The Arian controversy became a public issue in 318 and 319 when the elderly Arius preached a series of sermons in Alexandria.[65] In them he expounded on the relationship of the Father and the Son. Born in Libya (256), Arius had been trained in Antioch under Lucian, a well-respected exegete and theologian, and was serving the fairly well-to-do and "fashionable church Baucalis,"[66] a congregation in the port district of Alexandria. Reports describe Arius as "tall, austere, ascetically dressed, grim of countenance, urbane in manner."[67] He was a strong monotheist, but the way he spoke of the status and nature of the Son in sermons or lectures aroused the concerns of Alexander, Arius's bishop, and prompted him to pursue further discussion of the positions put forward by Arius.

To that end Alexander arranged for a public discussion or debate of Arius's views with a larger group of bishops and theologians. In those discussion Arius elaborated on his views and argued for the "monarchy" of the Father in such a way that he spoke of the Son as a creature. Thus, there was a time when he did not exist—prior to the Father begetting him, an event that took place before the creation of the universe itself. Others countered Arius by pointing out that his position meant that the Son was not truly God. Instead, Arius's opponents insisted that the Son was of one being with God. Agreeing with the latter, Alexander called upon Arius to stop promulgating his views. Arius responded by charging that Alexander was promoting Sabellianism.[68]

The dispute soon became a full-fledged controversy that spilled beyond the borders of Alexandria. In 320 Alexander convened a synod of bishops from Egypt and Libya (numbering about one hundred). They agreed with Alexander's excommunication of Arius and voted to send him into exile. Arius rejected the action of the synod and sought sanctuary with Eusebius of Casaerea. There he became a lightning rod as various bishops in Palestine rallied to his side while other bishops in Antioch and Jerusalem opposed him. Arius found an especially strong supporter in Eusebius of Nicomedia (across the Bosporus from Constantinople, modern day Istanbul), who had been a fellow student of Arius in Antioch. In the meantime Alexander sent letters to seventy bishops, informing them of Arius's excommunication and soliciting from them letters of communion that effectively excommunicated Arius throughout the church.[69] From Nicomedia, Arius enlisted the support of an increasing number of bishops who in turn held their own synod, in which they excommunicated Alexander.[70]

Within three to four years, the Arian controversy had spread throughout much of the church in the East. The matter caught the attention of Emperor Constantine, who had only recently become emperor of the Eastern empire in 324 by defeating the anti-Christian emperor of the East, Licinus. The theological controversy had become a threat to public peace and order as demonstrators took to the streets and the people deposed bishops and installed replacements. To quash the controversy, the emperor dispatched his sixty-seven year old ecclesiastical advisor, Ossius, bishop of Cordoba (Spain), to Alexandria with letters in which Constantine reprimanded Alexander and Arius for debating such matters and allowing their dispute to become matters of public disturbances. He urged them to reconcile.[71]

When that initial attempt to resolve the controversy failed, Constantine and his advisors decided to convene a general council of the church in order to restore unity within the church. In doing so, the emperor carried out the traditional role of a Roman emperor as the religious leader of his people. The council was to take place in Nicaea, a town in Asia Minor (modern-day Turkey). Prior to the council, Ossius attended a synod of fifty-nine bishops in Antioch, where he elicited the adoption of a statement of faith or creed.[72] Overall, the statement sided with Alexander and rejected the notion that the Son came "from what was not." Also, prior to the council, Ossius appears to have met with Alexander and came to agreement on the formula that the Son was "consubstantial with the Father,"[73] a point with which the council later concurred.

The Council of Nicaea

The Council of Nicaea convened in the early summer of 325. Due to distances and difficulties of travel, only a few bishops from Europe made the trip. As a result, those attending the council came primarily from churches bordering the Mediterranean Sea.[74] The prominent bishops who opposed Arius included Alexander of Alexandria, Eustathius of Antioch, Marcellus of Ancyra, and Macarius of Jerusalem. The prominent bishops who supported Arius included Eusebius of Casesarea, Eusebius of Nicomedia, Theognis of Nicaea, and Maris of Chalcedon. Pope Sylvester of Rome had asked to be excused from the council on account of his advanced age but sent personal envoys. Altogether, according to Athanasius (a twenty-five-year old deacon and secretary to Alexander), approximately three hundred bishops were in attendance. In the opening of the council, according to Eusebius's *Life of Constantine*,[75] the bishops were aligned down each side of a long hall and stood as the emperor, clothed in purple and gold, entered with three members of the imperial family and a few senior advisors. Eusebius describes the emperor as "distinguished by piety and godly fear." Constantine welcomed the bishops and urged them to help restore peace to the church by healing their divisions.[76]

According to Athanasius's *Epistola ad Afros*, the discussions of Arius's views took place in three stages.[77] The first stage entailed a discussion of the catchwords or slogans (for example, the Son "was from what was not") that summarized Arius's teaching that the Son was a creaturely being like other creaturely beings. Opponents of Arius looked for biblical expressions that stressed the unique status of the Son. The second stage apparently took place when debate ensued about whether or not various biblical expressions provided unequivocal rejections of Arius's teaching. In the third stage the bishops explored the use of more precise and unambiguous phrases such as "from the substance of the Father" and "of one substance with the Father." At this time the proposal to affirm that the Son is consubstantial (*homoousios*) with the Father was put forward. Although the term was not found in Scripture and had various shades of meaning, it clearly rejected any hint of creatureliness with respect to the Son. In his *Thalia*, Arius himself had declared that the Son was "not equal to nor, for that matter, *homoousion* with, the Father."

After the Creed was finished and adopted by the bishops, the emperor "stepped in firmly, even brutally, to ensure its acceptance."[78] When several bishops refused to state their agreement with it, Constantine threatened them with exile. In the end, Eusebius of Nicomedia, Theognis of Nicaea, and Maris of Chalcedon along with several others agreed to sign the creed but refused to accept its anathemas. Arius and a few others refused to sign anything and were subsequently sent into exile. The Creed reads:[79]

> We believe in one God, the Father, Almighty, Maker of all things visible and invisible;
> and in one Lord Jesus Christ, the Son of God, begotten from the Father, only-begotten, that is, from the substance of the Father, God from God, Light

from Light, true God from true God, begotten, not made, of one substance with the Father, through whom all things came into being, things in heaven and things on earth, who because of us human beings and because of our salvation came down and became incarnate, becoming man, suffered and rose again on the third day, ascended to the heavens, will come to judge the living and the dead;

And in the Holy Spirit.

But as for those who say, There was [a time when] when he was not, and, before being born He was not, and that he came into existence out of nothing, or who assert that the Son of God is of a different hypostasis or substance,[80] or is subject to alteration or change—these the Catholic and apostolic Church anathematizes.[81]

It becomes readily apparent in both its positive or thetic statements as well as their antitheses that the Creed addresses directly the key catchphrases used by Arius and his supporters. In particular, it focuses on stating the meaning that the Son is "begotten of the Father." If we reformat the second article visually, we can see what it was about theologically and better grasp its focus and emphases.

And in one Lord Jesus Christ,
    the Son of God, begotten from the Father, only-begotten, that is, from the substance of the Father, God from God, Light from Light, true God from true God, begotten, not made, of one substance with the Father,
through whom all things came into being,
    things in heaven and things on earth, who because of us human beings and because of our salvation came down and became incarnate, becoming man, suffered and rose again on the third day, ascended to the heavens, will come to judge the living and the dead.

The Creed uses 1 Corinthians 8, "one Lord Jesus Christ through whom all things came into being" (italicized text) as a framework. This passage brackets the statements regarding the answer to the question, "Who is Jesus?" More specifically, the indented text simply seeks to expand on what it means to say that the Son is "begotten" of the Father.

The decisions of Nicaea did not end the theological debates swirling around Arius as Constantine had hoped. The different positions taken over Arius's teachings hardened, and the controversy continued, at times violently, for the next fifty years. During these years bishops were installed and deposed—often by mobs or by the armed might of the authorities. One synod after another met to overturn the decisions of previous councils and produce new creeds. At times it appeared that the supporters of Arius would prevail and at other times that the supporters of the Nicene faith would triumph.[82]

Several new and influential thinkers arose within the church during this time and became key defenders of the Nicene faith as they further clarified the church's exposition of the Trinity and finally settled the issue. These included among others Athanasius, the Cappadocians (Gregory of Nazianzus, Gregory of Nyssa, Basil), and Hilary of Poitiers.

Athanasius, who started out as a deacon and served as secretary for Alexander at the council of Nicaea, became bishop of Alexandria upon Alexander's death in 328. His tenure proved to be tumultuous as Athanasius found himself accused repeatedly of false charges, such as immoral conduct, illegally taxing the Egyptians, tyrannizing bishops, interrupting grain supplies from Alexandria to Constantinople, and even murdering a rebellious priest.[83] He found himself exiled to Trier, in Germany, was forced to seek sanctuary in Rome, and fled to safety in the desert. When the council at Milan convened in 355, the emperor, Constantine's son Constantius II, pressured the bishops to depose Athanasius. When the pope, along with Hilary (recently elected bishop of Poitiers) and Ossius of Cordoba (now nearly one hundred years old) objected, they too found themselves in the next year either in exile (Hilary) or under house arrest (Ossius). In 356 Roman legions stormed the church of Theonas where Athanasius was holding a vigil service. During the ensuing melee Athanasius was whisked away into exile among the desert fathers in Egypt.[84] Altogether, Athanasius spent seventeen of his forty-six years as bishop in exile.[85]

In Athanasius's later years a group of young Cappadocians emerged as strong Nicene supporters and ultimately brought about the acceptance of the Nicene faith in the East. When Athanasius died in 373, leadership passed to Basil, who had become bishop of Caesarea in 370. From a wealthy, deeply pious family, he soon proved himself to be a capable administrator and a top-tier theologian with a commanding personality. From the beginning of his episcopate, Basil worked to forge a theological consensus between East and West. He installed his younger brother Gregory as bishop of Nyssa. Gregory proved to be only an adequate administrator but was a profound thinker and played a prominent role at the Council of Constantinople (381). Basil sent Gregory of Nazianzus to Constantinople to rally support for the faith of Nicaea. There he won renown as a preacher and shepherded a rapidly growing flock.[86]

Together, the Cappadocian theologians brought the Eastern bishops to the faith of Nicaea and its *homoousios* so that the Nicene Creed became the definitive statement of catholic orthodoxy. They accomplished this in part by working out the distinction between *ousia* ("substance") and *hypostasis* ("person") that enabled most of the Eastern bishops to embrace the Nicene Creed and thereby brought about the consolidation of Nicene Orthodoxy that was reaffirmed at the council of Constantinople. While Athanasius tended to see these terms as synonyms, the Cappadocians defined *ousia* as the essence common to the persons and *hypostasis* as referring to that which is proper and distinctive of a person. This Cappadocian solution grounded the distinctive characteristics of each person in its origins:

"begotten" distinguished the Son, "proceeding" the Spirit. The only acceptable formula was one *ousia* and three *hypostases*. The "one Godhead thus exists in three modes of being, three *hypostases*."[87]

The Creed of Constantinople

When the Eastern emperor Valens died in 378, the Western emperor Gratian appointed his Spanish general Theodosius (379–395) as emperor in the East. Under Theodosius the tide turned.[88] As a Westerner he was loyal to the Nicene faith, with the result that for the first time since 325 emperors from East and West adhered to the Nicene formula. Basil died in 379 before his fiftieth birthday. In 380 Theodosius issued an edict that all who lived according to the religion handed down from Christ through Peter to the Romans should believe "in the one divinity of the Father and the Son and the Holy Spirit in equal majesty and holy Trinity." All who failed to adhere to this were branded heretics and denied the name "catholic." This became significant for the princes at Augsburg, who argued that they were entitled to their princely rights within the empire as adherents of the Catholic faith, as confessed in the first article of the Augsburg Confession, which affirmed the Nicene Creed.[89] The churches of Constantinople were taken from the Arians, and Gregory of Nazianzus was installed as the new bishop in the presence of Theodosius.[90]

Theodosius identified his profession of 380 with the Nicene formula. In May 381 Theodosius convened a council that met at the imperial palace in Constantinople to resolve the Arian issue once and for all. The prominent participants of the council included Gregory of Nazianzus (elected president of the council), Basil's brothers Gregory of Nyssa and Peter of Sebaste, and Cyril of Jerusalem. For some time, the Council of Constantinople was seen as little more than a regional council of the Eastern church in that it was attended by about 150 bishops, mostly from the East. The Western church did not recognize it as ecumenical for a century or more. For example, Pope Felix (d. 493) recognized only Nicaea, Ephesus, and Chalcedon as ecumenical. Not until Pope Hormisdas (d. 523) did the West recognize it as an ecumenical council. Not until 1274 did the Western church recognize the canons of Constantinople. Not until Chalcedon in 451 was the faith set forth by 150 bishops affirmed as the faith of the church.[91]

The text of the Creed as we know it comes from Chalcedon. The following was read at the second session of Council of Chalcedon on October 10 and is the text used on September 16, 680, at the eighteenth session of the sixth ecumenical council at Constantinople.

> We believe in one God, the Father almighty, maker of heaven and earth, of
> all things visible and invisible;
> And in one Lord Jesus Christ, the only-begotten Son of God, begotten from
> the Father before all ages, light from light, true God from true God, begotten
> not made, of one substance with the Father, through whom all things came

into existence, who because of human beings and because of our salvation
came down from heaven, and was incarnate from the Holy Spirit and the
Virgin Mary and became human, and was crucified for us under Pontius
Pilate, and suffered and was buried, and rose again on the third day according to the Scriptures and ascended to heaven, and sits on the right hand of
the Father, and will come again with glory to judge living and dead, of whose
kingdom there will be no end;

And in the Holy Spirit, the Lord and life-giver, who proceeds from the Father,
Who with the Father and the Son is together worshipped and together glorified, Who spoke through the prophets; in one holy catholic and apostolic
Church. We confess one baptism to the remission of sins; we look forward to
the resurrection of the dead and the life of the world to come.[92]

The differences between the creeds of Nicaea and Constantinople can be seen most
clearly in the second and third articles.

In general, this creed restated the basic assertions of Nicaea. One notably new
clause was incorporated into the second article to address a situation that had
arisen since 325. The statement, "His kingdom shall have no end" (from Luke 1:33),
appears to be directed against Marcellus of Ancyra (d. 374), one of the staunchest
defenders of the Nicene *homoousios*. Some, however, suspected him of Sabellianism.
He and later his disciples had taught that the Word had become incarnate for the
purpose of redemption but would return all things to the Father. Thus, his kingdom
would end with the final judgment. This implied that the Logos was something of
a "transient projection" of the Father for the purpose of the incarnation.[93] Once he
accomplished the task of salvation, he would return all things to the Father and
again become what he had been from all eternity, immanent in the Father. Such a
position horrified many. Cyril of Jerusalem warned, "If ever you hear anyone saying
that there is an end to the kingship of Christ, hate the heresy."[94]

In addition to Marcellus, the Creed appears to take aim at the teachings of
Apollinaris, even though the Creed itself makes no explicit statement specifically
regarding Apollinaris's teaching. The first canon of the Council of Constantinople
did, however, anathematize the followers of Apollinaris (b. 310), who had served
as bishop of Laodicea (modern day Latakia) in Syria from 361–390. His views on
Christology began attracting attention after 362. By 375 he had broken with orthodoxy. Apollinaris and his followers denied that the Son assumed a genuine human
nature by stating that the Word took the role of the rational soul in Jesus and that
he brought with him a flesh that he had constructed in heaven rather than from
Mary,[95] who merely served as the "canal" through whom the Word passed.[96] His
teachings were condemned in several councils leading up to Constantinople.[97]

The most obvious difference between the Creed of Constantinople and the
Creed of Nicaea is readily seen in the much-expanded third article. Kelly notes
that it was not uncommon for Eastern baptismal creeds to include mention of the

catholic church, baptism, the resurrection of the body, and life everlasting. But its affirmation of the deity of the Spirit is quite striking. Herein lies the distinctive and lasting theological contribution of the Council of Constantinople. In the struggle to affirm the consubstantiality of the Son with the Father, an obvious next question would be, "What about the Spirit as well?" The Arians had apparently considered the matter and were prepared to speak also of the creatureliness of the Spirit. But such assertions remained in the background of the early fourth century discussion of the *homoousios* of the Son. By the second half of the fourth century, this issue burst into the open and became a hotly debated issue. Those who refused to speak of the Spirit as consubstantial with the Father came to be known as Pneumatomachians, or "spirit-fighters."[98]

The Council of Constantinople had to address head-on the issue of the Spirit's deity. While Basil did not want to add to the Nicene faith regarding the Son, he recognized that more needed to be said about the Spirit. In its first canon the Council of Constantinople not only anathematized the Pneumatomachians; it affirmed the full consubstantiality of the Spirit as well as the distinctive hypostasis of the Spirit. But apparently when it came time to approve the Creed, the emperor Theodosius asked for a more conciliatory tone to be struck. Therefore, the Creed does not use the more provocative *homoousios* language and state that the Spirit is consubstantial with the Father. Instead, it utilizes phrases from Scripture laid out in Basil's book *On the Holy Spirit*,[99] from which one can draw no other conclusion than that the Spirit is fully God.[100] Young concludes, "Paying attention to the doctrine of the Holy Spirit led to the formulation of a truly Trinitarian concept of God."[101]

The Text

The Creed included in the Book of Concord is, properly speaking, the Creed of Constantinople and not the Creed of Nicaea. The Creed of Constantinople is not merely a modified version of the Creed of Nicaea. They are two different texts.[102] The origins and composition of the second text are not entirely clear. It seems that the bishops at the Council of Constantinople did not write a new creed from scratch during the council itself but instead used an already existing baptismal creed that was used in or around Jerusalem or Antioch in the 370s. Kelly suggests that the style of the Creed, "its graceful balance and smooth flow, convey the impression of a liturgical piece that has emerged naturally in the life and worship of the Christian community rather than of a conciliar artifact."[103] To this creed those attending the council made a few alterations to meet their particular needs.

When the council in Constantinople adopted its confession of the faith, it did not see itself as propagating a new creed. Davis notes, "In the minds of the fathers of Constantinople, they were not thereby replacing the old sacrosanct Nicene Creed but rather ratifying the Nicene faith in the shape of the Creed of Constantinople."[104] Kelly comments, "that it should do this by adopting what was really a different formula from that of Nicaea may appear paradoxical to us, until we recall that at this stage importance attached to the Nicene teaching rather than to the literal wording of N [Nicene Creed]."[105] Such an approach continued for some time. The church tended to stress the content of teaching of Nicaea more than the specific wording of a particular formulary or text, which allowed for various creeds to be considered as "the faith of Nicaea."

The specific text of the creed endorsed at Constantinople fell into some obscurity between 381 and 451, partly because it was the view of many bishops that Constantinople was a regional council and not an ecumenical council,[106] partly because of the influence of Cyril of Alexandria. He was perhaps suspicious of new creeds, always cited the Nicene Creed only in its original, literal, and pure form, and claimed that no other creed could claim equality with it. Under his influence the council of Ephesus (431) clearly distinguished the Creed of Nicaea from the Creed of Constantinople. It was due to him "more than to anyone else that the obscurity of C[onstantinople] is due." In spite of Cyril's approach, "the habit of designating any orthodox formula constructed on Nicene principles as 'the faith of Nicaea' was never eradicated."[107]

The present text of the Creed of Constantinople first appeared in 451 at the second session of the Council of Chalcedon. The "Faith of the 318" (the Nicene Creed) was read aloud to great applause. The imperial commissioners then had the "Faith of the 150" read aloud to less applause but no dissent. Kelly suggests that there was some reticence to place it on the same level as the Creed of Nicaea, even though the participants regarded it as merely an expansion of the original Nicene Creed and did not deny its authenticity as the statement endorsed at Constantinople. It seems that the fathers simply preferred to use the Nicene Creed.[108] But the problem remained: it did not say enough about the Holy Spirit in response to those who denied his deity.

Throughout the fifth and well into the sixth century, it became increasingly common to regard the Creed of Constantinople as little more than an expanded version of the Nicene Creed, so that by the Middle Ages the original differences between the two creeds were largely forgotten and the Creed of Constantinople came to be known simply as the Nicene Creed.[109] Thus the Nicene Creed as we know it was admitted as authoritative in East and West alike from 451 onward. At first it was used primarily for baptisms but during the sixth century in Constantinople was used also within the communion service or as part of the preparation for communion during the sixth century in Constantinople. It appears that Charlemagne inserted it into the service after the Gospel around 798, a practice that came from Ireland and England. Around 1014, Rome placed it into the liturgy as well, where it has remained down to the present day.[110]

The Filioque Controversy

One new theological element later inserted into the text of the creed became the subject of significant controversy and a contributing cause to the Great Schism between the East and West (1054): the *filioque* [that the Holy Spirit proceeds from the Father *and the Son*] clause. Kelly notes that the theology of the procession of the Spirit from both the Father and the Son rose to prominence in the trinitarian thought of the fourth century through the impetus of Hilary and came to full expression in Augustine's theology. Due to Augustine's dominating influence, the double procession of the Spirit spread throughout the West in the following centuries. By the seventh century the double procession had taken such a hold on Spanish Christianity that at the third council of Toledo in 589 the Visigothic king (of Hispania, Septimania, and Gallicia) Reccared gave a brief exposition of the faith that spoke of the *filioque* in his address to the bishops.[111] It excluded any remnant of Arian teaching from the doctrine of Christ. For saying that the Spirit comes from the Son as well as the Father meant that whatever the Father does, the Son also does. Were the Father to do something that the Son does not, it might imply an inferior status for the Son. It is not clear whether the word *filioque* was actually inserted into the Nicene Creed at Toledo.

The *filioque* became a full-blown issue between the East and the West when Charlemagne became king of the Franks in 768 (and later, emperor). He soon became an advocate of the *filioque* and sought to persuade the papacy to support its introduction into the Creed. At the ecumenical council at Nicaea in 787, Pope Hadrian gave his approval to a creed circulated by the Patriarch of Constantinople that spoke of the Spirit proceeding from the Father alone. When Charlemagne rebuked the pope for supporting such a statement, the pope countered that this teaching was congruent with the statements of the church fathers from the beginning. In 796–797 at the synod of Cividale, Paulinus justified the insertion of the *filioque* into the Creed of Constantinople: "It no more violated the principle that new creeds must not be framed than did the alterations which the fathers of 381 had felt obliged to make in it. It had become necessary to interpolate 'and from the Son' on account of those heretics who whisper that the Holy Spirit is from the Father alone."[112]

By the ninth century the procession of the Spirit from the Father and the Son was taught throughout the Western Church. The *filioque* had been inserted into the Creed in Spain, France, Germany, and even northern Italy. In 809–810 Charlemagne assembled a council in Aachen that spoke in favor of the *filioque*. He then sent a delegation to convince Pope Leo III to insert it into the Creed but to no avail. Concerned about relations with the East, the pope acknowledged the orthodoxy of the *filioque* but added "not all essential truths were enshrined in the creed."[113] Rome declined to tamper with the authorized text for two more centuries. The exact date when the Western church actually authorized its inclusion remains cloudy.

The Athanasian Creed

Of the three ecumenical creeds, the Athanasian Creed (often called the *Quicunque Vult*, "whoever wishes"—the opening line of the Creed in Latin) probably is the least well known and appears as the most intimidating, both in terms of its length and its language.[114] Named after Athanasius, whose name is synonymous with orthodoxy (though Athanasius could not have written this creed, since it appeared a century and a half after his death), the Athanasian Creed came to be seen as a summary of the orthodox Christian faith. In recent centuries it has declined in popularity[115] and lost its place as a teaching tool in seminaries and as a confession within the liturgy in many churches. As a result, increasing numbers of pastors and people have little or no familiarity with this Creed. Nonetheless, Lutheran congregations continue to read the Creed, in whole or in part, on Trinity Sunday.

The history of how the Athanasian Creed came into existence remains shrouded in some mystery. This much seems certain. It is a creed of western origin. Westra notes that it has no "Greek or Eastern counterpart."[116] The Creed as we know it made its earliest appearance in the sermons of Caesarius, primate of Arles (502–542) in southern Gaul,[117] a famous preacher and churchman who collected texts in his "struggle to find a summary of catholic faith."[118] The Creed appears in a codex that includes a preface stating that since both clergy and lay people need to be familiar the faith, there is here written out the catholic faith according to the fathers, and "we ought both ourselves frequently to read it and to instruct others in it."[119] Caesarius and his contemporaries considered the Creed to be a medium of instruction, a handy summary of the orthodox faith of the previous two centuries. About this "there can be no reasonable doubt." The idea that it served as a hymn is a secondary development.[120]

Various theories have been put forward with regard to its authorship, theological origin, and historical context. Whoever wrote it drew heavily on Augustine's theology for its trinitarian section. The author also made use of Vincent of Lérin's *Excerpta*, the "quarry from which" the author drew the body of the Christological section in its argument and wording, with little revision. For this reason, the Monastery of Lérin must be regarded as the "cradle of the creed." Kelly contends Caesarius could have composed the Creed since he had been trained in school of Lérin, but in the end he believes that the author remains anonymous. He has little doubt that a single author was responsible for the text, probably a contemporary of Caesarius whom Caesarius might have asked to write it. Following "his usual practice," he attached the traditional title, "the Faith of Athanasius" on the ground that it embodied the teaching of the great defender of the Nicaean faith.[121]

After its appearance at Arles, references to the Athanasian Creed increase over the next several centuries, reflecting its growing prestige and status as a tool of instruction and a touchstone of orthodoxy. Kelly notes that by the time of Charlemagne, its prestige as a summary of orthodox teaching useful for improving the theological education of the clergy reached a pinnacle. It also began to find its way into Psalters along with the Apostles Creed and the Lord's Prayer. From there it moved into the divine office and began to be sung as a canticle.[122] By the sixteenth century it had taken its place alongside the Apostles and Nicene Creeds as one of the three classic or ecumenical creeds of the church. Within the Roman church it came to be used at prime on Sundays. Among Protestants it was given the same respect as the other two creeds by the Lutheran Book of Concord, and other Protestant statements of faith acknowledge it. The Book of Common Prayer called for it to be recited occasionally in place of the Apostles Creed. But in the twentieth century, such liturgical usage within Sunday services gradually became reduced to Trinity Sunday.[123]

Since the Athanasian Creed serves the important function of summarizing, preserving, and conveying the orthodox faith as set forth at Nicaea and the subsequent councils, it makes a different contribution than does the Nicene Creed. The fourth and fifth centuries were centuries of tremendous theological fervor and creativity. Some of the greatest bishops and theologians that the church has ever had lived during those years. These teachers—Athanasius, Basil the Great, Gregory of Nyssa, Gregory of Nazianzus, Hilary of Poitiers, Ambrose, and Augustine— weighed in on the most important theological issues of their day (not to mention contributing to the catechesis of the church as well). But after nearly two centuries of creative activity, the church had to let the dust settle, sift through it, and consolidate the gains that it had made.[124]

In this regard, the era of the Nicene Creed and the era of the Athanasian Creed resemble the sixteenth century. The 1520s were a period of theological revolution that sent shockwaves through the entire church. Luther's writings rolling off the printing press nearly every month provided new insight upon new insight, capturing and captivating theologians around Europe. By 1530 the Lutherans submitted something of a new way of conceiving the church and its faith with their presentation of the Augsburg Confession. But in the second half of the sixteenth-century, Lutherans had to step back, take stock of their gains, sift the wheat from the chaff, and define what it meant to be Lutheran. And so the Formula of Concord, as a summary and explication of the Augsburg Confession, lacks the "pizzaz" that many find in the Augsburg Confession. Yet it serves a critical function of passing on to the next generation the insights of Luther and the Augsburg Confession.

The Athanasian Creed serves a function for the era that preceded it similar to that which the Formula of Concord served for its preceding era. Thus, in both form and content, the Athanasian Creed provides an excellent summary and window into the theological activity and decisions of the fourth and fifth centuries of the church. As such, we should expect nothing particularly "new" in terms of its content or formulation. Instead, the Athanasian Creed seeks to restate what the creeds and councils had affirmed. Contrary to how many perceive it (because of its language), it simply seeks to lay out guidelines or boundaries for how one speaks of the Trinity and Christology.[125] It is as if to say, "if you go outside these boundaries, then you are no longer speaking of the Trinity or of Christ in the way that the Scriptures speak."

In structure, the Athanasian Creed follows the pattern of the *Te Deum Laudamus*, first confessing the Trinity and then confessing Christ. Accordingly, the first half of the Athanasian Creed deals with the Trinity by summarizing the

fourth-century discussions and decisions. The second half deals with the incarnation and person of Christ, thus summarizing the late-fourth-century (Council of
Constantinople) and fifth-century (Councils of Ephesus and Chalcedon) discussions and decisions regarding Christology. A brief statement introduces the Creed,
followed by a transitional statement between the trinitarian and Christological sections and a concluding statement that reaffirms the importance of confessing the
catholic faith.

The first half of the Athanasian Creed (par. 3–26) recapitulates the trinitarian
debates and controversies of the fourth century as reflected in the Nicene Creed,
the theology of the Cappadocians, and especially the theology and method of
Augustine. With regard to the Trinity, it lays out a very simple thesis (par. 3–4)
that states, "Do not speak of the Trinity so as to give the impression that there
are three Gods and do not speak of the Trinity so as to give the impression that
there are not three persons." In this we may see the boundaries set over and against
Arianism[126] and Sabellianism. The Father is God, the Son is God, the Spirit is God,
yet there are not three Gods but one God. The Creed affirms the unity of the three
persons first with a set of three attributes (uncreated, eternity, unending) and three
titles (Almighty, God, Lord). Similarly, it preserves the distinction of the persons
by affirming the different relations that they share within the Trinity. The Father
is both uncreated and unbegotten. The Son is uncreated but begotten. The Spirit
is uncreated, not begotten, but proceeding. The Creed does not attempt to define
these terms. It is enough to know that in some way these terms distinguish the persons from one another.

The second half of the Athanasian Creed (par. 28–39) turns to questions of
Christology and thus picks up the theological reflection on the Nicene Creed's affirmation that the Son of God became a human creature. It reiterates the decisions
of the three councils regarding the person of Christ. It affirms against Apollinaris
that Jesus was a complete and genuine human creature, possessing both body and
a rational soul. Similarly, it affirms against Nestorius that the Son is one person and
not two persons. Kelly contends that the Christological section has Nestorianism
deliberately and completely in its sights. This includes the affirmation that one
nature is not transformed into the other. Kelly cautions that even though it might be
interpreted against Eutyches (an outspoken opponent of Nestorius) and his followers (who tended to confuse the two natures), it is not explicitly directed against the
Eutychians, most of whom would have affirmed that the "humanity was taken into
deity."[127] Then it reiterates part of the Chalcedonian definition when it asserts that
Christ is one not by the confusion of substance but by a unity of person (though it
does not use the language of "two natures").

The text concludes by continuing with the narrative of Christ's biography in
the language of the Nicene Creed that speaks of Christ's suffering, resurrection, session at the right hand of the Father, and second coming. It also inserts the "descent
into hell" into the narrative. It speaks of Christ's return for judgment in words that

are likely to make the average Lutheran cringe with at least a little nervousness, for it speaks of Christ giving eternal life to those who have done good things and plunging into eternal fire those that have done evil things. Does this run contrary to the Reformation teaching that we are justified by grace alone, Christ alone, and faith alone? Two points have to be kept in mind. First, the Athanasian Creed here simply reflects the way in which the Gospel of Matthew speaks of the last judgment. Second, the last judgment portrays a public judgment, and in public judgments public evidence is brought forward—in this case, the fruits of faith or the lack of such fruits of faith. It reflects the public teaching of the time in which it was composed.

The confidence and uncompromising tone of the introduction (par. 1–2), the transition from the trinitarian to the Christological sections (par. 27), and the conclusion (par. 40) provide many a twenty-first-century reader a certain shock. The introduction states that whoever wants to be saved must "hold the catholic faith" and "keep it whole and inviolate" or will otherwise perish eternally. The transition also asserts that it is "necessary for eternal salvation" to believe the incarnation. The conclusion again states, "A person cannot be saved without believing this firmly and faithfully." Does this mean that one needs to know and understand intellectually all that is said here? Bray points out that the Creed is not speaking of a purely rationalistic or intellectual grasping of the faith. He notes that the introduction speaks of "holding"—we might say "treasuring and cherishing"—what is here spoken of. Similarly, he points out that to hold to the faith means that we "worship one God in trinity" (par. 3).[128] Thus a person clings to the confession of Christ, both as the Son of God who is equal to the Father and Spirit and as the incarnate man who died and rose for our salvation.

So in spite of the unease that some may experience when reading the Athanasian Creed, a considered reflection will yield a different conclusion. "No other official document of creed sets forth, so incisively and with such majestic clarity, the profound theology implicit in the New Testament affirmation that 'God was in Christ reconciling the world to Himself.'"[129]

Conclusion

The three "ecumenical" creeds embraced by the sixteenth-century reformers and incorporated into *The Book of Concord* have very different histories. These histories emerged from places across the continent of Europe from East to West and were composed over spans of time stretching from the early church into the Middle Ages. Despite these differences in cultural setting and despite the various controversies in which the three creeds arose, they each confess and safeguard the gospel, setting it within the biblical witness to the triune God and the incarnation of the second person of the Trinity. How they do that is the question to which we now turn.

2

The Theological Contributions of the Ancient Creeds

The creeds and confessions seek to be nothing less than answers to Jesus' question, "Who do you say that I am?" (Matt. 16:15). The three creeds (and for that matter the distinctively Lutheran confessional writings) all stand in the trajectory of the New Testament's confession of Christ. The very appearance of Jesus raises the question of who he is and why he matters. This comes through clearly in Matthew 11–16. John the Baptizer asks, "Are you the coming one or shall we seek another?" (11:3). Herod asks, "Is this John the Baptizer come back to life?" (14:2). When Jesus queries his disciples about what people are saying about him, they note that some think he is Elijah, others Jeremiah, and others, John the Baptizer. Then Jesus turns to his disciples and says, "Who do you say that I am?" (16:13-15). Herman Sasse noted that with this question Jesus calls upon the church to confess him.[1]

Only the church can answer Jesus' question. Jesus addresses the question to the disciples not only as individuals but as a group, as the church. Peter answers on behalf of the group; Jesus replies, "Blessed are you son of Jonah, for flesh and blood has not revealed this to you, but my father in heaven." It is to the church that God has entrusted his revelation. The answer given by Peter is an answer that states who Jesus is and why he matters. "You are the Christ, the Son of the living God." It is a doctrinal answer, a statement of doctrine—and a statement that matters. Upon it and by it the church is gathered. Against it the gates of hell cannot stand (Matt. 16:18). It is an answer for which the church will give an account on the Last Day.

The creeds stand in this trajectory of the various New Testament confessional statements when they seek to answer that question, "Who is Jesus?" How do the creeds confess Christ? One's identity is shaped by a story in which relationships take place. The creeds first answer the question by setting forth the Son's relationship to God and then to the human race. In doing so, they set forth a trinitarian and incarnational Christology. Within those relationships they set forth the story of God's entrance into the world in order to rescue his creation. These two affirmations provide the context for rightly understanding the story of Jesus. The Reformation built upon them to bring out the soteriology of the story. Luther's Small Catechism captures it first by affirming that Jesus is "true God born of the Father from eternity" and "true man born of the virgin Mary." The Reformer then tells how this Jesus Christ rescued us and made us his own.

The Trinitarian Confession of Christ[2]

The creeds first confess the Son's identity by setting forth his relationship to the Father and the Spirit. This is particularly true with respect to the debates that led up to and culminated in the adoption of the Nicene Creed in the fourth century. In doing so, the question of Christ's deity led to a clearer and more definitive confession of the Trinity. The church confessed the Trinity for the purpose of answering the question, "Who is Jesus?" The creeds answer that question by setting forth the Son's relationship to the Father and the Spirit in two ways. They utilize what scholars have come to refer to as economic and immanent patterns of language when speaking about Christ within the Trinity.[3]

Trinitarian reflection in the New Testament and in the three centuries leading up to Nicaea generally considered the Trinity within the framework of the three-fold structure of God's work within the world (*oikonomia*).[4] It focused attention on the way in which the three persons (Father, Son, Spirit) manifested themselves by their activity in the world (see, for example, Eph. 1:3-14 and Gal. 4). This approach begins with the revelation of the three persons and then asks, "How are they one?" This "economic" approach to the Trinity has several characteristics. First, it begins from the vantage point of speaking about the three persons—Father, Son, and Holy Spirit. Jesus appears on the scene in the first century and declares that Yahweh is his Father and that together they will send the Holy Spirit. Second, economic language stresses the relationship of the three persons to the world, the role that each plays within the economy or structure of God's work within the world. Thus the Father is frequently identified as the creator and the one who sends the Son into the world for our salvation. The Son is identified as redeemer and Lord, the one who rescues and reconciles us to the Father. The Spirit is described as the one who reveals all things to us and brings us to Christ. Finally, in the New Testament, "Father" is nearly always identified with God (see John 3:16, Gal. 4, and other passages). The words "God" and "Father" are used synonymously and provide the locus for the unity of the three. All things proceed from the Father and return to the Father (*a patre, ad patrem*). As Gregory of Nazianzus expressed it, "All action which comes upon the creature from God...begins with the Father and is present through the Son and is perfected in the Holy Spirit." These relationships can be expressed by the prepositions used for each. Generally, the Father receives the prepositions "from" and "to." The Son receives the preposition "through." The Spirit receives the preposition "in" or "by."[5] This provides the pattern for speaking of God's activity toward us as well as the church's prayer and worship toward God. Thus we generally pray to the Father through Christ and in the Holy Spirit.

The "immanent" or "ontological" language for the Trinity follows a different pattern, focusing on the relationship of the Father, Son, and Holy Spirit to each other apart from their activity within the world. It deals with the "inner life of God" or the "eternal being of God."[6] First, it begins with the "oneness of God" and then asks, "How are they three?" This became characteristic of the West since the time of

Augustine, who established the practice of considering *De Deo Uno* before taking up the topic *De Deo Trino*.[7] Second, instead of addressing explicitly their relationship to the world, it focuses on their relationship to each other and in doing so identifies the distinctiveness of each person by setting forth their intra-trinitarian relations. It does so by speaking of their "origins." Thus the Father is described as uncreated and unbegotten. He begets a Son. The Son in turn is described as uncreated but begotten of the Father. Finally, the Spirit is described as unbegotten and uncreated but as proceeding from both the Father and the Son. Third, an immanent approach to the Trinity identifies God with the divine being that all three persons share rather than identifying God primarily with the Father. Thus the Father is God, the Son is God, and the Spirit is God. This approach has its own potential difficulties, particularly with regard to piety (for example, does it really matter to whom we pray since they are all God?) and relevance (many scholars today believe that the perception of the Trinity's irrelevance for most people or some kind of prolegomena to the more interesting questions of Christian theology is due to the West's eclipse of the economic Trinity in its nearly exclusive focus on the immanent Trinity).[8]

We can see a shift within the creeds in the language they use for confessing Christ. For example, the Apostles Creed speaks in exclusively economic language. The Creed speaks of three persons—Father, Son, and Holy Spirit—and focuses on their activities toward the world (*opera ad extra*). The three persons are considered within a cosmological framework of God's activity within the world rather than an ontological framework, which presents the very nature and being of God. The Father is identified with creation. The Son is identified by his incarnation, death, and resurrection. The Spirit is confessed in connection with his ongoing activities in the church—the forgiveness of sins, the resurrection of the body, and life everlasting. God the Father creates. The Son suffers and dies. The Holy Spirit governs the church, forgives sin, and leads his people into the resurrection and life everlasting.

While the Apostles Creed speaks of the three persons along with their activities toward the world (*opera ad extra*), there is virtually no mention of their ontological or eternity unity. In the Apostles Creed the word "God" does not refer to an abstract divine essence but to a concrete person within the narrative. God is identified with the Father. This reflects the dominant usage of the word in the New Testament.[9] The only place where a link is mentioned between the three persons appears in the second article. There it confesses that Jesus Christ is the Father's "only son" and "is conceived by the Spirit." The first phrase identifies Jesus with the creator over and against Gnosticism's separation of the two, with its resulting disparagement of the creaturely. The latter confesses the miracle of the incarnation and points toward the redemption of creation.

The Nicene Creed follows the Apostles Creed in using primarily economic language (based as it was, in all likelihood, on a baptismal creed) and thus stressing the priority and prominence of the three persons revealed in history (Father, Son, and Holy Spirit) over the unity of an eternal divine essence. With its confession of

(margin annotations: "manifestations of the 3 persons" / "The differing manifestations and functions of the 3 persons" / "operating within")

"one God the Father" in the first article and "One Lord Jesus Christ," it reflects the language of Paul in 1 Corinthians 8. That the Father is God is taken to be axiomatic. The deity of the Son is thus referred to the Father (and not to some divine essence). The Spirit's deity is then also referred to the Father and the Son ("who together with the Father and Son is worshipped and glorified"). The deity of both the Son and the Spirit are confessed by their relationship of origin to the Father.

The challenge posed by Arius shifted the trinitarian discussion away from the economy of salvation to the ontology of God's existence. He argued that, since the Son is begotten (that is, created—according to Arius) by the Father, the Son must be inferior to the Father in his being. In fact, for Arius the two verbs—begotten (γεννάω) and to come into existence (γίνομαι)—were seen as synonyms. And so the Father is unbegotten and uncreated. It was only logical that since the Son is begotten, he must also be made.[10] As a result, the second article of the Nicene Creed focuses on the question, "What does it mean for the Son to be 'begotten' from the Father?" (John 3:16). Each of the phrases—"God from God, light from light, very God from very God, begotten not made, of the same substance as the Father"— were intended to confess what it means to be "begotten," namely, it does not mean "to be created"! The Spirit's deity is also defined by also finding his origin in the Father as one who "proceeds from the Father." As the Son is "begotten" and just so not created, so the Spirit "goes forth" from God or is sent by God without being created.[11] The Spirit proceeds from the Father without being created. The Spirit also comes from the Father in a manner differently than the Son, for the Spirit proceeds and is not begotten.[12]

As a result of Nicaea, how the three persons relate to each other and are distinguished from one another moved to the forefront of theological reflection. While the Nicene Creed generally follows the economic way of speaking about God, the Creed shifts to an immanent way of speaking about God in order to confess the co-equality of the three persons.[13] It remains rooted in economy, but its emphasis shifts as it refocuses on Arius's question regarding the inner life of God. Therefore, the Creed has to begin addressing questions such as how the three persons are related to one another so as to be distinguished from each other. In doing so, it concentrates on the inter-trinitarian relations of Father, Son, and Spirit. The language of *homoousios* also paved the way for shifting the focus away from the Father as the locus of unity to the one divine essence that is common to all three persons. This is hinted at already in the phrases, "God from God, true God from true God." Still to be sorted out was the distinction between *ousia* and *hypostasis*, terms that Athanasius assumed to be synonymous, a point reflected in the antithesis of the Nicene Creed (325). By the end of fourth century, the Cappadocians helped the church sort out these issues and molded all subsequent thinking on the Trinity. They distinguished the persons in such a way that the Trinity consists of one divine *ousia* and three distinct *hypostases*.[14] In the fifth century Augustine shaped all subsequent Western reflection on the Trinity with his emphasis on the immanent Trinity.

Thus the Nicene Creed shifted the focal point to the ontological Trinity with its confession of the eternal narrative/nativity of the Son of God and its significance for us (that is, in Christ we encounter the saving work of God himself). In doing so, however, it equipped the Reformation with the foundation for stressing the biblical narrative regarding the work of the Trinity within the economy of salvation. The Reformation could draw out the soteriological significance of the Nicene confession for the work of Christ, in which we encounter not only God but the loving heart of the Father. This becomes clear in Luther's Small Catechism, where he opens the second article by confessing that Jesus is "true God, born of the Father from eternity" and then speaks of our redemption. The economic Trinity was not lost on the Reformers and it may be said that it was recovered by Luther. This comes out perhaps most clearly at the end of Luther's explanation to Creed in the Large Catechism, where he uses economic language: "For this very purpose he [the Father] created us, so that he might redeem us and make us holy, and, moreover, having granted and bestowed upon us everything in heaven and on earth, he has also given us his Son and his Holy Spirit, through whom he brings us to himself. For, as we explained above, we could never come to recognize the Father's favor and grace were it not for the LORD Christ, who is a mirror of the Father's heart. Apart from him we see nothing but an angry and terrible judge. But neither could we know anything of Christ, had it not been revealed by the Holy Spirit."[15]

By the sixth century the author of the Athanasian Creed found it appropriate to use almost exclusively immanent trinitarian language. The Creed confesses the oneness of God by speaking of all three persons as God (though it does not use explicitly the language of a common divine essence), and it defines the relationship of the three persons in intra-trinitarian terms. As a Western creed, the Athanasian Creed reflects the theology of Augustine. One can see the Augustinian influence in the critical phrase "what the Father is, such is the Son, and such is the Holy Spirit." This Creed follows this pattern for ascribing both divine attributes and divine titles to each person. For example, in the Apostles and Nicene Creeds, the words "Almighty" and "God" were used to speak about the Father. Similarly, the word "Lord" was used in the previous two creeds to speak about the Son (though the Nicene Creed does speak of the Spirit as "Lord and Giver of life"). But in the Athanasian Creed, these terms are not used primarily with reference to one person over the other two persons. Each of these titles is interchangeable. Hence, the Father is God, the Son is God, the Spirit is God, yet there are not three Gods but one God.

The economic and immanent Trinity both capture important biblical thoughts. Both approaches deal with the same God—first in his works within the world and then in his essence. The direction for trinitarian talk from the Apostles through the Athanasian Creed moves from largely economic patterns of thought to immanent patterns for speaking about the Trinity. Perhaps there were few options for doing otherwise. The use of immanent or ontological language for the Trinity became necessary in order to make the clear confession that it is God who is at work in the world and God who has come to save his human creatures.[16] But both approaches are important and provide helpful guides for Christians.

Gerhard Forde's distinction between primary and secondary discourse can help clarify these two patterns for speaking about the Trinity. Primary discourse refers to the language used in interpersonal conversation, "I-you" exchanges. Within the church it is the language often used in preaching, prayer, and worship. Secondary discourse is the language of analysis and observation, in the third person, describing the essence of a thing or some actions. It reflects on the scriptural revelation of God and how to speak about God. Economic language for the Trinity follows the pattern of the New Testament and may be understood as the basis of interpersonal conversation, as primary discourse, even when it occurs in the form of third person descriptions of God and his activity in relationship to his world. The two forms of speech are not unrelated to each other but must be used in conjunction with each other. While we may use the primary discourse concerning God's relationship to his people and his action in their behalf in preaching and prayer, we keep in the back of our minds the secondary discourse of the immanent Trinity. It prevents us from falling into speaking in such a way as to suggest that the Son is in any way subordinate to the Father.[17]

The Confession of Christ's Incarnation[18]

The trinitarian discussion addressed the question "Who is Jesus Christ?" by confessing his relationship with the Father and the Son. Jesus' identity was defined in terms of his relationship to the Father and the Spirit. Therefore, confessing the doctrine of the Trinity is determined by how one confesses the divinity of Jesus. At stake in the entire debate was the answer to the question, "Is it God who saves or not?" If it is not God, then we are not saved. The orthodox were certain that Arius could not believe that God saves in as much as he believed that the Son was a creature. The creeds of Nicaea and Constantinople in the fourth century countered with a resounding yes. In Jesus it is God who has come "for us and for our salvation" and no other (Gal. 1:11; Rom. 1:1).

But the confession of Jesus' deity does not exhaust the biblical witness concerning Jesus. The question "Who is Jesus Christ?" also needed to address his relationship to the human race. The Apostles Creed affirmed that Jesus was conceived by the Holy Spirit and born of the virgin Mary. The Nicene Creed also affirmed that the Son was incarnate by the Holy Spirit but expressed the soteriological implications of such a statement when it confessed, "who for us human creatures and for our salvation, became a human creature." Again, the issue of salvation pushed itself into the foreground. What does it mean that he saved human creatures by becoming a human creature?[19] Many worked with the axiom that what the Son did not assume, he did not rescue and heal. Thus if the Son did not assume a complete human nature, he did not redeem our entire person or being.

So did the Son become a complete and genuine human creature and thereby suffer and die as a human creature? Neither the Apostles nor the Nicene Creed explored the relationship between the divine nature of the Son of God and his assumed human nature. Questions such as "What does it mean that the Son of God became human?" had not yet become the subject of debate. It would not be long, however, before they did. Already by the first council at Constantinople in 381, questions had been arising about the human nature of Jesus. The Arians could argue that references in Scripture to Jesus' "weaknesses"—such as not knowing the date of the last day, weeping, or growing weary—were creaturely and not divine attributes. But they could attribute them to the Logos in as much as the Logos was a creature. Some Arians argued that the Logos took the place of the soul (which is what made one a real person) within the flesh of Jesus.[20]

Athanasius shared the conviction with Arius that being tired, weak, thirsty, and weeping were creaturely attributes. But these could not be attributed to the Logos who was *homoousios* with the Father. He attributed them instead to the flesh that the Logos assumed. The Logos then remained immutable when he submitted himself to the weakness of the flesh—a view that has been misleadingly described as a "space suit" Christology.[21] As an alternative approach, Eustathius of Antioch believed that one needed to speak of a human soul in Jesus to account for the psychological weaknesses without saying that the Logos was fallible. Apollinaris of Laodicea, a friend of Athanasius, viewed that as a rejection of Athanasius's teaching. He argued that the soul or mind is the self-directing principle within a person and that it was not possible to have two self-directing minds in one person without conflict. Furthermore, Jesus needed a soul or mind that would not falter in the face of temptation. The Logos became that mind or self-directing principle in Jesus. Apollinaris's opponents countered that the human mind needed healing as well as the body (what is not restored is not healed). Apollinaris complicated the issue further with his tendency to speak of the Logos as bringing his flesh down from heaven with him. This seemed to make Christ something of a mixture of God and man, a diluted deity and a truncated humanity.[22]

The answer of Constantinople (381) as well as the councils that followed in the fifth and sixth centuries argued that the Son of God assumed a complete and genuine human creature. The councils answered the question of "Who is Jesus?" by confessing the union of the divine and human in the one person of Jesus Christ. The Christological statements affirmed: Yes, God did indeed suffer by means of a human nature (*qua homo*). Luther asserted this point in no uncertain terms (and thus it was incorporated into article VIII of the Formula of Concord), that unless we can say "God died" and "God was dead," we cannot be sure of our salvation.

During the first half of the fifth century, a controversy broke out between Nestorius of Antioch, who became bishop of Constantinople in 427, and Cyril of Alexandria that shaped the Christological debates for centuries to come. It began with the question of whether one should regard Mary as the mother of God (*theotokos*). The ascription of the title to her in no way implied that Mary was in some way divine. The issue was whether or not the child she carried in her womb for nine months was the Son of God or only a human being—the issue of the union of the divine and human in Jesus. Cyril argued that the "Logos united with himself, in his own being or *hypostasis*, flesh animated with a rational soul, and became man." This meant that the Logos, though immutable and impassible, acquired the ability to experience conception, birth, and suffering in his body. The Son/Logos himself went through the entire process. Nestorius countered that this would make the Son passible, thereby confusing the divine and human natures. He argued that in Christ the two natures dare not be confused. Thus Nestorius described the union of the divine and human in Christ more as a juxtaposition of two natures, just as a marriage brings about a union of two persons. "Christ can be called both impassible and subject to passion, being impassible in his Godhead and subject to passion in his body."[23] This means, "suffering should be attributed to his humanity, not to the Logos." This gave rise to the concern that he divided the person of Christ into two persons and that no genuine union truly existed. The Council of Ephesus in 431, under the leadership of Cyril, rejected Nestorius' position.

The council of Ephesus did not end the controversy. In 447 an older monk named Eutyches, a disciple of Cyril of Alexandria, was accused of saying that in the incarnation the humanity of Christ was absorbed into the one nature of the divinity. Eutyches maintained that the resulting human nature that Christ had received from Mary was no longer the same as ours or consubstantial with ours but was "taken up into the one nature of the Incarnate Word."[24] His position moved in the direction of saying that there were two natures prior to the incarnation but only one nature subsequent to the incarnation. This view came to be known as Monophysiticism— although many adherents insist that it is more accurately Miaphysitism[25]—and tended to characterize certain elements of Eastern Christology. The West adopted the position that the Son of God had one nature (divine) prior to the incarnation and two natures after the incarnation.

This issue came to a head at the Council of Chalcedon, which opened on October 8, 451. On October 22, 451, it published what has become known as the Chalcedonian Formula of Definition. The groundwork for this Definition had already been laid by Pope Leo's *Tomus* (letter) of May 21, 449, in which he agreed with the Alexandrians that the Logos was the subject who experienced the incarnation but agreed with the Antiochenes that Jesus was a man in fullest sense. The Chalecedonian Definition represented something of a compromise between the Antiochene position represented by Nestorius and the Alexandrian position represented by Cyril. The Definition was Antiochene in expression (two natures in one person) but Alexandrian in content.[26] After affirming that the Christ is perfect God and perfect human, and affirming Mary as *theotokos*, it declared that Christ must be confessed "in two natures, without confusion, without change, without division, without separation." The Chalcedonian Definition did not so much define the relationship of the two natures in the Son as it set boundaries or parameters for recognizing when one has gone out of bounds and is no longer speaking of the union of two natures in a way that is congruent with the Scriptural witness to Christ. It continued by affirming that each nature retains its distinctive characteristics within the one person of the Son of God. Frances Young argues that, as a compromise, it was doomed to failure, since it satisfied neither the Western insistence that two natures existed in Christ after the incarnation nor the alternative view that two natures existed before the incarnation but only one afterward, thus suggesting a preexistent humanity and a subsequent mixture of the natures.[27]

The followers of Cyril of Alexandria were not entirely content with how the unity of the two natures in Christ was confessed at Chalcedon. The Alexandrians continued to be concerned that the Chalcedonian Formula left open possible Nestorian interpretations. That Formula stated that each nature does what it is appropriate for it in communion with the other. For the followers of Cyril, this seemed to leave open the possibility of speaking of two "acting subjects." It could be understood to mean that "the Word performs the miracles and the human nature experiences the suffering." This suggests "that there are two separate acting subjects in Christ."[28] This in turn implies that the Son/Logos did not take part in the suffering and death and that only the human nature suffered as the "acting subject." The Alexandrians, to the contrary, insisted on the need to stress that Jesus had one center of operation, one consciousness, and one will, namely, the Logos.[29] They insisted that "it really was the divine Logos who experienced the limitations of human life, and suffered and died."[30] At stake was the issue of salvation, specifically whether God experienced what the human nature did. Especially critical was the question: Did God suffer in Christ and die or not?[31] This had long been a thorny issue, since nearly everyone took it as axiomatic that God does not suffer. Much of this was due to the influence of Plato, for whom perfection implied no change. Change suggests that something is moving toward perfection or away from perfection. Given that, the inevitable question arose: How can the Son of God suffer and still be God?

In order to make it clear that the Logos partook in the suffering and death, the Scythian monks of the sixth century advocated the unequivocal formula, "One of the Trinity was crucified in the flesh." Two points must be made. First, the second person of the Trinity must be regarded as the subject of all the actions of Jesus. Second, the Logos or second person of the Trinity suffered and died by means of the flesh. Maxwell notes that the debate occurred over how to understand the qualifiers "in the flesh" or "according to the humanity." For Nestorians, the clauses "in the flesh" or "according to humanity" could be used to mean that only the humanity suffered and died. But for the Scythians they designated the way or means by which the Logos suffered. "If God is to suffer, he must do it by means of the flesh because he cannot do it by means of the divine nature."[32] The Son of God acquired the ability to suffer and die by assuming a human nature in the incarnation.[33] Thus the Scythian "theopaschite formula" "is intended to be a genuine confession of divine suffering."[34] The Second Council of Constantinople (553) endorsed the theopaschite formula. Its tenth canon asserted, "If anyone does not confess that our Lord

Jesus Christ who was crucified in the flesh is true God and Lord of glory and one of the holy Trinity, let him be anathema."[35]

The church continued to wrestle with the union of the two natures in Christ in order to maintain, on the one hand, that the Logos was the self-directing subject in Jesus and, on the other hand, that the Son assumed a complete and genuine human nature. A century later the issue arose as to whether or not Jesus had both a divine will and a human will. A key text in this debate was the prayer that Jesus uttered in Gethsemane as he wrestled with the fate that awaited him, "not my will be done but your will be done" (Matt. 26:39). Bray points out that earlier some had believed that this verse proved Jesus was not truly God. A more nuanced understanding had emerged and with it a desire to emphasize the "voluntary nature of Christ's sacrifice." The sixth ecumenical council in 681 affirmed that the Son of God had two wills. With this assertion the church sought to maintain a balanced approach that took into account the entire picture of Christ as set forth in the Scriptures. By affirming two wills it could confess that the Son's will is one with the Father even as according to his human will he expressed reluctance, which "was the normal human fear of suffering and death which anyone in similar circumstances would feel."[36]

Finally, the seventh ecumenical council at Nicaea (787) dealt with the iconoclastic controversy involving the destruction of images that portrayed God in paintings or sculptures. When Pope Leo III ordered the destruction of images fifty years earlier (726), on the grounds that it violated the commandment prohibiting graven images, it sparked a full-blown controversy. On the one hand, God cannot be pictured. On the other hand, God became a man who can be portrayed in pictures or sculptures. In his case, was a painting "a representation of the divine person, or merely of the human nature?" Bray notes that the theology of Leontius of Jerusalem pointed the way forward. He adopted Leontius of Byzantium's doctrine of *enhypostasia* ("a nature exists within a person without exhausting its capacity") and argued that the divine person and divine nature were separate principles. "In his human nature the divine person lived a normal human life, not abandoning the attributes of his divine nature, but allowing them to distort the human nature by removing its limitations." In this way the "Logos gave an identity to the human nature of Jesus, and in this capacity he suffered and died on the cross."[37] This position became standard in both East and West. Since the "human nature of Jesus had a divine identity, or hypostasis," it was axiomatic that any portrayal of Jesus was a portrayal of God. It affirmed that since God became a human creature in the incarnation, it was appropriate for images to be made of God. In doing so, it saved Christian art for the church.[38]

The trinitarian and Christological framework within which the subsequent Lutheran confessional statements are considered and developed served fundamentally to provide more boundaries for the church's speaking about God; they did not intend to explain the mystery of the divine being.[39] This reflects the language of the Athanasian Creed. "Do not speak about the Father, Son, and Holy Spirit in such a way as to give the impression that there are three Gods. And do not speak about God in such a way as to give the impression that there is no distinction between the Father, Son, and Holy Spirit." To cross those boundaries is no longer to speak the way Scripture speaks. But these boundary markers do not exhaust the Scriptural witness to Christ. Within those boundaries any number of questions and answers can be considered. Within this framework the sixteenth-century Reformers considered further questions related to anthropology and our need for Christ as well as to soteriology and the benefits of Christ.

Taken together, the three creeds and seven ecumenical councils make clear two non-negotiable convictions of Christian theology. The first is that only God can save his human creatures. The trinitarian confession of the fourth century deals with this first truth and affirms that in the Son of God we come face to face with God himself. The second conviction is that by becoming a complete human creature, God has saved his human creatures. Gregory of Nazianzus responded to Apollinaris by stating, "What is not assumed, is not healed."[40]

Confessing the Story

It has been observed that, while the Apostles and Nicene Creeds are not strictly narratives, they do contain narrative elements.[41] Dorothy Sayers goes further and argues that creeds not only tell a story; they convey "the greatest drama ever staged." "The drama is summarized quite clearly in the Creeds of the Church, and if we think it dull, it is because we either have never really read those amazing documents, or have recited them so often and so mechanically as to have lost all sense of their meaning. The plot pivots upon a single character, and the whole action is the answer to a single central problem, *What think ye of Christ?*"[42] The creeds open the drama with God creating the heavens and earth, move to a focus on Christ's surprising and tragic death followed with his unexpected resurrection, and conclude with the Spirit's breathing new life into creation with the resurrection of the body. In this they provide something of an outline of the Scriptures that stretches from creation in Genesis 1, runs through the Gospels, and concludes with the new creation of Revelation 21. The Athanasian Creed follows a structure similar to the *Te Deum Laudamus* and thus concludes with a Christological narrative that takes us to the final judgment. Through it all, we discover that it is God whom we encounter in this story and it is God who is acting for his human creatures and his entire creation.

The First Article

One cannot overstate the theological importance of the confessional affirmation of the first article of the Creed—a point that we perhaps too often take for granted after two thousand years of Christian history. The confession that God is the almighty creator of heaven and earth sets the stage for everything that follows. It defines what makes God God. It locates the definition and identity of God within a narrative: God is the one who created everything that exists. If one did not create everything that exists, then that person is not God—period! The first article also lays the foundation for the first commandment that enjoins us not to confuse the creator with his creation. Crucially for the Nicene Creed, it also provides the backdrop for the debate with Arius, who had raised the question: Is the Son of God creator or creature? Finally, it shapes the Christian conception of salvation in terms of the resurrection of the body and the new creation.

The positive confession of creation in the first article of the creeds proved to be something of a radical countercultural confession in the first and second centuries. Young notes that the affirmation that God created everything out of nothing "came to distinguish Christianity from all other philosophies in the ancient world."[43] Christians lived in a world in which polytheism shaped popular culture and Platonism (and even Gnosticism) shaped the intellectual world of the philosophers.[44] Into this world Christians came proclaiming the belief that they had inherited from the Old Testament, namely, that the one God, the Father, created everything that exists. This was done by confessing that God created "heaven and earth," to which the Nicene Creed adds, "all things visible and invisible." By means of this merism (mentioning the extremes to include everything in between), they confessed that God created everything that is not God. God created everything from the smallest atom to the largest galaxy. This had far-reaching ramifications.

First, most pagan religions affirmed the eternity of matter or the eternity of the universe, even if it had its origins in something of a primordial soup. This was true for the pagan religions of Egypt and Babylon as well as Greece and Rome. Similarly, Platonism itself affirmed the eternity of matter. To be sure, it was chaotic and inherently unstable, but it had existed from eternity alongside the spiritual and invisible world of the forms. Nicaea's specification of "all things visible and invisible" was inserted in order to take into account the scientific worldview of Platonism as well as the spiritual beings.

Second, to say that God created *everything* implied that God created everything out of nothing (*ex nihilo*).[45] God did not create out of himself in such a way as to divide his being, nor did God give birth to the universe out of his being. The world is not part of God, and God is not part of the world. The world is not in some way divine and cannot be located along a spectrum of deity. Instead, there exists an absolute distinction between the creator and his creation. This provides the basis for a Christian worldview that organizes reality not into spiritual and material categories but around the distinction between the creator and his creation. In turn, that becomes the basis for the first commandment (do not confuse the creator with his creation!). This provided the critical framework for the Arian controversy. Arius identified the Son of God as the creator's creation; the council of Nicaea defined the Son of God as the creator.

Third, God does not create out of preexisting material. He is neither dependent upon preexisting material for creation, nor is he limited by the materials with which he has to work (much in the way that the medium in which a painter works—oils, acrylics, or watercolors—limit what that artist can accomplish). By contrast, Plato's "craftsman" is not truly creative. He imposes order upon a chaotic material world in light of the blueprint provided by the world of forms. The God confessed by the creeds, on the other hand, creates by speaking creation into existence. This insight carried far-reaching ramifications for a Reformation theology of the word of justification. For that same Word that spoke the world into existence, that Word that said, "let there be light"—and there was light—now says, "you are justified," and we are justified. God's Word is a performative word. God's Word does what it says.

Fourth, to say that God chose to create also means that God created because he wanted to create. There was no external necessity compelling him to create, nor was there any internal compulsion requiring him to create (that is, that he was lonely and needed companionship). All this is to say that God created freely and hence graciously. Creation is an act of sheer graciousness and extravagant generosity. Creation is a gift. This also highlights God's nature as a God of love. God's modus operandi continues through each of the three articles of the creeds. In fact, Luther used the same language to describe God's act of ongoing creating as he would for justification. At the conclusion of the first article in the Small Catechism, he writes, "all this out of sheer fatherly goodness and mercy without any merit or worthiness in me."[46]

Finally, the first article affirms the unconditional goodness of creation. A God who is love chose to create it freely and willingly. Creation is neither inherently chaotic and unstable (Plato) nor intrinsically evil (Gnosticism). In such cases, matter appeared as a "second principle alongside God, even opposed to God."[47] The affirmation of the goodness of creation carries with it ramifications for how one thinks about the incarnation of Jesus. Must one regard it as a sham or a phantom because it is somehow not appropriate that God associates himself directly with the material world (and "gets his hands dirty" with the material world, so to speak)? Similarly, it carries ramifications for the third article's affirmation that God continues to work through the creaturely elements in the sacraments for our salvation. It affects one's view of salvation. Does Jesus come to free us from the prison of our frail bodies, or does he come to restore us with a view toward the resurrection of the body on the last day at which point he will restore and renew his entire creation?

While the creeds' confession of God as creator of all things was a strong countercultural statement, it did not exhaust what the creeds had to say about God's relationship to his creation. The statement, "maker of heaven and earth" spoke of what theologians have come to call the initial creation (*creatio prima*). But the confession that God created everything does not stop there, as if God was finished with his creation and then let it run by itself. With the statement that God is the "almighty," it also speaks of God's ongoing involvement in and care for creation. More literally, the Greek speaks of God as *Pantokrator*, the all-ruling one. This suggests that the title "almighty" does not simply speak in an abstract way about an attribute of God (that is, "God can do whatever he wants"). Instead, by speaking of God as *Pantokrator*, it emphasizes that God is actively ruling and governing his creation. He remains intimately involved in maintaining, preserving, and providing for his creation. This came to be known later in terms of God's ongoing creation (*creatio continua*).

This emphasis on God's continuing care for his creation moved more into the foreground with the sixteenth-century Lutheran Confessions. Luther in particular would explore and unfold more fully what God's involvement with his creation here and now entails. For example, a cursory examination of his explanation of the first article in the Small Catechism quickly reveals that he is most interested in speaking about how God has "made me." In other words, Luther wants us to see that we ourselves are part of God's handiwork; we are his creatures! In fact, Luther exulted in the knowledge of being a creature. He also developed the concept of God's continuing work in his creation, particularly with Luther's concept of human creatures serving as the masks of God (*larvae dei*). Creatures are the gloves on God's hands. Luther speaks of them in the Large Catechism as the instruments and means through which he blesses us.[48] In fact, God working "in, with, and under" his creation becomes his characteristic way of working (*modus operandi*) in all three articles of the creeds. He works through the creaturely body of Jesus for salvation and through the first-article creaturely gifts (*dona creata*) in order to accomplish the third-article work of faith and sanctification. Finally, Luther's text even points the way forward toward addressing questions raised by the environmental movement regarding our place within creation. In the Small Catechism he states that God has made "me together with all creatures," suggesting that we share something in common with the rest of creation even as we are distinct from the rest of creation.[49]

The Second Article

Who is Jesus, and why does he matter? The creeds do not answer that question by citing the sayings of Jesus or by making specific references to the ministry of Jesus and his various miracles. Instead, they focus on key events in his life. Whatever else you need to know about Jesus, you need to know this. This suggests that his teachings are not the key to unlocking who he is and why he matters. Nor are his miracles. Such approaches may help determine the impact and significance of other founders of the world's various religions. But they do not perform that function in the case of Jesus. Instead, the essence of Christianity as set forth in the creeds and the Book of Concord does not center on how we are to live, with Jesus as the example of how we are to treat each other. The essence of Christianity is not what we do but what Christ has done for us!—the how, why, and for-what-purpose this person lived.

The Christological narrative or sequence of the second article of the creeds centers on three crucial events or narrative arcs, namely, the incarnation of the Son, the suffering and death of Christ, and his resurrection and exaltation. Not surprisingly, these three events have shaped and thus correspond to three major festivals of the church year, namely, Christmas, Good Friday, and Easter. Why these items?

They are hardly exhaustive of the New Testament witness. A number of seemingly important events are missing from this narrative. For example, there is no mention of the baptism of Jesus, the transfiguration of Jesus, or any of the miracles of Jesus.

Yet there is biblical warrant for focusing on these three narrative elements, since they were highlighted already by the Apostle Paul. Paul does not quote Jesus' sermons, nor does he refer to specific miracles that Jesus performed. Instead, when Paul summarizes the gospel of Jesus, he speaks of him as descended from David according to the flesh, dying, and rising again. Consider Romans 1: "concerning his Son, who was descended from David according to the flesh and was declared to be the Son of God in power according to the Spirit of holiness by his resurrection from the dead, Jesus Christ our Lord, through whom we have received grace" (Rom. 1:3-5). Paul provides another summary in his first letter to the Corinthians: "For I delivered to you as of first importance what I also received: that Christ died for our sins in accordance with the Scriptures, that he was buried, that he was raised on the third day in accordance with the Scriptures, and that he appeared to Cephas, then to the twelve. Then he appeared to more than five hundred brothers at one time, most of whom are still alive, though some have fallen asleep" (1 Cor. 15:3-5). Other examples can be found throughout other New Testament writings as well. They nearly always focus on his death and resurrection and occasionally include the incarnation as well.

These three narrative events within the creeds are supplemented and extended with the addition of a number of other statements that bring out more detail and clarity. The incarnation or birth of Christ is described as taking place by the Spirit's conception and by birth from the virgin Mary. Similarly, the death of Christ is described in various ways. The Nicene Creed simply uses the word "suffering" to encompass the entire event, including the death and burial. The Apostles Creed, on the other hand, emphasizes the reality of Christ's death with four expressions, "suffered under Pontius Pilate, crucified, dead, and buried." It does so in all likelihood to oppose the views of Marcion, who in line with earlier Docetists denied the reality of the Jesus' human nature. Marcion apparently argued that Jesus came down from heaven as a fully-grown man but did not have corporeal existence. Instead, he appeared as a ghostly figure. This rendered the death of Christ as little more than an illusion. The exaltation of Christ generally begins with the resurrection, although in the Apostles Creed it opens with the descent into hell, according to some sixteenth-century interpreters. From the resurrection it continues through the ascension of Christ, his session at the right hand of God, and then his return at the final judgment, at which time he will rule his kingdom without end.

In general, the creeds do not elaborate on the soteriological implications of this narrative. The Nicene Creed states that it was "for our salvation" that the Son became a human creature in order to die bodily and rise bodily for us. But in general, the creeds do not expand on how the death and resurrection of Christ accomplish our salvation. Early Christian theologians developed different approaches but seldom tried to explain his atoning work with elaborate theories. Gustav Aulen, in his classical study *Christus Victor,* examined several atonement motifs but perhaps did not take into account sufficiently the variety of motifs used in the early church.[50] Maxwell has noted that early church fathers such as Melito of Sardis and Athanasius at times interpreted the cross and resurrection in light of the Old Testament Day of Atonement narrative but more often interpreted them in light of the Passover narrative. For Melito, "Christ is the sacrificed Passover lamb whose blood conquers death. By His resurrection, He leads His people out of Egypt, that is, out of sin and death." He notes that the sacrifice occurs not to render atonement but to rescue from death. The Passover narrative also dominates Athanasius's thinking. Just as "the blood of the Passover lamb averted the angel of death, so also the blood of Christ conquers the power of death and Satan."[51] Both the death and resurrection of Christ constitute victory over death. Luther[52] would take this in a direction that Maxwell refers to as the "stomping narrative." Its genius lies in that it has a "place for the experience of defeat."[53] In his death, Jesus experienced defeat at the hands of Satan and death. But in the resurrection Christ turned the tables and crushed those powers that enslave us.

Perhaps the one clause in the Apostles Creed that has provoked more controversy than any other is the clause "descended into hell." It appears to have entered the Creed from the Eastern church. There it appears for the first time in the Fourth Formula of Sirmium, otherwise known as the Dated Creed of 359. But it had been a theme within the East for several centuries. Scholars are not sure precisely when the descent into hell entered the Apostles Creed in the West nor why. The scriptural basis for the descent into hell usually includes the following texts: Romans 10:7; Colossians 1:18; Acts 2:27-31 (Ps. 16:8-11), and 1 Peter 2:19. Historically, it was explained in two different ways.[54] The first and oldest, relying on 1 Peter 2:19, saw Christ descending into hell in order to spend three days proclaiming the gospel to the Old Testament saints. Christ went down into hell in order to give the Old Testament saints the opportunity to repent and thus be saved. Irenaeus, Justin, Origin, and Hippolytus tended to advocate this particular interpretation. The difficulty here is that it suggests that the people of the Old Testament knew nothing of Christ or the promises of his coming. The second interpretation saw Christ descending into hell in order to announce the defeat and subjugation of Satan and his minions (analogous to a conquering army entering its enemy's capitol).[55] This interpretation gained in popularity with thinkers like Rufinus and later Caesarius of Arles, who wrote, "He descended to hell in order to rescue us from the jaws of the cruel dragon." Kelly thus concludes that the inclusion of the descent provided the Apostles Creed with something that it had been lacking, namely, the act of redemption: by conquering Satan, he rescued us.[56]

In the sixteenth century the interpretation of the descent became a subject of debate that led to its inclusion in the Formula of Concord. Although the intention was to affirm that the entire Christ (the divine-human Son of God)[57] descended into hell, the Formula relied on Luther's interpretation that understood it as the first stage of Christ's exaltation, to be followed by the resurrection, ascension, and session at the right hand of God.

Perhaps most importantly, the Reformation confessions focus on how the salvation that Christ accomplished is applied to us, that is, accomplished for us (*pro nobis*). The Apostles Creed hints at it with its opening, "Jesus Christ *our* Lord." The Reformation confessions, especially Luther's Catechisms, pick up on the *pro me* ("for me") character of that confession and confess that Jesus has become *my* Lord. The Augsburg Confession defines the gospel as story plus promise. It uses the words of the Apostles Creed regarding the suffering of Jesus to say, "in order to be a sacrifice." Similarly, following the creeds' confession of Jesus' exaltation, the Augsburg Confession brings out the promise, "in order to rule, guard, and define his church through the Holy Spirit."[58] As seen earlier, the Nicene Creed does emphasize that the Son became incarnate as a human creature in order to save his human creatures.

The Third Article

Of the three articles of the creeds, the work of the Spirit comes across as the least developed. The church certainly did more with the doctrine of the Holy Spirit at Constantinople (381) than at Nicaea (325) by affirming the deity of the Holy Spirit. But it does not exhaust theological reflection on the Trinity. Nicaea had something of a "two hands" of God approach (Irenaeus): the Son is begotten from the Father and the Spirit proceeds from the Father. But it did not state how the Son and the Spirit relate to each other. The insertion of the *filioque* changed the balance of the Nicene Creed by affirming the complete deity of the Son. There is nothing that the Father does that the Son does not also do (such as sending the Spirit). But it could give the impression that the Spirit ends up in a somewhat subordinate position. What is the Spirit's role within the Trinity? For example, do the Spirit and the Father together send the Son?[59] Beyond that, the Nicene Creed does speak of the Spirit's work as the one who reveals the gospel to us (spoken by the prophets), which hints at his role in the inspiration of Scripture (2 Pet. 1:20-21). By characterizing him as the Lord and giver of life, it calls for consideration of the role of the Spirit as the one who gives life through creation, conversion, and the resurrection.

The Apostles Creed confesses this faith sparsely: "and the Holy Spirit." It offers no further elaboration on either the Spirit's deity or the Spirit's work. It simply follows this up with a list of items that appears to be more of an appendix, although they could be seen as the activities of the Spirit. These items include the "holy catholic church" (Luther rendered it "holy Christian church," following a northern European usage introduced in the fifteenth century), the communion of saints, the forgiveness of sins, resurrection of the body, and life everlasting, and they are not explicitly related to the Holy Spirit. Integrating them into a coherent unity as the Spirit's work would be left for later commentators, such as Luther, who calls this article "sanctification" in his catechisms. The Spirit is the one who brings us to the

Lord Jesus to receive his blessings,[60] and he does this by means of the church, the forgiveness of sins, the holy Christian church, the communion of saints, and the resurrection of the body.

Of the expressions in the third article of the Apostles Creed, perhaps the most debated in recent years involves the relationship between "holy catholic church" and "communion of saints." Are they two expressions of the same reality, or are they saying different things? The problem is that scholars cannot determine precisely when these expressions entered the Creed, or by whom they were added, thus authorial intent cannot be determined. For example, does the one refer to the church militant and the other to the church triumphant? In his rejection of an understanding of the church as a building or as polity, Luther contended in his Large Catechism that "communion of saints" (or "believers") was an explanation of "holy Christian church." Thus we believe in the holy Christian church, that is, the gathering of all believers. Since the liturgical renewal movement of the 1960s, some have suggested understanding *communio sanctorum* as "communion of sacred things" rather than "communion of saints." Doing so would suggest that it then refers the Lord's Supper. This then would complement the Nicene Creed's mention of "one baptism for the forgiveness of sins." Evidence from patristic sources for this usage, however, appears to be inconclusive.

Finally, the creeds conclude by directing our eyes to a future for which we long and hope, namely, the resurrection of the body and life everlasting. Here too, we can see an ongoing emphasis upon the value of the creaturely over and against any and every disparagement of material existence. It is worth emphasizing that the creeds do not speak of the Christian hope primarily in terms of dying and going to heaven. Instead, they capture the dominant note of the New Testament that frames the Christian hope in terms of the resurrection of the body (1 Cor. 15) and the renewal of creation (Rom. 8).[61] Kelly points out that in the Apostles Creed, the clause "everlasting life" is added to say something further about the resurrection. By itself, the resurrection of the body could imply that one rises up only to die again.[62] But with this emphasis on eternal life, it means that one will rise bodily never again to die. Kelly suggests that it was added to reassure troubled minds, to bring out the full significance of the resurrection of the body.

Conclusion

The creeds provide a framework for confessing Jesus in every age. They deal with questions regarding the person of Jesus Christ in his relation to the Trinity and in his union with humanity. The distinctively Lutheran confessions of the sixteenth century build on that foundation and proceed to confess the anthropological assumptions and soteriological implications of the three ecumenical creeds. As Bray points out, the creeds do not hinder theology but invite us into the Scriptures. "For a generation which cries out for fresh study and exploration, the creeds still offer an unexpected treasure-store of material waiting to be tapped by the adventurous and the creative."[63]

Part II

The Wittenberg Confessions, Luther's and Melanchthon's Confessions of the Faith

3

Luther's Small and Large Catechisms

Apocalypticists are not generally thought of as long-range planners. But when they do turn their minds to the particular, viewing everything in light of God's action toward the impending end, they produce some of the revolutionary literature of Western culture—the middle chapters of Isaiah, for example, or the letters of the Apostle Paul, and, for both their origin and impact, the catechisms of Martin Luther.[1]

Luther's apocalypticism has not always been recognized.[2] Some characteristic features of apocalyptic writings like Daniel, the Revelation of St. John, or Mark 13, with their divisions of time and vivid imagery, are altogether missing in Luther's writing. But Heiko Oberman's definition of apocalyptic in the late medieval world fits Luther exactly. "The waiting is for God to act," Oberman writes, with the reform itself being viewed in terms of God's in-breaking.[3]

Through the early years of the Lutheran Reformation, this expectation was clearly a factor in the way the reform proceeded. In fact, in the eyes of both Luther and his supporters, the events of the period between 1517 and 1527 gave credence to such hope. From a new and obscure faculty in a remote community situated on an ethnic divide in Saxony, Luther was catapulted to the very center of European attention, within a few years standing before the emperor himself to confess the faith just as the old order was apparently breaking down.

Realities of a Reformation

If they seem proportional from the distance of centuries, in the eyes of the Reformers, events of the ensuing years continued the apocalyptic roll, even if in a more threatening way. Already an excommunicant, Luther was outlawed and then faced with one crisis after another: divisions in Wittenberg itself; theological conflicts with a series of opponents, including in 1524–1526 the leading academic light in Europe, Erasmus of Rotterdam; then in 1524, the Peasants' War broke out. It appeared to Luther as the opening of the floodgates of chaos and conflagration.

But even while the accumulating strains fed apocalyptic expectation, Luther had eyes for everyday realities. Amid all the chaos, among other things, he got married—"to make the angels laugh and the devils weep," as he put it. But he also took steps toward bringing reform into the parishes of Saxony, steps that would eventually lead him to write the first of the Lutheran confessional documents, the Small and the German, or Large, Catechisms.

A Movement in Transition

It took only a short while for the Lutheran reformers to begin thinking about the practical realities of renewing parish life in their region though a number of factors combined to restrain such interests. When the possibility of organized reform on a wider basis began to emerge, they took steps to get an assessment of the actual conditions prevailing in the congregations. As the reports came in, however, there was some deep disagreement about how to proceed. By 1528 it was clear that Luther himself was going to have to formulate a way of bringing the reform down to earth.

In fact, concern for the everyday life of the people gathered in medieval Saxon parishes lay deep in the origins of the Lutheran reform. Teaching at the University of Wittenberg, overseeing several area Augustinian monasteries, in 1517 Luther was also preaching a couple of times a week and taking a turn hearing confessions. A lot of priestly help was required in the confessional because it was an annual requirement for virtually the whole population. It was as he took his turns hearing confessions that Luther encountered the abuse of indulgences that fired his initial protest at the door of the Wittenberg church. This, of course, turned out to be a match in a service station, the explosion spreading across Germany and into surrounding countries.

The concern for the practice of the faith was more than occasional. Through the late 1510s and early 1520s, Luther regularly wrote and preached on such matters. The *Flugschriften*, pamphlets that could be quickly printed and easily distributed, carried the Lutheran witness into the emerging cities and the surrounding countryside. Like *The Freedom of a Christian*, one of the five great treatises of 1520–1522 and the classical formulation of Luther's understanding of the gospel, these writings were directly accessible to the public, even in a semi-literate context. By the same token, Luther regularly preached on key elements of Christian life and practice, such as the Apostles Creed and the sacraments, baptism and the Lord's Supper.[4]

Inherent as this down-to-earth-ness was in Luther's reform, a combination of factors and forces prevented it from becoming programmatic. Some of these factors were basic to the nature of the Lutheran reform, others were situational. Reform was a perennial topic in later fifteenth- and sixteenth-century Europe. The biblical humanism that had swept the academic world, capturing its imagination, was driven by a determination to recover the literary power of the ancient world and reshape public life accordingly. Leo X, the pope who excommunicated Luther in 1520, was elected by the College of Cardinals to reform the papacy itself. The name of Jan Hus, a fifteenth-century reformer from Prague, not so far southeast of Wittenberg, was so familiar in the region even a hundred years later that Luther was widely understood to be in his succession.

But reform-minded as the times were, Luther's apocalyptic gave such hopes a different twist, undermining the attempt to make it a human project. "While Philip and Amsdorf and I drank Wittenberg beer,"[5] he later reminisced, "the Word reformed the church." Conceived in the light of eternity, the only appropriate reform of the church would be God's work. Anything else would simply be more evidence, as if any additional were needed, of human pretense.

Thus, unlike other reformers of the time, Luther did not set out systematically to overhaul the life of the church or the community. In 1522 Ignatius Loyola lay wounded in Spain writing his *Spiritual Exercises*, a program of self-reform that through the Society of Jesus—the Jesuits—he offered as a pattern for the whole church. In 1542 John Calvin published his *Ecclesiastical Ordinances for the City of Geneva*, a blueprint for transforming his community into a beacon on the hill that would shed its light to the whole world. Luther, in contrast, convinced that God was transforming all things, went to work on a much more proximate goal proportional to the doctoral oath he had taken in 1512: his project was to improve the preaching of parish priests. He began by composing model sermons for them, his postils, while at the Wartburg in 1521/1522.[6]

At the same time there was another factor in Luther's understanding of reform related to his understanding of the church. He had no idea of the kind of denominationalism that later developed in North America, and if he had, he probably would have regarded it with horror. He was a Catholic in every sense of the word, identifying himself with the larger church even long after his own excommunication. He never abandoned his view of the church as universal.[7]

This ecumenical orientation is responsible for what has been classically termed "the conservative reformation." Forswearing the language of transformation, Luther saw himself as going to the origins—the Word of God incarnate in Christ Jesus, which approaches now out of the Scriptures—to declare it once more and to support its continued declaration in Saxony. Thus, the Lutheran Reformation was conservative in the sense that it moved within the framework of the catholic tradition instead of attempting something novel and also in that it sought to preserve what it regarded as definitive, namely, the word prior to all tradition in Christ himself. Such an understanding of the church made programmatic attempts at reform appear pretentious and divisive.

In addition to the internal factors, there were also some external restraints that blocked the way to a more systematic attempt at reform. The most immediate was the Edict of Worms. Promulgated by Charles V after Luther's appearance before him in 1521, the Edict not only outlawed Luther but proscribed his followers. In fact, Lutheranism—as it came to be called—was illegal, and the threat remained that Charles would use the force of the Holy Roman Empire as well as his own considerable power to implement the edict. As it turned out, for various reasons, Charles was not able to make good on it for almost two more decades. But for the first several years following the Diet of Worms, the proscription effectively stymied any possibility of organizational efforts by the Lutheran Reformers and the authorities who supported them.

If the Edict of Worms represented the official disposition of the political force of the empire toward the Lutheran Reformation, ecclesiastical powers were equally adamant. The papacy was commonly preoccupied with other pursuits—just prior to Luther's time, Pope Julius II had launched a series of wars for his own benefit; Leo handed down Luther's excommunication from his hunting cabin. Cardinals, archbishops, and bishops frequently purchased their offices for the attached benefices, with little or no interest in the ecclesiastical function, but, collectively or individually, they recognized a threat when they saw one. If the reformers associated with Luther were intent on staying within the tradition and its structures, those empowered by it were equally intent on driving them out. With just one possible exception and that minor, not a single German bishop supported the Lutheran reform in its initial decade.

Eugene R. Fairweather once observed offhandedly that the history of the church in the Middle Ages is the story of one failed reformation after another, and then, finally, one that worked. The combined authorities of church and political forces eventually absorbed or stopped every prior reforming effort. That was the way it was supposed to work. The papacy provided spiritual oversight for Christendom while political authorities provided for its physical well-being. Spontaneous reform efforts threatened the unity of both church and state. But in the sixteenth century the combination was breaking down. Ongoing corruption undermined the church's claims for itself. In Germany particularly, local authorities, whether mayors and town councils or sovereigns of larger territories like Brandenburg or electoral Saxony, were increasingly jealous about both imperial and papal interference in their affairs. Frederick the Wise of Saxony shared interests with many other sovereigns in his efforts to carve out, increasingly, prerogatives for his governance in both religious and political matters.

Originally in Switzerland, later in Strasbourg and parts of southwestern Germany, reformers worked out their own variation on the traditional combination of religious and political authorities.[8] In Zurich, when Roman Catholic officials opposed the reform, Ulrich Zwingli, who was city pastor, met with the town council and arranged a series of debates, with the councilmen deciding the outcome. When the council held for Zwingli, they joined in affecting the reform of the city. So too in Geneva, the council called John Calvin back to the city parish for the expressed purpose of reformation, having previously dismissed him and a senior colleague. The ideal was a Christian commonwealth, with ecclesiastical and political authorities linked to transform their communities.

Luther's Pauline apocalyptic asserted itself here, too. If the Word reforms the church, then accordingly the Word expressed in the flesh in Christ Jesus and set forth in Scripture must prevail within it. To those grounded in the give and take of politics, such confidence may appear naive. But given his intense expectation of an imminent end, Luther was convinced that the long term had already been provided for, and decisively. All that was needed was something provisional. The church would provide for the proclamation of the word and administration of the sacraments; the secular authorities would help out, like the deacons in the book of Acts, making sure the tables would be set.

Tending to business in the local congregations could not be assumed, however. So in 1526, following up on the earlier suggestion of another pastor, Luther made a proposal to the offices of the Elector of Saxony for what came to be known as the Saxon Church Visitation. He suggested that teams of parish visitors be established, consisting of theologians and political officials (canon lawyers, who had a combined interest) to go and investigate the conditions of the churches. The assessment would then become the basis for recommendations leading toward the improvement Luther and his Wittenberg colleagues sought.[9]

The visitation was a fateful step in a couple of different ways. To begin with, it signaled the first steps toward formal organization among the Lutherans. To this point, since the beginnings of the reform, Lutheranism had been a loosely affiliated reforming movement of preachers and professors with some sympathetic support from various politicians. Through their preaching and publications, they had gathered a large public following. Examination and oversight by visitation committees, however provisional they may have been, set footings for the development of church governance outside of the Roman hierarchy. According to Roman Catholicism's definitions of authority, at this point Lutheranism became something other than a reform movement within the Catholic tradition—taking on responsibilities reserved for the bishops, it separated itself.[10] Further, when sympathetic support turned to formal provisions by the government, another line was crossed. Though they took a more passive role among the Lutherans than they would in the Reformed traditions, once they got a foothold, the politicians became long-term participants in church governance. As Lutheranism spread to other parts of Germany and beyond, the visitations became standard practice. In fact, those who exercised the authority formally held exclusively by the bishops came to be known as **Parish Visitors**.

The Visitations

In 1526 another event crystallized the factors that had come together to promote the Saxon Church Visitation. Charles V called a diet, summoning the political sovereigns of Germany and some surrounding territories to meet with him in the southwestern German city of Speyer. When the dignitaries assembled, Charles himself was otherwise detained. He was battling one of the most brilliant strategists in the history of warfare, Suleiman the Magnificent. Marshalling his Turkish warriors, Suleiman had moved across the Balkans into southeastern Europe, capturing Buda and Pest in Hungary and in 1529 laying siege to Vienna itself. Not that far from Wittenberg, Vienna was the eastern door to Western Europe. It was a political but, even more, a huge religious threat. Suleiman's Islamic faith made his victorious incursions a direct affront to Christian claims to world preeminence, further fueling already inflamed fears of apocalyptic conflagration.

The German political leaders sympathetic to the Lutheran reform did not let whatever fears they may have had blind them, however. They had a legally constituted assembly of the Holy Roman Empire meeting without the supervision of one of the most powerful opponents of reform, giving them a great opportunity to move in their own direction. A principle was ratified at the Diet of Speyer that was later interpreted, if not originally intended, to provide a local option clause. This holding, stated as *cuius regio, eius religio*, can be roughly translated "whose region, his religion." It strongly implied, if it did not state outright, that the political leaders in their own territories could legally align with the reform. The blockade set by the Edict of Worms in 1521 was breached.

It took a while for Charles to recover his initiative. He called another diet in Speyer to assemble in 1529. This time when he could not attend, he sent his brother, Ferdinand, as his emissary. Using Charles's authority without the customary diplomacy, Ferdinand summarily revoked the holdings of the first diet. As a result, the politicians who had supported the reformation walked out—the original incident from which "Protestants" have gotten their name. In the Latin of the sixteenth century, however, the term *protestatio* could refer to a statement of official position or faith, the driving force behind the walkout. The Protestants of that time were not simply protesters but confessors of the evangelical faith at stake in the Reformation. The resulting conflict occasioned negotiations that eventually led to another diet, one of the most significant in the Lutheran reform, the Diet of Augsburg in 1530.

The Diet of Speyer of 1526 was fateful in its own way, however. On the basis of the claimed local option, Saxon officials gave full support to Luther's proposal for parish visitations. Teams of parish visitors, the first one including Luther himself, went into towns and villages, seeking reliable indications of circumstance and necessity.

If apocalypticists generally do not make good long-range planners, the Reformers were not necessarily independent observers. Problem and solution danced together so closely in their eyes that one could hardly be distinguished from the other. Reading the results of the parish visitations, as reported back to Wittenberg, require some salt. But even so qualified contemporary pastoral experience or work in a helping profession appears to corroborate the general results of the visitation. "The devil, the world, and the sinful self," the three powers Luther refers to in his Small Catechism explanations of the Lord's Prayer, do not commonly want for employment. Even if the exact proportions can be debated, there was compelling evidence of difficulty, both in behavior and in knowledge of the basics of the biblical message, among the laity and the clergy.[11]

One common problem among the laity was drunkenness. The French had fairly recently established a market in Germany for fortified wines—brandy—adding further kick to the beer most commonly consumed in Luther's region. Though he drank copious amounts of beer and wine himself, especially in his later life, Luther was deeply concerned about the problem of widespread inebriation and regularly inveighed against his "swilling Germans," as he called them. With the alcohol abuse, there was the normal range of other difficulties—sexual, familial, and social.

The parish visitors also reported widespread ignorance of defining features of the Christian faith. Knowledge certainly is not everything there is to faith, but at the same time faith must know of the one in whom it believes. The visitors were alarmed accordingly. In one congregation the people had refused to memorize the Lord's Prayer because they considered it too long to remember. Most commonly, people had only a passing understanding, if any at all, of the Christian witness.

The situation was not that much better among the clergy. The requirement of clerical celibacy was some four centuries old by this time, but church officials—many of whom had no contact at all with their territories, frequently living else-where—generally winked at violations. In the most common ruse, priests had live-in cooks who also had bedroom duties. In one district the visitors surveyed, over ninety percent of the pastors were living in such arrangements. The hypocrisy had serious consequences for the women involved. They had no legal protection and their children were considered illegitimate. Erasmus of Rotterdam, Luther's sup-porter before he became one of his main opponents, was one such child.

Though somewhat more knowledgeable than the laity, the pastors did not fare much better with the parish visitors. In one parish, the sacrament had not been administered in two years. Two common manuals of already prepared sermons were entitled *Sleep Soundly* and *Sermons That Preach Themselves*. The general igno-rance of the clergy was a common source of humor. Chaucer's *Canterbury Tales* and Boccoccio's *Decameron* both provide some good examples.

A Divided House

As the reports came back to Wittenberg, the first significant, public controversy broke out among the Lutheran reformers. Bound together in one of the deepest and most complex friendships in the Lutheran reform, Luther and Philip Melanchthon remained close despite some persistent tensions. But a mutual friend of the two proved even more difficult, and lastingly so.

Luther's and Melanchthon's friendship developed out of their first meeting, when Melanchthon arrived in Wittenberg in 1518 as professor of Greek. Luther was deeply impressed by the twenty-one-year-old scholar's erudition. Melanchthon was captured by the force of Luther's declaration of the gospel. In 1521 he wrote one of the classical expressions of Lutheran theology, the first edition of his *Loci Communes*. Luther once said that it should be added to the canon of the New Testament.[12] They worked closely all the way through the Lutheran reform until Luther's death. Melanchthon preached at his funeral, comparing Luther with the prophet Elijah.[13]

The friendship was tested at several points through the 1520s. When Luther was hidden away in the Wartburg Castle, Melanchthon had trouble maintaining the leadership in Wittenberg. His inability to maintain a steady hand with some of the more radical forces emerging in the theological faculty compelled Luther to return to the city. Apparently put off by Luther's marriage to Katherine von Bora in 1525, Melanchthon was even more troubled by Luther's rough polemics against Erasmus in *The Bondage of the Will* although not, at this point, with his theological position.[14] Although some later scholars have argued that deep theological differences emerged at this time between the two Wittenberg professors, the two seem not to have noticed. Their own perception of each other's theological positions and their friendship proved elastic enough to accommodate variations,[15] although even in the 1520s Melanchthon sometimes expressed the "Wittenberg theology" in different terms than Luther did. He did not feel the necessity of being Luther's clone, a measure often used later to assess his thought. Instead, though demonstrating his older colleague's influence at every turn, he responded to the biblical and patristic texts and to the circumstances of church and society on the basis of his own background and his own situation. As an ecclesiastical diplomat for the Evangelical governments and as an instructor of rhetoric and dialectic, his vantage points for viewing reform differed at times from Luther's.

Luther came to his theological convictions in the crucible, caught up in the biblical Word as he battled with the grasping temptations of despair. Immersed in the Psalms by monastic practice, driven by close study of Paul's Letter to the Romans in preparation for his lectures in 1516–1517, Luther began to absorb Paul's apocalyptic witness to Christ Jesus and to mature in his own convictions, a process that continued throughout his life but was largely in place by 1518–1520.[16] His teachers had taught him to understand justification as a process in which God graces people who have done everything that is within themselves to do, thereby making up for what the self has not been able to achieve. Paul's apocalyptic literally changed the subject. Whereas in late-medieval Catholicism the acting subject was basically the self with some divine supplement, in Paul's preaching the subject is the triune God, who creates out of nothing, loves his enemies, and raises the dead (Romans 3–5). Justifying the godless through the forgiveness of sins, God realigns sinners by faith in Christ Jesus. So doing, God attacks the powers of this age—sin, death, the devil, and the law run amuck—to reclaim the creation from their distortions and destructions.

Feasting on the Psalms and Romans, Luther ran through the rest of Scripture, reevaluating the traditional theological method. When Christianity moved out of its Palestinian origins into the Greco-Roman world, it took over key assumptions originally set by the Greeks—Platonists and, later, Neoplatonists and Aristotle—and attempted to fit Christ Jesus into these presuppositions. Luther's *Heidelberg Disputation*, written in 1518, opened a sustained attack on what he came to call thinking *ad modum Aristotelis*. This is a way of thinking theologically that begins without a personal creator as the absolute and ultimate. It presumes that the law provides the original way of salvation, eternally ordering all things, while human free will enables individuals to cooperate with God to some degree in obeying the law, thereby meriting a merciful grace from God. Instead, speaking of what he called the theology of the cross, Luther proposed a different method shaped by Paul's apocalyptic. He proposed to begin with the death and resurrection of Christ Jesus as, in effect, the first premise in the theological syllogism and then to ask what must be assumed and concluded accordingly. For example, since Christ's death justifies, it must be assumed that the law cannot—the logic that Paul follows in Galatians 2:21. Similarly, since Christ's justifies, "free will, after the fall, exists in name only"—one of the theses set forth in the *Heidelberg Disputation* that was also cited in Luther's excommunication. Again, the logic follows with compelling simplicity: if Christ's death was necessary to justification, humanity has no inherent capacity to justify itself.[17]

Compared to Luther, Melanchthon was in some regards a much more traditional theological thinker. Brilliantly gifted in the languages, Melanchthon was a teacher, not a pastor. He is remembered as the "preceptor of Germany" for his great contribution to university curriculum reform. Such a reform was the topic of his first lecture in Wittenberg in 1518. As an ordained priest assigned to teach on the university faculty, Luther was never far from the pulpit and parish practice. Melanchthon's point of reference was the classroom, the education of pastors on a firm academic foundation, the cultivation of the effective communication skills that the reformers believed necessary for pastors who were to function above all as ministers of the Word of God.

Given this difference, generations of scholars have attempted to pinpoint more precisely the source of the theological differences that developed between the two leading Wittenbergers. The last great generation of Luther scholars, led by theologians such as Lauri Haikola—a leading Finnish scholar—and Wilhelm Pauck, pointed to Melanchthon's deeper loyalties to the biblical humanism of Erasmus and his associates throughout Northern Europe. As Pauck pointed out, Melanchthon told his first biographer toward the end of his life that he had striven in everything he did to contribute to the actual improvement of community life, a boast Luther often made of himself as well—a statement that demonstrates his loyalty to the agenda of biblical humanism, though it stemmed also from the Reformer's Old Testament studies. For in its pages Luther found God revealing himself in his creation and engaging his people deeply in family and community life.

Since the critique of Melanchthon's dogmatic approach launched by the "classical liberal" theologians around Albrecht Ritschl at the end of the nineteenth century, scholars across the dogmatic spectrum, from the Ritschlians to existentialists like the early Jaroslav Pelikan, have criticized Melanchthon's use of Aristotle. According to this argument, Melanchthon's program was to take Luther's witness to the unconditional act of God in Christ Jesus and repackage it for academic purposes in Aristotle's rhetorical forms. In the end, however, this interpretation of Melanchthon contends, as the patriarch Isaac once observed, "the voice is Jacob's, the hands are Esau's." Again and again in the development of the Lutheran Confessions, Melanchthon found himself in trouble attempting to bring off the combination.

More recent scholars have viewed this development from another perspective. In his pedagogy, they argue, Melanchthon assumed that Aristotle's rhetoric was theologically neutral and could be refashioned as a tool for the professor of the liberal arts assigned to cultivate good communication skills among his students, many of whom would become preachers of God's Word. Clearly, Melanchthon was committed to Aristotle's theory of rhetoric, absorbing with it Aristotelian dialectics. Some scholars view this as a use of culture in line with Luther's understanding of the realm of active righteousness.[18]

Wherever the fault lines perceived by many of their students in the sixteenth century as well as the many scholars of the twentieth century actually fell, the two stood together in their rejection of the first major deviation within the Wittenberg circle from the professorial promulgation of the gospel—more precisely, the dispute with Johann Agricola focused on the proper distinction of law and gospel. The problem in the controversy precipitated by the reports of the visitation committee involved the law. In fact, it was the first of three installments in what has come to be known as the Antinomian Controversy. The trouble erupted again in the later 1530s and still once more in the early 1550s.

In this first installment the conflict began following Melanchthon's publication of the *Instructions for Parish Visitors*, written in September of 1527. Intended as something of a handbook for the visitations and parish life, the document begins with Melanchthon's complaints about preachers who so emphasize faith that they neglect the doctrine of law and so encourage what he calls "carnal security."[19] Over and against this, Melanchthon urged the pastors the use the Ten Commandments to drive people to repentance. "At some point they should explain the whole Decalogue because the preaching of the law rouses to penitence. At some time they should censure certain vices and should plentifully declare that God is gravely offended and [declare] which he threatens."[20]

Melanchthon's instructions triggered a reaction from Johann Agricola, a longtime companion who was also close to Luther. Remembered primarily for the second stage of the antinomian controversy, between 1537 and 1540, Agricola had originally arrived in Wittenberg about the same time as Melanchthon. He had joined his two better-known companions at several of the key events in the early reformation and in fact still played a prominent, though mischievous, role—though from a distance—into the later 1540s.[21] A school rector until he was formally called to an adjunct position on the faculty at Wittenberg in 1536, he was overmatched theologically. But polemics was part of an academic job description in the sixteenth century, and he did not mind mixing it up, even against long odds.[22]

So Agricola went after Melanchthon in a series of sharp exchanges that extended into the summer of 1528. The target of his attack was what he saw as Melanchthon's recourse to the law. He insisted, as he also argued in the later 1530s, that while the law may affect a change in outward behavior, it does not address the heart. Consequently, it brings about no genuine change in its hearer. In fact, he argued, a repentance born of the law is indistinguishable from any other fear-driven activity: it is mere self-protection. If there is going to be a real change of heart, the gospel must be preached "in all of its sweetness." Hearing of Christ's self-sacrifice, the hearer will be moved to self-examination and so, repenting of all that required Christ's death, assay a new life. Lacking Luther's theological and pastoral sophistication, Agricola understood both law and gospel in formulaic terms, as though the law was a linguistic form that could be put away in favor of the gospel as a sweeter, more influential way of talking.

Some contemporary observers suspected that a non-theological factor had as much to do with the controversy as the stated issue. Not so long before the conflict began, Melanchthon had assumed, alongside his assignment on the arts faculty, a second position on the theological faculty for which Agricola considered himself the prime candidate. Jealousy may have tinged the conflict. Not everyone was convinced of the significance of the issue either, at least not as it was framed in the debate. At first Luther dismissed the whole exchange as a *pugna verborum*, a war of words, and let it go, assuming the disputants would eventually come to an understanding. But as the exchanges escalated, they attracted wider notice. Finally, the elector became concerned and asked Luther to step in and settle the issue. In the fall of 1528, the disputants were taken with Luther to a residence of the elector's in Torgau and the whole thing was settled, at least for the time being.

In the settlement Luther carefully sought a formulation to which both sides could agree. He made a distinction between what he termed public and justifying faith. Public faith could be considered the equivalent of what has now commonly been termed "civil religion": it is the general conviction that God prefers good behavior to bad, rewarding the righteous and punishing bad behavior. Justifying faith holds fast to Christ Jesus, recognizing and trusting in him as God's righteousness for the sinner. The law, not simply as formula but as the force that confronts humanity in the circumstances of every day, must be proclaimed in the church. But the law cannot by itself create faith. That is work carried out through the gospel by the Spirit of the risen Christ.[23]

The settlement acknowledged the propriety and necessity of Melanchthon's encouragement of preaching the commandments, as Luther had in his postils and in his practice, but it also recognized the law's limits, though in another way than Agricola had contended. The apparent compromise shows Luther's sensitivity to the concerns of both of his colleagues and the basis of his apparent disinterest in the conflict. This stance, however, was belied by the fact that he wrote his catechisms, at least in part, as a critique and rejection of Agricola's position as expressed in his own manuals for the instruction of the young.[24] Luther's settlement sunders the connection between the law and the righteousness that gives human creatures their core identity before God. The law pertains to human performance and to earthly, personal, and public disciplines, not the righteousness that avails before God, a distinction that Melanchthon made but that Agricola had obscured. Over and against

Agricola, Luther insisted that as the law cannot be reduced to mere moral demand, the gospel cannot be reduced to moral influence. Faith involves a living relationship in which the hearer, confronted by the accusing voice of the law, gets grasped by the word of forgiveness and resurrection and is, thereby, freed to live as Adam and Eve were originally intended to live—in the freedom of creatureliness.

When the conflict broke out between Luther and Agricola again in 1537–1540, Luther reacted vehemently and vociferously against Agricola, in part because he seemed to believe that others could use Agricola's position as an excuse for not practicing the Christian life of obedience to God but even more so because he believed that Agricola confused law and gospel by making the gospel of forgiveness do the work of the law, both in accusing sinners of their sin and in instructing them in how to live in faith.[25]

The Catechisms

Being asked to deal with his feuding colleagues, Luther still had his eye on his original goals and the intent of the visitation—to reach the people in the congregations and to improve the preaching. To serve these purposes, he began to mull over the possibilities of writing a handbook for "catechism," the word used to designate initial instruction in the Christian faith since the early church.

Catechism appears in the church's history all the way back to the New Testament itself. It has sometimes been suggested that 1 Peter, one of Luther's favorite epistles, was originally a catechism preached and then written to be circulated among suffering Christians in Asia Minor. Though no document survives, Origen was a catechist. Augustine wrote a handbook for catechesis; after him, there was a trove of medieval documents, generally centering on the faith, hope, and love expressed in the Apostles Creed, the Lord's Prayer, and common forms of Catholic devotion.[26] Though it took a different approach, even Erasmus wrote something of the sort, a *Handbook for the Militant Christian*. As Luther knew and used the term out of the tradition, he generally grouped the Commandments, the Apostles Creed, and Lord's Prayer, calling them "the catechism," that is, a program for instruction.

Traditionally, catechisms were put to several general uses, both public and personal. Commonly read aloud or preached from the pulpit, they provided basic instruction in the Christian use of Scripture and practices of the faith. On a personal basis, the medieval catechisms were used in preparation for confession and absolution, for prayer, and for other forms of devotion, such as the Hail Mary.[27] Luther turned this tradition in his own direction. Knowing the history of the tradition, Luther urged several of them to write catechisms, as he and the other Wittenberg reformers debated ways to reach the level of parish life. In the end, Luther was not satisfied with any of the other efforts and decided to take up the challenge himself.

One of Luther's great advantages over others before him in the church's catechetical tradition was the printing press. Discovered for European purposes in the fifteenth century, it was the first mass media, and as such its public power had not yet been fully recognized. Luther saw the potential and used it to the best of his ability. At one point in the early 1520s, over three-fourths of the books in print in Germany had been written by Luther himself. In fact, when Luther and Katherine von Bora took over the Black Cloister, the former home of the Augustinian monks in Wittenberg, Luther's printer maintained a shop in the basement. Oftentimes, he was setting the beginning of a treatise in type before Luther had finished the end of it. The power of print, especially in a culture just beginning to recognize its potential, was a major factor in the effectiveness of the Lutheran reform.[28]

Having already had extensive experience with it, Luther turned to print to bring home his reform literally. So in 1528, after failing to find a colleague who could work on the assignment,[29] he went to work on a catechism of his own. Characteristically, before he had finished one, he was at work on another for a different audience. The first, the Large Catechism, was written for pastors and teachers; the second or Small Catechism was for families to use in the instruction of their children. The Large also assumed the name German Catechism because it was written in Luther's own Middle High German rather than the church's Latin.

Though perhaps not originally conceived as such, the combination of the two catechetical handbooks proved to be a simple but in the end highly effective strategy. The pastors and teachers held critical positions in the life of their communities. The Large Catechism made it possible for them to learn even as they were teaching. In teaching the Commandments, the creed, and the Lord's Prayer to their children, using the wall charts provided, the parents would be learning these symbols of the faith themselves.

The effectiveness of Luther's strategy can be measured by the aftermath of the defeat of the Smalcald League, the military alliance that shielded the Lutherans into the 1540s. Even though Charles V finally succeeded, at least in a limited way, in carrying out intentions announced in the earlier Edict of Worms, he could not overcome what had happened in the homes. The kind of moral transformation for which Luther and Melanchthon had hoped may not have been accomplished. Sin, death, and the devil do not just surrender, even to that which is "most certainly true." If Luther's apocalyptically tinged hopes made him wary of transformation schemes, he was nonetheless convinced of the power of the Word to hold in the face of any opposition. So he taught the church to sing, in an older translation of the words to "A Mighty Fortress," "that Word above all earthly powers, no thanks to them abideth." The catechisms sounded the Word even as the Reformation appeared to be collapsing.

Closely linked by timing and structure, the Small and Large Catechisms also share common sources. In May, again in September, still again in November and December of 1528, and finally in March of 1529, Luther preached series of sermons on parts of the catechism. The sermons may look like an experiment in field-testing. But in fact, sometimes his work on the catechism may have provided resources for his preaching. Multitasking as usual, he began work on the text of the Large Catechism before the last series of sermons was completed. The Large Catechism was completed in April 1529, portions of it getting into print before the rest was completed.

Luther still was not satisfied. Before the year was out, a second edition of the Large Catechism followed. It included a lengthy "Exhortation to Confession," reflecting the fact that while they opposed the requirement of annual confession, the Lutheran Reformers still wanted to emphasize its regular practice. Luther also added to the introduction to the explanations of the Lord's Prayer and provided some marginal notes. And then there were some illustrations, among them wood-cuts depicting, for example, biblical stories of transgressions of the commandments. Lucas Cranach the Elder, a great Wittenberg artist and Luther's close friend, provided some of the cuts.[30]

Two more editions followed. One issued in 1530 included a new introduction. It was written probably while Luther was staying in a castle at the Saxon town of Coburg, as close as he would get to the city of Augsburg when Melanchthon went there with the rest of the Lutheran delegation to present the Augsburg Confession. A final edition from Luther's hand appeared in 1538.

Luther went to work on the Small Catechism initially in December of 1528 and continued, intermittently, until May of the next year, when his explanations of the five chief parts were assembled and, together with illustrations, published as a pamphlet. Luther also wrote a preface and provided a program for daily meditation and prayer as well as a Table of Christian Callings, formally "The Household Chart of Some Bible Passages for All Kinds of Holy Orders and Walks of Life," setting out the obligations pertinent to the various callings of life. As they were originally written, each of the parts had already appeared in chart form for home use.

Small as it was and remained, the catechism did grow some in subsequent editions, not always at Luther's own hand. He did some of his own revision, in 1531 for example, changing the statement on confession to its present form. But additions were also made by others, sometimes with and sometimes without Luther's permission. Short forms for marriage and baptism and a litany soon were bound in. There were also some additions to the Household Chart, those more likely with Luther's consent. After Luther's death other items were sometimes attached to printings of his catechisms, including the "questions for those who wish to receive the Lord's Supper" that first appeared, separately, in print in 1549 and were first incorporated into a printing of Luther's catechism in 1551.[31]

Both the Large and the Small Catechisms quickly gained the authority of use. No formal action was taken providing them with a special standing in the Lutheran community; there was no agency to take such action. But the fact that they were Luther's writing along with the down-to-earth way in which they set out the Christian faith gave them a practical power among those who adhered to the reform. Portions of the Large Catechism were commonly read in worship in parts of Germany. By the time of the Formula of Concord, the Small Catechism had come to be known as "the layman's Bible."[32]

The Structure of Luther's Catechism

Written over the same period for different audiences, the two catechisms also share a common structure, two features of which should be noted. One is the ecumenical orientation, the other the order. Both closely reflect the situation of the Lutheran reform at that particular time, though both also have larger implications.

Even if Luther gave them greater priority, the chief parts of the catechism—the Commandments, Apostles Creed, Lord's Prayer, the sacraments, and absolution—had long been central to the Catholic tradition. Following standard usage of the Western church, Luther used a form of the Ten Commandments that omitted what the Hebrew tradition had regarded as the second—the commandment against graven images in Exodus 20—and divided its tenth commandment into two. The commandments had been taught in that form by the Western church for centuries. The Apostles Creed, with roots extending back into the second century, became the creed of Western Christendom at the time of Charlemagne, at the turn of the ninth century. The Lord's Prayer, with baptism and the Lord's Supper, go back to the New Testament and have always been central to Christianity. Organized around these defining elements, Luther's catechism is ecumenically Catholic to the core.

Appropriating the heritage in this structure, the catechisms also closely reflected their origins in the pulpit. They are structured for preaching. The Large Catechism was lifted from sermons Luther had preached during the previous year and was addressed to an audience that could handle some theological discursions. The pastors and teachers, even if their training was rudimentary, could deal with some abstractions. But there as well as in the tighter discipline required in writing the Small Catechism, Luther was concerned to literally bring home the Word. He not only translated the Christian faith into the vernacular language from the Latin that had carried it north. He translated the faith culturally into the parlance of everyday living among the German-speaking faithful.[33] In both catechisms but particularly the smaller, Luther generally assumes the doctrinal basis for his statements to emphasize the personal confession of faith. So in the explanation of the Second Article of the Creed, for example, he states the doctrine of the two natures of Christ in two quick phrases, "true man," "true God." To emphasize the victory Christ won by his death and resurrection direct, personal terms sufficed: "He has saved me, a lost and condemned person." Even the doctrine of justification by faith, as important as was to him and the Lutheran reform, is rendered in language suitable for proclamation to children, "that Jesus Christ freed...that I may be his own."[34]

The proclamatory character of the catechisms also shows still another feature of the structure, the orientation to everyday life and experience. While the explanations, as they have traditionally been called, are oriented by the biblical Word as it had been received the church, they consistently touch on points where the Word and experience meet in daily life. Evident throughout, this becomes particularly clear in the treatment of the Commandments and the Lord's Prayer. Even some five centuries later, readers of the explanations of the commandments, especially in the

Large Catechism, commonly comment that it seems like Luther has been reading the daily news. In the explanations of the Lord's Prayer, Luther plumbs the essential conflicts of life in faith, up to and including the struggles between hope and despair. A scholar trained in the interpretation of Scripture, Luther is at the same time a pastor who knows first hand where the battles between faith and unbelief rage. So for instance, "we pray that the devil, the world and our sinful self will not deceive us and so lead us into" sins like despair. Faith is formed by the Word in the crucible of everyday life.

This orientation to the everyday experience of life also set the order of the parts of the catechisms, one of the unique and still controversial features of the catechisms' structure. Luther transformed the order of the medieval catechism, abandoning the outline of faith (the Creed), hope (the Lord's Prayer), and love (the Ten Commandments—though earlier love had been elucidated through lists of virtues and vices). The Reformer explained his reasoning for placing the Decalogue first, the Creed second, and the Lord's Prayer third, with a comparison to a sick person who must first diagnose the illness and find a prescription for cure, then find the medicine which will restore to health, and then seek and obtain the medicine: "First, a person must know what to do and what to leave undone. Second, when he realizes that he cannot measure up to what he should do or leave undone, he needs to know where to go to find the strength he requires. Third, he must know how to seek and obtain strength."[35]

As this statement demonstrates, Luther follows an experiential order. He begins with the commandments because that is where life begins, under the *nomos*, in the context of demands and conditions that bear down from birth to death. As Luther understands and interprets them, the Ten Commandments codify and summarize the essential requirements of life in relation to both God and the neighbor. The Apostles Creed follows the Ten Commandments as proclamation of the gospel. The gospel declares that Christ has broken into the world of the law to take it upon himself in his death and resurrection to make sinners his own, thereby freeing them from the powers of sin, death and the devil. The Lord's Prayer follows the Creed, expositing the shape of life as it is lived out in the tension between the claims of the law and the gospel, teaching sinners to call out to Christ Jesus for his assistance. In this way each of the first three parts of the catechism posts a defining part of the life of faith—demand, gift, and consolation in the struggles of life.

Karl Barth and others who want to begin the discussion of law and gospel on the level of knowledge—epistemology—have fiercely criticized Luther's law-gospel order as it is reflected among other places in the catechisms.[36] For them, the true knowledge of God bestowed by Christ Jesus through the gospel sets a necessary precondition for a proper understanding of the law. For this reason, Barth insisted, the proper order should be gospel-law. Whatever standing the criticism is given on theological or pastoral grounds, it is critical to note the different starting points. For the Calvinist tradition, including Barth, the issue remains true knowledge of

God; for Luther, the true issue is both prior and larger, faith itself. Ignorance or mis-understanding both point to deeper problem, unbelief—the all-pervasive distrust exposed by the First Commandment that characterizes the sinner.

The Witness

It can be helpful, examining what the catechisms actually say, to make a distinction between first- and second-order discourse. First-order discourse declares, bestows, gives; second-order discourse takes place one step in the remove, talking about declaring, bestowing, or giving. Preaching moves to first-order; theology, which reflects on the Word that has been heard so that it can be declared once more, is classically second-order.[37]

The catechisms, especially the Small but also the Large, are preaching docu-ments—aimed at cultivating trust in God and the life that flows from it—confes-sions in the fullest sense of the word. In them Luther passes on what he has also received, again and again specifying those for whom God acts in law and gospel—God acts *pro me, pro nobis*, for me, for us, and above all, "for you." Though he occa-sionally moves back to second-order discourse in the Large Catechism, addressing pastors and teachers, it never takes long for him to get back to the level of direct witness. In both catechisms Luther literally hands over the goods, speaking from faith to faith.

In this light the most recent translation of the Book of Concord makes a very important move when it changes the standard translation of Luther's repeated catechetical question from "What does this mean?" to "What is this?" Meaning immediately moves to second-order, giving the interpreter a measure of control over what has been said. Luther's original question, "*Was ist das?*," sets up an answer that declares what God is doing, perhaps reflecting Luther's own experience at the time he was writing the catechism, as he heard precisely that question from his not quite three-year-old son Hans.[38] For this reason, in the explanations of the Small Catechism, God claims virtually every verb. The triune God, who creates out of nothing and raises the dead, exercises control over all that is and every moment.

Thus, as strategically important as they were to the Lutheran reform, with Reformers beginning to take a more direct hand in the life of the congregations, the Small and Large Catechisms are not, properly speaking, theological documents. The standard vocabulary of Lutheran theology—justification by faith alone, *simul iustus et peccator*, the bondage of the will, the uses of the law, and so forth—is conspicuously absent. This language is suitable for theological discourse but not for everyday conversation, where God meets his children of all ages. Preaching, the declaration of God's ceaseless activity for both creation and creature, has literally put theology in its place. Throughout his life Luther continued the medieval custom that he had practiced as a monk, preaching the catechism or parts of it with some frequency.[39] He also rendered its parts into hymns, so that the fundamentals of the faith might be sung into the people's thinking and living.[40]

At the same time, while preaching, Luther obviously retains his theological concerns. *Reine lehre*, "sound doctrine," remained at the forefront of Lutheran concerns throughout the reformation—every bit as much in Luther as in the authors of the Formula of Concord. For Luther sound doctrine was not an end in itself, as if the doctrine of justification by faith itself justifies. Rather, doctrine, as a second order pursuit reflecting on God's words of law and gospel, informs their faithful first order declaration. Recognizing this, the theological assumptions informing Luther's witness can be examined.

Luther's explanations of the Ten Commandments reflect the same assumptions that informed his settlement of the earlier conflict between Agricola and Melanchthon. Instead of moving from the gospel to the law, the classical procedure of the western theological tradition, Luther in effect reversed the order. The law precedes the gospel pastorally. Sinners do not reconsider without a reason. But theologically, Christ's death and resurrection sets the center, presuming the lordship of the Word made flesh, who set existence in place through his creative Word; in his action in behalf of sinners lies the first premise of every theological argument.[41] Since Christ justifies, therefore, it must be assumed from the beginning that the law cannot. The law is God's Word about our activities, and neither the creation of the human being nor our re-creation in justification is an activity accomplished by human will or action. As Luther wrote in his later conflict with Agricola, in the later 1530s, "the law was not given that it might justify, vivify or prescribe anything for righteousness." Rather, "the law was given to reveal sin and effect wrath."[42] So Paul writes in Romans 10:4, "Christ is the end of the law, that all who believe may be justified." The gospel reduces the law to terms. It has no standing in relation to salvation.

But if Christ Jesus has stepped on the law's fingers to keep it out of heaven, it still has its place on earth. Like Adam and Eve, creatures are created with limits. They depend on their creator, on one another, and on the creation itself. These limits have no particularly Christian dimension; neither are they in any sense of the term particularly religious. Rather, they arise out of the actual demands and conditions of creaturely life and so are found, stated or unstated, in various forms among believers and unbelievers of all kinds. The Ten Commandments gain their authority from their clear statement of the essential demands and conditions of creatureliness. Each of the explanations of the commandments proceeds from this assumption.[43] In the Small Catechism, Luther elaborated his ethical instruction in the "Table of Christian Callings," but in the Large Catechism he shows how the Ten Commandments and the structure of callings come together, as he explained in the Small Catechism's instruction for confession of sins when he combined the Ten Commandments with the vocational structure of human life as an instrument for examining oneself.[44]

The first table, which includes the first three commandments, states the essential requirements of creaturely life in relation to the creator. Not having life in themselves, having a birthday and anticipating at some uncertain point a death day, creatures have to be in line with the source of life, their creator. This is the First Commandment—you shall have no others gods before me because other gods, even though they invariably claim to be life giving, depend on their adherent's lives to sustain them. When that runs out, both die. The Second Commandment follows. Since creatures must be in touch with their creator, they must know the creator's name so that they can call out confidently, anticipating an answer. So too the Third Commandment: since creatures must be in touch with their creator, they should at some point shut up and listen so that they can hear the creator's voice.

The explanations of the second table, which describes the relationships of creatures among themselves, proceed along the same lines. Each of the remaining seven commandments states and protects a fundamental dimension of life: the family, life itself, sexual relations, property, language, and, in the Ninth and Tenth, trustworthiness. When and where these conditions and limits are observed, life prospers; violated, they rebound in consequences, seen and unseen, which continue to ripple through the human community.

In this way Luther's explanations provide a down-to-earth, descriptive analysis of how the law actually works. Agricola, understanding the law terminologically, thought it could be simply dismissed. Where people live and breathe, the law retains its force. Only Christ Jesus can finally master it.

For all of its descriptive character, however, at one point in his exposition of the Ten Commandments it appears that he has the sense that Christ Jesus is looking over his shoulder: his explanation of the First Commandment in the Large Catechism. As he himself says in this classic statement of the Lutheran witness, the First Commandment is "the clasp that holds the wreath together."[45] Thus each of his explanations in the Small Catechism begins with a reference, "we should so fear and love God that . . ." The creator determines all relationships, both with creatures and between them. But as Luther works his analysis, "the creator" is not merely a job description or the anonymous "higher power" of addiction therapy. Rather, the creator is the Father who raised Jesus from the dead. So the gospel begins to spill over.

This is not an accident. Luther considered the First Commandment both the "highest sum of the law, in which all things are required, and the highest sum of the gospel, in which all things are given." His conviction roots in the language itself: "I am the Lord your God. You shall have no other gods before me." The preface states a promise that God has entered into relationship with us, an event that for Christians can only be a reference to Christ Jesus. It is because God has entered into this relationship that the command follows, in effect radicalizing the promise: because the triune God has become your God, God will tolerate no other. As Charles Arand has emphatically stated, this understanding of the First Commandment makes it fundamental to the whole witness of the catechisms and to the larger witness of the confessions, that the core of God's human creature lies in faith, in fearing, loving, and trusting God above all things.[46]

As the commandments declare the law, the creed proclaims the gospel.[47] Though completely certain of the oneness of the triune God, Luther arranged his explanations around the work of each of the three persons. The God who creates redeems in Christ Jesus and sanctifies by his Holy Spirit; the God who redeems in Christ Jesus also creates as God the Father and sanctifies in the Spirit of the risen Christ; the God who sanctifies by the work of the Holy Spirit equally creates as God the Father and redeems in Christ. The triune work of God can neither be distinguished nor separated from the identity of the triune God; neither can it be reduced to a series of job descriptions. There are many other contenders for the bare titles, for example, the mere job descriptions of creator, redeemer, and sanctifier.

Hidden away amid all the verbs Luther set out to declare the work of the Trinity are a couple of quiet transitions that, when put together, declare the work God does in Christ through the gospel. The explanation of the First Article affirms what Luther had learned from Ockhamistic instructors, that God freely decided to create human creatures totally independent of any external coercion, to love them as his children, and to rescue them from their rejection of him and the life he gives when they sin. Luther did so with the words that describe our failure to explain his gift of life to his creatures: "all this is done out of pure, fatherly, and divine goodness and mercy, without any merit or worthiness of mine at all!"[48] This explanation ends at about the same point that the commandments do: "therefore, surely we ought to thank, praise, serve and obey" God, binding together God's gift of life with his expectations for human performance. In the creed this "ought" grows out of a double root. The demands and conditions of creatureliness obligate service to the creator, other creatures, and the creation—an inescapable requirement of humanity itself. At the same time God the Father's gifts given in and through such relationships, for all of their bloom, bring with them obligations all around.

But in the second article the "ought" disappears, having been replaced with a different, a creative, word, "may." This word fashions a new reality in place of sin's hostility toward the creator. The first phrase in the explanation of the Second Article in the Small Catechism declares what God has done in Christ Jesus—he has become my Lord. The next several phrases declare how this has happened: fully God, fully man, Christ Jesus took on all of the other powers that contend for lordship over me, being crucified and raised from the dead to break their grip and establish his own. Death and resurrection effect a new creation, a return of sinners to Eden. God restores their identity as creatures who fear, love, and trust in God above all things. The explanation's last phrase makes all the difference. Whereas other lords, reflecting the power of the law, operate in relationships of dominance and submission, Christ Jesus has become my lord so that "I may be his own, live under him and serve him in everlasting innocence, righteousness and blessedness." Displacing the "ought," with its focus on human action, the word "may," especially in combination with "be his own," brings about a new relational reality, the gift of the relationship of God's child to the creator and redeemer. As Jesus says in John's Gospel, "I no longer call you servants but friends" (John 15:15). At the same time it sets out capability: what under the "ought" sinners could never accomplish until the gospel brought it into range. The German behind the English "may" carries a creative force when it proceeds from the mouth and work of the creator and redeemer. God's "may"—like his "let there be" in Genesis 1—establishes the new reality of his—his resurrection's—new creation. The "ought" simply reflects what God designed human creatures to be, not what they can do apart from God on their own. The "may"—a subjunctive in German—indicates what the Holy Spirit enables God's children to do when they live by faith.

The word "may," like the month with the same name, has another dimension, however—it may happen, but the possibility of another stormy morning still remains. So the explanation of the Third Article, concerning the work of the Holy Spirit, opens with a double confession in which the *simul justus et peccator* gets stated in personal terms. The presence of Christ and his gifts, the newness he brings, exposes the presence of the old with all of its pretenses and illusions. The heart is driven to confess, "I believe that I cannot…believe in Jesus Christ my Lord or come to him," a reaffirmation of Luther's understanding of the human will's boundness when making choices about its god(s), as Luther expressed it in his *On Bound Choice* [*De servo arbitrio*]. At the same time, my understanding and effort, reason and strength are no longer all-definitive. So having displaced the ought of the first article, the may of the second undergoes its own transition, becoming the "has" of the third: the Holy Spirit has called, has gathered, has enlightened, has sanctified, and has kept—has established a new reality and continues to maintain the identity of the child of God in both faith and obedience.[49]

The simultaneity of the explanation of the Third Article also shapes the explanations of the Lord's Prayer.[50] As creatures of the earth, Christians live in a creation shaped by the conditions and demands of their own lives, the lives of those around them, and the environment of the earth itself. What pulses in one aspect of life, reverberates in others. So the law shapes the context of life, making its inevitable claims. At the same time, grasped and held by the Spirit of the risen Christ, Christians live in the forgiveness of sin and the hope of the resurrection. So grasped, as Luther argued, they gladly do without the law what the law requires—that is, carried beyond obligation, Christians freely give of themselves in service to God, the neighbor, and the earth. But this happens in contention. As Luther wrote in his *Antinomian Disputations*, the last series of arguments with Agricola, "insofar as Christ is raised in us, so far are we without the law; insofar as Christ is not raised in us, so far are we under the law."[51] Christians are confronted by both realities, of the law bearing down and the gospel breaking in to heal and free.

With this in mind, Luther wrote his explanations of the Lord's Prayer on two levels. On the one hand, they provide a simple and straightforward explanation of what is being asked for in each of the petitions. But on the other, they also exposit the shape of life under the *simul*—dying with Christ under the force of the law, being raised him daily under the power of the gospel. As such, the explanations of the Lord's Prayer are the catechism's statement of what Luther sometimes called his theology of the cross.

As Luther explains them, the petitions focus on the most basic requirements of everyday life in faith: in the first and second petitions, the Word and faith; in the fourth and fifth, daily bread and forgiveness. Being carried beyond ourselves, having to ask for what we presume to control, already involves a death for the sinful self, the old Adam or Eve. But the implicit conflict in these petitions explodes into open warfare in the third and sixth petitions, both of which name the opposition: the devil and the world as well as the sinful self. We are battlegrounds open to all comers, batted back and forth by opposing forces even as we imagine ourselves self-possessed, whole, free, and alive. But in Christ Jesus, the dying always gets joined by the rising. "God indeed gives daily bread," as everything else, "without our prayer, but we pray in this petition" as in every other "that we might realize this."[52] This realization sees the first rays of Easter; the trust that goes with it cries out in the joyful groaning of hope, "deliver us from evil."

The first three chief parts make up what might be called the "Word" section of Luther's catechisms. He added the explanations of baptism and the Lord's Supper,[53] and still later the section on confession and absolution, because his understanding of the Word of God in all its forms—oral, written, and sacramental—remained fundamental for his understanding of God and of humanity. The majority of Germans in 1529 could not read or write. Therefore the sacraments, which had stood at the heart of medieval piety, would always remain controversial. Luther poured his understanding of the Word of God as the power of God for salvation into his treatment of them. In each of the sacraments, the oral word clothes itself as a visible word as God embodies or materializes the gospel by joining the Word with the visible stuff of everyday life. If the hands of confession and absolution cannot be compared directly with the water of baptism or the bread and wine of the Lord's Supper, the touch of the hand and the sign of the cross nevertheless express in physical form what the Word has declared.

The Small Catechism's treatment of baptism and the Lord's Supper are parallel. "What is it?" Against the Anabaptists who were emerging in the late 1520s Luther wrote, "not simply plain water." "It is water enclosed in God's command and connected with God's Word." Likewise, the Lord's Supper is not just bread and wine but "the true body and blood of our Lord Jesus Christ under the bread and wine"—with the power of God's Word behind it: "instituted by Christ himself." What does each sacrament do for you? Both give "the forgiveness of sins, life, and salvation," three synonyms that mean human life is restored to its original relationship with its creator.

"But how is that possible? the catechumen was then to ask. "It's the Word," God's power in verbal form, placed into the setting of physical elements because, as Luther once had a peasant speaking in his treatise on absolution, "to receive God's Word in many ways is so much better."[54]

The fourth question on these two sacraments diverges. On the Lord's Supper the Reformer addressed the important medieval question, "How can I be worthy of receiving Christ's body and blood?" His answer: trust the words "given for you," "shed for you for the forgiveness of sins." Christ serves his supper to the hungry and starving, not to those who can take it or leave it or who think they have to earn it. The last question on baptism extends the Holy Spirit's baptismal action of restoring life and salvation through the forgiveness of sins into daily life. The rhythm of baptism, according to Paul in Romans 6:3-11 or Colossians 2:11-15, is the rhythm of dying and rising, of the action of God's Word as both law and gospel. In the mystery of the continuation of sin and evil in the lives of the baptized, the threat of death returns, and it must be voided by the baptismal promise (Rom. 6:23). The promise is as sure as God himself. True, the Holy Spirit must repeatedly reactivate the faith he creates in the midst of the struggle of believers against their own recurring sinfulness (Rom. 7:7-25). Thus, baptism fills its own meaning full when "the old creature in us with all sins and evil desires" is drowned and dies through repentance, and "daily a new person . . . comes forth and rises up to live before God in righteousness and purity forever."[55] Luther then followed up with instructions on "how simple people are to be taught to confess" their sins, with the emphasis on trust in the promise of forgiveness through the work of Jesus Christ.[56]

With this, Luther reverses the order in traditional understandings of the sacraments. Because the Word is God's self-expression, it accomplishes what it declares. So the sacraments have no meaning whatsoever, no matter how pious the packaging may become, apart from the promise of Christ, which they convey, but they do everything that the Word of the gospel in oral or written forms does. Baptism is a dress rehearsal for the Last Day, and it is more. It is the actual enactment of the promise of God that finds fulfillment in that day, no day of judgment for those made alive in Christ as the judgment of being buried in Christ's tomb fell upon them in baptism. The oral declaration of the gospel, with the hands firmly grasping the head, resolves all ambiguity about the beneficiary of this gift. The Lord's Supper gets stripped clean of every sacrificial connotation to be set out as originally, among and for his betrayers, as embodied testament. God's Word, also in sacramental form, determines reality.

The Goal of the Catechism

The goal of catechesis is to live out the Christian life in devotion to God and and in one's callings for the neighbor. Luther's students recognized that his design for the catechism, placing law first and gospel following, with the Lord's Prayer setting forth the contours of the Christian life, aimed at cultivating much more than a knowledge of Christian doctrine. Luther conceived of his catechism as a handbook for Christian living.[57] Joachim Mörlin, who is sometimes called Luther's "chaplain" and did function as a student helper during his time in Wittenberg, guided readers of his expansion of the Small Catechism into learning God's law, his gospel in Christ, and "the chart of Christian callings."[58] Luther himself added two sections to his treat-ment of his revision of the medieval catechism, one instructing believers in their life of daily meditation and devotion, one applying biblical passages to the structure of their lives as he taught about Christians' fulfillment of their humanity in exercising the God-given callings he gives so that all people can care for each other.

Luther believed that the faith-filled life to which Christ has brought us through his death and resurrection means walking in the Lord's footsteps (Rom. 6:4). That involved first of all the discipline of daily meditation on God's Word and respond-ing to him in prayer. Therefore, the reformer sketched "how the head of the house is to teach the members of the household to say morning and evening blessings," and "table blessings."[59] Morning begins with the sign of the holy cross, a reminder of God's claim through his recreating Word in baptism, and evening ends in the same way. The day should be framed, Luther taught, by meditation on the catechism as a summary of God's Word—since few could read the Scriptures, which has become an activity suitable for applying Luther's discipline to twenty-first century lives—and by praying oneself into God's hands and the protection of his angel. Pleas for God's protection and the confession of sins are a part of this approach to God.

The devotion to God of this section of the catechism is followed by Luther's application of his teaching on the Christian's "vocation" or "calling" to daily life.[60] The Small Catechism calls the walks of life that constitute normal human life "holy orders," transforming the language of medieval appreciation for the monastic way of life into the designation for all God-structured activities. The "vocations" of monks and nuns and priests into "holy orders" lost their privileged place. Everything done in faith is God-pleasing, Luther taught, reversing Romans 14:23 into a positive eval-uation of daily life as the creator shaped it.[61]

Luther adopted the medieval social theory with which he had grown up, view-ing human life as taking place in three "walks of life," or "estates," as the term is usu-ally translated: the home, which included both family and economic life; the political community; and the church. In the "Household Chart of Some Bible Passages for All Kinds of holy orders" in the Small Catechism, he discussed the "offices"—the role and the functions involved in those roles to which God "calls" all human creatures for the exercise of care and responsibility toward each other. All people have such offices or responsibilities; only believers recognize that they are given by God as his invitation to serve him by serving others.[62]

Because Luther intended his Small Catechism as a handbook for the home, for parents to instruct their children and their servants, printers also included two liturgical rites for which he had composed new forms, for marriage and for bap-tism, to deepen family's understanding of the calling of marriage and of the impor-tance of baptism in their children's lives.[63]

The "Household Chart" and these booklets on marriage and baptism were intended to give instruction on God's expectations for those who lived by faith and in joy and peace wished to serve their God. But they expressed God's will for human actions; they functioned as law. Luther pointed that out in his 1531 revision of instruction on how to confess sin and receive absolution in the Small Catechism. He combined the Ten Commandments with his understanding of the callings of daily life to assist sinners in recognizing their need to repent: "reflect on your walk of life in the light of the Ten Commandments: whether you are father, mother, son, daughter, master, mistress, servant" (callings); "whether you have been disobedient, unfaithful, lazy, whether you have harmed anyone…stolen, neglected, wasted, or injured anything" (commandments). God's expectations remain his law, also when it instructs us about his will for us.[64]

Luther's Way of Instructing

Luther altered the order of the parts of the traditional catechism of the medieval church because he believed that God's Word that bestows new life through Christ, as summarized in the Apostles Creed, makes sense only if it speaks to those who know that they have miserably failed to meet God's expectations, especially that his human creatures fear, love, and trust in him above all things. If the gospel's saving word is to take root in human consciousness, there must be a consciousness of the need for a redeemer named Jesus. Therefore, Luther's understanding that God's law addresses sinners before his gospel can penetrate their hearts shaped his reformulation of the introduction to the life lived in Christ for beginners. This catechetical text also reflects his conviction that God's righteousness consists of his being faithful to his promises to be the loving father of his human creatures. It reflects the anthropology that Luther came to see as a key to grasping what it means to be human: in God's sight human beings are truly human when they fear, love, and trust in the one who made, redeemed, and sanctifies them. They fulfill their humanity in relationship to one another and God's earth through the actions and attitudes of love that meet God's expectations for their exercise of the responsibilities attached by him to humanness. In the forgiveness of sins, deliverance from death and the devil, the Christian is released from the power of the law to live by faith, serving the rhythm of day, dying and rising with Christ until the new day dawns.

4

The Augsburg Confession

The parish visitations in 1526 and the years following made good sense to the Lutheran Reformers and their political leaders, dedicated as they were to strengthening the faith of their people and promoting their faithful living. In the circumstances of the time, the visitations also carried an overtone that reverberated into the Holy Roman Empire and beyond. By assuming responsibility for the Saxon parishes, suggesting changes up to and including the use of German with other modifications in the universally employed liturgy, the Wittenberg reformers took over prerogatives long reserved for the Roman Catholic hierarchy. In this way the visitations represented a breach, in teaching to be sure, but also in the ritual which had formed the heart of popular belief in late medieval Europe. Consequently, while Luther was working on some of the softer tones of his catechisms, larger forces deployed to muffle the threat to the old order. The result was another dramatic diet, this one in the southern German city of Augsburg. It elicited the defining Lutheran confession, commonly called the *Augustana* from the Latin name of the town.

The Politics of Liturgy

Contemporary assumptions obscure a presupposition basic to premodern Europe, that religious unity provides an essential condition for political peace. For a millennium prior to the Reformation, language, liturgy, and politics had been linked to symbolize Christendom, the hopes of European unity and preeminence. So even while the church commemorated Pentecost yearly, the papacy enforced Latin as the common tongue of the church. Other languages evolved, Romance across the south and, with the exception of Finno-Ugric and Baltic, Germanic in the north. But no matter what was spoken in the homes or on the street, in the mass, in academics, and in trade, Latin held. Saint Jerome's fifth-century Vulgate set the mandatory biblical standard. The Western liturgy, a form that had evolved in the third and fourth centuries, defined Christian worship across Europe. Simultaneously, as politicians had recognized going back to Charlemagne and beyond, the liturgy symbolized a political commons that putatively spread from southern Italy to the northern reaches of Scandinavia. It conveyed religious identity to the common people as well in an age when an insufficient number of educated priests were available.

Whether in Wittenberg, Strasbourg, or southwest Germany and Switzerland, the reformers were linguists. Trained to one degree or another in the assumptions of biblical humanism, they took it for granted that the ancient languages—Hebrew, Greek, and classical Latin—gave them access to the wellsprings of culture. By translating, and thus passing over the Vulgate and the medieval Latin that had developed from it, they hoped to release the original purity and power of the biblical texts. So Johannes Reuchlin, a friend of Melanchthon's family and later his mentor, risked going to the rabbis to recover biblical Hebrew, a step that quickly brought him under attack. In 1516 Erasmus, the crown prince of later biblical humanism, made an equally radical move. He published a Greek recension of the New Testament based on a text he claimed to have found in an attic in Basel. Not so long after, Luther and his Swiss counterpart Ulrich Zwingli used these resources to begin translations into their own dialects of German.

There was ample biblical precedent for this enterprise in Pentecost, a festival of translation. Instead of erecting a linguistic preserve around the good news of Jesus' death and resurrection, the early church carried out its mission in the conviction that the Holy Spirit was breaking all of the boundaries, linguistic and otherwise.[1] So Jesus' own Aramaic gave way to Koine Greek, a broad-shouldered, brawling street language spoken in the marketplaces of New Testament times. It in turn yielded to the other languages of the Mediterranean world, eventually Latin. While biblical humanism provided some of the impetus along with the tools, the texts themselves propelled the reformers to translate into their mother tongues. Published, their Bibles not only gave wider access to the texts of Scripture but also established their dialects.

Biblical precedents and gospel impetus notwithstanding, in the early sixteenth century translation amounted to sedition. But that did not deter the Reformers. Luther published his first of several translations of the New Testament in 1522, bringing the bulk of it back to Wittenberg from his stay at the Wartburg Castle.[2] In 1526 he compounded the linguistic offence liturgically by publishing his *Deutsche Messe*,[3] going beyond his abolition of the canon of the mass in his *Formula missae et communionis* three years earlier.[4] It not only set out the mass in Luther's Saxon dialect of German and in hymnic form rather than the traditional liturgical settings; it also included several other revisions that reoriented worship.

The issue was more than formal. As Luther saw it, the mass itself had become perverted. Centuries of theological development had, according to his interpretation of the New Testament, reversed the poles in the sacrament of the Lord's Supper. Instead of being set out as Christ's act in which the benefits of his death and resurrection are distributed to his people, the sacrament had become, in both theology and practice, a sacrifice—a merit acquiring performance by the church in which God is placated by the offering of the transubstantiated elements. The medieval Christian mission had not possessed sufficient personnel to bring the biblical message in the form of proclamation and instruction to the masses of people converted largely by political decision of their leaders. Therefore, the understanding and practice of the Christian faith slipped into patterns familiar to the populace from their traditional religions. Those religions were based on a ritualistic rhythm that dictated that the human approach to the divine shaped personal and public life. Luther believed that the Christian faith is an understanding of reality based on the presupposition that life comes from the Creator God, who creates through speaking and who relates to his human creatures as a God of conversation and community.[5] Luther and Melanchthon never ceased criticizing the ritualistic religious practice of their day. At their worst, these practices had reduced the center of Christian life, the mass, to mere trafficking in religious gullibility, with its merits offered to the highest bidders. Even more seriously, such practices had perverted the use of the sacrament from the delivery of God's life-renewing Word, and through it the benefits of Christ's death and resurrection, into a human action intended to manipulate God's grace. Attacking this reversal both for itself and its implication for papal power, Luther insisted that the eschatology of the New Testament be restored in theology and practice. So in his liturgical settings of 1523 and 1526, he removed the prayer in which the words of institution had been enclosed in the canon of the mass—the Eucharistic prayer—for sacrificial purposes. Luther substituted forms in which the words would be proclaimed to the congregation. In the sacrament the living and present Christ bestows the gifts of his death and resurrection, given with his body and blood to eat and drink, on sinners assembled by his Word.

In addition to translating and introducing changes in the liturgy, in the visitations the Reformers made still more recommendations for altering the church's life. The people were to receive both the bread and the wine, not the bread only as was common in medieval Roman Catholic practice of the sacrament. Private confession and absolution, a notoriously abusive instrument of social control in late medieval life, was stripped of its compulsion. Its focus was shifted from the satisfactions performed by the sinner to the absolution that conveyed forgiveness of sins. The clergy were allowed, if not encouraged, to marry. Monasteries and convents, already emptying at a phenomenal rate, were being taken over for other charitable public purposes. If Luther was a conservative reformer, the religious life of Saxony and other sovereignties joining in the visitation process was nevertheless transformed.

But for all of the religious implication of the visitation, Charles V, his bureaucrats, and the papal curia saw something even more alarming. In *To the German Nobility*, one of the great treatises of 1520, Luther had argued that if the church does not proceed to reform itself, political leaders in the empire should arrogate the authority necessary to do so.[6] In the visitation John the Constant, the elector of Saxony from 1525 to 1532, did exactly that. So did a few neighboring sovereigns. They made themselves in effect emergency bishops, taking a hand in the selection and supervision of the clergy in their territories. Such a step may have had implications that Luther did not envision. He apparently hoped for a more democratic form of leadership in congregations assembled under the authority of the Word alone. But the source of some restlessness in Wittenberg was seen in much larger proportion beyond. Linguistically, liturgically, and in terms of church governance, the Lutherans were moving in directions that threatened the unity of the church and the empire.

Attempts at Reunion

From 1517 until into the later 1520s, the leadership of both church and empire had dealt with the Lutheran reform the way large scale institutions generally deal with dissent: repressively. The failure of escalating attempts to silence him had made Luther both an excommunicant and an outlaw. From the Diet of Worms in 1521 until the first diet of Speyer in 1526, the movement that had generated out of Luther's protest remained under the ban.

A variety of factors, some of them involving the empire as a whole, others more local, came together to give Luther and the Lutheran movement shelter. Charles V, though he had enough power of his own to make the office of emperor more than it had been for some time, was hamstrung by a combination of enemies. A Habsburg, Charles had a familial power base in three corners of Europe: the Low Countries in the Northwest, Spain in the Southwest, and through his brother, Ferdinand, claims in what is now Hungary toward the Southeast. The Holy Roman Empire, which included most of what is now Germany and some adjoining territories (including, officially, the Low Countries), was the fourth corner. Because of such power the papacy had strongly opposed Charles's election as emperor even though he was very young in 1519 and the office had more wallop in title than in substance. Charles's relations with the papacy were strained throughout his tenure: they were not helped at all when in 1527 his troops sacked the city of Rome and carried off the pope as their prisoner.[7]

If his conflict with the papacy was not trouble enough, Charles had other enemies who were even more of a problem. His rivalry with Francis I, a member of the Valois family who was king of France, broke into open warfare four times during his reign. Suleiman the Magnificent of Turkey outdid all of Charles's opponents, moving his troops across the Balkans all the way to Vienna, where he laid siege to the city in 1529. Suleiman was also in league with a pirate named Barbarossa, who troubled shipping lanes in the Mediterranean, a serious problem for the great Italian cities. It was Suleiman's threat that occasioned Charles's absence from the first diet of Speyer and made him hesitant about simply forcing the Lutherans' hands. Charles needed them as allies against the Turks, a critical consideration in his attempts at conciliation.

The Lutherans could also count on some force of their own. Between 1517 and 1548 three Saxon electors in succession supported the Lutheran Reformation. Frederick the Wise had originally used his office to shield Luther, amongst other things because of his pride in his new university at Wittenberg. Taking over in 1525, his brother John, remembered as the Constant or the Steadfast, had taken the support the next step, actively underwriting the visitation. His son, John Frederick, who took over in 1532, would become an eager supporter. He studied with Luther and was more ardently convicted, though sometimes his problems with drink made him erratic.

Other German sovereigns also lent their support, especially following Ferdinand's summary rejection in the second Diet of Speyer in 1529. Six rulers and

Archduke of Austria

fourteen imperial cities joined in the protest, among them John of Saxony; Philip of Hesse, who was to play a key role in the 1530s and 1540s; and the Margrave George of Brandenburg-Ansbach. Braunschweig-Lüneburg and Anhalt also joined in, along with cities like Strasbourg, Nuremburg, Ulm, and Reutlingen. In fact, the German free cities soon became hotbeds of the Reformation. Thus, even if he had been able to get his hands free of his other enemies, Charles V would have had to get past some significant opposition to get at Luther. After the failure of Ferdinand's power play at the Diet of Speyer in 1529, he needed to find a way to get the Lutherans back to the table.

One such possible forum for settling the issues raised by the Lutheran reformers was a council of the church. Early in what became the Reformation, somewhat overwhelmed by the widespread response to his protest, Luther went to the city church in Wittenberg and formally appealed for a council. He hoped that such a council would include all the bishops of the church and that it would consider the issues on the basis of God's Word without papal meddling.

There was both historic and fairly contemporary precedent for such an appeal. The ancient ecumenical councils, assembling in places like Jerusalem, Nicaea, and Chalcedon, were instrumental in defining the church's theological tradition. In the fourteenth and fifteenth centuries, as the papacy became mired in itself, reform minded leaders had advocated the restoration of the council as an institution. A series of councils resulted. The most critical one, at Constance in 1414–1418, actually succeeded in some restoration of the papal office. Thus, there was in theory, anyway, sound footing for Luther's hope of a conciliar settlement. Through the 1520s, the appeal was reiterated by Luther and his supporters to the point that it became a *sine qua non*, an essential condition for any settlement. But Charles V could read the political realties, churchly and otherwise. Clement VII, who had been elected pope in 1523, was unalterably opposed to such an assembly of the bishops. Relations between pope and emperor already severely strained, the notion of a council became a focal point of further conflict. Charles pushed, Clement balked. It was not until the mid-1530s that a new pope, Paul III, accepted the idea of a council and then on terms that the Lutherans could not accept.

Politics being the art of the possible, however, Charles V and his imperial advisors began to look for some intermediate possibility. The default position was a resort to force, which he threatened at Speyer by renewing the Edict of Worms. But in the conflict charged atmosphere of 1529–1530, that could be catastrophic, as much for Charles as for the empire. So Charles temporized still more, looking for an opening.

Setting Off Alone

While Charles and his advisors were sorting through the possibilities of negotiation, the Lutherans and those supporting them to one degree or another faced problems of their own. Even though the threat of force that had hung over their heads had not materialized for some eight or nine years, the Lutherans still had to consider the possibility that Charles might actually get loose and do what he vowed to do in the Edict of Worms. If he did, the odds stood strongly against them. So they had to take steps.

In the immediate aftermath of the second diet of Speyer in 1529, the political leaders of the reform quickly sought to forge an alliance. Under the leadership of John of Saxony and Philip of Hesse, they formed a working agreement for mutual protection. As Philip of Hesse saw it, religious differences could wait; Charles V's threat demanded two-feet-on-the-ground realism. But it did not take long for other differences to claim renewed importance. Especially in Saxony, theological concerns asserted primacy, particularly issues concerning the nature of Christ's presence in the sacrament.

But there were other divisive factors as well. Old tensions emerged between the eastern and northeastern Germans of Saxony and Brandenburg Ansbach and the Germans of the Upper Rhine Valley, which runs along the southern border of Switzerland and moves north on what is now the French-German border to Strasbourg. By connections through the universities, the southwest Germans had much in common with the Swiss. Political differences also produced different perspectives—Elector John of Saxony and Margrave George of Brandenburg-Ansbach were anxious to preserve the power of the princes; the cities were more inclined toward an aristocratic form of governance. As these differences surfaced, the possibilities for alliance waned.

Margrave George and John of Saxony both argued, though John less consistently, that religious unity was a necessary condition of alliance. They had Luther's support. Translating the Old Testament, he was closely familiar with the prophetic denunciation of Israel's and Judah's search for alliances. He had also developed some distrust of the southwest Germans and the Swiss through previous dealings. For the time being, Melanchthon joined him in opposition.

That did not settle the issue, however. Hesitant though some of them were, the political leaders had committed themselves to the alliance formed immediately after the second Diet of Speyer to appeal Ferdinand's ruling to the emperor. Still, they called a meeting in early June of 1529 for further consideration of the terms of their agreement. Philip of Hesse was the only one who argued for a more broadly based alliance. He had enough influence to gain a delay; the meeting resumed in August in the town of Schwabach.

In the meantime both George and John expressed interest in a document that would publicly state their religious unity. Two statements were already available for this purpose. One was the *Instructions for Parish Visitors* written by Melanchthon in 1528 with some revision by Luther.[8] The other statement was more personal. In the third part of his *Confession concerning Christ's Supper*, also written in 1528, Luther had set out his own confession of faith, using the Apostles Creed as a basis.[9] But the margrave and the elector wanted a statement of their own. So in June the

Wittenberg theologians agreed to prepare such a statement, this one more directly applicable to the situation at hand.

The new statement was written sometime in July. Little is known of the actual process: the drafting procedure was closely guarded, leaving no historical record. The evidence available strongly suggests that Melanchthon was the principal author, though when it was published, it bore Luther's name.[10] Whatever the case, the Wittenberg faculty worked together as a team, and Melanchthon undoubtedly consulted the third part of *Confession concerning Christ's Supper* as he worked. Luther mentions having assisted: occasional formulations, such as the statement on the fruits of faith in Article VI, reflect his idiom. Justas Jonas, trained in both canon law and theology, also helped out. The resulting document has been called the Schwabach Articles.

Two characteristics of the new statement should be noted. For one thing, it was clearly drafted over and against the Zwinglians, leaving little room for compromise. Article X confesses that "there is truly present in the bread and wine, the true Body and Blood of Christ" and that "it is not only bread and wine, as even now the other side asserts." This excluded several cities, including Strasbourg and Ulm, and for tactical reasons, Nuremburg demurred.

Another characteristic feature to be noted in the Schwabach Articles concerns the structure of the argument. Luther's confession in the third part of *Confession concerning Christ's Supper*, like his explanations of the Creed in the Small Catechism, is fully and simply trinitarian. The Schwabach Articles follow a different order. The first three articles set out the trinitarian formulas of the larger Catholic tradition. Thereafter, the focus follows a somewhat traditional outline of public teaching, while at the same time reflecting Melanchthon's alteration of that outline in his *Loci communes* of 1521. The Schwabach confession's remaining articles follow a roughly experiential sequence from sin to grace (4–6) to the means of grace (7–11); the church, the return of Christ to judge, and the government's penultimate authority (12–14) and finally, disputed ceremonies (15–17).

The Schwabach Articles is in one sense the first Lutheran confession even though it was superseded shortly after its publication. It served a limited purpose, marking out a particularly Lutheran stance over and against those who were making overtures to the reformers of the Upper Rhine Valley. But it also laid foundations for the first seventeen articles of the Augsburg Confession as Melanchthon edited and revised it. Whatever hesitations he may have had about Margrave George's unyielding particularity, once he set his feet, John the Constant remained just as firm. Right into the negotiations as Augsburg, he made no effort to build alliances.

Seeking a Wider Alliance

Before the Wittenbergers started work on the Schwabach Articles, Philip of Hesse had already embarked on his own efforts towards a more wide ranging alternative. He had several incentives, among them the central location of Hesse between the rival reforming factions as well as the defense of his sprawling territory. He was not at all convinced that the practicalities of warfare demanded theological agreement. But if others were convinced of it, he was willing to make an effort. Therefore, late in June he wrote the first letters setting up a meeting that would become one of the legendary encounters of the Reformation, putting Luther and Zwingli face to face at the same table. Philip of Hesse hoped that such a direct meeting would overcome their mutual opposition, clearing the way for compromise.

The meetings, which took place in late September and early October of 1529, included some other significant participants: Melanchthon and with Zwingli, one of Melanchthon's old friends, Oecolampadius. He had taken the Latin as a literal translation of his German name, "house light." Martin Bucer from Strasbourg also attended. The meetings themselves began dramatically, climaxed in a showdown and ended in pedantry.

In the preliminary meeting Luther and Oecolampadius confronted one another on the nature of language, a seemingly innocent but decisive issue. The Swiss argued that words can only signify, that the interpreter supplies the connection between the signifying word and the ultimate reality behind it. Luther insisted that words also can accomplish what they declare in and of themselves, that God's Word in particular does what it says. Zwingli and Oecolampadius were operating with the medieval tradition of "realism," which placed reality in the heavenly forms or ideas and devalued the created, material order.[11] Luther's education by "Ockhamist" instructors found the focus of reality in God's revelation of himself and in that which he had created. Separated by fundamental presuppositions about the nature of reality and language, neither the conversation between Luther and Oecolampadius nor that between Melanchthon and Zwingli made much headway.

Preliminaries completed, on October 2 a plenary session was called. The theologians quickly agreed on many points. But then conflict took over. Much of the dispute revolved around John 6. Zwingli presented verse 63, "the flesh is of no avail," as his ultimate weapon against Luther's doctrine of the bodily presence of Christ in the sacrament. Luther retorted that John 6 plainly has no reference to the Lord's Supper, that the words of institution which Christ spoke on the night in which he was betrayed have to taken in their plain sense: "this is my body," by Christ's own promise, makes the bread just that. Before the session, Luther had chalked the Latin words of the Lord's Supper—*hoc est corpus meum*—onto the table. At the decisive moment in the conversation, he would whisk back the tablecloth to reveal them there, stating his refusal to yield.

Jots and tittles took over thereafter, sparring over metaphysics and quotations from the church fathers supporting the different points of view. After a few days of such footnote chasing, the theologians themselves were bored. Oecolampadius moved that the conversations be suspended. It looked like old hostilities had carried the day.[12]

But Marburg made something of a breakthrough, if not of the proportion Philip of Hesse desired, still significant. Luther was asked to draw up a statement summarizing what had been achieved. For this purpose, he used a copy of the Schwabach Articles, pruning off excesses, refocusing the statement pastorally and giving it a more positive cast. The result was a fifteen-article statement; on fourteen of them, Lutherans and Zwinglians had found accord; on the fifteenth, concerning the Lord's Supper, they did not. The real presence of the theologians themselves had overcome some long term suspicions, showing the broad range of agreement already in place between them. But the real presence of Christ's body and blood in the Supper was another matter: neither the Lutherans nor the Zwinglians could give at that point. So, in the end, Philip of Hesse went away disappointed. The way to further alliance had been blocked. But Luther's summary of the Marburg Colloquy remained. Doing his own editorial trimming and patching, he had turned the Schwabach Articles into a much more succinct and direct statement.

A New Possibility

In the last months of 1529, several factors combined to further complicate matters for the Lutheran reformers on both fronts. As it happens often enough, interpretations of conflict generate even more of it. So Zwinglians and Lutherans went home blaming one another. Even Chancellor Gregor Brück, a seasoned diplomat serving the elector, got into the act. He compared an alliance with the Zwinglians to carrying a mouse in your pocket. Then there was more trouble with the emperor. When the envoys delivered the Speyer Protestation, the formal appeal of the revocation of the holdings of the earlier diet, Charles V had them arrested and imprisoned.

The question of the propriety of political resistance had been on the theological docket in Wittenberg ever since Frederick the Wise asked about it following the original promulgation of the Edict of Worms in 1521.[13] Charles's reaction to the Speyer appeal gave it a new urgency. The theologians debated it closely. Lazarus Spengler, the municipal secretary of Nuremburg; Johannes Brenz of Schwäbisch Hall, the theologian who advised Margrave George; and the Wittenbergers were largely agreed, even if they argued some fine points. Though they regarded the claims of faith as prior to political demands, they were still hesitant about anything more than passive resistance. Yet Luther was beginning to make some distinctions that opened up the possibilities of military defense, particularly if the emperor were to actually resort to force to impose a religious settlement.[14]

Then, in January of 1530, Charles V made a surprising announcement. He scheduled another diet, this one to meet in April at Augsburg though it was eventually postponed until June. His trouble with the Turks was at the top of the emperor's considerations,[15] but he also realized that the protestors of Speyer would have to be addressed. Apparently still working on the possibility of the council, Charles had some conversations with Clement VII in Bologna. There, Charles formally received the imperial crown from Clement, evidence of improving relations between them. This may account for the surprisingly conciliatory tone of the summons to the diet. Charles V promised that "all care [would be] taken to give a charitable hearing to every man's opinion, thoughts, and notions, to understand them, to weight them, to bring and reconcile men to a unity in Christian truth."[16]

It took a couple of months and some bitter disappointments for the Saxons to realize the extent of Charles's welcome. Not surprisingly, it did not extend as far as they originally thought. But from March into April, even into May, John remained convinced that there was a new possibility for working things out. If this appears illusory, he had his reasons: Charles did need military support; there had been talk at the second diet of Speyer about calling a German council in the absence of a wider conciliar discussion; the Wittenberg theologians were obviously more willing to move back towards Rome than they were to hold on for the Zwinglians. In addition, John also had some personal and political reasons. Charles's Habsburg family owed him a sizable debt incurred in Charles's election as emperor, and John needed to have his own succession from his brother Frederick ratified before granting succession to his own son.

But if John found a variety of reasons to push forward, his friends were most hesitant. Disappointed with his inability to form a fuller alliance, Philip of Hesse held back from plans for the diet. He did not arrive in Augsburg until the middle of May. The cities of Nuremburg and Ulm also held back, not wanting to complicate matters with Philip. Margrave George was not available for his own reasons. As a result, the Saxons were forced to go ahead alone.

Luther's summary of the Marburg Colloquy and the Schwabach Articles in fact provided raw materials for the writing of the Augsburg Confession, but the emperor's invitation had not required the kind of confession Melanchthon finally decided to compose. The emperor demanded an explanation of the practical reforms introduced in the lands of the Wittenberg Reformation, an account of the liturgical and ceremonial changes that had been made in Wittenberg and the surrounding regions. The elector put the theologians to work on this in March, shortly after receiving the summons. The results have commonly been called the Torgau Articles, more recent terminology, but the drafts produced in Saxony in preparation for Augsburg remained unfinished.[17] At least two different drafts were prepared, the second written by Melanchthon in April with a fuller account of the theological justification for the changes. Melanchthon had the second draft with him at Augsburg where one of his first tasks was completing the statement. The final form, after considerable revision, appears in Articles XXII to XXVIII of the Augsburg Confession, now grouped together as "Articles in which an Account is Given of Abuses that have been Corrected." Article VII of the Augustana states the guiding assumption for these changes. Given the sufficiency of the gospel, "it is not necessary that human traditions, rites, or ceremonies instituted by human beings be alike everywhere" (Latin text).[18] The Wittenberg theologians had redefined Christianity: they viewed it no longer as primarily a matter of human performance, certainly not of ritual. Rituals only served to enhance the conversation between the creator and his human creatures.

Trouble in the Making

Preliminary documents in hand, the Saxon delegation left for Augsburg in April, journeying southwesterly. It included with the elector and his son John Frederick, Melanchthon, Johann Agricola, whose preaching at Speyer had impressed John, Chancellor Brück, and some other officials. They arrived in Coburg, on the border of electoral Saxony, the day before Easter.

Luther was also part of the retinue to that point but could not go any further. Still an outlaw, he lost the protection of law outside of John's territory. Not wanting him at risk, John had hoped to take him as far as Nuremburg where Luther would have been close enough for regular consultation, but the Nuremburg authorities refused, fearing potential complications. So Luther preached at services Easter evening and then stayed behind, nearly 150 miles away from the proceedings at Augsburg—close enough to be reachable by messenger but still too far for easy communication.

His stay was challenging. As usual, Luther worked prodigiously, writing among other things a commentary on Psalm 118 and a polemic, *An Exhortation to the Clergy Assembled at Augsburg*.[19] But soon his work was not enough to distract him. He received word that his father had passed away. He missed his family. And then his grief was compounded by the inactivity. He complained in letters to Melanchthon of being tortured by silence, worrying that his younger colleague would not be able to withstand the pressures brought to bear on him. It was a difficult time.

Arriving in the city of Augsburg, the Saxons immediately encountered the first of several disappointments concerning the openness that Charles had led them to expect. Archduke Ferdinand, who had already been such a problem at Speyer, had taken some steps of his own to prepare for the diet. Working with Lorenzo Campeggio, the papal legate, he had asked the faculty at the University of Vienna to prepare a list of Lutheran theological errors. The assignment had passed to the faculty at Ingolstadt, where it had been assigned to none other than Dr. Johann Eck, or *Dreck* ("filth") as Luther had called him. Eck had set about to portray the Lutherans in the most heretical, seditious, and incendiary light possible.

Eck is not celebrated in the history of Roman Catholicism as one of its great or even notable theologians. A controversialist first, last, and always, he made a career for himself out of his opposition to Luther and the reformers. Sixteenth-century popular polemics being what they were—commonly generously overstated, harsh, and more than a little crude—Eck was hardly alone in his vituperations. But he was not noticeably slowed by considerations like fairness or evenhandedness. Since Luther was already both outlaw and excommunicant, all that remained was to tar his associates with the same brush.

So, relying on a long memory and extended experience of conflict, Eck had quickly compiled a document already in circulation on the streets of Augsburg. Addressed to the emperor, it was entitled the *404 Theses*.[20] Eck announced in the preface that he wished to provide a complete picture of the people with whom

Bitter abusive language [margin annotation]

Charles proposed to enter into conversation. The document consisted of excerpts from the writings of Luther, Zwingli, the radical reformers and others, all of them edited and pruned to support Eck's charge that Wittenberg reform was guilty of every imaginable heresy. It has commonly been said that Eck's *Theses* led directly to Melanchthon's recasting of the documents that the Saxons had brought with them to the diet. Receiving a copy shortly after his arrival, Melanchthon set to work immediately. In fact, a second series of disappointing events proved to be an even more serious threat.

If John's hope for openness leaves him looking a little gullible, the elector still had enough political experience to realize that critical decisions are not always made in open meetings. Early on, John started looking for ways to arrange some more private consultations. Both he and John Frederick could count on connections close enough to reach the emperor's ear. One of them in fact had been Charles V's tutor. Asking that another of John's courtiers be sent to join the talks, the contacts agreed to set up a meeting between John and Charles in late March for closed-door consultation.

Prudent as such an effort may have been, it turned into something slapstick. The emissaries to Charles wandered into Innsbruck several days late; the messenger sent to find them arrived ahead of them and delivered the message into the wrong hands; the emperor had in the meantime chosen another representative. On May 8 it all fell through. Charles V was angry that provisions had been made for Lutheran preaching in Augsburg, ordered it to stop, and flat out refused to meet with the elector.

While trying to make contact in person, John had also tried to initiate something through the mail. He sent the emperor a copy of the Schwabach Articles, hoping thereby to demonstrate the Lutheran reform's place within the larger Roman Catholic consensus. Charles got the document May 8 but quickly condemned it, among other things because it recognized only two sacraments. The next day Campeggio appealed to the emperor's improving relations with the papacy, insisting that there be no private consultations with the Saxons and that Lutheran preaching stop.

When John got word from Innsbruck of the emperor's reaction, he was so disappointed that he threatened to leave Augsburg for Coburg. In the place of openness he had found unrelenting resistance. When his emissaries shuttled the threat back to the emperor, John got in return an even sterner reaction. Charles denounced John for rejecting the Edict of Worms, a course that had damaged the empire, condemned him for seeking other alliances, and again demanded the immediate cessation of all Lutheran preaching. It may not be over until it's over, but for all intents and purposes, it sure looked over, the emperor's denunciation signaling what could be anticipated in the diet itself.

With this, the Saxon delegation changed course. The emperor had called the diet. The Saxons had arrived in good faith. Even with the outcome all but set, they had to go ahead. But given such realities, the reformers had to emphasize their loyalties to the Catholic tradition and the political order associated with it. Given

Eck's salacious misrepresentations and the emperor's repudiation, Melanchthon had his work cut out for him in revising the document. In addition to composing for the princes and municipal governments an explanation of the reform measures the reformers had undertaken, he also had to make a defense of the catholicity and orthodoxy of their teaching. Such a defense involved both positive statements of biblical teaching and condemnations of the false teachings that the church through the ages had rejected. Above all, these condemnations appear in article I, the rejection of the classic heresies, in articles V, IX, XII, XVI, and XVII, in which Anabaptist views of the means of grace, forgiveness and perfection, civil government, and Christ's return are rejected; in article VII, with its condemnation of Donatism; and in articles II and XII, where the Pelagian understanding of sin and justification are condemned. In article X all opposing doctrine is condemned without specific reference to any named group. Other condemnations were added in later printed editions of the Confession.[21]

The Editorial Process

With Luther at a distance, failing diplomatic efforts, other political leaders arriving in Augsburg after the middle of the month, and Melanchthon's own agenda, the final editing of what became the Augsburg Confession, was an extraordinarily complicated process.[22] Even if Luther complained about the mail, he and Melanchthon corresponded regularly. John's efforts with Charles registered their impact along the way. As these efforts foundered, the Saxons realized that they had to bring others, including Philip of Hesse and some of the cities, into things with them.

The classic analysis of the drafting was written in 1976 by Wilhelm Maurer. Entitled *Historical Commentary on the Augsburg Confession*, this work offers a detailed analysis of the various versions the Augustana went through before assuming its final form just before it was presented to the diet on June 25.[23] Summarizing Maurer's closely detailed analysis, the process can be said to have gone through four stages.

The first stage began with the Saxons' arrival in Augsburg in early May and ended on May 22, with the articles on disputed practices virtually complete. Several factors combined to make these articles his first concern. To begin with, the emperor himself had prioritized the issues. What the Lutherans had treated as local options had added up in his eyes to a major disruption. Further, while there had been drafts and probably an extended discussion along the way as the Saxon delegation traveled to Augsburg, the document was still incomplete. But still more, the practices involved were ecumenically ticklish, among them communion in both kinds (lay reception of the wine with the bread); marriage of the clergy; the mass; the practice of confession; dietary laws concerning the use of fish, meat, and butter; monastic vows, and the authority of the bishops. In fact, even after Melanchthon eliminated some even more provocative issues and applied all of his considerable diplomatic skill to those that remained, Roman Catholic representatives after the diet rejected all of articles that resulted.

Completing the articles on disputed practices, Melanchthon attached them to the text of the Schwabach Articles. Though he initially hoped to finish his revisions by May 4 so that Luther would have plenty of time to make any revisions he considered necessary, Melanchthon did not get it done until May 11. Luther turned it around by May 15 with a famous statement that Maurer finds both positive and negative. Calling the assembled document an "apology"—the term for their statement that all the Wittenberg colleagues had been using until Melanchthon recognized that he was not just *defending* Wittenberg reform but much more *confessing* biblical truth—Luther wrote to Elector John on May 15: "I have read through Master Philip's 'Apology' and it really does please me, and I do not know anything that can be improved or changed, and I would not attempt it anyway, for I cannot step so softly and quietly as he."[24] To the comment, he added something of a prayer: "May Christ our Lord help it to bear much and great fruit, as we hope and pray. Amen."[25] The German word that Luther used to describe light stepping literally, often translated as to "pussyfoot," could also mean in the sixteenth century "to step softly"—diplomatically—in a positive sense.[26] It remains certain that, while giving the document his endorsement and recognizing the diplomatic necessities of Melanchthon's situation in Augsburg, he was apprehensive about the diplomacy involved.

Luther's discouraging of further editorial work did not forestall further efforts to refine the confession. When word of Charles's refusal of the Schwabach Articles got to Augsburg, sometime between May 13 and 15 according to Maurer's calculations, Melanchthon further rewrote the article on monastic vows and the office of the bishop, which became Articles XXVII and XXVIII of the Augustana. Though Melanchthon and those working with him continued to finesse some of the fine points well into June, the articles concerning disputed practices—XXII through XXVIII, which amount to the second part of the Augsburg Confession—were all but complete at this time.

After the Confession had been presented, Luther expressed widely varying assessments of it. On the one hand, Luther wrote several times during July of his pleasure at the confession Melanchthon and his colleagues had made in Augsburg.[27] But he also grew impatient and wrote of his fears that the Evangelical negotiators in Augsburg would concede too much.[28] He sent a sharply worded complaint to Justus Jonas about this second part of the Augsburg Confession on July 21. By that time his memory had elided differences between the various versions Luther had seen, but he wanted a clearer, more forceful statement of the issues. Specifically, he said, he missed the rejection of the Roman Catholic notion of purgatory, praying to the saints, and any declaration that the pope had become the Antichrist.[29] Though references to purgatory are missing, Article XXI does reject the invocation of the saints, something Luther had apparently forgotten. Maurer suggests that there may have been a statement on the papacy in one of the various editions that had been set aside for diplomatic reasons. Given the joint force of Eck's critique and Charles's repudiation, Melanchthon and his colleagues, along with the political leaders, probably considered the issue too hot to handle. The elector and his colleagues in other governments needed a settlement with the emperor.

On or about May 22 in Maurer's analysis, a second stage in the editorial process began, this one involving what became the first seventeen articles of the Augustana. Up to this time, the plan had been to set the Schwabach Articles together with the new document just reaching completion in Articles XXII through XXVIII. Several factors were involved in the reconsideration. Charles's rejection of Schwabach was one of them. It made little or no sense to present statements he had already declared inadequate. But Philip of Hesse's arrival was another. When he weighed in on the process, he exerted pressure to broaden what the Wittenberg theologians had made so deliberately particular, making room for those more sympathetic to the Swiss.

Revising Schwabach was a major undertaking. Melanchthon went to work on the project with some colleagues, maintaining his oversight throughout. Maurer maintains that through this stage and what followed, Melanchthon paid much closer attention to Luther's statement in the third part of *Confession concerning Christ's Supper* than he had in originally drafting Schwabach. The goal was to effectively improve the arguments ecumenically, stressing even further convergence with the Catholic tradition. Given Philip of Hesse's pressures, Article X on the Lord's Supper was particularly ticklish. For both ecumenical concerns and the conviction of the Wittenberg theologians regarding Christ's presence dictated that there could be no concession on the real presence of Christ's body and blood in the sacrament. At the same time Philip of Hesse and the south German cities had to be given some room for difference, of emphasis if not of substance.

The revision of Schwabach was still in the works when another of Maurer's stages began on May 30. The change making it still a third stage in the editorial process that produced the Augustana was the arrival of the Nuremburg delegation. With Philip of Hesse, they found the Saxons too parochial and pushed to broaden the revisions still further to provide room for themselves and other southern German cities supportive of the Lutheran reform. By June 15 they were satisfied that they had done just that.

The fourth stage, beginning June 15, involved translation. To that point the language was German. It would also be the language of the diet. By June 15 the German version of the Augsburg Confession was all but complete, lacking only some points of finesse later applied in fussing to the finish. Completed, it became the text that was to be read to the estates and presented to the emperor. Latin was the international academic and diplomatic language, however. So earlier in June some Saxon officials had begun preparing a Latin translation of the disputed articles. From June 15 on, Melanchthon himself translated. He had a gift for the language, writing cleanly and concisely. Because both the German and the Latin were used diplomatically, both assumed official status in representing the position of those practicing reform in the Wittenberg manner.

The final form and content of the Augsburg Confession fell into place, on the basis of Luther's confession of 1528, the Schwabach Articles, the Marburg Articles, and the electoral Saxon work on the issues of reform with a view toward both the scholastic teaching of the medieval church and, in the last seven articles, its practices. The first article affirms the ancient doctrine of the Trinity, the cornerstone of orthodox catholic Christian faith. The second treats original sin, a key element in the anthropology which the Wittenberg theologians presumed as they treated the central problem of salvation. Their answer to that fundamental question of human life, how can I become and remain in God's favor, begins in article three, affirming both the redeeming work of Christ and the delivery of his benefits by the Holy Spirit, again in terms of the ancient creeds. Articles IV through VI treat how the Holy Spirit delivers these benefits, by fostering faith; how he fosters faith, through the means of grace in the preaching of the Word; and what faith does in terms of Christian living in new obedience. He also creates the community of believers, the church, the subject of articles seven and eight. In each of these articles Melanchthon crafted the essentials of Wittenberg theology in such a way that they confronted and sometimes contradicted widespread scholastic conclusions, but did so in a manner designed to create as little offense as possible.

That policy continued in articles IX through XIV, which expressed the central Wittenberg premise that God works through his Word to accomplish his saving purposes, but it did so on the field of medieval sacramental theology and its practical focal point in the understanding of penance and repentance. Luther's and Melanchthon's doctrine of God's Word stands implicitly behind these articles even though it is not elaborated. That emphasis on God's Word resulted in a reevaluation of the sacred, ritual works central to medieval piety, and article XV dismisses them as means of salvation. Article XVI affirms the goodness of God's created order in its social structures; article XVII affirms the return of Christ to judge the world. In this last article as well as in several others the positions of the "radical" reformers of the medieval tradition of biblicistic, moralistic, anti-clerical, anti-sacramental, millenarian reform are explicitly rejected.

Sometime during the process of revision, Melanchthon took the opportunity to add three articles of his own. Articles XVIII, XIX, and XX have no precedent in the antecedent documents. While not simply personal—these additions had to be approved along with all the other revisions by those involved in the process—they concern points that either troubled Melanchthon theologically or focused particular concern. They also reflect Melanchthon's engagement with the accusation of the Roman Catholics, who had been particularly critical of Wittenberg views of freedom of the will and of salvation by faith alone because they feared the collapse of moral order if the people believed that their good works did not contribute to their salvation.

The title of Article XVIII, "the Freedom of the Will," may seem curious since in fact it states a form of Luther's argument on the bondage of the will. It also reveals that Melanchthon approached the question from a different angle than Luther had in his debate with Erasmus. Luther's concern focused on the nature of God and his relationship as Creator to his human creatures. Melanchthon had recognized in his exchanges with Roman Catholic opponents that their concern was one of anthropology and the integrity of human beings as creatures fashioned by God to exercise the responsibilities he had given them.[30] For Luther himself, the logic was straightforwardly simple: since Christ Jesus frees, in relation to God the will must be bound. But such simplicity sparked a couple of decisive turns in the Lutheran reform. It was cited in his excommunication and became the issue in the great theological battle between him and Erasmus in 1525, a conflict that put Melanchthon in a delicate position between two men whom he admired. While earlier scholars held that Melanchthon and Erasmus came to some understanding on the issue in 1527, Timothy Wengert has shown that this is false.[31] His continuing disagreement with Erasmus may be one reason Melanchthon wanted to single the topic out for closer attention in Article XVIII.

Since the free will argument was traditionally used to account for evil in the world, Article XIX addresses the causes of sin. The harsh criticism of Roman Catholic foes had convinced Melanchthon that, having recast the historic treatment of the freedom of the will, he must register the impact of the Lutheran argument on the origin of sin. Thus, Article XIX carries on the argument begun in Article XVIII.

Connected to this critique of the Wittenberg way of thinking was the frequently voiced Roman Catholic critique of the insistence that salvation comes by faith alone. This criticism found resonance with Erasmus and his concern, reflecting his brand of biblical humanism, for moral reform of both personal and public life. When Erasmus published his *Diatribe* against Luther in 1524, he repeated the charge of Roman Catholic leaders concerned that no one would strive to be good if the conviction of the bondage of the will took hold. Luther answered with equal force, arguing that in relation to God, no one is good now. Melanchthon saw the necessity of expanding the argument originally stated in Article VI concerning the relationship of faith and good works in Article XX. He and Luther and their colleagues had repeatedly argued, as does this article, that good works can proceed only from the faith given by the Holy Spirit, which moves believers to love their neighbors for Christ's sake.

Articles XXII to XXVIII embrace the issues raised by the practical aspects of Wittenberg reform. For the Wittenberg theologians they were the secondary results to their understanding of God's creative and re-creative Word as it justified by creating faith in Christ in sinners. For the Roman Catholic theologians, these issues of sacral ritual performance were critical for proper Christian living, and because they held a quite difference basis for structuring their thought, the two sides collided but also talked past each other at many times.

The composition of the preface formed a vital part of Melanchthon's activities in formulating the statement of the Evangelical governments during May and early June. For the preface placed the contents of their confession in context. Beginning with a draft intended only to represent the particular stance and interests of the electoral Saxon government, the preface evolved into an appeal to the emperor for understanding for their concerns and support. Their explanation grew out of the emperor's own demand that they account for the reforms that they had introduced. The followers of Luther committed themselves to strive for Christian unity and harmony and pledged to participate in a council should that be the only way to restore that unity and harmony to the church.[32]

The German edition of the Confession was already completed by June 15. Melanchthon continued to work on the Latin daily, completing his work during the last week before the diet assembled to consider it. All of the parties involved expressed their final approval for the formal presentation June 25, 1530.

The Presentation

Already hanging by tenterhooks, the diet nearly collapsed in on itself when the emperor was arriving in Augsburg from Innsbruck. Several incidents took place when the imperial entourage approached the city, one outside of town along the river Lech, one in the city itself. Both were promoted by Campeggio; together, they made it appear certain that either the emperor himself or John would back out before the diet met.

Still hoping to make early contact with Charles, John sent envoys to meet his party before they arrived in Augsburg. They met some miles out of town. When John's men approached, Campeggio saw to it that the papal colors were struck. Charles and his delegation promptly dismounted and went to a knee, indicating their loyalty to the papacy. John's representatives remained firmly in their saddles. Charles took deep offense at this display of what he took to be sedition. It looked for a while as though the diet would be prorogued.

Then when Charles V and company actually entered the city, at Campeggio's urging, he announced a *corpus Christi* procession. A medieval custom involving the reserved host or bread of the sacrament, understood to have been transubstantiated, the procession amounted to a parade. The host was carried in a monstrance, the box on traditional Roman Catholic altars for the bread remaining from the mass, which was mounted on a pole. If the flag struck along the Lech represented the papacy, the transubstantiated host was Christ Jesus himself, to be reverenced accordingly. Pious as such a practice may have been to traditional Roman Catholics, it could hardly have been more offensive to the Lutherans. They had long argued, as had Luther in the Small Catechism, that it is the Word that makes the sacrament, not the elements; that Christ's real presence is in and with the elements as they are eaten and drunk, and that consequently, when the sacrament has been completed, the elements are just that, bread and wine to be respected but not adored. So offended, they became even more offensive by refusing to participate, thereby adding to their sedition what the Catholic officials could only consider publicly displayed infidelity.

If cooler heads prevailed against those tempted to bolt the diet, further finesse was demanded. Lutheran preaching and publishing had carried the reformation from the congregations into the public mobilizing support throughout Germany. Given the two confrontations that had already developed, the authorities in Augsburg and the diet itself feared an uproar that would break into rioting. So it was arranged that the Augsburg Confession would be presented to Charles V and the diet itself in a smaller episcopal palace, the bishop's residence which had an auditorium-sized main hall. That automatically limited public attendance. The Lutherans countered with a ploy of their own. The weather being unseasonably warm that June, they knew that the windows would have to be opened. So they asked Elector John's vice-chancellor, Christian Beyer, known for his stentorian voice, to read the confession aloud. He did so with such volume that the crowds gathered at the windows heard the whole thing. But it was not enough to bother Charles V. Seated prominently at the center of the room, as Beyer read, his imperial majesty slumped forward, head bobbing, sound asleep.

If Charles was not impressed, others more attentive immediately recognized the theological diplomacy that Luther had also observed in an earlier version. The bishop of Augsburg is said to have exclaimed when Beyer finished, "This is nothing but the pure truth."[33] Centrists at the diet saw in it a basis for further negotiation. Standing in the face of all the efforts to portray the Lutherans as seditious blasphemers, a public threat, Melanchthon and those who had joined him succeeded in getting the hearing they sought. The negotiations that followed very nearly closed the breach that the reformation had opened.

"Very nearly" was not, however, near enough. Given the Wittenberg insistence on the radically Word-centered way of thinking of reality and the Roman Catholic insistence that hierarchy and ritual held the church together, it was probably unrealistic to have thought that the medieval model for the structure of western Christendom could have maintained itself in the wake of Luther's challenge. The unfolding of reactions to the failure of negotiations in Augsburg, chronicled in the next chapter, gave Melanchthon a chance to write a commentary on the confession of the princes and municipal governments, which he had composed, and in it to define the heart of Wittenberg teaching personally—but also eventually for the wider Christian public.

5

The Apology of the Augsburg Confession

After the maneuvering that had led up to Christian Beyer's dramatic declamation of the Augustana on June 25, all of a sudden things quieted down. There were no riots in Augsburg, a possibility some of the authorities had feared. In fact, for a while there was not even a rejoinder, at least officially. But for all the public silence, privately many different hands were at work. When things broke into the open again, the various parties had indeed come close to a settlement. Philip Melanchthon's Apology of the Augsburg Confession testifies to the failure of these efforts. But it also laid foundations for what was to become Lutheranism.

Less communal, clearly the work of an individual, the Apology has from its origins been identified with its author. Both the catechisms and the Smalcald Articles bear Luther's name and his marks, but they were written for public use and were quickly taken for that purpose. Melanchthon composed the Augsburg Confession for the governments that were introducing Wittenberg reforms to use as an explanation of their churches' position. In contrast, the Apology was Melanchthon's personal response to the theological negotiations of the summer of 1530. He worked on it largely alone into April of 1531, when it was published under his name, addressed as a formal defense to Charles V.

But Luther's comments moved him to revise it within a few months, and a second edition, which remained the edition in use until the 1580s, appeared in September 1531, reflecting Luther's input and affirming the fact that the Wittenberg colleagues worked together as a team.[1] It clearly exhibited Melanchthon's trademark, although particularly this second edition, issued in <u>octavo</u> format instead of <u>quarto</u> format, as was the April 1531 *editio princeps*, bore Luther's fingerprints. The document gained confessional standing alongside the Augsburg Confession and became formational for the emerging generation of Lutheran theologians. It was the first of many commentaries on the Augsburg Confession. Some scholars have argued that the Apology already betrays that Luther and Melanchthon were following differing trajectories on key issues in their public teaching. More recent scholarship has disputed this.[2] Certainly throughout the sixteenth century, the Apology did not reap any criticism of Melanchthon of the sort that arose against him after Charles V's defeat of the Evangelical military forces in 1547. All sides in the intra-Lutheran conflicts after 1548 acknowledged the authority of the Apology and sometimes cited it against the positions they attributed to the Melanchthon of their (later) time.

The Cast of Characters

Historical developments are clearly bigger than the jealousies, animosities, and hatreds that infest them, but still personalities and their problems provide some clues to the unfolding of theological debates. Some people involved in the conflicts of the Reformation really did not like one another. Their feuds fueled the acrimony of larger encounters, involving institutions, structures, and other forces of the time. Commonly expressed according to the canons of sixteenth-century academic debate, which mixed generous portions of invective with references shoveled out of the gutter or the barnyard, the polemics nowadays appear overstated and scatological, at best humorous, at worst, vulgar and intolerant. Such modern judgments betray a lack of understanding of the academic and ecclesiastical culture from which they arose.[3] Still, it is necessary to get acquainted with some of the people involved.

Among those supporting the papacy against Luther and the Wittenberg reformers, by far the best qualified academically as well as in his standing in Rome was Thomas Cardinal Cajetan. A member of the mendicant order of the Dominicans who had spent a lifetime studying the work of Saint Thomas Aquinas, the greatest of the Dominican theologians and the officially definitive theologian of Catholicism since 1879, Cajetan wrote a commentary on Thomas' work that still commands respect. His leadership helped restore Thomas's prominence among the medieval theologians in early modern Roman Catholic theology. Cajetan's meeting with Luther at Augsburg in 1518 was one of the classic encounters of the reform, the learned cardinal realizing even before the earnest monk in front of him some of the radical implications of their discussion. For all of its potential for greater understanding, however, it hardly had been an ecumenical conversation.[4] Cajetan had an arrest warrant already prepared; Luther escaped by night on a horse provided by the elector of Saxony. That was the extent of their contact. Cajetan returned to his studies, dropping out of the public debates that followed. Though he had departed from the German stage, his theological influence lingered. By historical consensus, the theologians who arose after him representing historic Catholicism, in their own minds if not those of Roman Catholic officials, were not of the same caliber as Cajetan—not by a long shot.

Luther's most persistent critic was Johan Eck, whose academic title and last name Luther elided to form the word *Dreck*, a barnyard term. Eck taught at the University of Ingolstadt from 1510 to his death in 1543, but he made his career and reputation as Luther's opponent. He represented a kind of generic scholastic position, blending Ockhamist and Thomist insights. Luther and Eck first met in public debate at Leipzig in 1518, an exchange arranged by Duke George, who was sovereign over ducal Saxony and a cousin of Elector John. In the debate Eck used a tactic that he employed throughout his opposition to Luther, tarring him as an associate of heretics. This ploy succeeded at several points along the way—with Duke George; later in Rome, where Eck advocated Luther's excommunication; and still later, when Eck smeared the Wittenberg reformation in his *Four Hundred Four Articles*. Such an approach also obviated any real theological exchange. Instead of engaging difference, Eck magnified every nuance of variation into a threat to all things sacred.[5]

Standing with Eck at Augsburg against the Lutherans was another controversialist, Johannes Cochlaeus. Holding a theological degree from Cologne, one of the last late medieval Thomistic faculties, Cochlaeus had also studied law. But for all of his education, he became something of an itinerant polemicist. After service at the court of the archbishop of Mainz, he had attained a position at the court of George of Saxony in 1529. This implacable foe of Luther and the reformation took the apparent inconsistencies in Luther's dialectically driven, relationally oriented way of thinking as evidence of theological degeneration, and made a career of such attacks. Cochlaeus was Luther's first Catholic biographer, opening his work with the story that Luther's mother was a bath-house attendant and his father an *incubus*, a devil in the form of a man.[6] As with Eck, contemporary scholars are fairly well agreed that Cochlaeus' work did not match his self-estimate.

A third figure involved in the aftermath of the presentation of the Augustana was Johannes Heigerlin Fabri. Swiss, Fabri took his Latin name from his father's trade—he was a blacksmith—and used the same imagery in his best-known work, *Hammer against Lutheran Heresy*. He had initially been cordial to both Luther and Zwingli, the Zurich reformer, but in the early 1520s took a hardening line that solidified even further when he was appointed advisor to Charles V's brother, King Ferdinand, in 1523. Thereafter, Fabri emerged as a constant foe of the reformation, alienating his old humanist friends in Switzerland by leading advocacy at the Diet of Speyer in 1529 to impose the death penalty on Anabaptists. He attended the Diet of Augsburg with Ferdinand, having been appointed bishop of Vienna the same year.

If Eck, Cochlaeus, and Fabri could be termed a Roman Catholic ecumenical second team, there were some other theologians involved for whom even such lesser standing would be a stretch: Konrad Wimpina, Johann Dietenberger, and Julius Pflug. Of these, Pflug drew the most interest because of his association with Erasmian humanism. He brought a distinct theological perspective to the group of, for the most part, older theologians, whose orientation, whatever brushes with new humanistic breezes they may have had, arose largely out of the medieval scholastic traditions. However, even that designation does not fully enable us to define their specific positions and approaches to debated issues. It has been frequently said that "Ockhamism" dominated the scholastic scene, and certainly Gabriel Biel, one of the leading "scholastic" theologians of the late fifteenth century in Germany, represented the thought of William of Ockham as it had been processed by the intervening generations of over a century quite well. However, even Biel knew Thomas Aquinas and Duns Scotus well and was influenced by the biblical humanism of the Brethren of the Common Life.[7] Studies of Biel's contemporaries and the generation between him and Luther show repeatedly how the mixing and matching of the inheritances they had received was at the turn of the sixteenth century the order of the day for theologians like Eck and his colleagues, as it is in every era.[8] Furthermore, the reformers wished to deal not only with the thought of their professors but also the ways in which popular piety functioned in the minds and lives of the common people.

For all of its theological significance for Lutherans, the Diet of Augsburg was a political assembly before anything else. Some of the most important voices, even in the theological discussions, belonged to politicians and their advisors. Of these, Charles V had the greatest authority, and he used it directly and through his advisors in shaping the Roman Catholic response to the Augsburg Confession. His own relations with the papacy had been strained. After years of conflict, going back to his election to the office of emperor, Charles sent his troops into Rome in 1527, taking Pope Clement VII prisoner for a year. But personal quarrels notwithstanding, Charles understood his vocation as emperor as giving him responsibility for implementing Catholic faith in the political life of the community. This put his office in line with the papacy, even if he and Clement were personally at odds. Charles moved accordingly. He also strove zealously for an end to religious division because he knew that this would strengthen his forces against the Turks. This fired his resolve to end religious division within his German lands.

Though the papacy styled itself as far above the pettiness of a German political assembly, it was not about to leave to chance its own interests in the outcome. So it was represented, as it had been at the Diet of Worms, by its legate, the canon lawyer Lorenzo Campeggio. As a diplomat, he was not as concerned theologically as he was politically, having long represented papal interests at the emperor's court. But he knew, with the kind of Italian worldly wisdom evident in the work of Machiavelli, that theological texts spill political implications over into their context. His task was to guard papal primacy and with it, the vested interests of the prominent Italian commercial families that had long controlled the papacy.

If the Roman Catholic delegation at Augsburg can be called a second team, the Lutheran contingent also included some lesser-known figures. Though not as prominent historically, they still contributed to the conversations that took place. Three stood out. Gregor Brück served as chief political advisor in his office as the elector's chancellor, having already contributed to the preface to the Augsburg Confession. He was primarily responsible for the politics of the negotiations. Georg Spalatin, a long time friend of Luther's, was chaplain to the elector; former secretary to Elector Frederick the Wise, he was now pastor in Altenburg. In the early days of the reformation, when Frederick the Wise was elector, Spalatin interpreted Luther's protest to his prince and provided critical support.[9] He also contributed to the theological discussions. Justas Jonas, trained as a canon lawyer, served on the Wittenberg faculty, holding the office of dean for a time.[10] His expertise in the law of the church and experience with the visitation gave him an eye for the details. Still, Luther's preeminence and Melanchthon's growing influence made these three effectively no more than consultants.

Luther looms so large in contemporary consideration that Melanchthon often gets lost in his shadow. But in the actual drafting of the Augustana and its aftermath, the proportions reversed. Luther remained far in the background while Melanchthon took the center. Though he remained in Coburg until August and was kept informed of developments, after the first couple of weeks in May, Luther had little to do with the proceedings.

Surprising though it may be, a number of factors helped to limit Luther's apparent role the final form of the Augustana and subsequent negotiations. For one thing, though it was as close as he could get, given the risks, Coburg was still far enough away to frustrate quick communications. His absence may not have displeased his princely supporters, for they must have recognized that Luther was correct in saying that Melanchthon had the diplomatic skill needed for negotiations that were to prevent the emperor from executing the Edict of Worms. With all of this and personal concerns as well, Luther also had work to do. He wrote a commentary on Psalm 118 and also set to work on a new edition of a longtime favorite, *Aesop's Fables*.[11] But the details of Luther's Coburg calendar do not tell the whole story. Some scholars have argued that, given the importance of the events unfolding at Augsburg along with his expressed concern about Melanchthon's ability to hold in the face of pressure, something else was holding Luther back.[12] They argue that longer-term differences having to do with the orientations of the two men may have played a role already in 1530. Others counter that argument by noting Luther's support for the efforts in Augsburg in most of his letters from the Coburg. They further argue that if the two of them did not take what is now perceived to be a difference in orientation seriously enough to leave more of a written record behind, those viewing their relationship from the distance of almost five hundred years should proceed cautiously in judging their relationship.

Luther and Melanchthon: A Relationship beyond Description?

The two Wittenberg reformers viewed their own roles within their call for reform as different, and they both had literary gifts sufficient to permit them to use a variety of genre in a variety of situations. That makes it very easy for scholars to compare apples and oranges when setting the two alongside each other under a magnifying glass that is not always historically sensitive. Nonetheless, in the course of twentieth-century interpretation of Luther and/or Melanchthon four areas of difference have received treatment: the Lord's Supper, and the related topics of justification, the role of the human will in salvation, and the role of the law in the Christian life.

Regarding the Lord's Supper and its related Christological dimensions, all seem to agree that the two colleagues shared a common view of the vital issues under debate in the 1520s even though they may have used slightly different terms and placed somewhat different accents on their specific development of their doctrine. Anticipating Zwingli's refusal to compromise at Marburg in 1529, the Wittenberg theologians included in the Schwabach Articles a strong assertion of Christ's bodily presence in the Lord's Supper. Melanchthon prepared the final draft of this statement and carried it over in Article X of the Augsburg Confession. Though the Lutherans understood the reality of Christ's presence differently than Roman Catholics, in the negotiations at Augsburg the statement passed without exception. But as the Smalcald League expanded, variations on Zwingli's objections surfaced once more, still blocking the way.

Martin Bucer, the Strasbourg reformer, worked tirelessly to mitigate the differences. In 1536 he traveled all the way to Wittenberg to talk directly with Luther about it. Distrustful, Luther at first tried to avoid the meeting but eventually relented. Melanchthon drafted and then negotiated assent from both sides to a document, the Wittenberg Concord. Its view was translated into his revision of Article X of the Augsburg Confession in 1540. There he used language that Luther and his other Wittenberg colleagues believed represented the view that they had always held, and probably Melanchthon himself believed he was only sharpening what the entire Wittenberg team wanted to say.[13]

Timothy Wengert has recently argued that a key passage that has been used since the sixteenth century to argue that Melanchthon abandoned Luther's view of Christ's ascension into heaven and therefore the very nature of his presence in the Lord's Supper did not indicate a divergence as great as had been interpreted then and now.[14] Others, including Johannes Hund, argue that even in the 1520s the two theologians accentuated different elements of their understanding of the Lord's Supper. Hund contends that by 1536, in the Wittenberg Concord, Melanchthon had largely abandoned certain of Luther's key phrases, including the "partaking of the body and blood of Christ through the mouth" and "the reception of Christ's body and blood by the impious" and had begun to emphasize the presence of the entire person of Christ rather than the presence of his body and blood in the elements of the sacrament. The final stage in Melanchthon's sacramental doctrine according to Hund's analysis began after Luther's death.[15]

The other three topics on which Luther and Melanchthon are often said to have differed all relate to questions regarding God's grace and the human response to it. Robert Kolb has argued that both men, along with their colleagues and disciples, wanted to emphasize God's total responsibility as Creator for everything, and this fundamental presupposition grounded their emphasis on God's grace or favor as the only and exclusive reason for his goodness to humankind. At the same time the Wittenberg theologians all wished to accentuate that God holds every human creature totally responsible for being the creature God designed him or her to be. Every Christian thinker has struggled with the tension between these two—different but total—responsibilities. Most have resolved that tension in favor of God for the most part but have striven to find some role for human responsibilities with a grand variety of systems that Lutherans began already in the sixteenth century to label "semi-pelagian" or "synergistic." According to Kolb's interpretation, the Wittenberg theologians refused to resolve the tension systematically but instead laid down the

distinction of law—the demand for human exercise of God-given responsibility—
and gospel—the call for reliance on the totally responsible and loving God—as
the practical way of dealing with the irresolvable tension imposed by the biblical
address to human creatures.[16] Indeed, it is true that Melanchthon became ever more
concerned about human responsibility, but he never lost his focus on justification
by faith as the point of orientation of his thought process. Furthermore, Luther also
never lost the concern for the new obedience of his hearers, which he expressed
from his first postil of 1521–1522 onward, especially in his sermons.

The Apology demonstrates more clearly than the Augsburg Confession itself
that Melanchthon's central concern in representing Wittenberg theology revolved
around the issues raised by Luther's understanding of the justification of sinners
by God's unconditional grace, received by these human creatures through trust in
Jesus Christ. The Apology's fourth article is the first fully developed theological
statement of justification by faith in the Lutheran Confessions as a whole and perhaps the most important. As critical as the doctrine was to the Lutheran confessors,
as frequently as he discussed it in passing references, Luther never did write a fully
developed statement devoted to justification alone, apart from *The Freedom of a
Christian* (1520)[17] and his *Disputation on Justification* (1536);[18] the latter was not
published during his lifetime. Significantly, later in his life, Luther suggested that
he was going to write a rhapsody on justification, using a form that would thereby
appeal to both head and heart.[19] But he did not follow through on his plans. It
fell to Melanchthon, therefore, writing in a situation that demanded it, to define
more fully how the Lutherans used this language. Thus Article IV of the Apology
became a classical text in the reformation itself. This article treats what later editors
divided into three articles, on justification, the office of preaching or the means of
grace, and new obedience, along with the Augustana's twentieth article, on how the
Evangelical churches proclaimed faith and works. Thus several vital elements of
Wittenberg thinking come into consideration in Apology Article IV.

Wilhelm Maurer expressed some regret that already in the Schwabach Articles
one does not find a clearer trinitarian theology although he does minimize the significance of what he views as its additional failure to fully work out a "christological replacement."[20] In so far as this is true, it reflects both the genre of the confession as a brief public statement rather than a dogmatic textbook and also the issues
under discussion. (It also reflects Maurer's involvement in the theological discussions of his own time.) Often, readers of the Confession initially miss its use of the
Wittenberg doctrine of creation, in its affirmation of the holiness of normal daily
life, lived out in faith, and they often ignore that the Holy Spirit is at work in every
mention of the Word of God in its oral, written, and sacramental forms, as well as its
presentations of the believer's new obedience and of the life of the church.

Danish Reformation scholar Leif Grane is a good example of those who refined
the earlier argument of Albrecht Ritschl that Luther and Melanchthon did not share
the same doctrine of justification by faith.[21] That point of view was sharpened by

disciples of Karl Holl in the "Luther Renaissance."[22] These schools of interpretation sought to emphasize the ethical dimension of Luther's teaching and so suggested that Melanchthon had separated God's "forensic" act of justification from
the sanctification that provided that ethical dimension. Others took up the argument for a variety of reasons, often including those at odds with Ritschl's and Holl's
concerns. In interpreting the Augsburg Confession, Grane also found that, on the
one hand, Melanchthon separated justification and sanctification in a manner that
Luther did not, refashioning Luther's unified picture of the believer into a divided
image, through an emphasis on the *forensic* nature of God's declaration of forgiveness. On the other hand, Melanchthon is said to have emphasized the law, and new
obedience, in a manner other than Luther, placing too much emphasis on human
performance.[23] Grane died before the new focus of attention on the octavo edition,
with its extensive input from Luther, commanded scholarly attention, so he could
not take this research and argumentation into consideration.

Another reading of the texts in their historical context has emerged since
Grane and others advanced their interpretation. More recently some students of the
Wittenberg Reformation have contended that while both Luther and Melanchthon
continued to experiment with the expression of their convictions, there is good
reason for the absence of public disagreement between them. Their fundamental
perception of God's re-creative working through his Word, their common concern
for the sharp distinction of God's justifying action in the gospel from his sanctifying
action that produces new obedience in the believer, and their similar insistence that
faith issues its fruits in the new obedience of the faithful placed them in underlying
agreement on these matters, however different the details of their formulation may
be.[24] Above all, it is important to remember that the modern scholars' definition of
"forensic" often does not correspond to Luther's and Melanchthon's way of thinking. They shared a strong doctrine of God's performative, re-creative Word, and so
both believed, in the words of Gerhard Forde, "The absolutely forensic character of
justification renders it effective—justification actually kills and makes alive. It is, to
be sure, 'not only' forensic but that is the case only because the more forensic it is,
the more effective it is!"[25]

Furthermore, Melanchthon's reiteration of Luther's fundamental anthropological insight that the human creature exists in two distinct modes of relationship,
expressed in "two kinds of righteousness," dare not be ignored. This distinction,
which Luther once labeled "our theology,"[26] also informed Melanchthon's definition of what it means to be human and of God's relationship with his human creatures. Melanchthon's "righteousness of the law" corresponded to Luther's "active
righteousness," or "righteousness produced by oneself," while his "righteousness
of faith" corresponded to Luther's "passive righteousness" or "righteousness given
from outside oneself."[27] Both Luther and Melanchthon continued to shape their
exposition of the faith within the fields of tension they labeled the distinction of law
and gospel and the distinction of two kinds of human righteousness.

These considerations do not necessarily answer the question of whether later emphases in the formulations of the two may have drifted apart, but in the text of the Apology it is clear why Luther found a more than adequate expression of their theological efforts over the previous decade.

From the later sixteenth century on, many have regarded Melanchthon's view of the human will and its role in "conversion"—understood in sixteenth-century Latin chiefly as the conversion of daily repentance of those already claimed by the Holy Spirit—as divergent from Luther's.[28] That viewpoint continues to be argued, with strong evidence in individual quotations from Melanchthon's works, from the 1530s on. Kolb maintains, however, that these quotations must be seen in their larger contexts, in which Melanchthon consistently maintained that God's grace and the Holy Spirit's work are solely responsible for the initial conversion of the human will to faith in Christ. Kolb attributes the charges of synergism to Melanchthon's emphasis on the human responsibility that was the concern of both Wittenberg theologians and an occasional lack of clarity of expression in the younger partner.[29]

Closely related to the questions of justification by faith and the role of the human will in conversion is the issue of the Wittenberg theologians' understanding of the role of God's law in the Christian life. This debate has focused on Melanchthon's use of the term "third use of the law." In the 1534 edition of his *Scholia* on Paul's Letter to the Colossians, Melanchthon took over Luther's language of the uses of the law—terminology Luther had developed over the 1520s, defining the law by its intended impact. In the second edition of the *Loci communes* (1535), Melanchthon codified a system of three uses under the assumption that while God uses the law to restrain and drive, the Christian in turn uses the law in a third way, as a guide to new obedience.[30] Some contend that with this development Melanchthon also gave increasing emphasis to the power of human choice in doing the good although always within the context of God's grace.[31] Though these developments were incremental, Melanchthon was clearly following the track laid down in the Apology, it is contended.

In a meticulous analysis of the development of the third use, Timothy J. Wengert argues that two ecumenical conversations provided the occasion for it. One took place early in 1534 at the behest of the Albrecht, archbishop of Mainz, to whom Melanchthon had dedicated his Romans commentary of 1532. The other followed that summer, when Melanchthon met with a French contact dispatched by the bishop of Paris seeking enough common religious ground for an alliance between Francis I, the French king, and the Lutherans against Charles V.[32] In both instances the need for some defense against the charges of antinomianism from the Roman Catholic side became clear.

In these conversations Melanchthon was caught in a familiar dilemma, between Scylla and Charybdis. On the one side, he did not want to make any concessions to the medieval Catholicism he had met in similar discussions at Augsburg. It held that faith yields the love that in turn produces the good works that justify. As

Melanchthon had long argued, this both dishonors the work of Christ and leaves the conscience dependent on its own achievements, an intolerable combination. Rather, as Melanchthon argued with even greater clarity than in the Apology, justification is a purely forensic act in which God reputes or declares the sinner righteous for Christ's sake. He therefore could allow no formulation that made good works necessary for justification.

But Scylla cleared, Charybdis still loomed. Both the Archbishop and the French were concerned about the Lutheran willingness to fill out theologically the necessity of good works—a requirement Melanchthon stated in the imperative of Article VI and amplified once more at the conclusion of Article XX of the Augustana, developing it further in the Apology. Faced with this pressure, Melanchthon also wanted to repudiate his old nemesis, John Agricola, who had reduced Luther's nuanced dialectic of the end of law to a chronological termination. He thus obscured that dialectic of faith with the necessity of both the accusing force of the law and the need for specific instruction for Christian living. Melanchthon saw Agricola's teaching as antinomian. Melanchthon found his way around this side of the dilemma by following a familiar route, Aristotelian natural law theory. While Christ silences the accusing voice of the law, the law eternally remains in the order of things to give knowledge of what is morally required. Summarizing natural law, the Ten Commandments show the way to the earthly righteousness required—so the third use, further amplifying the absolute necessity of obedience to the law.

As Wengert writes surveying the development of Melanchthon's argument in the *Scholia*, "Again, Melanchthon tried to ground his discussion of good works in the consolation of God's mercy. However, he wanted to do this without compromising the necessity of good works. The very order of his argument—from the necessity of knowing how we are forgiven, to the necessity of obeying the law, to the necessity of knowing how this obedience pleases God—placed the law squarely at the center of Melanchthon's theology. Not death and resurrection or even repentance and faith, but knowing [that we are declared righteous and that our imperfect works are accepted] and obeying [the law] had become the centerpiece of his theology."[33] With this center established in the 1534 *Scholia* and his ecumenical conversations, Melanchthon cemented it in the 1535 edition of the *Loci Communes*. The gospel having been reduced to a heavenly declaration, the law and with it, a concomitant assertion of the human will's power to comply shaped a doctrinal theology in which the freedom of the gospel had become virtually theoretical. As Wengert notes, everything that fired the great Lutheran controversies of the 1550s was already on the table in 1534.[34]

In assessing the divergence between Luther and Melanchthon, however, one dare not overlook the very frequent use made by Luther of the law not only as the evaluating standard that accuses sinners of transgressing the bounds God set for their own humanity but also as a guide for the behavior of those who know that they are justified by Christ through their faith. In the first of his postils, the sermons prepared for modeling regular preaching, Luther often concentrated on the behavior he expected the gospel to produce. His instruction in the ways to walk in the law of the Lord did presume that the accusing force of the law would guide people, but often his instruction took the path of positive portrayal of what the Christian life should be. This task of moral instruction fell upon him as an urgent priority, along with bringing clarity to the question of God's exclusive role in saving sinners and making them his children.[35] The failure of his people to follow that instruction deeply troubled him, to the point he wished to threatened to leave Wittenberg because its population was not following his moral instruction.

Therefore, it is difficult to drive too sharp a wedge between Luther and Melanchthon simply on the basis of differing terminology. For they did not always share their terminology with each other just as they continued to tinker with their own expressions throughout their lives. Wittenberg took on the character of a theological laboratory with the advent of the Reformation, and the experimentation did not cease in Luther's lab nor in Melanchthon's. Furthermore, no one had informed either one of them that Melanchthon was supposed to be Luther's clone.

The Wittenberg Team of Confessors

For Luther and Melanchthon, "confession" was a verb—proclamation or first-order discourse in which the living God is literally at work bestowing himself in relation to the hearer. The noun "confession" functioned for both men as a "verbal noun," in the terminology of Peter Fraenkel in a study of Melanchthon's thinking.[36] So in parallel form, for instance, in the Small Catechism, where he was patterning the Christian life (and thus the daily confessing of the faith for children), Luther assumed that the doctrines at stake in the three articles of the Apostles' Creed emphasize the gifts that the triune God to God's people. For Melanchthon, confession was also a verb, and he conceived of it as such in the stance he and his colleagues took at Augsburg. But for both men it could also be a noun—second order discourse one step in the remove from witness, words about the Word—when the situation called for the presentation of the content of what was being confessed.[37] For all the Wittenberg reformers, theology—like doctrine itself—served as a discipline undertaken for the sake of preaching. Luther also frequently proved his mastery of second order discourse, in treatises such as his writings on the Lord's Supper and his book on the bondage of the will, *On Bound Choice*, and so did Melanchthon. First order discourse was not appropriate for a statement that laid the Evangelical faith and Wittenberg understanding of the biblical message before the emperor and the estates of the empire. In general, for Melanchthon theology was oriented to doctrine as more of an end itself, that is, truthful knowledge, though he always delivered this knowledge for the purpose of enabling proclamation. That is why he dedicated himself to the study of effective communication.

Melanchthon could also be a powerful witness at a personal level, as Luther knew full well through years of friendship. If only coincidentally a preacher,

Melanchthon was at heart a teacher—the so-called "German preceptor." So when the cart that carried him rumbled out of Augsburg on its way back to Wittenberg after the break down of the negotiations that followed the presentation of the Augustana, he was already at work on a teaching document—a defense to be sure, as the Apology might also be called, but above all an explanation or clarification of what had been believed, taught, and confessed in the Augsburg Confession.

Luther recognized that his own manner of confessing the faith would have had a different impact than that of the practiced diplomat of the Evangelical princes, his colleague Philip. The contemporary portrait of Luther as a reluctant Lutheran, struggling against countervailing forces to stay within Roman Catholicism, may be true to a point, but it does not do historical justice to Luther's efforts to widen the reform and have it translated into institutional form. He wrote voluminously to people in Germany and in northern and eastern Europe recommending visitations and other provisional structures. That task he assigned to his colleague Johannes Bugenhagen to a large extent. Yet for all of this, he understood such efforts as a natural outgrowth of the Word and faith, improvising and seeking adjustments rather than setting up programs and structures. Apocalypticists work from the conviction that the future unfolds from God's hands. On the other hand, it has often been too easy for some scholars to forget how deeply involved Luther was in plans for church life. Recent analysis of the political attitudes of the two Wittenberg reformers has emphasized how close to each other they stood in their understanding of the secular government's involvement with the church's life even if their political activities took different forms.[38] Both men's theological interests always had a programmatic political dimension that was more than programmatic. Melanchthon did receive certain assignments from his electors to carry out the vital tasks of an ecclesiastical diplomat. Luther himself could not have played this role as an outlaw, and his personality was perhaps not suited to it, as was Melanchthon's.

Whatever the differences between the two leaders of Wittenberg reform were, they stood together in the minds of their Roman Catholic opponents in 1530. With Luther at the Coburg, out of the daily contact they shared in Wittenberg, Melanchthon, Jonas, Spalatin, and other colleagues confronted the imperial and papal front ranged against them, intent on executing the Edict of Worms and rooting out Lutheran heresy.

The Confutation

In the summons to the Diet of Augsburg, Charles V promised an open hearing. The Wittenberg reformers, with Melanchthon leading the theologians and Chancellor Brück looking after the practicalities, responded accordingly. The Augustana emphasized convergence, stepping lightly if at all on some of the most divisive issues such as papal primacy. It was classical peacemaking, in line with the nature of the task at the Diet and its goal of explaining to the emperor the basis of their reform. But not everybody was eager for peace and, among those predisposed, the eagerness was not always present in the same measure. So as is generally the case in public controversy, once the Augustana was presented, things got even more complicated.

The immediate response was somewhat promising. On June 25 the Augustana was submitted to those estates of the empire that had remained with the papacy and the emperor. The day following, responding to the conciliatory language of the Lutheran confession, they asked that it be passed on for the judgment of the theologians, specifying that they be people of good will and that the response follow the moderate tone that had already been struck. At the same time they asked if the Lutherans had anything that they would like to add to the Augustana, a request that may have been an attempt to make the Wittenberg reformers show a more polemical hand. At least, Luther certainly took it that way. Writing to Jonas nearly a month after the presentation, he expressed his wish for articles "concerning purgatory, the adoration of the saints, and especially Antichrist, the Pope,"[39] forgetting that the veneration of the saints is indeed the subject of Augustana Article XXI. In another letter to Jonas written earlier in July, he expressed his conviction that doctrinal agreement was impossible but that politically the followers of Wittenberg reform might win some kind of toleration. He was wary of the emperor's claims to authority in doctrinal matters, asserting the prior authority of God's Word.[40] Luther's apprehensions notwithstanding, the reformers assembled in Augsburg, mindful of the footing that they obtained for further negotiation, declined the invitation for additional submissions.

But it was quickly apparent that the politicians seeking reconciliation did not represent a consensus of the Roman Catholic voices at Augsburg. Eck, Cochlaeus, and colleagues argued that it is never appropriate to negotiate with heresy. Charles V had been attempting for some nine years to enforce the Edict of Worms against the Lutherans. Negotiation was still a long way from the submission he had been seeking. He demanded compulsory agreement to whatever the negotiations achieved. Campeggio, while recognizing the political necessities in honoring the request of the Catholic estates seeking peace, was also concerned about the precedent. So in standard diplomatic style, what he gave with one hand, he sought to retrieve with the other. If Luther had some hesitation about the course of negotiations, the combined Roman Catholic apprehensions also elongated the process of negotiation.

Finally, on July 5, the emperor announced his acceptance of the appeal of the Roman Catholic political leaders, at the same time rattling his saber. Making official the appointment of the group assigned to reply to the Augsburg Confession, he set some strict conditions. Charles would issue the Catholic response in his own name, demanding full submission by all involved under terms of the Edict of Worms. The trouble had gone on long enough; it was time to resolve the issue, if not voluntarily then involuntarily. Mindful of papal primacy, he appointed Campeggio to constitute a group of the Catholic theologians to write a reply to the Augsburg Confession. Campeggio's subsequent selections demonstrate his own reluctance. Assembling a group that numbered somewhere between nineteen and twenty-four, large enough to bog down on any number of issues, he included among them Eck, Cochlaeus, and Fabri.

Shortly after opening the conversations at Augsburg, Charles tried to upstage them. On July 14 he once again appealed to Pope Clement VII to immediately convene a church council to revolve the theological conflict. There was not much of chance; the pope and his advisors in the curia had long opposed the idea, fearing the larger ramifications of conciliar action. But since 1518 the Luther and his allies had argued that there could not be a settlement without a council, and Charles knew too that without direct papal ratification, the negotiations at Augsburg would at best be provisional. With this, perhaps anticipating denial, he made the appeal.

In the meantime Campeggio and his committee still had a mandate to prepare a response to the Augsburg Confession. It did not take much time for the theologians to prepare the first draft. With prior compilations of the Lutheran heresies ready at hand, Eck, Cochlaeus, Fabri and their colleagues went right to work. Following patterns that had been hardened by some twelve years of polemics, they were ready to present the results to the emperor by the end of the second week in July. One wag described the document in terms of wagonloads, some 280 folios by one count, including extended selections of Luther's most outrageous statements and some nine or ten essays proving the Lutheran variations from Catholic faith. The Augsburg Confession was apparently a tough act to follow.[41]

Whatever pride the theologians may have taken in their speed and dispatch, the emperor and the leaders of the Catholic estates were not at all satisfied. The contrast between the lean and irenic Augustana and the bulging hostilities of the theologians' draft compromised it. So the emperor returned their work, asking for reductions in size, moderation in tone, and some reconsideration of the whole approach. Charles also ruled out the attacks on Luther because he had not been directly involved in the proceedings.

The rest of July was spent in editorial work. Reportedly, the emperor's advisors told Eck to take a third off the original edition immediately, but they wanted much more. Reluctantly, complaining of repudiation, holding out for everything they could, Eck, Cochlaeus, Fabri, and company gave ground like an army giving up territory. With Eck assuming more leadership as the process went on, there were four revisions in the remaining weeks of July.

Receiving the fourth attempt at the end of the month, Campeggio along with a couple of Charles V's counselors worked through the early days of August to finish a fifth revision. The haste was evident. A German translation of the original Latin text omitted part of it; an erasure still showed through so clearly that the imperial secretary who read the document aloud took it as part of the text. But after a month's efforts and the repeated misstarts, the emperor pushed ahead. On August 3 those still present assembled in the same hall where the Augustana had been presented; the new document was declaimed, mistakes and all.[42] Charles V fell asleep during the two-hour reading, just as he had dozed off during the presentation of the Augustana. Campeggio complained that the Lutherans had greeted the reading with open laughter.

However, it should be noted that the Confuation's final form did not condemn every article of the Augsburg Confession. It approved and expressed agreement with articles I (God), III (Christ and the Holy Spirit), VIII (the mixed nature of the church), IX (baptism), XIII (the use of the sacraments), XVI (civil life), XVII (Christ's return to judge), and XIX (the cause of the evil). It expressed partial or conditional and critical acknowledgement of articles II (original sin), V (office of preaching and means of grace), VI (new obedience), VII (the church), X (the Lord's Supper), XI (confession and absolution), XIV (ecclesiastical order), XV (ceremonies), XVIII (freedom of the will), and XX (faith and works). Extensive critique was lodged against articles IV (justification), XII (repentance), XXI (invocation of the saints), and the last seven articles, on the reform of practices and ecclesiastical structures.

In the end the document got mired in the conflicting claims of authority. Charles V's advisors demanded that the Lutherans submit even before hearing the reading, additionally insisting that the reformers agree in advance not to write a reply. When they refused, they were denied a written copy. Perhaps, even after the revisions, the emperor and his advisors recognized the shortcomings of the theologians' work. Even if they had been satisfied, Campeggio could not yield to Charles V the authority to speak in the name of the church.

Rendered something of a step-child by the problems of authority, the Confutation has always retained this status. The Council of Trent, which approached the Lutheran reform in much the same way, ratified the holdings of the document, giving it some quasi-official footing in Catholic tradition. But contemporary Roman Catholic scholars, mindful of the disparity between classical Thomism and late medieval Ockhamist theology, see the Confutation as a less than adequate statement. Historical scholarship views it in terms of the polemics of its authors. David V. N. Bagchi describes the Confutation as "imitative in style, reactive in content, and directed at those with religious and political power," calling it "a paradigm of the controversialists' policy of the preceding debate."[43] When the Lutherans nicknamed it the *Confutatio Pontifica*, they gave it a status its original authors may have claimed but that no other Catholic authority would fully endorse.

The Committee of Fourteen

Confronted with the imperial demand for submission, denied close access to the document that Charles declared refuted their positions, the Lutheran delegation in Augsburg took the one alternative available to them. They balked. But the imperial advisors were already prepared. Anticipating impasse, they had preserved room in the language for further negotiation.

So in mid-August a new commission went to work, this one consisting of fourteen members. From each side, Charles appointed two princes, two canon lawyers and three theologians. Given the prior dealings at Augsburg, Melanchthon was the obvious candidate to lead the Lutheran side. Charles apparently had some additional considerations in his appointment. Committed to achieving the Evangelical princes' ardent desire for a negotiated settlement, Melanchthon is understood to have already minimized a number of issues; the continued stress was allegedly also wearing him down. The combination suggested the possibility of further yielding even though his Evangelical contemporaries viewed him as bold and defiant, like Daniel in the lion's den. Eck was the lead Roman Catholic theologian.

The Committee of Fourteen made some progress. With agreement on eight of the doctrinal articles of the Augsburg Confession accepted, more or less wholly, and with another ten acknowledged with some reservations, it made sense to precede article by article addressing difficulties as they arose. On August 14 the committee came to Articles IV through VI of the Augustana, concerning justification, the office of the ministry, and the relationship of faith and good works. Several of Eck's long standing issues with the Lutheran reform came to head at these points: the place of the law in Christian life, the relationship of faith and charity, the Lutheran assertion of the *sola fide,* along with the traditional Roman Catholic understanding of merit. Eck and his colleagues argued for the continuing significance of the law in the Christian life, insisting that the charity or love infused in faith produces the merit that justifies. According to Spalatin, Melanchthon sidestepped the concept of merit, using the term but placing its accomplishment totally in Christ, to emphasize the primacy of faith. The Lutheran theologians further argued that the New Testament itself suspends Old Testament law and that there was precedence in the church fathers for use of the term *alone.*

Given the nature of the negotiations and its subsequent fate, it is difficult to determine the strength of the agreement. Estimates varied from the beginning. The Roman Catholic theologians claimed that the Lutherans had conceded the "alone" in justification, while Lutherans claimed they had restricted their yielding to the language of charity. But with that, at least for the time being, both sides were willing to say that they had agreed on the doctrinal points in the first twenty-one articles of the Augustana, with the one possible exception in Article XXI, concerning the invocation of the saints.

For whatever progress was made doctrinally, the negotiations strained and finally bogged down when it came to matters of practice. They, of course, expressed the doctrinal issues in concrete form. Charles V had asked the Lutherans to prepare an accounting of the ceremonial changes that they had made to be presented at Augsburg. This the Saxons had done in Augsburg Confession Articles XXII through XXVIII on the basis of their earlier deliberations that prepared the so-called Torgau Articles. The Lutheran reformers regarded matters of church practice, including liturgy, governance and the like, as *adiaphora*—matters of liberty left open by Scripture and so aspects of church life where local options could be exercised.[44] Neither Roman Catholic theologians nor Charles V recognized such freedom. The theologians viewed the articles like so many dominoes, convinced that if one tipped, in the end the primacy of the papacy would also fall. The emperor regarded liturgical uniformity and ecclesiastical unity as visible expressions of the oneness of the empire and Christendom itself. In fact, Charles considered these the central matter.

Given such high priorities on the Roman Catholic side, not surprisingly the Confutation had taken issue with every one of the articles concerning "Abuses That Have Been Corrected": communion in one kind, in which the cup was withheld from the laity at the sacrament; celibacy of the clergy; the sacrifice of the mass; requirements of private confession; dietary regulations; monastic vows, and the authority of the bishops. As subsidiary as they may have appeared to the Lutherans, on the Catholic side they were individually and collectively articles that drew a line in the sand, reflecting their fundamentally different conceptions of the Christian faith, the one centering the relationship between God and human creatures on human ritual approaches to God, the other on God's Word coming to the human creature.

But the Lutheran negotiators were apparently also under some pressure at these points. The two free cities among the seven original signers of the Augustana, Nuremberg and Reutlingen, included populations who had found Lutheran assertions of the freedom of the gospel particularly appealing. The desacralizing of late medieval piety, in which an overlay of religious regulations imposed by the church was thrown off, made the last articles of the Augustana particularly important to urban peoples. Melanchthon complained of this in a letter to Luther written late in August, noting that the "free cities in particular hate [the] authority" of the bishops. "They are not concerned about doctrine and religion but only about power and liberty."[45]

With such an impasse developing, Charles V reduced the size of the committee to seven, including one canon lawyer and two theologians from each side. In an August 24 session, this smaller group took up two of the most contentious issues, the sacrifice of the mass and the marriage of clergy. Enough progress was made for historians to suggest that Melanchthon and his colleagues from electoral Saxony were willing to accept an agreement in the whole on condition that Lutherans could continue the practices they had reformed and preach as they had been.[46] But for the Roman Catholic authorities there was no compromise available on church governance. For both papacy and empire, there could be no agreement without the reassertion of papal primacy. The negotiations broke off at that point.

Aftermath

Though they had been refused a text of the Confutation, the Lutheran theologians at Augsburg had other resources. For some reason Melanchthon himself appears not to have been present when it was read. Others had notes, however. One and possibly more of them amounted to stenographic transcription. That was enough to begin work. Later in the fall Melanchthon obtained a copy of the complete text, apparently from someone who would now be called a leak. Though both Eck and

Cochlaeus had urged publication of the Confutation, when he found out about the leaked text, Eck complained that Melanchthon had laid hands on it by fraud.

Relayed to city officials in Nuremburg, one of the free cities supporting the Lutheran reform, the notes prompted a quick reply. Andreas Osiander, then pastor in Nuremburg and a celebrated character who would later provoke a bitter controversy over the doctrine of justification, wrote a refutation based on the notes. In it, he set out the argument dear to Nuremburg citizens, asserting the priority of the Word over church officials.[47]

While duly appreciative of the Nuremberg response, the Lutheran parties at Augsburg wanted another statement. They had played politics with the imperial court on the issue of a Lutheran reply to the Confutation. Now they clearly needed one. So on August 29 Chancellor Brück and the Saxon representatives were instructed to prepare something further. It was understood that much of the responsibility would fall to Melanchthon, but the politics also required some consideration. So Brück and Melanchthon went to work on a refutation of the Confutation, completing it by September 20.

On September 22 the die was cast. Charles V formally announced that the Augsburg Confession had been refuted on the basis of Scripture and gave the Lutherans until April 15, 1531, almost ten years from the deadline he had originally promulgated in the Edict of Worms, to submit to his judgment. The new refutation in hand, Chancellor Brück stood in the name of the elector of Saxony to object. Complaining of the bad faith with which the Confutation had been handed down, he announced that the Lutherans were prepared to refute it. But having already declared his unwillingness to hear anything further from them, Charles refused to accept the new document. The next day he left the diet.

Virtually all who had attended the diet, whether adherents of the traditional faith or reform minded, anticipated that the breakdown of negotiations would be the beginning of war. Once more, however, Charles proved unable to make good on his threat to take military action. Hamstrung by other opponents, including the Turks and the French, he had to temporize with the Lutherans. In 1531 he negotiated with them the so-called Nuremberg Armistice, recognizing what was effectively a stalemate. He sweetened the pot somewhat with a promise to ask papacy to call a council of the church for further negotiation. The Lutherans were so publicly committed to a conciliar settlement that they believed they had no alternative but to agree to attend should such a council materialize. But the chances appeared from slim to the point of nonexistent. So the Lutherans continued efforts they had already begun in the late 1520s, seeking a formal alliance. The seven original signers of the Augustana—including Electoral Saxony and the city of Nuremburg—formed a military arm they called the Smalcald League. Armistice or no, it grew throughout the 1530s until a significant majority of German governments embraced some form of Evangelical reform.

The Apology

The negotiations having failed, Melanchthon faced a double challenge when he left Augsburg later in September. He had stood as spokesman for the Lutheran reformation at a decisive point, editing to its final form a statement that the Lutherans had hoped would demonstrate the reform's standing within the larger catholic consensus of the faith. This claim had been formally repudiated by the emperor himself. So Melanchthon had to demonstrate the truth of the original confession, documenting its validity. At the same time, in order to gain the settlement for which he had made such a considerable effort, Melanchthon had stepped lightly over some of the most critical convictions of the reformers. As noted above, some scholars contend that he apparently compromised on justification by faith itself although neither Luther nor any of their students seems to have noticed. Thus reasserting the claim to ecumenical standing, he had to clarify the core of Lutheran teaching, as he and Luther saw it, the teaching of justification by faith in Christ alone, as well as meet his critics' objections to other elements of the Augustana.

Going home, Melanchthon had some sources to carry along. One was Osiander's reply to the Confutation, as forwarded by Nuremberg city officials. Another was the document that Melanchthon and Brück, with some additions through unknown hands, had prepared. Rankled in particular by the imperial claim to scriptural authority for the Confutation, he was not satisfied with either but wanted a fuller, harder-hitting statement. So he set to work.

The project possessed Melanchthon. He worked on the new document through the fall and into the spring of 1531, noting his progress and complaining of delays frequently in letters to friends. According to an apparently apocryphal story, Luther grabbed the pen out of Melanchthon's hand one Sunday, pointing out the necessity of rest.[48] Luther later joked that "Philip would have never published his Apology if he had not been forced to—he always wanted to improve on it,"[49] but the older colleague himself provided much counsel. The document was completed in April.

As usual with Philip Melanchthon, the consummate linguistic tinkerer, "finishing" did not necessarily bring his efforts to an end. To the undoubted exasperation of the printer, he continued to revise even while the type was being set. When finally published, this version of the Apology came to be called the quarto edition, for its format. Still unsatisfied, Melanchthon consulted with several other theologians, including his opponent of the late 1520s, Johann Agricola; Johannes Brenz, who had been with him in Augsburg; and Martin Bucer, the reformer of Strasbourg. Most importantly, Luther made extensive suggestions, on both how to sharpen the argument and where to abbreviate it.[50] The result of these consultations was a second or octavo edition, published in September of 1531. Printed in a smaller format that also gave it its designation, the later addition was much more satisfactory in Melanchthon's eyes and was later signed by several theologians. Justas Jonas used the octavo edition to make most of his German translation that became in the process a further amplification, with Melanchthon's assistance.[51]

The Structure of the Argument and Its Foundations

Melanchthon pursued several distinct goals, each pursuit with its own tactics, in providing a defense or justification of the teaching of the Augsburg Confession. From correspondence during the time of its composition, it is clear that the author of the Apology was intending to clarify the justification of the sinner in God's sight as he fashioned his defense of the Confession at Augsburg.[52] At times he clarified the Confession's teaching and the language used to convey it. At other times he expanded or elaborated on the succinct wording in the Confession to elucidate its intention and meaning. He also proceeded into detailed exegetical and historical arguments to buttress the brief summaries of Wittenberg teaching and practice in the Confession.[53]

In presenting his argument he followed closely the rules he had laid down for public addresses in his rhetorical textbooks. He could choose from four rhetorical genres the ancient three—the *genus demonstrativum*, used to praise or criticize a person; the *genus deliberativum*, used to persuade or dissuade; and the *genus iudicale*, used to pursue a legal case in court or in the political arena—or Melanchthon's own invention, the *genus didascalium*, used to instruct with the aid of several tools, including logic and organization by topics. Not without some characteristics of the last of these, the Apology is structured according to the *genus iudicale*, as the Wittenberg professor argued his legal case to the emperor (for example, Ap Preface, II, 35, 51; XII, 2, 122; XXI, 44; XXIII, 2–4; XXVII, 18). In arguing the case the speaker, or in this case author, defined a *scopus* or *status* of the argument, "the principal question or proposition, which contains a summary of the point of contention, to which all proofs and arguments are to be referred, or the principal conclusion."[54] The *dispositio*, or outline, of the argument embraced six parts, which followed each other and functioned to build the case. In the instance of the fourth article of the Apology, the *exordium*, designed to set the stage for the argument and prepare hearers or readers to appeal to the truth, embraces the first four paragraphs, as numbered in modern editions. The *narratio* or *amplificatio* fills in details; in the example of Apology IV the *propositio*, the statement of the thesis in detail, is embodied within the *narratio* (paragraphs 4–48). Paragraphs 40 through 48 contain the main proposition, that human righteousness in God's sight is restored through the word of promise that delivers the benefits of Christ and must be received by trust in that promise. The *confirmatio* then presents supporting evidence and reasoning which confirms the thesis (paragraphs 49–182).

The function of the Apology centered on the defense of the Augsburg Confession and its contention that "we cannot obtain forgiveness of sin and righteousness before God through our merit, work, or satisfactions, but we receive forgiveness of sin and become righteous before God out of grace for Christ's sake through faith."[55] Therefore, the fifth part of such a "judicial" presentation, the *confutatio*, extended from paragraph 183 to 400 in disposing of the opponents' accusations, misrepresentations, and errors. This *genus* brought its argument to a conclusion with a *peroratio*, which repeated the thesis or *propositio*, a brief summary or *confirmatio* of the thesis, and an emotive appeal for agreement. In the first edition of the Apology article IV had only a brief *peroratio*, but in the second edition it was expanded significantly.[56] Not all articles followed the form of the *genus iudicale*, at least not in the detail of the fourth and twelfth articles. Nonetheless, all the articles belong to the larger case Melanchthon was making in the emperor's personal presence, with the Latin-reading public listening in.

Presenting his case in this way required Melanchthon to present his evidence. As in the Augsburg Confession, but in much more detailed and extensive fashion, he based his presentation in the Apology on Scripture. The Confutation fashioned its arguments without an appeal to tradition, attempting to meet the Wittenberg theology on the grounds it claimed for itself. This made it urgent for Melanchthon to counter their contentions on the basis of Scripture. Therefore, in his rebuttal of the Confutation's case, based on some one hundred ninety Scripture passages, Melanchthon cited nearly three times as many, with five hundred forty references to Scripture.

The placement of the Bible passages betrays which issues were of most importance to the two sides. The Confutation, concerned about the defense of the ritual practice of the faith, concentrated its texts on such issues and on the general topic of good works, with twenty-five passages defending clerical celibacy (article XXIII), twenty-one supporting its critique of the Lutheran understanding of good works (article VI), nineteen its criticism of the Lutheran rejection of the veneration of saints (article XXI), eighteen on monastic vows (article XXVII), and nine on the distinction of foods (article XXVI). Melanchthon marshaled over two hundred fifty on justification and its related topics of the means of grace and new obedience (articles IV–VI) and eighty on repentance (article XII). The Apology did take the dispute over the ritual forms of the practice of Christianity seriously, however, and called on Scripture fifty times in treating the Mass (article XXIV), thirty-one times each on monastic vows (article XXVII) and clerical marriage or celibacy (article XXIII), the latter two with a defense of the Lutheran understanding of the goodness of the created order and God's pleasure at the normal conduct of daily life.[57] Melanchthon drew his evidence from twenty-one books of the Old Testament and twenty-two of the New, with four references from the Apocrypha. Old Testament favorites included the Psalms (41), the Penteteuch (26), and Isaiah (21), with Jeremiah (14) and Daniel (10) trailing them. Romans provided Melanchthon the basis of his case with more than one hundred citations; with sixty, Matthew provided formidable support as well. First Corinthians (42), John (31), Galatians and Luke (each 23), and Colossians (19) supplied a variety of foundations for Melanchthon's argumentation as well.

At Augsburg Melanchthon had insisted that "nothing disagrees [in our Confession] with the Scriptures, or with the catholic church, or with the Roman church as we know it from the Fathers."[58] As had the scholastic theologians before him, Melanchthon buttressed what he had grounded in Scripture with evidence from the tradition of the church, moving onto his opponents' field even as they had avoided patristic citation in the Confutation to carry the battle to those who claimed to teach *sola Scriptura*. In citing the Fathers he was directly refuting the claim of John Eck in this *Four Hundred Four Articles* that the Wittenberg theologians had deserted the tradition of the church. The Apology denied this at several points quite directly[59] and turned the charge against the Roman party by demonstrating that its doctrinal formulations and its practices were of recent origin.[60] Not all Fathers could claim equal faithfulness to biblical truth, in Melanchthon's view, and in different situations he could praise different ancient authorities, although Augustine remained his most cited Father.[61]

Sixteenth-century students of the ancient church did not distinguish East and West as sharply as most scholars do today. Chronology played some role in Melanchthon's selection of the Fathers since, all else considered, the older, the better, was considered a rough rule of thumb. But for the Wittenberg colleagues, correspondence to their own analogy of faith decided which Fathers and which of their citations would guide the contemporary exposition of the faith.[62] Augustine corroborated the Apology's most often, some thirty times (for example, Ap II, 22, 24, 36, 38, 41; IV, 29–30, 33, 87, 179+, 358+; XII, 167; XIII, 5, 23; XVIII, 3; XXI, 36). It cited Ambrose eight times (Ap II, 19; IV, 340, 389; XII, 91, 96, 171; XXIII, 20; XXIV, 75), Jerome seven (Ap IV, 173, 264, 318; VII/VIII, 11; XII, 171; XXI, 2; XXII, 4), Epiphanius six (Ap VII/VIII, 42, 43; XXIII, 49; XXIV, 8, 96), once each to Irenaeus (Ap II, 18); Origen (Ap XVI, 6); Gregory of Nazianzus (Ap XVI, 6); Chrysostom (Ap XII, 88); and Cyril of Jerusalem (Ap X, 3).

Melanchthon may have generally given the church fathers more place and space in his writings than Luther did, but such a judgment dare not obscure the fact that the former asserted the principle of biblical authority alone as warmly as the latter and that Luther used patristic evidence extensively, in accord with the way of thinking theologically he had learned as a student. The Apology reflects the Wittenberg appeal to the foundational authority of Scripture and a kind of secondary authority in selected passages from the Fathers that can be found throughout the writings of both reformers and their colleagues.

The Tone and Method of Melanchthon's Defense and Refutation

When he read the Apology in 1534, Cochlaeus marked out Melanchthon's use of terms like "asses," "sycophants," "worthless hypocrites," and "windbags" to observe, "Fierce and vicious he is, a barking dog toward those who are absent, but to those who were present at Augsburg, Philip was more gentle than a pup."[63] Even if such a comment is discounted for its source, it indicates a remarkable shift in tone in the Apology, one that reflects the rhetorical definition of his shift in genre. No longer writing a document for Evangelical governments to use in a public forum, Melanchthon took up the argument before the emperor as an individual advocate, presenting a defense, an apology, of his cause, his legal case. The extensive editorial process that the Apology went through makes its hostilities all the more striking. With a printer's devil picking up pages of the manuscript as he finished them, the first parts of Luther's treatises were commonly in print before he wrote the remainder. He did not have the opportunity to retrieve some of his polemical excesses. Writing, editing, revising and revising again, Melanchthon carefully measured all the language in the Apology, even that which might appear to be gratuitous. The hardening tone was calculated.

Explaining the difference in a letter written to Johannes Brenz on April 8, 1531, close to the publication of the quarto edition, Melanchthon said, "I have entirely laid aside the mildness which I formerly exercised toward the opponents. Since they will not employ me as a peacemaker, but would rather have me as their enemy, I shall do what the matter requires and faithfully defend our cause."[64] This would suggest that the hardening tone reflects that changed situation after the breakdown of negotiations at Augsburg. But the last clause of the final sentence may suggest an additional, more personal factor. Given Luther's comment about his pussy footing, Melanchthon's harsher language might be interpreted as an attempt to demonstrate his willingness to maintain a tougher position. It certainly reflects the changed situation in the empire. No longer searching for a settlement, Melanchthon turned again to confessing his faith in detail.

However, Melanchthon's defense through offense typified the way in which medieval theologians conducted their enterprise, above all through public disputations. Scholastic method had dictated citation of those whose positions were being rejected, and the humanistic Melanchthon needed material to argue his judicial case before the emperor. His polemical examination of opponents' positions clarified his own teaching and thus strengthened his confession of the faith.[65] Therefore, the "scholastics" won mention as the opponents with whom the disputation continued, even in Charles V's court. General mentions of the "schoolmen" or "sophists," always as false teachers, dotted the Apology (Ap Pref, 17; II, 4, 7, 8, 10, 12, 13, 15, 23, 43, 46; IV, 9, 11, 121, 229, 271, 289, 304, 312, 344, 379, 383; XI, 2; XII, 3, 16, 28, 41, 91, 117, 120, 131, 132, 133; XIII, 18, 23; XXI, 40, 41; XXIV, 13, 31, 64). Specific medieval theologians earned criticism as well, Gabriel Biel some eleven times, once directly, most often through allusion (Ap XXII, 22–23; and Ap II, 2, 7, 8–9; IV, 9, 210; Ap XII, 7, 68, 75, 117; XXI, 11; XXII, 9, 22–23). Duns Scotus was cited three times (Ap XXII, 68, 143, 148), and Thomas Aquinas fourteen, occasionally for support (Ap II, 27, Ap IV, 304), most often critically (Ap II, 4, 43; IV, 105, 288, 289; XII, 13, 63, 118; XIII, 6; XV, 24; XXIV, 62; XXVII, 20). Wittenberg's contemporary critics did not come under Melanchthon's explicit attack although their positions won condemnation in the very fact that he was refuting their Confutation.

It should also be noted, however, that the polemics are directed at other theologians, not against Charles V. Both Melanchthon and Luther went to some pains to demonstrate their continuing loyalty to the emperor. This reflects the state of the ecumenical dialog and the political situation within the empire in the early 1530s.

Lutheranism was no longer simply a reform movement. The reformers with their political advisors had set up institutional forms in the Saxon Visitation that they would continue to employ in church governance as the reformation expanded. Despite problems with his health that severely limited his preaching, Luther could still write, using letters to guide the spreading Lutheran reform. The Smalcald League opened a political-military umbrella over the expansion that continued through the 1530s. But for all of this, both Melanchthon and Luther remained firmly committed to a settlement that would preserve the place of the Lutheran reform within Catholicism, hoping that the emperor would make good on the promised church council that could accomplish this purpose.

These hopes may have been another factor in the sharpening polemics. Convinced that they had the support of both Bible and tradition for their position within the church, Melanchthon was thoroughly exasperated with those who lacked both the expertise and the imagination to recognize the basis of their theological arguments. Descriptions like "crude asses" may not be part of the usually recommended ecumenical vocabulary—though certainly not foreign to the medieval art of university disputation. And even as he examined and reexamined the offerings of the Roman Catholic second team, Melanchthon was convinced that the use of such terms was justified.[66]

Given the shape of the negotiations and current academic custom, Melanchthon had a ready-made format for his response to the emperor's declaration. Both the Confutation and the negotiations had used the organization of the Augustana; Melanchthon followed the same procedure, once again taking up the argument article by article. As he did so, he used the late medieval formula for academic dispute and the state-of-the-art humanist tools for communication,[67] stating the Lutheran teaching at stake, summarizing the objections registered by the Confutation and then replying, both to fault the objection and to reestablish the point. The method is thorough to the point of being at times seemingly ponderous because it was following a form designed for oral argument. At the same time, this method freed Melanchthon to concentrate of the issues that he regarded as decisive. This explains the distribution of the argumentation in the Apology. Affirmations no longer in dispute are passed over quickly, with minimal discussion. The articles on original sin (II), the church (VII), and human traditions or ecclesiastical practices (XXII–XXVIII) get further development because of their closer correlation to the center of the argument, justification by faith, or their prominence in the negotiations. Article IV, on justification, and article XII, on repentance, are the real heart of the Apology.

In its text the honor of Christ and the consolation of troubled consciences head the list of Melanchthon's concerns in presenting the Wittenberg theology. Christ's honor was at stake when his sole responsibility for the salvation of sinners was brought into question by various schemes of establishing, conditioning, or completing the faithful believer's relationship to God. In the fourth article of the Apology Melanchthon went on the offensive against those whose positions "bury

The Apology of the Augsburg Confession

Christ completely" (Ap IV, 81, 18), "obscure the glory and blessings of Christ" (Ap IV, 3), fail to make use of Christ (Ap IV, 12), "insult Christ" (Ap IV, 149, 150), "abolish Christ" (Ap IV, 229), and "rob Christ" of his glory as mediator and propitiator (Ap IV, 157, 214–15). Conversely, "Christ's glory becomes brighter when we teach people to make use of him as mediator and propitiator" (Ap IV, 299; cf. Ap II, 50; Ap XII, 43; XV, 4, 10). When Christ's sole responsibility for salvation is not made clear, dismay, disquiet, and despair can overwhelm the pious (Ap XI, 7, 9; cf Ap IV, 24, 157, 165, 213, 215, 257, 269, 285, 317; XX, 4). That Melanchthon, like Luther, wished to avoid at all costs. He aimed every effort at conveying the benefits of Christ to God's people. The word *beneficium* had a rich field of meaning in medieval thought, ranging a wide variety of payments and property holdings, through gifts of every form, to its older sense of favor, kindness, a benefit freely given. The "benefits of Christ" signified the forgiveness of sins, life, and salvation for Melanchthon and his colleagues. To counteract the tendency to diminish the honor of Christ by limiting his significance for the restoration of righteousness to God's faithful, the Apology insists that God alone justifies, that is, restores righteousness in God's sight to sinners through forgiveness and the gift of new life, a new identity, before God.

The Wittenberg understanding of God's performative Word, as it condemns sin and restores human righteousness, lies behind Melanchthon's confession that God speaks of his expectations of his human creatures in his law and that he restores the relationship that stands at the heart of the human relationship with the creator through his promise of salvation in Christ. This distinction of the law's demands and the promises of the gospel guided all proclamation of God's Word, according to both Melanchthon and Luther. In the Apology Melanchthon made clear that all Scripture should be divided into these two chief ways of teaching. He regarded the promises of the coming Christ in the Old Testament and of the Messiah who has come in the New Testament as equally effective in restoring God's relationship with sinners (Ap IV, 5–6, 102). In the structure and organization of Apology IV, Melanchthon referred to this distinction both when he introduced the positive treatment of the Lutheran teaching on justification (Ap IV, 5) and when he began to address the arguments of his opponents: "with the acknowledgment of the fundamentals in this issue (namely, the distinction between the law and the promises or gospel), it will be easy to refute the opponents' objections. For they quote passages about law and works but omit passages about the promise" (Ap IV, 183). He faulted the opponents for this and compared them to the Israelites who confused God's expectations for the life the creator gives with the cause of that life; they were like the people of Israel as they gazed upon the veiled face of Moses (Ap IV, 21, 133–35, 229). They completely overlooked the promises and failed to see the benefits of Christ. In addition they focused only on the commands that involve human actions, not on the first commandment and the original sin of doubt of God and his Word that is the source of all other sins (Ap IV, 7–9). They had succumbed to the thought patterns of the philosophers outside the faith, who could assess humanity only on the basis of works (Ap IV, 12–13).

A proper focus on the relationship with God as the center of what it means to be human turned believers to Christ, to the promises within their framework of the distinction between law and gospel. "Since Christ is set forth to be the propitiator, through whom the Father is reconciled to us, we cannot appease God's wrath by setting forth our own works" (Ap IV, 80; cf. Ap IV 31, 43). By selecting the law as the basis for justification, Melanchthon contended that the opponents "bury Christ completely" (Ap IV, 81, 18). For they failed to understand that "the law cannot be kept without Christ, and that if civil works are done without Christ, they do not please God. In commending works, therefore, we must add that faith is necessary, and that they are commended because of faith as its fruit or testimony" (Ap IV, 183). He then drew out the ramifications of this Christological principle, contending in his discussion of the opponents' use of Colossians 3:14, "If it is love that makes people perfect, Christ, the propitiator will be unnecessary. . . . Paul would never permit Christ, the propitiator, to be excluded, and hence this view is far removed from his intention" (Ap IV, 231). A little later he repeated this point: "wherever good works are praised and the law preached," we must hold fast to the principle "that the law is not kept without Christ—as he himself has said, 'Apart from me you can do nothing'" (Ap IV, 269). Again, the "teaching of the law is certainly not intended to abolish the gospel of Christ, the propitiator" (Ap IV, 269).

The Christological principle, in its law-gospel framework, is most especially used in order to support the confessors' position that justification takes place through faith. The passages that deal with the promises of Christ are given their due when brought into conjunction with the passages that deal with faith. "For it is only by faith that Christ is accepted as the mediator" (Ap IV, 80). Only faith takes hold of Christ the propitiator (Ap IV, 231). It is by faith that we apprehend Christ's benefits and set him against the wrath of God. So faith gives Christ the glory due him because it lets him remain the sole mediator and propitiator. Luther's understanding of justification rested upon his anthropological definition of what it means to be human as consisting of two dimensions, two "kinds of righteousness."[68] Melanchthon assumed this distinction into his own anthropology and argued throughout the Apology on the basis of its definition of human identity or righteousness in relationship to God as a righteousness of trust, created by the Holy Spirit, and a righteousness of works in relationship to God's creatures. Only trust in Christ makes God's children righteous in God's sight.

This trust produces the righteousness of love and service to other creatures as well as that of praise and prayer toward God. In the Apology Melanchthon focused largely on the righteousness of faith or trust although he met Roman Catholic criticism of Wittenberg theology as antinomian by showing how faith produces new obedience. In article XVI and in several of the reform articles particularly he also reflected Luther's appreciation of the created order as the place of everyday service to God's world.[69] God places all people into different walks of life, which Christians recognize as callings from God, as these walks of life take a variety of forms in different cultures (Ap XXVII, 49). In this world both false believers and believers may formulate articulations of God's will and plan for human life (Ap XVI, 3). Melanchthon conceded to the opponents who lived from Aristotle's program for education and thinking that the Stagarite had "written so eruditely about social ethics that nothing further needs to be added" (Ap IV, 14). He affirmed the goodness of all God's many created gifts, including medicine, meteorology, and art as well as civic virtues, skills such as rhetoric, and the like (Ap XVI, 1–3; 13; cf. Ap XXIII, 37–39). God's commands brought people into the normal practice of everyday life. But the sinful tendency to regard works done directly for God as more meritorious and worthwhile in God's sight diverted the attention of medieval Christians from their vocations and led them to specializing in "human commands," inventions of religious leaders, which served neither God nor neighbor. Melanchthon rejected these "sacred" or "religious" works and the popular idea that mere performance of the outward ritual of such works produces spiritual benefit (Ap IV, 10, XXIII, 7–13; XXVIII, 23). The Apology follows Luther in using language applied only to the monastic life in the Middle Ages in order to praise the God-pleasing nature of carrying out one's vocation in everyday life: they are "states for acquiring perfection" (Ap XXVIII, 37), where, though justification and sanctification are not to be earned, believers may grow in trusting the mercy promised in Christ and in dedication to their callings (Ap XXVII, 8, 27).

For all his praise of Aristotle's explanation of what is good in human actions, Melanchthon regarded it as his opponents' fatal flaw that they followed Aristotle in his anthropological foundation, which defined humanity only in terms of human performance (Ap II, 12, 43, IV, 12–16, 43, 134). Aristotle had no personal God who created through his Word, and therefore, the Wittenberg theologians rejected his definition of humanity decisively, even while accepting his estimate of much of what is proper for human action. The righteousness of human performance did not win merit before God, Melanchthon insisted, for "God does not regard a person as righteous in the way that a court or philosophy does (that is, because of the righteousness of one's own works). Instead, he regards a person as righteous through mercy because of Christ when anyone clings to him by faith" (Ap IV, 283+).

The gospel defines the source of true human righteousness at the core of humanity as God's desire to forgive and save on the account of Christ (Ap IV, 283+). Though he did not cite the First Commandment in particular or develop it in the way Luther does in the Large Catechism, it along with the other two commandments of the first table provides the driving force in his argument. "Meanwhile, they [the traditional theologians] fail to notice the first table, which instructs us to love God, to conclude that God is angry with sin, truly to fear God, truly to hear that God hears our prayers" (Ap IV, 34). The Decalogue "requires other works that are placed far beyond the reach of reason, such as, truly to fear God, truly to love God, truly to call upon God, truly to be convinced he hears us, and to expect help from God in death and all afflictions. Finally, it requires obedience to God in death and all afflictions so that we do not flee or avoid these things when God imposes them" (Ap IV, 8). What remains less than clear in Melanchthon's formulation, even in the octavo edition, is whether his use of the distinction of two kinds of righteousness is operative when he claims that "obedience to the law would be righteousness if we kept the law" (Ap IV, 159 octavo). If the law here includes the first commandment, which "commands" trust that the Holy Spirit produces, this statement can be understood as consistent with Melanchthon's distinction of the righteousness of faith and that of works. That he does not make this clear at this point gives some basis for seeing another focus than that which he and Luther otherwise often had. That Luther expressed himself in a similar way at times makes a clear analysis more difficult. In the midst of their battle they were not calculating dogmatic expressions as carefully as their subsequent readers would.

The Apology raised the question, in one form or another, countless times, "whether human traditions [or works in any other form] are necessary acts of worship for righteousness before God" (Ap VII, 37). Here it is clear that Melanchthon shared Luther's distinction of the two kinds of righteousness. His designations for the kind of righteousness God designed for human beings to perform included "the righteousness of reason" or "philosophical righteousness" (for example, Ap IV, 9, 22), pointing to its potential source in God's gift of rationality; "the righteousness of the law" (Ap IV, 21, 39, 43, 47, 49, 106; VII, 31, 21, 24), pointing to God's Word which defines it; "one's own righteousness" (Ap IV, 20, 283; XII, 79, 108; XV, 9; XXIV, 23), that is, that which human beings perform themselves; "civil righteousness" (Ap IV, 34, 183; XII, 142; XVIII, 4, 5, 9), the righteousness which functions in civil society, whether motivated by faith or not; "carnal righteousness" (Ap IV, 179, XVIII, 4; XXIII, 4), acts of conformity to God's law performed for selfish reasons; and "the righteousness of works" (Ap XVIII, 40). The core of human righteousness, however, is "spiritual" (Ap XVIII, 2, 9, 7, 31); "eternal" (Ap IV, 132; XVI, 2, 8; XVIII, 10, 23); and "Christian" (Ap IV, 12, 16), in contrast to civil and carnal righteousness, which proceed from other roots than faith. This righteousness is constituted by faith (Ap IV, 18, 20, 39, 43, 47, 155, 211, 358; VII, 31, 45; XII, 10, 15, 16, 29; XV, 4, 10, 16, 22, 25, 32, 42, 43, 50; XXIII, 37; XXIV, 27, 43, 57, 60, 63, 77, 96, 96–98; XXVII, 23, 54); it is produced by the gospel (Ap IV, 27, 47) and by God (Ap IV, 30, 32, 41). It is a righteousness not of outward performance but of the heart, that is, of the trust that determines human personality and personhood (Ap IV, 92; VII, 13, 31, 32, 36).

Melanchthon's anthropology brought the biblical image of being human in these two dimensions together with the medieval Aristotelian analysis of human functioning in the realms of the mind or reason, the will, and the emotions. Some medieval theologians had made reason the locus of control in the human creature, and the Wittenberg reformers certainly criticized a reliance on reason in place of revelation regarding God and his actions. Nonetheless, they expressed high appreciation for God's gift of rationality and the necessity of using it properly and wisely, also in recognizing proper forms of behavior in the temporal realm (Ap XVIII, 4).

However, the Ockhamist tradition had emphasized the primacy of the will, and Melanchthon recognized that the opponents of Luther's thought had believed that the will produces human righteousness (Ap IV, 283). The Apology argued that neither reason nor will can produce the faith that constitutes true human righteousness (Ap II, 11–13, 26, 42). He was, however, willing to place faith within the realm of the will so long as it is understood that the Holy Spirit moves the will to trust Christ and receive his benefits (Ap IV, 125, 127, 132, 135). Melanchthon reaffirmed that the origin of the trust of which Luther spoke so eloquently in the Large Catechism[70] lies in the power of the Holy Spirit. He bestows the key to righteousness in God's sight; he bestows the faith that constitutes true human righteousness. This human trust "can be called righteousness because it is that which is reckoned as righteousness (as we say with Paul) regardless in which part of a person it may finally be located" since faith in Christ embraces and defines the whole person (Ap IV: 283+). This confidence in God's mercy rests on the recognition that God's reckoning establishes reality. God's pronouncing forgiveness creates reality. Melanchthon and Luther shared a strong doctrine of God's performative, re-creative Word, and so both believed that, in Gerhard Forde's words, "the absolutely forensic character of justification renders it effective—justification actually kills and makes alive." They further insisted that this forensically bestowed gift of righteousness is "'not only' forensic but that is the case only because the more forensic it is, the more effective it is!"[71]

Melanchthon's "forensic" form of God's re-creative power took form in the promise that God gives by sending his Son Jesus Christ to die for the sins of the world and to rise from the dead to restore righteousness and bestow new life as children of God upon his people. Faith hearkens to the gospel that conveys the benefits of Christ—his righteousness—for faith is the only reaction that can respond to a promise (Ap IV, 48–60, 252+). Like Luther, Melanchthon found Abraham as God's outstanding example of the faith that clings to the Word of promise, and the second edition of the Apology expanded the treatment of Abraham's faith, as Paul commented on it in Romans 4:3.[72]

Article XV of the Augustana, on ecclesiastical rites and regulations, affirmed that ceremonies cannot constitute an element of that which is necessary for salvation. Melanchthon's sharp rejection of ritualistic good works as meritorious for salvation reinforced his rejection of the human claim to power in the church (Ap XXVIII). Article XV of the Apology reiterated his insistence that sinners receive forgiveness and justification only by God's grace through faith. It also revealed that he was willing to permit a variety of ceremonies so long as that gospel of Christ could be proclaimed.[73]

Though often in less dramatic images than those Luther used, Melanchthon also depicted the entire life of the Christian as a life of struggle against the deception of the devil, and so he shared with Luther the conviction that the entire life of the Christian is a life in which the proclamation of law and gospel continues to produce repentance. He regarded the proper practice of repentance as a critical issue for pastoral care and directly correlated to justification. The two reformers shared the view of repentance as a repetition of baptismal dying and rising, as Luther stated in his Small Catechism.[74] Christ's justifying act radicalizes repentance, tying it directly to the freedom of the gospel so that it is no longer an occasional necessity brought on by personal failures but a lifelong rhythm of daily death and resurrection, as he made clear in the statement on "The False Repentance of the Papists" in the Smalcald Articles as well as in the *Antinomian Disputations* of the later 1530s.[75]

Recognizing the strategic place of repentance in the Lutheran witness, Melanchthon devoted major attention to it in article XII, spelling it out with close attention to the major premises and conclusions to be drawn. In article XI he had affirmed that Lutheran pastors continued to hear confession of sins from their people, rejecting many practices of the medieval church, which had focused on human performance of satisfactions to attain merit in God's sight, embracing the pronouncement of absolution for the comfort and consolation of troubled consciences. This practice arose out of the teaching on repentance elaborated in article XII. The Confutation's dismissal of faith's role in repentance set the tone for the article, with a rhetorical appeal to the emperor, "what are we to do here?" "This is the very voice of the gospel itself, that we receive the forgiveness of sins by faith." Melanchthon read the opponents' critique as "contempt for the blood and death of Christ" (Ap XII, 2–3). As in article IV, Melanchthon followed the guidelines of the *genus iudicale* to unfold his petition for the emperor's approval of the Lutheran position. He rejected the "endless questions" and "great darkness" of scholastic discussions of how sorrowful sinners should be and what limits had to be put upon the keys to heaven and hell exercised by the priest, to say nothing of the accent on the performance of satisfactions, to concentrate on the forgiveness of sins (Ap XII, 4–7).

Apology XII rejected the three-fold medieval division of the sacrament of penance into contrition, confession and absolution by the priest, and works of satisfaction to set aside the temporal punishment for the sins, the guilt of which had been set aside in the absolution (Ap XII, 8–16). Eleven specific doctrines of scholastic theology, largely revolving around the meriting of grace through proper contrition or proper performance of the human actions related to repentance, won mention and rejection (Ap XII, 17–27). Melanchthon focused on the sorrow over sin which the law effects and the trust and consolation which the gospel bestows, "a putting to death and a raising to life." In addition, Melanchthon raised no objection to discussing "fruits worthy of repentance, that is, the good works that follow conversion" in connection with faith (Ap XII, 28 octavo). He did object to the manner of treating repentance in the past that had led to terror and despair (Ap XII, 29–34), so without ignoring God's wrath against sin, he concentrated on the gospel of Christ, which "freely promises the forgiveness of sins through Christ." The Wittenberg understanding of repentance "increases the value of the sacraments and power of the keys, illumines the benefits of Christ, and teaches us to make use of Christ as our mediator and propitiator" (Ap XII, 35–43). Melanchthon's pastoral concerns stood at the heart of his treatment of the topic.

Having established his *confirmatio* in this manner, Melanchthon proceeded to the *refutatio* or *confutatio* of the Confutation's treatment of article XII and its definition of repentance. In it he actually reinforced his position to prove its criticism false. Matthew 11:28 teaches the two parts of repentance: "being weary and carrying heavy burdens refers to contrition, anxieties, and the terrors of sin and death; to come to Christ is to believe that on account of Christ sins are forgiven. When we believe, our hearts are made alive by the Holy Spirit through the Word of Christ" (Ap XII, 44). On this basis he marshaled arguments from Scripture, including the story of David's repentance in 2 Samuel 12, and, in the octavo edition, a judgment from Bernard of Clairvaux (Ap XII, 56–58), as well as Peter in Acts 10 (Ap XII, 63–67). The Wittenberg rejection of any automatic or magical use of the sacraments apart from trust in Christ forms another element of Melanchthon's refutation (Ap XII, 59–60). The rhetorical interweaving of defense and critique continued at length as Article XII laid down its fundamental principles for the practice of pastoral care and proclamation of the gospel.

Intimately connected to the formulation of the biblical understanding of the justification of the sinner for Luther was his assertion that the sinful will is bound in its ability to exercise free choice in its relationship with God.[76] Melanchthon's expressions regarding the bound choice of the will evolved over the years, but in 1530 the two of them agreed that the will was not free to choose God over false gods as the object of its ultimate trust. This issue had reaped Melanchthon sharp criticism from Roman Catholic opponents because, they charged, it fostered moral and thus societal disorder. Therefore, Melanchthon sometimes changed the focus from the bound-ness of human choice and the relationship of human creature with Creator to the integrity of God's human creature as a responsible individual. The Confutation had accepted Article XVIII of the Augustana while trying to avoid a pelagian position. In the Apology Melanchthon found that its rejection of Pelagianism was not consonant with its authors' own teaching, following Gabriel Biel's way of thinking, that "apart from the Holy Spirit people can love God and keep the commandments of God 'according to the substance of the act' and can merit grace and justification by works that reason can produce itself" (Ap XVIII, 2) a summary of Gabriel Biel's doctrine. Melanchthon affirmed that human beings exercise a certain, limited freedom of choice in the horizontal realm of life. To clarify the difference between that claim and the claim to be able to love God and keep his commandments apart from the power of the Holy Spirit, he repeated the distinction of "civil righteousness, which is ascribed to the free will, and spiritual righteousness, which is ascribed to the operation of the Holy Spirit in the regenerate" (Ap XVIII, 9).

Melanchthon, of course, understood the operation of the Holy Spirit as his re-creative action through the gospel, God's Word. The Wittenberg theologians dedicated no larger work to the topic "means of grace" though their theology rested and rode upon the Holy Spirit's action in applying law and gospel to the lives of his hearers, as his Word becomes concrete in oral, written, and sacramental forms. In fact, in the 1520s the reformers had made little use of the medieval expression "means of grace" that would become so important to their students later. Though it seems curious that the Augsburg Confession and its Apology contain no theoretical treatment of God's Word (nor do Luther's Catechisms, and Smalcald Articles III.iv offers but a brief, undeveloped reference to it), Melanchthon did address the Word of the gospel in sacramental form, in the Confession in brief summaries, in the Apology with somewhat more extensive detail. Luther and Melanchthon waged an unremitting battle against the false concept of Christianity that they found lodged in the ritualistic practices of the medieval church. They centered their critique on the concept of automatic sacramental effect, through rote external use of or partici- pation in sacramental actions, as summarized in the phrase *ex opere operato*.

The Apology rejects the Confutation's insistence on the seven sacraments of late medieval practice because of its definition of a sacrament as rites which God commands and uses as a means of bestowing his grace (Ap XIII, 3). The Augsburg Confession's affirmation of baptism as a channel of God's grace, open enough to embrace a Roman ritualistic understanding as well as the Lutheran teaching that God effects his saving will through the Word connected with the water of bap- tism, had occasioned no objections; Melanchthon reaffirmed the sacrament's sav- ing power as a form of God's Word and the validity of infant baptism (Ap IX). Likewise, the Confutation of Augustana Article X on the Lord's Supper summoned only Melanchthon's reaffirmation that "in the Lord's Supper the body and blood of Christ are truly and substantially present and are truly offered with those things that are seen, the bread and wine, to those who receive the sacrament" (Ap X, 1, 4). Disagreement over practices connected with the celebration and use of the Lord's Supper, treated in article XXII, on the lay reception of both body and blood, and XXIV, on the sacrifice of the mass, invited Melanchthon to a fuller exposition of the proper practice of the Lord's Supper for the strengthening of faith and the consola- tion of consciences. This concern guided Melanchthon's defense of the Lutheran understanding of confession and absolution in a treatment that focused on pastoral care (Ap XI).

Like Luther, Melanchthon continued to search the Scriptures and teach the gospel he found there—along with God's plan for human living that played a vital role in the repentant life. His theological writings in the last three decades of his life reveal much of the path he took. His three treatises from the 1530s, however—the Augustana, the Apology, and the *Treatise on the Power and Primacy of the Pope*— rose above the others in terms of the role they played in the church. They became secondary authorities in determining Lutheran teaching and ecclesiastical life.

6

The Smalcald Articles and the Treatise on the Power and Primacy of the Pope

When in August of 1530 Charles V declared the Augsburg Confession repudiated and announced his intention to enforce the Edict of Worms by the next spring, he precipitated a three-dimensional crisis for the Wittenberg Reformers and their allies. The first dimension was political and military. The leaders of the five territories and two cities who had signed the Augustana knew that in order to resist Charles's renewed threat successfully, they had to have a larger and more solid alliance. They went to work on the problem immediately, forming the Smalcald League. As it spread a power umbrella over the reform, the league also gave the politicians footing for practicing their vocations. They took responsibility for the larger political implications of the reform as well as some of the day-to-day necessities of the church.[1]

The second dimension was churchly. Like many other Germans of the time, Luther and his colleagues were commonly and caustically critical of the power structures of the Mediterranean world, centrally the papacy itself. At the same time they stressed their allegiance to the Catholic tradition of the church. At Augsburg Melanchthon had muted the criticism, making several concessions in hopes of a settlement. When the emperor suspended negotiation, the critical side of the Lutheran reform re-emerged forcefully, hardened by the disappointment. They still considered themselves Catholic, but in the 1530s the adjective "Roman" had lost considerable power.

Thirdly, the name "Lutheran" itself indicates a common criticism of the Reformation, both at the time and since, that it was merely personal—Luther breaking the unity of the church for the sake of his own agenda. Whatever the standing of such a critique, there certainly was some personal dimension to the reform, as became evident once more in the Apology, which Melanchthon composed and then revised under Luther's direction. Indeed, persons and personalities played a role both in the case of individuals and of groups, such as the team that constituted the Wittenberg theological faculty. In the mid-1530s these personal concerns fused with an impending public occasion to produce two more of the Lutheran Confessions, the Smalcald Articles and the *Treatise on the Power and Primacy of the Pope*. Luther wrote one, Melanchthon the other.

Necessities of Defense: The Smalcald League

Dramatic as it was in terms of its impact, Charles V's announced intention to enforce the Edict of Worms by April 15, 1531, still contained a softer overture. The emperor promised that he would use his influence, for what it was worth, to persuade the pope to call a council of the bishops in search of a settlement. Even with that possibility open, the threat that the emperor would use violence to stop the reform dominated considerations. Charles V still had some troubles with the Turks, with the French, and with the papacy. But he had enough power of his own to be a real problem to the Lutherans. All the emperor needed was opportunity, and the Lutherans could quickly go the way of a whole succession of medieval reforms: into the trash heap.

But the Lutherans had some advantages of their own. To begin with, they had some effective political leadership. John Frederick, the son of John the Constant and nephew of Frederick the Wise, had taken over in electoral Saxony. He was well-versed theologically and eager to support the reform, not only within his territory but beyond, into the politics of the empire. He also proved effective in his office. John Frederick's chief cohort in leadership was Philip, landgrave of Hesse, who had already been involved in the political side of the reform for some years. If Philip was not as sophisticated theologically, he was a little more experienced in the affairs—in more than one sense of the term—of power. The location of his territory, toward the southwest from Wittenberg, around the city of Frankfurt, put him in a position to broker relations with the Upper Rhine Valley Germans, between Basel and Strasbourg, and the Swiss. His inclinations to dynasty also whetted his appetites to build a larger alliance, even if they eventually proved problematic.

Together, John Frederick and Philip of Hesse set about expanding their support. Philip of Hesse had led such efforts in the late 1520s, foundering on the doctrine of the true presence of Christ's body and blood in the Lord's Supper when Luther and Zwingli met at Marburg. So this time the two political leaders decided to begin with what they had at hand: the seven signatories of the Augsburg Confession. They were not yet a very large group—after Saxony and Hesse, some smaller territories and a few independent cities. But they did agree amongst themselves theologically and offered, however tentatively, the leavening for a larger lump.

Another advantage immediately available to the Lutherans was sympathy among other Germanic language speaking peoples. Even with the earlier breakdown of negotiations, there were still enough prospects among the southwestern Germans and Swiss to drive a decade long effort with increasing levels of success. Concentrated in and toward the eastern and northern parts of Germany, the Lutherans had plenty of room and grow in those directions. They had already made progress in Denmark, through which they would reach into the territories it governed, chiefly Norway and Iceland; Sweden with its eastern appendage, Finland, were also becoming officially committed to Wittenberg reform. Capitalizing on Luther's effective use of the printing press to disseminate the reform and gain popular support, especially among dislocated farm families moving into the imperial cities of Germany, the leadership of the Smalcald League quickly began to gain new members. By the end of the 1530s a significant number of German princes and municipalities had officially become part of the league. Even if not formally included, both Scandinavian monarchs could be considered potential allies as well. Efforts to bring King Henry VIII and his England into the League seemed within reach of success for a time in 1536.[2] As the league grew, Charles V's saber rattling about the Edict of Worms mattered less and less, or so it seemed.

Significant as such advantages were to the Lutheran reform in the 1530s, the direct involvement of the political authorities in oversight of the reform and the life of the church also posed some problems. On the one side, there was ample precedent for it, going all the way back to the Constantinian settlement in the early fourth century. But on the other, as much as they depended on political support, the Lutherans had some of their own reasons for apprehension about it. Consequently, a different pattern of church state relations emerged.

In the centuries following the church's establishment by the Roman Empire, a tradition shaping the relation of church and state emerged that controlled medieval life. Remembered as the two swords theory, it effectively divided authority and responsibility: the church held the spiritual sword, overseeing religious and moral life while the state wielded the political sword, restraining the flesh in all of its forms. But it was a distinction more than a separation. The papacy commonly intervened in political affairs. Charles V appealed to the tradition of the German kings to claim religious authority over the reformation. Whatever the various proportions, political and religious authority had been linked in Europe for over a millennium.

In a variety of ways, some southwestern Germans and Swiss developed their own versions of the two swords tradition, bringing church and state together for the establishment of Christendom. This started with Zwingli's reform in Zurich, where city officials took a critical voice both in decision-making and implementation of church affairs. Later, Calvin's Geneva followed a pattern that formally left ecclesiastical and secular affairs distinct tasks, given respectively to church and municipal government though at the level of personnel the two leaderships were closely intertwined.[3] After exiling Calvin in 1538, the city council called him back to Geneva in 1541. While there were occasional tensions, civic leadership worked with him to legislate reform.

Luther had also appealed to and gained critical support from political figures earlier in the reformation. One of his classical treatises of 1520, *To the German Nobility*, was a foundational call for political support. Even while outlawed by one political authority, the empire, Luther was dependent for his protection on another, Electoral Saxony. The support of the electors was instrumental in both preserving and extending the Lutheran reform. There was thus ample precedent in the Lutheran reform for the organization of something like the Smalcald League as well as for its direct participation in critical decision-making.[4]

Yet at another level, for Luther and some of his colleagues, the issue was considerably more complicated. One factor was Luther's ecclesiology. Apocalyptically driven, Luther thought of the church as a remnant within the larger society. As Melanchthon put it in Article VII of the Augsburg Confession, reflecting Luther, the church is the people of God, gathered together to hear the Word and receive the sacraments. The preached and sacramental Word defines the church, rendering all the accompanying institutions and structures provisional. "It is not necessary that human traditions, rites, or ceremonies instituted by human beings be alike everywhere," the article states.[5] But Luther's apocalyptic also produced some skepticism about the nature of the state's involvement. While he interpreted conservatively Paul's admonition in Romans 13 to honor the emperor, leading him to counsel obedience, Luther was sharply critical of the use of coercion in matters of faith. The emperor's threat exacerbated this concern, so that through the 1530s the Reformer became increasingly willing to support armed resistance. The critique of coercion stood throughout, however. Faith is the fruit of the Word and cannot be produced on demand.[6]

On the basis of these considerations and related matters, a different pattern of church-state relations developed among the Lutherans. In the course of the Lutheran reform, the participation of the politicians was often more than passive. They looked after matters like organization and support, as in the church visitation. They took on issues of political and military defense, as seen in the organization of the Smalcald League. They could even make the call in an important ecumenical issue, as they did when the pope finally called a council. At the same time the integrity of theological issues and some churchly matters were recognized as being of a different order, to be handled by the theologians themselves or within an emerging structure, the consistories, which were assemblies of pastors and secular counselors meeting under the supervision of an officer loosely equivalent of a bishop, significantly called a "Superintendent," a German translation via Latin of the Greek *episkopos*. The virtually unanimous opposition of the bishops to the reform effectively suspended the office among Lutherans, though many of the functions remained. Sweden was the major exception, retaining the title "bishop."

Jesus' offhand observation that the children of darkness are wiser in the ways of the world than the children of light (Luke 16:8) is not to be taken as a distinction between politicians and theologians. But the elector, the princes, dukes, mayors, and other political officials knew the ins and outs of power politics a little more immediately than the professors and pastors. So the league brought with it another quality. To defense it added some political savvy—the adjustments, accommodation, and compromise—necessary to growth and survival.

Conciliar Hopes and Illusions   idealistic

There had always been something quixotic about the Lutheran Reformers' talk of a council. They could appeal to historical precedent. The seven ancient ecumenical councils of the church, following a pattern begun with the Jerusalem Council in

Acts 15, defined the church's tradition at critical points theologically. In more recent European memory, in the fourteenth and fifteenth centuries, a conciliar movement succeeded to some extent, among other things, reducing the number of popes to the original one at a time. The Council of Constance in 1414–1418 also laid the basis for continuing conciliar governance, to the ongoing annoyance of the papacy. Thus, it made some sense in 1518 when Luther went to the town church in Wittenberg and formally appealed for such an assembly of bishops to settle the issues raised by his protest. There was also a political advantage to be gained from continuing the appeal, especially as controversy mounted. But as sensible as it may have been, in the end the appeal turned out to be more hope than reality.

Luther expressed some reservation about the prospects even when he went to the altar in Wittenberg to formally request a council. He was even charier in the early 1530s. But still, he spelled out some hope for what the council would be. Luther and the Wittenberg theologians, with the politicians, wanted it free, so that the bishops could proceed without papal meddling; they wanted it general, so that there would be open to the whole church, not merely an Italian operation; and they wanted it Christian in the sense that it would be subject to the Word of God as final authority. There was not a chance at any of these points. In fact, no precedent could move Clement VII, who held office from 1523 to 1534, to take the first step. The papacy had effectively controlled a council earlier in the sixteenth century, but he was not about to take another chance. He was unalterably opposed.

Still, despite the history of tense relations between them, Charles V had some leverage with Clement VII—enough to demand appearances if not the reality. His continued pressure shifted the issue from calling a council to locating it, Clement delaying the prospects by angling to keep any council close enough to Rome for easy oversight. The Reformers pressed for more distance. Bologna was proposed, then Mantua, in northern Italy. Conversations about the council began as the newly elected pope, Paul III, began efforts at reform shortly after his election in 1534.[7] A papal diplomat, Pier Paulo Vergerio, was dispatched to Wittenberg to start negotiations with Luther.

In *Luther: An Experiment in Biography*, Harry G. Haile recounted the encounter between Vergerio and Luther with a wonderful eye for the medieval color. Concerned that illness may have sapped his appearance, Luther took some unusual steps to give the impression of virility. He got his teeth fixed, his hair darkened; he donned a large codpiece, an item of medieval attire assumed to emphasize the quality of masculinity. Vergerio found this amusing but was more impressed by Luther's eyes, black, piercing and intense. Since the location for the council still had not been fixed, Vergerio pushed Luther to come to Bologna but above all to attend. "See to it that you come to such a council, then," he said as the two prepared to part. "I will be there," Luther replied, "holding my neck out!" The Saxons remembered well what had happened when Jan Hus, the Czech reformer, went to Constance on a safe-conduct pass. Such provisions notwithstanding, he was burned at the stake.[8]

Ecumenical negotiation proceeding by the same clock as normal politics, it was 1536 before Charles V's efforts were finally productive. While somewhat more proactive than his predecessor, Clement VII, who had by every standard been unqualifiedly reactive, Paul III was no more eager to meet the Lutherans on the terms proposed. But given the Holy Roman Emperor's continuing pressures and the spreading reforming influence north of the Alps, something clearly had to be done. So in the summer of 1536, Paul III finally issued a formal call for a council. It was scheduled to meet in Mantua in May of 1537. The pope left no doubt about any possibility of openness, however. The express purpose of the council, as he stated it in the summons, was "the utter extirpation of poisonous and pestilential heresy."[9]

It did not take long for John Frederick and Gregory Brück, his chancellor, to measure the political proportions of such an invitation. The statement of purpose only made explicit what was implicit in the location. With an already dispropor- tionate number of bishops in Mediterranean Europe, a majority of them Italian, meeting in Italy would simply put another lock on the assured results. Thus, as John Frederick argued, even to accept the invitation would be to concede. After all of the efforts expended, he may have regretted coming to such a conclusion. But John Frederick knew from the beginning that the Lutherans could not possibly attend such a council without submission and so resolutely opposed it.

As certain as John Frederick's reasoning was, there was some political risk to it. In the Nuremberg Armistice of 1531, the Lutheran politicians had committed them- selves to attending a council. More, after nearly eighteen years of appeals, having gained Charles V's initially reluctant but later unswerving support for one, it would be something of an embarrassment to refuse. More still, there was a widespread concern for preserving the unity of the church, deeply held among the Lutherans even through their protests. So, John Frederick's quick assessment notwithstanding, through the summer and fall of 1536 and even into the winter of 1537, the question of attending the council remained open.

Personal Considerations

John Frederick and the other Evangelical governments needed a united front among the theologians, so the elector specifically forbade the theologians from publishing their own opinions about one another's arguments after the fact in the negotiations surrounding the council at Mantua. Above all, the Saxon elector wanted a statement of Evangelical teaching from the pen of his friend and leading theologian, Martin Luther. Against the background of these discussions, movement in direction of the council continued, with Luther's personal situation, particularly his health, haunt- ing the preparations. For all the stresses and strains of his years as a reformer, he had lived into his fifties, surviving among other things his own work habits. Before his marriage to Katherine von Bora he did not take care of himself, working in extended fits of productivity that lasted sometimes up to 72 hours, collapsing and then going again. His wife's medical sophistication had made him at least somewhat more responsible. But after some apparently serious heart trouble in the later 1520s, in the early 1530s his health began to deteriorate. Some of the difficulties might seem comparatively minor, but he also suffered from insomnia, tinnitus (a ringing in his ears), vertigo, and respiratory difficulties brought on by a cold that in the absence of antibiotics set in and stayed. He also complained of a pain in the hip that laid him up. But while none of this was life threatening, the cumulative effect slowed him down, making it difficult to preach and hindering other work.

There was another, more serious problem, however, that beset Luther increasingly, beginning in May of 1536 and, more dramatically, through the summer into the fall and winter that followed. It was a kidney stone, or "the stone," as Luther called it. Excruciatingly painful, it also brought on uremic poisoning, leaving him desperately ill. The stones eventually would pass, allowing some recovery, but H. G. Haile has found medical documentation connecting the poisoning with the irritability and explosiveness that dogged Luther's last decade of life. All of these problems came to a head late in 1536. On December 18, Luther suffered a heart attack. He made some progress initially at the hands of a barber, who, following common medical procedures of the time, had bled him. The following day, however, he had a deep pain in his chest that resulted in a convulsion and left him close to death. Though he recovered sufficiently to continue work, he was substantially weakened.[10]

Luther's health difficulties along with apprehensions about potential misinterpretations of his message by friends and foes alike combined to provoke his interest in a suggestion originally made by John Frederick, that he write a theological last will and testament. Some of the concern was protective. The events of the reformation, especially his stand before the emperor at the Diet of Worms in 1521, had made Luther a hugely popular public figure, a symbol at several different levels in German-speaking Europe. His status fed rumor mongering, among them a repeated report that he had finally recanted his faith. With John Frederick's suggestion Luther saw a chance to finally set the records straight. He welcomed another chance to confess. So he had begun to mull over a statement.

Melanchthon and Luther clearly agreed on the necessity of attending the proposed council. It was nearly a decade since the Lutheran reform had begun taking on more institutional forms. Though the forms were provisional and charismatic in the sense that efforts were so much driven by and concentrated around the person of Luther, the practice of visitation and the formulation of constitutions for territorial and municipal churches (*Kirchenordnungen*), many of them authored by Luther's pastor and colleague, Johannes Bugenhagen, had been put into use by those governments in order to make reform a reality at the congregational level. Still, after steady efforts to spread the reform and some worldly-wise assessment of the possibilities at a council, neither Melanchthon nor Luther was willing to give up on the unity of the church. They had grown up with only one image of the church, and that image viewed it as one single institution in the West. As a result, the theologians agitated to accept Paul III's summons, despite its stated intention.

The Smalcald Articles

Luther and Melanchthon were not the only people in Wittenberg or the Smalcald League who had agendas. Chancellor Brück shuttled back and forth between the elector and the Luther household, sharing reports of political considerations and the progress of Luther's health. At the same time John Frederick consulted with Philip of Hesse and the other politicians of the league, debating strategies. The scholarly debate regarding the underlying reason and impetus for the composition of what came to be known as the Smalcald Articles has noted evidence that already in 1535 John Frederick was pressing Luther to update his doctrinal "last will and testament."[11] He had prepared such a document in 1528 and appended it to his *Confession concerning Christ's Supper*.[12] That work reveals how Luther might have written such a will apart from the circumstances of the papal invitation to council in 1536. In 1528 he structured his parting confession according to the Creed, in three articles. The first rather briefly confesses the Trinity against the ancient heretics. The second not only treats the person and work of Christ but also touches on original sin, the bondage of the will, abuses of medieval piety that divert attention from Christ, and the God-given structure for proper human living in home, church, and society. The third article confesses Luther's faith in the Holy Spirit and his gift of faith through the proclamation of the gospel, baptism, and the Lord's Supper, as "means" or "ways" of coming to us to his people, applying Christ's sufferings to them, and bringing salvation to its fruits. He followed the Creed further in confessing his belief that the Holy Spirit works in and through the church. The confession closes with a conclusion regarding the abuses connected with indulgences, purgatory, the invocation of the saints, the identification of marriage and ordination as sacraments, the Mass, and other aspects of medieval church life. But in 1536, eight years later, John Frederick shared Luther's fear that after his death, despite this confession, some would misrepresent his views, and so both of them agreed that some kind of summary of the reformer's teaching was necessary.[13]

However, Luther himself explained the Articles as an agenda for council when he revised them for publication in 1538,[14] a year after they had been subscribed at the meeting of the Smalcald League in Smalcald. The correspondence between the court and the theologians in electoral Saxony confirms that all sides also viewed them as an agenda for the Evangelical representatives to use in negotiations at a council with their Roman Catholic counterparts. The structure of the Articles, divided into three sections, confirm this. Its initial affirmation of common commitment to the ancient doctrine of the Trinity and the person of Christ, followed by a confession of the heart of the faith, the person and work of Christ, and then an agenda for addressing other critical doctrinal issues points to the document's first intended function as an agenda for council while in no way minimizing its parallel function as Luther's doctrinal last will and testament.[15]

In addition to Luther's own concerns, Elector John Frederick wished to use the Articles as an instrument in his own pursuit of strengthening Saxon leadership within the Smalcald League. The elector had no hopes that the council could bring any benefits to the Evangelical churches and was trying to frustrate the League's participation in the gathering. He also desired to determine the doctrinal stance of the League with a firmer affirmation of Luther's own theology. He expected that the Articles would accomplish that goal, and with it Saxon dominance among its allies.

So the public or political and the personal came together, but not without the help of some friends. If John Frederick was going to take Luther's statement to Smalcald, he needed to have a united group of theologians behind him. If, in fact, the league was going to join in the statement and have representatives actually attend the council, there could not be evident dissent back in Wittenberg. So just as the Wittenberg theologians had joined in the preparations for Augsburg in 1530, several theologians were appointed to help Luther: Nicholas von Amsdorf, John Agricola, George Spalatin, Melanchthon, Justas Jonas, Casper Cruciger Sr., and Johannes Bugenhagen. With the possibility of negotiations in mind, Luther was told to distinguish in the statement between matters where no compromise was possible and points open to further discussion.

When Luther started work on December 11, a meeting of the Smalcald League had already been scheduled to assemble in the town of Smalcald the next February. The theologians and the politicians would meet separately, the theologians to pass on Luther's statement, the politicians to take up the political ramifications of the pope's invitation. When Luther went to work on the statement, he had recovered his health sufficiently to work fairly quickly. By December 18 and 19, when he suffered heart attacks, he had already completed large parts of the statement. Despite his health problems the tone of the text is bold, direct, expansive, sometimes humorous, and, as the section entitled "Concerning the False Repentance of the Papists,"[16] reminiscing on his personal struggles a quarter century earlier. Perhaps more than the other Lutheran Confessions, the Smalcald Articles reveals the personality of its author and his disposition at the time of writing.

Following the heart attack and convulsion, Luther gained enough strength to finish as the colleagues gathered around him on December 28 and the subsequent days. Some of the remainder was taken by dictation with the help of the other theologians. Though there are not many details available from the meeting, there is evidence of some pointed discussion of the statement on the Lord's Supper. Given his negotiations with Bucer and others, Melanchthon appears to be the likely source of this concern. The theologians also asked Luther to include and amplify a statement on the issue said to have seriously blocked the negotiations at Augsburg, the invocation of the saints.

As he approached the task of writing, Luther did not follow the elector's instructions precisely. Instead of starting with the non-negotiables, he began with four brief, creedally shaped statements concerning "the sublime articles of the divine majesty" recapitulating the basic, trinitarian affirmations of catholic faith. This comprises the first part, which identified what is common to all and lays the basis for what follows. It also identified the Lutheran movement's standing in the tradition of the Western church and pointed to the common public confession of that tradition that provided a basis for conversation at the council.[17]

The second and third parts then follow along the lines suggested by John Frederick. The second part treats the "office and work of Jesus Christ, or our redemption." After briefly recapitulating the doctrine of justification by faith, Luther states, "Nothing in this article can be conceded or given up, even if heaven and earth should pass away." In section II, article 2, Luther then draws out—placing it among the matters that cannot be negotiated—the critique of medieval Roman Catholic practices generated by the doctrine of justification, including the mass, monasticism, the papacy and related matters.[18] In Part III, identified as addressing matters that can be discussed, the corollaries of justification are considered. These include such doctrinal matters as sin, the law, repentance, the gospel, the sacraments, and several aspects of ecclesiastical practice.[19]

Four aspects of the argument in the Smalcald Articles should be noted. First, Luther recorded for the context he was addressing a summary of what he had been teaching for more than fifteen years. At point after point in his review of its content, Werner Führer provides painstaking detail on precisely how Luther's formulations in 1536/1537 reiterated the teaching he had found in Scripture since the late 1510s and early 1520s.[20]

Second, Luther's theological method, immediately evident in the starting point, commands our attention. Unlike the explanations of the Apostles Creed in the Small Catechism or in the *Confession* of 1528, where each article begins with one of the persons of the Trinity, Luther summarizes the doctrine of the Trinity in its classic formulations in the first part. But he was sensitive to the different settings in which he was writing. Here the Roman Catholic negotiators across the conciliar table determined the agenda. Luther lays down the trinitarian assumptions and goes immediately to the justification of the godless. This is Christ's work, which takes priority not only for faith but in the classical work of theology, reflection on the Word for the sake of its speaking. Once again, Luther's apocalypticism shaped his understanding, and the context determined his method.

Third, it is critical to note the correlation of affirmation and condemnation in the second part. The critique of medieval Catholicism's "belief and practice," as Luther links the two in his comment, is neither accidental nor additional to the Lutheran reform but stems directly out of the justifying word of faith. In other words, the critique itself is a function of the gospel, which has exposed the fraudulence of long standing Roman Catholic practice, and just for this reason has to be placed beyond any kind of compromise. As Part I of the Smalcald Articles makes transparently clear, Luther sees himself as a catholic. But his catholic faith, as expressed in the biblical assertion of justification by faith in Christ Jesus, would not allow any concession on the mass and accompanying practices that had become idolatrous any more than it will tolerate compromise on an institution like monasticism or an office such as the papacy. Precisely these practices, within the context of the ritual-istic conception of religion that dominated the western European medieval church, had undercut and obscured the gospel. The critique itself is a non-negotiable con-sequence of the gospel of Christ's justification.

Fourth, once the Christological priority was asserted in the statement on jus-tification, theological issues became "matters which we may discuss with learned and sensible men, or even among ourselves," as Luther calls them, introducing the third part. At one level, this may seem to underestimate the significance of state-ments concerning matters like sin, the law, repentance, and the like. As Luther rea-sons them through, however, each is a direct consequence of justification: since Christ saves sinners, people must not be able to save themselves in any other way. Given Christ's promise to save, the law clearly cannot contribute to their salvation. Because Christ's saves, sinners must become aware of their need for him. But at another level, theological formulations are always secondary. The promise that the truth of the gospel is a person, Jesus of Nazareth, crucified and risen from the dead, relativizes the claim to the truth of every propositional statement, which in seek-ing to bear witness to the person always reveals itself as less than the person who embodies the truth. Such matters are therefore discussable, not only with others but even and especially with those who identify themselves as part of the reform. Luther was ever eager for clarity and precision in the theological discipline that serves the proclamation of the gospel; he was not convinced that theological state-ments must be always and everywhere the same. His confession for Smalcald, like all the Lutheran confessions of the faith composed in the sixteenth century, did not attempt to serve as a doctrinal textbook or summary of the whole counsel of God. They all addressed the specific issues raised by and in specific situations. None in itself was adequate for the larger task of giving instruction in the whole of biblical teaching. Each was designed to proceed from the heart of that teaching to the issues under consideration at the time and provide a model for confessing the faith in other situations.

Though it is not structural, another feature of Luther's argument in the Smalcald Articles that should be noted is his attack on "enthusiasm," the view that the Holy Spirit does not work through external means, such as human language and sacra-mental elements, or at least does not place his power in such elements. Luther added a detailed criticism of the *Schwärmer* in an addition to the text that he formulated when it was to be published in 1538. It concluded his treatment of confession of sins (SA III, viii, 3–13). The problem began to emerge much earlier in the reform, while Luther was secreted away in the Wartburg. One source was Andreas Karlstadt, a highly educated colleague on the Wittenberg faculty;[21] another sprung out of Zwingli's reform in Zurich. Developing out of these roots, enthusiasm or the enthu-siasts—alternatively called anachronistically in modern scholarship the "left wing of the Reformation" or the "radical" reformers—were labeled *Schwärmer* by Luther. The word means "to swarm" or "to rave." These "ravers," in the language of Luther and his followers, became the underground of the Reformation, routinely harassed, heavily persecuted by both Roman Catholic and Lutheran authorities yet surfacing repeatedly. George Hunston Williams has identified three forms among them: the Anabaptists, the Spiritualists, and the Anti-Trinitarian Rationalists. Interestingly, these three groups were identified in the Lutheran Late Reformation as three aberrant forms of reform, with which the followers of Luther and Melanchthon did not wish to be identified in any way. They have relatively little in common even though Luther, too, grouped Anabaptists and Spiritualists together. Williams assigned the nomenclature "radical" to the three disparate groups because they rejected what he termed the "magisterial" Reformation, refusing to submit to human religious "masters" or authorities and to political authorities as well.[22]

For all of their subterranean activities, the enthusiasts—or *Schwärmer*, as Luther polemically called them, after the image of bees swarming their hives—had a far loftier sense of their place in things. Enthusiasm, the term used by Ronald Knox in a definitive study,[23] literally means god-within-ism. Classically, its adherents believed that the Holy Spirit becomes available to the faithful directly, from within, without means, in an unmediated presence. Thus, the Anabaptists, the largest group of them, were named for the practice of what has come to be called "believer's baptism." They despised the sacraments as merely outward, gathering the genuinely committed into communities organized to take themselves beyond the ordinary routines and responsibilities of everyday life as fellowships of the just. The Spiritualists claimed that personal possession of the Spirit laid the basis of a invisible fellowship of those so endowed. For example, Karlstadt, a canon lawyer with a couple of doctorates, read the Scripture aloud to illiterate peasants he met in the streets, seeking their interpretation in the conviction of such direct inspiration. The Anti-Trinitarian Rationalists regarded the doctrine of the Trinity as the source of the church's difficulties and sought to replace it with the simple teachings of Jesus. Forerunners of the Unitarians, their best-known proponent in the reformation was Miguel Servetus, Spanish physician, who ventured into print with two variations on an alternative to trinitarian teaching. Several streams of anti-trinitarian critique revived a wide palette of ancient arguments against the creedal doctrine of God. They continued to attract repudiation by Lutherans throughout the sixteenth century.

Though there are occasional implicit references, for example, in the catechisms' treatments of baptism, the Augustana explicitly rejected enthusiast teaching in the anathemas at the end of several articles (for example, Articles V, IX, XVI, and XVII). In one of the most noted discussions in the Smalcald Articles, Luther picked up the issue in the context of his considerations of confession and absolution. As Luther understood it, the absolution is an external word; the believer does not possess it, as though it were an installation, but hears it on the lips of a neighbor who says, "Your sin is forgiven for Jesus' sake." This external character of the Word brings the enthusiasts to Luther's mind, for that, in his analysis, is the problem with enthusiasm. Assuming the possession of the Spirit, it despises the external. So Luther launches his critique with these words, "In these matters, which concern the external, spoken Word, it must be firmly maintained that God gives no one his spirit or grace apart from the external Word, which goes before. We say this to protect ourselves from the enthusiasts."[24]

Characteristically, the concept expanded for Luther as he worked with it. Thomas Müntzer, a key figure in the Peasants' Revolt of 1525, is named; he had invoked the power of the Spirit to endorse his own plans for the reformation. But with the key assumption exposed, that special revelations of one kind or another, not Scripture, sets the norm for public teaching, Luther could see over the shoulders of Müntzer, Karlstadt and the others, the pope. "The papacy also is purely religious raving in that the pope boasts that 'all laws are in the shrine of his heart' and that what he decides and commands in his churches is supposed to be Spirit and law—even when it is above or contrary to the Scriptures or the spoken Word."[25] The link between the left and right, the enthusiasts and the papacy, rests in the conviction of unqualified possession of the Holy Spirit, which resulted in the loss of what has been termed the *extra nos*, the God who stands beyond us in judgment, whether of condemnation or grace.

The February Meeting

When the theologians and politicians, with all their pomp and colorful attire, found their way to Smalcald for the planned assembly of the league, a couple of dramatic changes awaited them. The surprises combined to detour the Smalcald Articles and call forth another Lutheran confessional document.

The first was in Luther's health. He had recovered sufficiently from his heart troubles to make the trip; the elector wanted him present, no matter how fragile his health had been, to lead the theological considerations involved in the question of attending the papal council. The trouble began again, however, the day after he arrived. He had two minor bouts with stone, February 8 and the 11, before a major blockage developed six days later. This time, Luther became desperately ill, uremic poisoning setting in quickly so that the combination of pain and sickness incapacitated him. After several days of this, convinced that Luther was at death's door, the elector provided his own coach to send Luther home—if he could make it. The combination of mountain roads and medieval coach springs accomplished what the barbers had been unable to do, even though they had seemingly spared nothing in their attempts to break the stone. Ten miles from Smalcald, Luther joyfully reported to Katherine and friends, he was finally able to relieve himself, passing by his own report at least a gallon. He survived another brief bout in better shape, but he was not in any condition to return to the proceedings he had so ingloriously left behind.

While Luther's own personal drama was unfolding, the political back and forth between John Frederick and Philip of Hesse continued on the field of the Smalcald Articles. Philip opted for a less specifically determined theological foundation for the League in order to remain as open as possible to the South Germans and the Swiss. Melanchthon favored the Hessian solution himself, having worked hard in the previous year to attain accord with Martin Bucer and his south German allies. Particularly Luther's graphically specific formulation of Christ's sacramental presence in the Lord's Supper, that "the true body and blood of Christ...are given and received not only by godly but by wicked Christians," seemed to depart from the settlement of 1536. The *manducatio impiorum*, as it is called, the eating by the impious, served as an exclamation point to the true presence of Christ's body and blood, not only present to faith but actually and physically for all, because Christ said it was so. As Melanchthon and Philip of Hesse read it, it threatened to derail further expansion of the League.[26]

In this connection, Luther's absence was both a possibility and a problem. With him removed, Melanchthon and Philip of Hesse did not have to meet him head on. But his worsening condition, as word of it passed around the assemblies, gave his statement even greater symbolic force. The two Philips could hardly come right out and oppose a document so intimately linked to him when Luther appeared to be a death's door. A number of leaders at Smalcald hit upon a method familiar in assemblies of both the politically and the theologically minded, resorting to parliamentary maneuvering to keep the Smalcald Articles off the floor and therefore not subject to formal discussion. In the meantime, the princes offered a counterproposal Melanchthon long had kept in mind, that the Augsburg Confession be used as the statement that already had attained public recognition as the "symbol" of the Wittenberg reform. This was agreed, with the provision that Melanchthon provide what amounted to a twenty-ninth article to the Augustana, addressing a topic he had scrupulously minimized in 1530: the papacy. Given the change of the times, it would hardly do to ignore one of the main bones of contention.

If this left Luther's document hanging, it still had his authority and could be published as John Frederick had originally intended, as Luther's last will and testament. So the articles were placed before the theologians present. As Führer points out, the subscription of the Articles had begun already in Wittenberg, when first Luther affixed his signature, and then the other members of the committee assembled there joined in affirming that the document represented their faith as well.[27] Melanchthon, apparently hoping that some reconciliation might be yet possible at the council and conscious that he would be leading the League's negotiators, signed with a proviso indicating his willingness to acknowledge papal superiority over the bishops provided it was recognized as established by the usual political convention, human right, as opposed to divine. When the theologians subscribed, they set in motion a process that gave confessional status to the Smalcald Articles.

In the end, however, the princes made all of the proceedings at Smalcald moot. The pope had submitted to Charles V's pressure, but the announced council was hardly to be free, general or even Christian, as the Lutherans had hoped. Instead, it was another power play in which participation and capitulation were indissolubly linked. Recognizing this, the assembly of the princes and other political leaders in the Smalcald League decided that attendance was impossible.

By the previous December Paul III had already decided that Mantua was an unacceptable meeting place, moving it to a then unspecified location. The Smalcald League's refusal took the pressure off both Charles V and the papacy. When the council did finally assemble, in 1545, it met in the city of Trent, German-speaking and within the borders of the German empire, but on the southern side of the divide of the Alps. That facilitated travel between Rome and the council and kept the council under strict papal and southern European control. It was agreed from the beginning that Luther's heresies made it unnecessary to examine the Lutheran proposals directly. They were quickly condemned on the basis on common caricatures. Meeting on-again, off-again over the next two decades, the Council of Trent reformed the practices of the medieval church, leaving its name imprinted on what followed until the second Vatican Council of the 1960s, Tridentine Catholicism.

The Problem of the Papacy

In a culture that values openness to an extent that it excludes all those not considered sufficiently indiscriminate, Luther's denunciation of the pope as the Antichrist immediately appears as overblown, personal polemics. For this reason, willingness to accept Luther's assessment has sometimes become a test of genuine confessional subscription. Both sides, the truly open and the genuinely committed, miss the historical character of this problem that the Lutheran Reformation addressed, not only in the middle 1530s but throughout.

Though they never regained the power the office had in the thirteenth century, when Innocent III declared papal sovereignty over all creatures, later medieval popes had certainly not surrendered such claims. Boniface VIII, at the beginning of the fourteenth century, had made allegiance to the papacy a condition of salvation. In fact, when the great voyages of European exploration exposed routes to the Americas and the Far East, it was a matter of course for the pope to call in southern European sovereigns and divide the newly found regions among them. Jesus' eschatological claim of the resurrection, "All authority in heaven and earth has been given to me" (Matt. 28:19), gave his earthly vicar, in papal interpretation, the power to assign rights to anything and everything, whether it was gold for the Spanish in far off Peru or slaves for the Portuguese in Africa.

While the corruption and tyranny attendant to these inflated claims was recognized throughout Europe, Germans and other northern Europeans felt the squeeze with particular sensitivity. They were the primary producers in an economic chain that moved inevitably southward, ending in the dominance of a Mediterranean power structure that included the Roman bishop. By no coincidence, Clement VII was a de Medici, part of a powerful Italian family that with others had long contended for papal power to advance a compound of other interests. At one level, the papacy was a religious problem. But in an extractive economy where the mouth of the horn of plenty opened toward the South, the problem was clearly also economic, political, social, and national. Luther tapped into German resentment of these forces early in the Reformation. More by happenstance than intention, the Reformation became such a widespread and powerful movement because it gave focus to so much of the larger complaint as well as the aspirations of Germanic-language-speaking peoples.

If this combination of conditions was not enough, from the beginning the papacy made itself a focal issue. In the larger scale of things, Luther's original attack on the abuse of indulgences perpetrated by Tetzel and his sponsors could hardly have been more minor. At the time, Luther was an unknown monk teaching on an obscure faculty at the far edges of nowhere. But bureaucracies have a fine tuned ability to detect perceived threats, no matter how minor. Before Luther himself recognized it as such, his opponents interpreted his protest as a direct attempt to undermine the office and moved quickly to respond to it as such. For the papal curia, the reformation was an all out attack on papal supremacy. In the confluence of forces and circumstances, even in the early 1520s, it had become just exactly that.

As at the outset of his reforming career, so in the 1530s Luther thought through the theological implications of the justification of the godless; as he came under the increasingly vitriolic attacks and papal forces in the church as well as the empire; he began to draw dramatically more radical conclusions about the hierarchical struc-ture of the medieval church. He railed against papal abuses as well as the office itself to the end of his life although, according to the analysis of Scott Hendrix, his view of the papacy was quite fixed by 1522.[28]

In common with Zwingli and other renaissance humanists, Luther was con-vinced that the key to papal claims to supremacy was the sacrifice of the mass. Identifying themselves as by office standing in an historical succession stretching back to the first bishop of Rome, the Apostle Peter, the popes asserted the right to legitimize all forms of Christian ministry. This legitimization was necessary, as it remains in Roman Catholicism, for the administration of a valid sacrament. God will only accept the sacrifices of those whom he has appointed, who stand in the properly defined relationship to Peter's successors. By the same token, God will only confer his grace through the channels he has established. Thus, as Christ's vicar on earth the papacy controlled traffic both directions, whether heavenward or earth-bound. This entire conception of Christianity was fundamentally ritualistic and hierarchical.

Zwingli and company attacked papal claims by challenging what they saw as the underlying premise, Christ's physical presence in the Eucharist, the appropriate name for the sacrament when it is understood sacrificially as an act of thanksgiving. In a simple but direct argument, Zwingli held that because Christ has ascended into heaven, he cannot be physically present in earthly elements like bread and wine. Rather, Christ is present in the hearts and minds of the faithful who gather in com-mon memory of the night in which he was betrayed. Since Christ is not physically present, the legitimizing authorization of the papacy is not necessary to affect the sacrament. The sacrament becomes effective in the faith of the participants.

Luther attacked at the same point but predictably, his argument was not onto-logical—a matter of being, as in both medieval Catholicism itself and Zwingli—but eschatological. The crucified and risen Christ who is even now reclaiming all things joins his people in the present through the external Word, whether that Word be preached or administered sacramentally. The sacrament of the Lord's Supper is therefore no sacrifice directed toward God; neither is it an act of pious remem-brance. Rather, it is God's act in Christ in his ongoing restoration of creation and creature. The physical nature of Christ's presence "in, with and under" the bread and wine is thus crucial. He comes down to earth, gathering the godless as his very own. His presence is assured by his promise and therefore stands independent of any theory or explanation attempting to ascertain it. At the same time Christ's prom-ise makes the sacrament independent of personal perception; he is there, whether apprehended in faith or unknown to unbelief. Neither a hierarchy of offices nor the piety of the pious but God's Word makes the sacrament.

Thus, as Luther argues it in Part II of the Smalcald Articles, the doctrine of justification by faith alone apart from works of the law is the theological source of his critique of the papacy. God's justifying work in Christ becomes a reality in the faithful through the Word preached and administered. In that light, the claims to define and control God's work in the restoration of all things can only appear as ultimate hubris or, as Luther argued it, enthusiasm. By the same token, wresting such claims to sovereignty from the papacy and then making the sacrament the confection of the piety of the pious accomplishes nothing. The Word makes the sacrament, nothing else.

Luther had another source ready to hand in this conflict. A long-standing tra-dition had linked individual popes with the office of the Antichrist; a linkage sug-gested by the very passage the papacy traditionally invoked to establish its claims, Matthew 16.[29] If Peter was in fact identified personally as the rock upon which Christ would build his church, the papal claim, he was also named in the verses immediately following as the tool of Satan. The Antichrist is just such a religious figure, eschatologically. He appears under the cover of religiosity to undermine the reality of faith. Overheated, overblown, harsh, and petulant as he could be, when Luther called the papacy the Antichrist, he was not simply indulging his hostilities. Rather, he was taking up an older tradition rendered particularly attractive by the apocalyptic of the time to expose an office that in the name of the faith itself had become tyrannical and destructive.

The crucial position of the papacy in late medieval life along with the centrality of the issue in the Lutheran reform also explains why the princes and theologians agreed that it had to be dealt with if there was going to be a council in the later 1530s. Given the course of polemics early in the reform and through the 1520s, the surprise is that the Augsburg Confession did not include anything more than a discussion of the power of the bishops, in Article XXVIII. Granting the benefit of the doubt, the omission may have been an ecumenical gesture; more likely, avoiding the issue had more to do with the delicate state of relations with Charles V. Melanchthon knew as well as anyone, with greater sensitivity, that attacking the papacy was no way to cultivate relations, even if the emperor himself had developed a bad habit in that regard.

Without diplomatic niceties for constraint and holding a transparently hostile invitation to the council, the politicians were convinced that the papacy demanded attention. Originally, the pastors and theologians at Smalcald were asked to provide a statement; they handed the request on to Melanchthon, who within a couple of days had prepared what became the *Treatise on the Power and Primacy of the Pope*. It was slated to serve as a supplement to the Augsburg Confession because the Confession had not treated the papacy directly. It was formally subscribed to by those present for that purpose. The decision of the politicians to refuse the invitation left the document without an immediate historical purpose. It has since been linked with the Smalcald Articles more by shared timing than by any other direct connection between them.

The Structure of the Argument in the Treatise

Taking up the request of the pastors and theologians, Melanchthon once again drew on a standard form for medieval polemics. He opened with a statement of the arguments advanced by the papacy, refuted them from Scripture, the historical tradition of the church, and by examination of the substance of the arguments themselves. This completed, he took up the claim that the pope has become the Antichrist, before finally exposing further what the Augsburg Confession and the Apology had argued concerning the positive use of ecclesiastical power.

Melanchthon summarized the objectionable papal claims in three: supremacy over other pastors and bishops, the assertion that spiritual authority brings with it the consequent right to use the political sword, and that believing these things is necessary to salvation. Examining the biblical evidence, he sorted through several passages to indicate that "neither Peter nor the other ministers should assume lordship or authority of the church," making the Word subservient to their office (*TPPP*, 11). The history of the church offers several illustrations of the fact that the Bishop of Rome was one among many others. Further, when the substance of the papal argument from Matthew 16:18-19 is examined, it is clear that the rock upon which Christ promises to build his church is neither Peter nor any other person but the word Peter confessed.

Given the tradition associated with the Antichrist and the polemical context, Melanchthon employed particular care with the Reformers' claim that the pope has filled the office. In fact, to start with, he asserted it more by indirection, beginning with a definition of the term, taken out of 2 Thessalonians 2:3, 4 and then listing four characteristics of the papacy which compellingly illustrate the definition. This much said, the indirection yields to a direct warning: Christians "ought rather to abandon and curse the pope and his minions as the realm of the Antichrist" (*TPPP*, 41). Abuses of papal authority, along with perceived idolatries, are then cited to justify the Reformers' rejection of the papacy.

In the final section (*TPPP*, 60–82), Melanchthon spelled out a definition of Christian ministry based on the priority of the Word. The Word defines the office: ministry exists for the sake of the proclaimed Word and the administered sacrament and therefore includes the authority to bind and release, that is, to deal with public sin as necessary by either absolving or withholding forgiveness. The priority of the Word obviates rank and degree among pastors; all who are called to preach the Word and administer the sacraments are effectively bishops. At the same time it entitles the church, collectively and individually, to call and ordain pastors who will preach the Word. Ministry is thus defined neither by hierarchical relations nor by the person of the preacher but by the act of handing over the gifts of Christ at pulpit, altar and in the straits of everyday life.

While the *Treatise on the Power and Primacy of the Pope* never did become a formal part of the Augustana and lost its original purpose, it gained confessional status through its attachment to the Smalcald Articles in print and the resulting use in the churches of the Lutheran reformation. This status was formally recognized when the authors of the Formula of Concord included it in the Book of Concord. Its value continues in its specific considerations of the office of ministry, a perennial issue.

Finalizing the Text of the Smalcald Articles for Publication

Luther reworked his document for publication in the summer of 1538. He added sections to the articles on the mass, purgatory, invocation of the saints, repentance, and confession and absolution.[30] He completed the document with a preface. In the preface he told readers that he had composed the articles to prepare for negotiations with the papal party, specifically to state where concessions might be possible and where "we definitely intended to persist and remain firm."[31] He held out little hope that the Roman Catholic opponents would negotiate in good faith, and so he "wanted to publicize these articles through the public press, in case (as I fully expect and hope) I should die before a council could take place," an indication that he did see this agenda for council as a doctrinal last will and testimony, his "testimony and confession," for he recognized how "shamelessly they have slandered us," as the followers of Luther increased in number, as was the case in the late 1530s. He confidently asserted that his side did not need a council, for "through God's grace our churches are now enlightened and supplied with the pure Word and right use of the sacraments, an understanding of the various walks of life, and true works."[32] For Luther, pure and undefiled religion consisted of listening to God's address to his human creatures and practicing the human life God created them to live.

Significant is his decision to include comments on the pressing issues of the secular world, of morality and public order, in the preface. The text of the Articles dealt with the reform of the church, but Luther had never separated the concerns of daily life from his agenda for proclaiming God's Word and will. He had set them alongside each other in 1520,[33] and in 1537 he repeated some of the same societal challenges or offenses: general quarreling and tensions among responsible political authorities, greed and usury, wantonness, extravagant dress, gluttony, gambling, conspicuous consumption, general refusal to obey orders, and extortion were among those he listed. Of particular interest is "conspicuous consumption" (in German, *Prangen*), an indication of Luther's belief that the lifestyle of Christians should be modest and moderate, not indulging in wasteful use of God's gifts for satisfying earthly desires or for trying to exalt oneself through display of wealth. Such profligacy and intemperance in the secular side of life reflected the ritualistic parading and display of clergy, who counted pomp and ceremony as more important than faithful delivery of God's Word.[34]

At the end of his extensive study of the Smalcald Articles, Werner Führer affirms that the Smalcald Articles—and by implication the *Treatise on the Power and Primacy of the Pope* that accompanied them—aimed at giving biblical witness to what form the church takes when the gospel of Jesus Christ determines that form. Therefore, Führer argues, it is not part of the theological legacy of the "Lutheran church" alone but of all Christians.[35] That was indeed Luther's goal.

Part III

The Formula of Concord

7

Theological Tensions among Luther's Followers before His Death

Every movement that has sought to change human society through the propagation of ideas has experienced a period of reflection, reformulation, and reorganization. The original vision of the founder or founders of such movements must be more rigorously or precisely defined, clarified, and refined. Such adaptations of the ideas of charismatic leaders are necessary for these ideas to find their place within the institutions of society, which they reshape and by which they are reshaped. These refinements are also necessary in order to convey the ideas to successive generations. Leaders whose insights offer new paradigms and whose charisma popularizes these insights must have followers who interpret, codify, and institutionalize their ideas for long-term use. At least four elements—the institutions within which the ideas are to function, competing traditions from the past, contemporary circumstances, and changing situations or contexts—all tug and tear at the ideas of such leaders as they test and transform them for future use and application. This historical process also took place within the Reformation that Martin Luther set in motion.

The Formula of Concord and Its Setting in the Late Reformation

In the case of the Lutheran Reformation, the reprocessing of his ideas for use in specific circumstances on the popular level began almost immediately.[1] It continued through Luther's own lifetime. But the precise definition of Luther's legacy had to be worked out within the peculiar circumstances in German ecclesiastical life in the second half of the sixteenth century, in the second generation of Luther's movement—in controversies over what he had indeed meant and taught.

These controversies would have had to develop in some form or other, no doubt. They did develop within the political context shaped by the attempt of the German imperial government under Emperor Charles V to eradicate the Lutheran confession of the faith by sword and fire. This political pressure brought to the surface disagreements among Luther's heirs that had only festered in discussions and disputes around the reformer during his lifetime. For a generation they hammered out their definition of his doctrine as they hammered at each other in the polemical style of seeking the truth common in the period. The results of their disputes over his legacy were codified in part in the Formula of Concord.

"Late Reformation" and "Confessionalization": Scholars Assess Process and Period

Since about 1980 Reformation scholarship has focused much attention upon the process that led from the dynamic period labeled "Reformation" to the more (though not completely) settled period traditionally called "Orthodoxy." Earlier scholars had placed the process within the latter period, designating it as "early Orthodoxy."[2] More accurate is its placement at the end of the Reformation, under the label "Late Reformation."[3] Recent studies have sharpened their focus through the use of the term "Confessionalization."[4]

This approach places dogmatic and ecclesiastical developments within a larger framework defined by Heinz Schilling as "a fundamental process in society, which ploughed up the public and private life of Europe in thoroughgoing fashion," by redefining society not only theologically and ecclesiastically but also in terms of political, social, economic, and cultural attitudes and structures.[5] The term "confessionalization" must be understood within the German academic and ecclesiastical context in which it arose. Most "confessionalization" scholars understand "confession" not in its primary sense of a theological position codified in a document written in the form of a "confession of faith" but rather in the derived meaning of "church body," something roughly equivalent to "denomination" (although differences between the sociological structures of the church in North America or the United Kingdom and those in traditionally Lutheran lands in central and northern Europe make this equivalence quite rough). They understand "confessionalization" as a process of mutual influence and integration of the institutional concerns of church and state. In Germany the fact that Luther's followers had defined themselves by their use of the Augsburg Confession led to their legalization as "the estates of the Augsburg Confession." As a result, Roman Catholic and later Reformed churches were designated *Konfessionen*, even though written confessions of faith played different roles in their church life than in that of Lutheran churches.[6]

It remains true, however, that one central and vital part of this larger cultural and political phenomenon now under study as "confessionalization" revolved around the definition of core values for culture and *politia* by theologians. For the Lutherans of Germany in the sixteenth century, this process did play itself out to a significant extent in theological debates that aimed at sharpening public consensus on what the biblical message was, as Luther had understood it. The process almost inevitably aimed at reaching a common written formulation that would legally and authoritatively define that message for the churches. Given the political situation of Germany in the third quarter of the sixteenth century and the habits of pursuing the truth inculcated in its academic institutions, that consensus could only be reached through fierce disputes and adversarial exchanges of ideas.

Polemic as Theological Method

The sharp polemic that shaped theological discussion in the sixteenth century seems repugnant to those who take part in the gentler conversations at the turn of the twenty-first. The strident tones of the earliest theological storms that swirled around Luther did not abate when the discussion shifted to the exchanges that his disciples conducted among themselves to define what he had really taught. In the 1520s this tone was set by a number of factors that were still present in one form or other in the 1550s.[7]

Alongside the presentation of the biblical truth, the Christian search for the proper expression of the message of Scripture has always been concerned to condemn false ideas that challenge the biblical truth, alongside the presentation of that truth. From the early church on, Christians in all ages have recognized that God's message of salvation in Christ is easily undercut and perverted by the stealthy challenges and subtle alternatives from ideologies that clothe themselves as angels of light.[8] The search for the best expression of the truth—called "pure teaching" by sixteenth-century Lutherans—was conducted at Wittenberg under the leadership of the biblical humanists, with Melanchthon at their head.[9] Their efforts to develop a rhetoric suitable for conveying the good news of the gospel also involved seeking clarity through condemnation of every form of false news. Luther had been trained by the medieval scholastic system that tested truth and the ability to communicate through adversarial challenges. The university disputations—the intellectual equivalent of the tournaments in which the knights proved their worthiness for their profession—provided students and professors alike the opportunity to show their argumentative prowess. That Luther and his foes traded blows in public discussions of theology seemed natural to those who had been educated in this system.[10]

Indeed, as E. Gordon Rupp noted, "Luther has never received sufficient credit for the nasty things he did not say."[11] By this Rupp meant that Luther's enemies, both in the Roman curia and in the leadership of the Roman party in Germany, attacked him with tongues as hot and as sharp as the fire and sword with which they threatened him as they condemned him to death for heresy. That Luther reacted in kind is not surprising, also because of the eschatological urgency and the sense of betrayal that framed his replies to their attacks. He believed that the world would soon end and that the political and theological aggression of his papal opponents was no more than a tool of Satan, who employed them to prevent the salvation of those who should hear his exposition of the biblical message of salvation. He further believed that precisely those who claimed that God had entrusted them with the protection of his message and the care of his people's souls—popes and bishops—were betraying God and his church through their perversion of the gospel and their persecution of those who taught it properly.[12]

Thus, when Luther's followers set out to define and refine his message in public forums in the three decades following his death, their recourse to polemic came naturally to them. Luther and Melanchthon had reintroduced the practice of academic examination through public disputation at the University of Wittenberg, and so their students had learned to think in the same adversarial fashion as their medieval predecessors. Luther, Melanchthon, and their Wittenberg associates had taught the next generation that in the history of the church condemnation of false teaching had provided necessary clarification for the exposition of the truth.

In addition, a significant group of their students developed a deep sense of outrage at what they perceived as betrayal of the truth by Melanchthon and some of their former student colleagues in Wittenberg. For the Preceptor and his closest disciples had cooperated with the duke of Saxony, Moritz, in the effort to work out a compromise with the papal party in Germany in the wake of the Smalcald War (1546–1547), and Moritz himself had betrayed the Wittenberg cause by siding with Emperor Charles V in that war. He had thrown his troops on the imperial side, thus sharing responsibility for the imprisonment of his own father-in-law, Philip of Hesse, and his own cousin, Elector John Frederick of Saxony. Many of those in the Wittenberg circle began to nurse a profound sense of betrayal because of these events. It expressed itself in the sharp tones of theological polemic. Those Wittenberg graduates who understood Luther's thought in a more radical way linked this political betrayal with their objections to the differing interpretations of Luther's theology which Melanchthon and his closest associates were developing. Melanchthon and those who remained loyal to him had acted in good faith to save the Evangelical church and Luther's university, and they reacted to criticism with increasing frustration and bitterness. A generation of debate ensued. One result of this debate was the process of negotiation that produced the Formula of Concord.[13]

Luther's Paradigm Shift and His Students' Effort to Define It

The figure of Luther hangs over the entire Reformation. His paradigm for theology—the manner in which he framed the critical questions of biblical teaching—shaped the thought of both his supporters and his opponents in the church in the early modern period with a power that permeated the teaching and life of both church and society. Many of his contemporaries regarded him as an eschatological prophet who would fulfill hopes for a radical break with the past and a new and brighter future. These hopes had fed and been fed by popular discontent and dreams for several generations, in Germany and beyond. During his lifetime princes and theologians looked to him for advice. Indeed, he functioned as a substitute for popes and councils as an adjudicator of problems and an interpreter of the meaning of Scripture. When he died, German Evangelicals lost a living voice of authority as well as a symbolic figure of incomparable significance.[14] At the conclusion of their work the authors of the Formula of Concord observed about the situation after Luther's death,

> The following things are common knowledge, obvious and no secret: What kind of very dangerous situations and troublesome disturbances arose in our beloved fatherland, the German nation, soon after the Christian death of that highly enlightened and pious man, Dr. Martin Luther; how, given the alarming conditions and destruction of well-ordered government, the

enemy of the human race endeavored to scatter his seeds of false doctrine and disunity, to excite harmful and aggravating divisions in churches and schools, and thereby to adulterate the pure teaching of God's Word, to break the bond of Christian love and unity, and in this way to prevent and impede noticeably the course of the holy gospel. (Preface to the Book of Concord 4)[15]

Luther's own understanding of the biblical message developed slowly over the first decade of his career in Wittenberg. Thereafter, he shaped and reshaped his proclamation of God's Word under a variety of influences, including that of his colleague and conversation partner Philip Melanchthon,[16] as he addressed the ever-changing situations of the church in the three decades following the publication of the Ninety-Five Theses. It is therefore little wonder that among his students differing interpretations of his understanding of Christian teaching developed. For they, too, were influenced by a variety of intellectual and ecclesiastical concerns and forces in addition to the words and personality of their Preceptor and prophet, Martin Luther. The radical change of paradigm he offered Western Christendom around the year 1520 centered in his theology of the cross and his distinction of law and gospel and of the two kinds of righteousness.[17] Hearers and readers inevitably mixed and massaged these foundational insights with a variety of ideas and instincts from their medieval background as they wrestled with the formulation of the message from Wittenberg that had excited their souls and aroused their minds. Inevitably, they debated and quarreled over the differing ways in which they were weaving the threads of his thought together for display and use in their own individual contexts.

The Role of the Law in the Christian Life

One of the earliest examples of this arose in the tension and conflict between Philip Melanchthon and Johann Agricola. About Melanchthon's age, Agricola represented the first generation of Luther's students. He arrived in Wittenberg in 1515, just as Luther's rejection of scholastic method and his affirmation of the unconditional grace of God, apart from the works of the law, were arousing interest and controversy at the university and beyond. Among the brightest and best of the Wittenberg students of the late 1510s, Agricola grasped Luther's rejection of salvation through human merit and the works of the law; he understood Luther's insistence on the gospel's unconditioned promise of salvation through Christ. However, he did not absorb the dynamic of Luther's distinction between law and gospel. Therefore, as he began to propagate his understanding of Luther's message in his own published works, before and after his departure from Wittenberg to become school rector in his native Eisleben, Agricola inevitably set his ideas on a course toward conflict with the brightest and best of Luther's colleagues, Melanchthon.[18]

In articles prepared to guide the visitors who were to inspect the parishes of electoral Saxony in 1527, Melanchthon took precautions against what he had observed as a crude, wild, dissipatious way of life in Saxon villages. He emphasized the need to preach the law to work repentance in the daily lives of those who were hearing Luther's message of freedom and forgiveness in the gospel. He knew there would be no end of offense against God and others if the law was not preached along with the teaching of faith. In his sharply critical response to Melanchthon's position Agricola elaborated on ideas he had already been formulating. He saw Melanchthon's emphasis on the law as a return to medieval piety under the burden of legal requirements for human performance. Agricola lodged his objections; the two exchanged arguments, in published catechisms and in biblical commentary, as well as in polemical exchanges over the Visitation Articles.[19] With Luther's aid and the arbitration of Elector John, a formal reconciliation was worked out between Agricola and the Wittenberg theologians at Torgau in November 1527.[20]

A decade later Agricola's abhorrence of the legalistic religion with which he had grown up was kindled again by another resident of Eisleben, Georg Witzel, an Evangelical pastor who had returned to the Roman Catholic fold. When Luther invited Agricola to come to Wittenberg to assist with the composition of the Smalcald Articles at the end of 1536, Agricola abandoned his call, moved his family, and hoped for a position in Wittenberg. Luther had always been fond of his former student and obtained a lectureship for him. But Agricola's denial of the functioning of the law in the Christian life created tensions between the two almost immediately. Luther felt himself betrayed by a disciple. He feared that Agricola's perversion of his teaching of the law and confusion of the law/gospel framework for the entire study of theology would only cause havoc in both theological discussion and parish life. In a series of disputations Luther tried to correct Agricola's theology.[21] Agricola conceded his misunderstanding, repented, but then immediately returned to his old teaching.

After Agricola had falsely claimed that he had obtained Luther's approval of the ideas he was publishing, Luther lost all patience and turned sharply against Agricola. Luther's colleagues had tried to dissuade him from permitting Agricola to come to the university, but now they tried to restrain the reformer's wrath. He published a critique of Agricola's theology as he understood it, *Against the Antinomians*.[22] Agricola filed countercharges against Luther before the elector. The prince placed the plaintiff under a kind of city arrest until the matter could be settled. Agricola fled to Berlin in 1540 and lived the rest of his life as a preacher at the court of Elector Joachim II.

Agricola was driven by a single-minded rejection of medieval works-righteousness. As bright as he had seemed to be, he did not understand the dynamic of Luther's proper distinction between law and gospel. Agricola taught that the law has no place in the life of the Christian, that is, it serves only to preserve civil order in the societal or political sphere of life. In Christ God had set aside his attempt to direct human lives through the threats and coercion of the law. God's only message for Christians is the gospel. Agricola did not deny that Christians also sin and need to repent. But he believed that the love of God in Christ moves them to recognize their sinfulness and thus leads them to repentance. For he saw in the gospel a glimpse of God's wrath sufficient to work contrition in faithful hearts.

Agricola emphasized that the transgression against the law was secondary to "transgression against the Son" (of God), catching Luther's emphasis on the first commandment but missing the larger context in Luther's use of the law, also in the Christian life. For Luther recognized that law and gospel cannot be defined simply by their superficial content—God's demands in the form of injunctions and God's love in sending Christ to the cross, for instance—but must also be defined by the impact which the Holy Spirit accomplishes through that content.[23] If God's love in Christ places a crushing burden of guilt upon a sinner, its message is functioning theologically as law. Agricola's failure to realize what was for Luther the very basis of the practice of theology and good pastoral care struck the Wittenberg colleagues as a theological and pastoral disaster. Luther and Agricola never reconciled. Agricola went on to play another mischievous game in the composition of the Augsburg Interim.

The Role of Contrition in Salvation

Questions of the relationship between human works and salvation led to another controversy among Luther's followers within a few years. Born in Austrian Habsburg domains, the child of Hussite parents, Conrad Cordatus, seven years Luther's senior, had recognized the truth in Luther's ideas as a young priest and had spent time in jail for spreading those ideas. After he became pastor in Niemegk, not far from Wittenberg, he took advantage of the proximity to attend lectures at the university. There the pastor of Niemegk took exception to the assertion of one of his instructors, Luther's and Melanchthon's young colleague and former student, Caspar Cruciger, that "contrition is a *sine qua non* [necessary part] of salvation." That sounded too much like the false teaching Cordatus had opposed at the cost of his freedom. Cruciger appealed to Melanchthon as the source of his view. The sharp exchanges between Cordatus and his instructors came to an end only when Luther intervened with theses for a disputation that affirmed that good works are a necessary part of Christian living but not "necessary for salvation."[24]

Disagreements between Friends

This topic of good works and their role in salvation was but one of the topics that troubled the relationship between Melanchthon and his friend and former colleague Nikolaus von Amsdorf. Luther had claimed in 1522 that he, Melanchthon, and Amsdorf only appeared to be the leaders of the Reformation; the Holy Spirit had actually been responsible for everything that had happened in Wittenberg during the previous four years, acting while the three of them had drunk beer together.[25] Amsdorf and Melanchthon had shared both the joy of Luther's cause and the troubles and frustrations of challenges to it. Left "in charge" in Wittenberg while Luther was "in exile" at the Wartburg, the two of them had shakily leaned on each other when the so-called Zwickau prophets visited Wittenberg and contended that they had special revelations which would supplement and improve on Luther's proclamation. At that time they had stood together, of one mind, but in the last decade of Luther's life his two companions had private disagreements on a number of topics. These differences foreshadowed many of the issues that would plague the entire Lutheran community in the years after Luther's death.

The two comrades came from different backgrounds, and their careers led them in different directions. Melanchthon came from a well-placed artisan family; as the son of a skilled armor smith of superb reputation, he had a strong appreciation for princes, who ordered armor. Amsdorf sprang from the lower nobility and at times exhibited the independence and contempt that that type can show toward a prince. Amsdorf's mind had been shaped by scholastic training, in the way of Duns Scotus, but Melanchthon's way of thinking much more reflected the principles of biblical humanism. Amsdorf had left his university position in Wittenberg to move to the city of Magdeburg in 1524; there he led and guided the introduction of the Reformation. He was a pastor, whose care of and concern for parishioners expressed itself in different ways than did the concerns of Professor Melanchthon, who had to concentrate his attention on making his ideas clear to students or to theologians from other camps.[26]

Despite his absence from Wittenberg, Amsdorf kept in contact with his friends there and closely followed developments at the university. He did not like Cruciger's ambiguous language regarding human action and salvation, for local Roman Catholic leaders had threatened him and his Evangelical colleagues with death for failing to teach that "good works are necessary for salvation." With the help of his school rector and former student in Wittenberg, Georg Major, he was hardly finished with that battle when from his own camp he felt the pointed edge of Cruciger's claim regarding the necessity of contrition for salvation in his back. He reacted somewhat vehemently in correspondence with Luther.[27]

Melanchthon's attempt to come to terms with Luther's use of the philosophical category of absolute necessity in describing the bondage of the human will and God's unconditional grace (for example, in his dispute with Erasmus, above all, in his *On Bound Choice* [*De servo arbitrio*])[28] also brought Melanchthon into quiet conflict with Amsdorf. Melanchthon wanted to avoid assigning responsibility for evil to God, and he wanted to take cognizance of human psychological reactions in mind and will to God's Word. Therefore, even though he had criticized Erasmus sharply and supported Luther in the dispute between these two in the mid 1520s,[29] in the second edition of his great textbook of doctrinal theology, his *Theological Topics* [*Loci communes theologici*] (1535) he had suggested that the difference between David, who was saved, and Saul, who was damned, lay in their differing reactions to the Word. Amsdorf ignored these aspects of Melanchthon's argument, apparently believing that they could fit within his own view of Luther's and Melanchthon's careful holding in tension both God's total responsibility for salvation and the human responsibility to which God holds his creatures in the performance of his will. But Melanchthon's view of contingency, Amsdorf feared, threatened the heart of Luther's message. In his 1535 *Loci communes*, Melanchthon insisted on mitigating that tension between divine and human responsibility with the contention that God leaves certain things open to human determination, that is, contingent on human decision. Amsdorf could forego a public attack on his former comrade in Wittenberg, but he had to criticize his position. He did so in a critique of Philip's rejection of Luther's concept of absolute necessity. In defending Luther's understanding of the sovereignty of God and the unconditional nature of his promise, Amsdorf argued that God has predestined those whom he wants to save without condition from before the creation of the world; he also argued that God has predestined the damned to their damnation.[30]

Not only differing focuses on Luther's teaching regarding grace and works brought the two former colleagues into conflict. They had differing views of how leaders of the church, as well as the church itself, ought to relate to political figures and secular government. Melanchthon tried to accommodate the desire of his friend Landgrave Philip of Hesse, one of the strongest supporters of Luther's cause among the German princes, for a solution to marital problems through approval of his bigamy. Luther went along, but Amsdorf did not. His contempt for the landgrave can be felt in his memorandum on the subject, in which he ironically suggested that if Philip needed a second wife, his first wife must need the companionship of a young courtier just as badly.[31]

Melanchthon and Amsdorf had differing perceptions of how best the Lutheran churches might relate to the medieval papacy. Melanchthon worked hard at reconciliation, particularly at the imperial diet at Regensburg in 1541, at which Philip led an Evangelical delegation in negotiations with the papal party. Amsdorf rejected the effort as hopeless, foolhardy, and dangerous.[32]

The two also barely avoided a public confrontation less than two years before Luther's death when Melanchthon became involved with the reformer of Strasbourg, Martin Bucer, in composing a constitution for the reform of the archdiocese of Cologne, under the leadership of its archbishop, Hermann von Wied. Imperial troops ended that effort in any case (1546), but in 1544 Bucer and Melanchthon had cooperated in writing a plan for teaching and organization of church life for Cologne. Amsdorf believed that their document agreed with Luther's teaching, but he objected to certain unclear elements in its presentation of biblical doctrine. He believed that a program for reformation should appeal clearly to Luther's ideas and his personal authority; the Cologne constitution did not. It taught that sinning against conscience could forfeit grace, an idea Amsdorf held as synergistic. The document did not sufficiently repudiate the papacy and others who were propagating error. Above all, Amsdorf found its doctrine of the Lord's Supper ambiguous. Bucer had played a mediating role in the earlier disputes over the true presence of Christ's body and blood in the sacrament between Luther and Zwingli, the Wittenbergers and the Swiss. The climax of his efforts to bridge the differences between the two came with his journey to Wittenberg in 1536 and the Wittenberg Concord, which his group of south German theologians and the Wittenbergers had formulated in their meeting. The Concord left itself open to interpretation in the critical question of the reception of the body and blood by those who receive it without faith, and Amsdorf had criticized Bucer sharply in print at that time. In 1544 he found that Melanchthon had been drawn into a formulation of sacramental teaching that obscured the biblical definition of how God gives himself to believers in the Lord's Supper. He privately put pressure on Luther to repudiate the formulation of Bucer and Melanchthon in the Cologne constitution, but he did not present his views publicly.[33] He and Melanchthon remained in friendly correspondence in spite of their theological differences.[34]

Nonetheless, Amsdorf and Melanchthon represent different poles of interpretation and understanding in the process of digesting Luther's many-faceted challenge to the theological paradigm of Western Christendom. Inevitably, sparks had to fly between such poles. The tensions between Amsdorf and Melanchthon foreshadowed the very public controversies that broke out after Luther's death. Coincident with the reformer's death Charles V was able to set in motion his plans to eradicate the Lutheran churches and their theological point of view. This created the arena in which this inevitable confrontation actually took place.

8

The "Culture of Controversy"

The Smalcald War, the "Interims," and the Adiaphoristic Controversy

On February 18, 1546, Martin Luther died, a quarter century after Emperor Charles V had declared him an outlaw in the Edict of Worms. That decree had placed the very limited power of his imperial throne behind the Roman church's effort to eradicate Luther's followers and execute him for heresy. The emperor, scion of the Habsburg line, had inherited the kingdoms of Aragon and of Leon and Castile from his maternal grandparents, Ferdinand and Isabella. His father, Philip, had died before his own father, the German emperor Maximilian of Austria. Philip bequeathed to his eldest son, Charles, not only the lands German lands of Maximilian but also the territories of his grandmother, Mary of Burgundy, which included one of the industrial heartlands of medieval Europe, the Netherlands.

Charles V and the Threat of Luther's Reformation

Charles ruled more land and people than any European ruler between Charlemagne and Napoleon, and he commanded not inconsiderable financial resources. The emperor had grown up at the Burgundian court in the Netherlands and had been influenced by the ideals of Erasmian biblical humanism. He was concerned about abuses in the church and desired the kind of institutional and moral reform that Erasmus and his circle had promoted. He had no conception whatsoever of what Luther's call for reform of the central teachings of the church really meant. He knew only that he could not abide such challenges as Luther's to public authority. If the pope's authority could be challenged and frustrated, so could that of the emperor.

Charles treasured his own authority. He lived at a time in which all Western European rulers were trying to consolidate, centralize, rationalize, and aggrandize their power. Martin Luther threatened those plans for Germany, and not only through his own challenge to the ecclesiastical paradigm of the age. The German princes, as intent as Charles on strengthening their own territorial governments, were combating the emperor's plans for a more powerful centralized imperial administration. Some attempted to do so also by increasing their control over the churches of their lands through reform according to Luther's model.

The emperor's desire to wipe the name of Luther from the face of the earth was frustrated, however, by a constellation of factors. Though powerful in the lands that belonged directly to his family, he possessed relatively little power as German emperor. The widespread nature of his empires, which extended over Spain into the New World as well as into Spanish holdings in Italy, diluted his attention and his power. A stubborn Spanish nobility fought the centralizing tendency of Charles' new royal court in the years immediately following the Diet of Worms. Charles won that battle and established a strong "early modern" monarchy for his newly united Iberian lands. But that victory distracted him from dealing decisively with his problems in Germany, represented by Luther's call for reform. The Habsburg family's long-standing rivalry with the royal Valois family of France kept Charles' diplomats and armies busy for much of the three decades following Worms, as did tensions with the popes, whom he acknowledged as heads of the church but also wanted to keep submissive to his own policies. The threat of Turkish armies, which actually laid siege to the chief city in his Austrian domains, Vienna, in 1529, and continued skirmishes with pirates in the Mediterranean Sea also frustrated his desire to end schism in his German lands.

The Smalcald War and the Attempt to Eradicate the Lutherans

Twenty-five years after the Lutheran confession of the faith had been outlawed with the Edict of Worms, the emperor finally had sufficient resources and an absence of distracting commitments elsewhere in his far-flung empire to move against the Lutherans. His decision had nothing to do with Luther's death. His government negotiated with the papal curia on how to proceed against the German heretics, but the emperor did not make war directly against the Evangelical faith. Instead, he singled out the two leading princes in the Protestant league of Smalcald, Elector John Frederick of Saxony and Landgrave Philip of Hesse, and charged them with a series of offenses in order to win some of their Lutheran peers for the war against them.

He had reason enough to send troops against them. Philip was guilty of bigamy, specifically forbidden in Charles' newly decreed legal code of 1532. John Frederick had used illegal force against the clerical foundation at Würzen and the episcopal chapter in Naumburg to extend the influence of the Reformation in those areas adjacent to or within his domains. Both had broken imperial law by going to war against the duke of Braunschweig-Wolfenbüttel, Heinrich, whose own military forces had burned the Evangelical city of Einbeck in an effort to win it back to the Roman Catholic fold. They had jailed Heinrich, occupied his lands, and promoted popular reform there. Neither prince had shown the proper enthusiasm or support for the emperor's crusade against the Turk.

With his brother Ferdinand, Charles successfully courted Philip's son-in-law and John Frederick's cousin, Duke Moritz, of the Albertine branch of the Saxon ducal family, as well as a number of other younger Evangelical princes. Moritz was a happy warrior who had fought as a part of the Habsburg forces in the war against the Turk and had served as the emperor's mediator between Heinrich of Braunschweig-Wolfenbüttel and his cousin and father-in-law. In June 1546 Moritz signed a treaty of support with the Habsburg brothers. He pressed for written guarantees that he would not have to abandon his Lutheran beliefs after the war, but he received only oral promises that he was pledging himself neither to fight against nor to renounce his own Lutheran faith.[1]

With support from Pope Paul III and from Moritz, and with pledges of neutrality from most other German princes, Charles outlawed John Frederick and Philip on July 20. They took their armies south, with support from some Evangelical cities, but frittered away their early strategic advantage against Charles's and Ferdinand's forces, composed of troops from their Iberian and Italian as well as their German domains. Moritz's occupation of electoral Saxony in November and early December brought John Frederick back to his lands, and he cleared his cousin's forces from his territory with dispatch, by Christmas. He besieged Moritz's troops in Leipzig during the winter. In the spring Charles led his Spanish contingents into Saxony. A country urchin showed the emperor's army a ford on the Elbe River; they pursued John Frederick's and Philip's cohorts and caught them at Mühlberg on April 24, 1547.

At the end of the battle the two Lutheran leaders were led from the field in chains. Charles rewarded Moritz for his support with John Frederick's title and position as elector of Saxony and much of his territory. Although the emperor did not carry out his threat to execute John Frederick and Philip, he kept them in prison for seven and five years respectively. Charles seemed supreme in his German lands, and it was clear that he was set to break the back of Lutheran reform.

Charles was not as supreme as he seemed. His alliance with the pope collapsed in early 1547. Tensions broke out between Charles and his brother Ferdinand, who feared he would be excluded from the succession to the imperial throne which had been granted him in 1532 with the crown of the "kingdom of the Romans," the title for the heir apparent in the Empire. Roman Catholic and Evangelical princes in Germany saw the specter of imperial control bounding over the horizon and began to work together to put brakes on the emperor's steamroller. Nonetheless, the emperor attempted to suppress the Lutheran confession of the faith through the implementation of his own plan for reform. It was composed at the imperial diet in Augsburg in early 1548 and embodied in a document popularly called "the Augsburg Interim."

This policy statement drove his Evangelical allies into opposition. With Moritz in their company by late 1551, they leagued with the Habsburg's traditional enemy, the Valois family, specifically King Henry II, and defeated the imperial forces in 1552. Ferdinand negotiated a peace with the Lutheran forces that provided them with provisional freedom to practice their confession of the faith legally, in the Truce of Passau. Negotiations continued, even after Moritz fell on the field of battle against one of his Evangelical comrades from the Smalcald War, Margrave Albert Alcibiades of Brandenburg-Kulmbach, in July 1553, at age thirty-two. Moritz's brother August assumed the electoral title and the mantle of leadership among the estates of the Augsburg Confession.

The Religious Peace of Augsburg

An imperial diet began in Augsburg in February 1555. Negotiations over the settle-ment of the religious question in Germany lasted six months. Charles, supported by papal legates and some German bishops, steadfastly opposed any compromise with the Lutherans. The emperor's brother and designated successor, Ferdinand, usually with the support of a majority of ecclesiastical princes (bishops and abbots) and Bavaria—the most powerful of the Roman Catholic principalities—sought accommodation with the Protestant estates. Under the leadership of August of Saxony, who wanted peace and security for his own lands, the Evangelical princes sought to retain good relationships with the Habsburgs and the status quo. In his willingness to forego spreading the Reformation in return for the safety of his own position, August was supported by the other two secular electors, the conservative Joachim II of Brandenburg and Frederick II of the Palatinate, who had not openly declared his lands reformed although he had permitted Evangelical preaching for some time. Idealists such as Duke Christoph of Württemberg, Philip of Hesse, John Frederick's sons in ducal Saxony, and others promoted a more favorable situation for the Lutheran churches.

The Religious Peace that the negotiations produced guaranteed the adherents of the Augsburg Confession legal status, inferior to that of Roman Catholics, but secure from persecution and prosecution. By establishing the right of princes to reform the church and the right of subjects to emigrate because of their faith, the Peace established the practice later summarized with the phrase *cuius regio, eius religio* ("whose region, his religion"). Lutherans were permitted to retain lands that had belonged to the church before 1552. Any ecclesiastical princes (bishops and abbots) who wanted to change from allegiance to the pope to the Evangelical faith would have to forfeit their lands.

Confessio Augustana Variata

The definition of legality for Evangelical princes and cities now rested upon the understanding and interpretation of the text of the Augsburg Confession. Since 1533 an altered version of the German Confession had been in general use among the Evangelicals, and in 1540 Melanchthon prepared an updated, more extensive Latin text that was accepted by all in Wittenberg as the valid text of their public statement of belief.[2] None regarded his revisions as a betrayal of his original purpose or of Luther's teaching. All recognized that the Evangelical governments had the right, and Melanchthon, as their chief diplomat, the obligation, to sharpen the argu-ment of their "mission statement" for the dialogues with Roman Catholics that the imperial government was mandating at the end of the 1530s. All in the Wittenberg circle understood the "Augsburg Confession" as an on-going process of confessing God's teaching; it had not attained formal status as a secondary authority in 1540 (although the process of establishing it as such had begun in some lands). In 1530 the Evangelical governments had claimed it as their own. By 1540 Melanchthon's own prince, John Frederick the Elder, wanted his formal religious policy statement updated. Melanchthon did so especially with an extensive expansion on the doctrine of justification. He had no idea that his original text was sacred. He believed it was a tool that the Evangelical estates had to use in public negotiations with the Roman Catholic party. At the time the revised text was first published, only John Eck, Roman Catholic representative at the Colloquy of Regensburg in 1541, challenged the Lutherans regarding the official text of their Confession.

But in 1561 Elector Frederick III of the Palatinate used the tenth article of the altered Latin Confession to justify his introducing Calvinist views of the Lord's Supper into his lands.[3] This political use of the revised version after 1561 made the issue of its proper text highly significant, and those who adhered to Luther's understanding of the true presence of Christ's body and blood rejected the altered versions of the Confession in order to close the door to the Calvinist interpretation. Before that interpretation was offered by the government of the Palatinate, all in the Wittenberg circle appeared to understand the language of the revised tenth article in Luther's understanding of the critical expression which his colleague Philip had used. Melanchthon had altered the text's confession regarding the Lord's Supper[4]

From	To
Our churches teach that the body and blood of Christ are truly present and are distributed to those who eat in the Supper of the Lord. They disapprove of those who teach otherwise.	On the Lord's Supper they teach that with the bread and wine the body and blood of Christ are truly exhibited[5] to those who eat in the Lord's Supper.

But Frederick III's claim to adhere to the text with a different teaching on Christ's presence in the Supper demanded new precision, with implications for the text of the Augsburg Confession. By 1577 its "unaltered" text, that of the first printing of 1531, became standard for Lutherans, a shibboleth in their defense of their teaching.

The Augsburg Interim

Before these political developments led to the legalization of the Lutheran confession of the faith, however, the adherents of the Augsburg Confession had experienced eight very difficult years, in which the existence of the Lutheran church was on the line. After defeating the armies of John Frederick and Philip, Charles proceeded to implement his plans for consolidating his control of German religious life by returning all his subjects to the Roman obedience. He convened an imperial diet in September 1547, once again in Augsburg. He appointed a commission under the archbishop of Mainz to draw up a solution to the religious problem of his German lands that would establish religious policy in the Empire until the Council of Trent had completed work on the reform of the Western church. Then all Germans would be expected to submit to the council and pope. The archbishop named a committee, which included two Spanish theologians, Ferdinand's court preacher, two leading Erasmian humanists—the suffragan bishop of Mainz, Michael Helding, and the bishop of Naumburg-Zeitz, Julius Pflug—as well as one Evangelical representative. He was Johann Agricola, Luther's renegade student, who since 1540 had been assisting Elector Joachim II of Brandenburg implement a very conservative version of Luther's reformation in his lands. On the basis of a proposal composed by another reform-minded Erasmian Roman Catholic, Johann Gropper, the group hammered out its interim solution for German religious life, which was popularly called "the Augsburg Interim."[6]

The Augsburg Interim reflected the vision of the church that Helding, Pflug, Gropper, and others from Erasmian circles had sought to implement for a generation. It remained faithful to the theology of medieval Catholicism, repudiating superstitious folk belief (against which the reformers often directed their criticism) while embracing the positions of scholastic theologians whose views the reformers had also rejected. This school of thought misunderstood and rejected the basis of Luther's teaching on justification, the distinction between two kinds of righteousness, and therefore affirmed that justification of sinners takes place through faith formed by love, not by faith alone.

The Interim firmly adhered to the authority of the pope and of the bishops; the interpretation of Scripture was to lie only in the hands of the hierarchy. Although the authors of the Interim affirmed that the performance of the mass in itself does not merit forgiveness of sins, they emphasized its sacrificial nature, and they insisted on explaining the presence of Christ's body and blood in the Lord's Supper with the theory of transubstantiation. The imperial settlement insisted on the use of the traditional seven sacraments, all of which were said to convey sacramental grace. It reaffirmed a host of medieval practices in ceremony, festivals, sacramentals, and similar ritual practices. Two concessions were granted to the Evangelical churches: the right to commune the laity in both kinds and the right to permit priests to marry (reforms that might well have been introduced by reform-minded adherents of the papacy in the sixteenth century had they not become symbols of the Protestant Reformation).

Scholars have debated whether Emperor Charles intended to promulgate the Augsburg Interim as a program for religious life throughout his German lands or to prescribe it only as a temporary solution for the Lutheran heresy in Evangelical lands. Whatever his intentions, in fact it was imposed only in those places where the imperial will could be implemented, either by military occupation or by political coercion. No Roman Catholic government introduced its measures. One month after its formal promulgation, on May 15, 1548, Charles also published a *Formula for Reformation*, which prescribed reform of congregational and monastic life.

The presence or threat of Spanish troops caused the imposition of the Interim or some compromise with it in southern Evangelical German cities such as Constance, Strasbourg, Nuremberg, Regensburg, in the dukedom of Württemberg,[7] and in a few other territories. Duke Erich of Braunschweig-Calenberg made the Interim law in his lands, against the fierce opposition of his mother, Elizabeth. Hundreds of pastors were sent into exile. Most of their pulpits stood empty, for the Roman Catholic leadership had not prepared personnel to implement a Counter-Reformation. Increasing disregard for the Interim in the areas in which it had been initially forced upon the population plagued imperial officials after 1550. The governments of the Palatinate, Brandenburg, and Hesse, for example, made efforts to comply with the emperor's religious program, but enforcement was occasional and irregular.[8]

However, although some territorial and municipal governments attempted compromise with imperial policies, in several north German lands and cities the Interim was not accepted.[9] Open defiance flared. In fact, Philip Melanchthon was the first to compose a memorandum on the Augsburg solution for his new sovereign. (As one of the prizes Moritz received for his support of the Habsburg cause, the University of Wittenberg stood now within his domains, and its theologians had become his ecclesiastical advisors.[10]) Melanchthon urged rejection of the Interim, noting the many points at which it deviated from biblical truth, as understood by the Wittenberg theology which he and Luther had been teaching for three decades.[11] This memorandum appeared in print, was "leaked" to printers in Magdeburg and elsewhere, and also was published as part of the internal maneuvering against Agricola within the Brandenburg court in Berlin.

Melanchthon's prince was reluctant to break with the emperor who had just awarded him the electorate and extensive new territories. Other north German rulers had no such reservations. The nobility of ducal Saxony supported John Frederick's sons in their refusal to implement it.[12] The municipal governments of Hamburg, Magdeburg, and other Lutheran urban centers rejected it.[13] The negative reactions of the Lutheran theologians appeared in print quickly. Nikolaus von Amsdorf tore apart the theology of the Interim article by article. From southern Germany Johannes Brenz and Andreas Osiander issued sharp critiques, even as they went into hiding or exile respectively. Caspar Aquila, who had lent Johann Agricola some moral support in his quarrels with Luther and Melanchthon, chastised the Brandenburg court preacher caustically and repudiated the teaching of the Interim with specific theological arguments. Erasmus Alber applied his literary skills to the public criticism of the Interim's program.[14]

But Amsdorf, Aquila, and Alber could criticize more freely because they had become exiles,[15] reluctantly but more or less willingly, because of the imperial victory. Melanchthon had decided to make every effort to preserve the university to which he had dedicated his career, and so he was trying to serve his new prince. Despite his sharp rejection of the Augsburg Interim, the professor was caught in a difficult situation, in a web of intrigue.

The Leipzig "Proposal"—Also Known as the "Leipzig Interim"
Melanchthon's new prince, Elector Moritz, was in a difficult situation. The Habsburg brothers could not remember that they had promised Moritz that he would not have to abandon his Lutheran confession of the faith. They insisted that electoral Saxony

implement the Augsburg Interim. Whatever Moritz's personal inclinations might have been, the nobility and towns of his lands made clear their opposition to any deviation from the teaching and practice to which they had pledged themselves as Luther's followers. In this corner between rock and hard place the new elector turned to both secular and ecclesiastical advisors to find a way out. In the months between the promulgation of the Augsburg Interim in April 1548 and the diet of his estates at Christmas Moritz had them forge a compromise settlement which would appear as compliance with the new imperial law of religion but would at the same time preserve the heart of the Evangelical reform in the preaching and practice of his lands.

Melanchthon was willing to work on this compromise. His astrological reckonings suggested that Charles V was not long for this world, and the preceptor was willing to buy time with negotiations on a compromise. He believed that some concessions could be made in nonessential matters to preserve the security of Saxony: better to yield a little in the life of the church than to let Spanish occupation forces invade and drive all Evangelical pastors from their pulpits, as had happened in the South. For he was convinced that Luther's principle of Christian liberty permitted yielding in regard to "adiaphora," neutral practices neither commanded nor forbidden by God, for the sake of weaker fellow believers and for the sake of peace in the church. In his treatment of ceremonies and usages in article fifteen of the Augsburg Confession, he had set down the principle of openness to a variety of approaches to those aspects of the life of the church,[16] and his paraphrases of the Confession for the French king, Francis I, in 1534, and for the English king, Henry VIII, in 1536 demonstrated his willingness to allow variations in the ritual of the church.[17]

In fact, Melanchthon and his colleagues at Wittenberg, together with other leading Saxon churchmen such as Johann Pfeffinger (superintendent of the churches in Leipzig and since 1541 theological advisor for Moritz and for his father Heinrich before him) withstood severe pressure from some of Moritz's secular counselors. They sought the theologians' support for more compromises. In a series of meetings during the summer and fall of 1548, with occasional advice from the new bishop of Naumburg-Zeitz, Julius Pflug, Moritz's government formulated a new religious policy and prepared it as a "proposal" for the territorial diet that met in the last week of December 1548. Though the entire text of this document was never officially published, its contents became known through printed excerpts and through rumor and report. Many former students of Melanchthon found it an appalling betrayal of God, Luther, and their Praeceptor's own integrity. They labeled the settlement "the Leipzig Interim." They found its doctrinal content inadequate, confusing, and at points heretical. Moreover, they were convinced that its compromises in various areas of church life were dishonest and could only confuse the common people.[18]

The Leipzig "Proposal" set forth a doctrine of justification through faith (although it omitted the Lutheran "alone") on the basis of God's grace and mercy, but this doctrine was ambiguously stated according to its critics. Good works—the virtues of faith, love, and hope—were labeled "necessary for salvation." Avoiding the term "sacrament," the document treated confirmation, penance, marriage, ordination, and extreme unction in connection with baptism and the Lord's Supper, permitting the inference that all seven of the medieval sacraments were accepted as such.[19]

In the realm of the ceremonial life of the church, the Latin rite was restored, all but eliminating German from the liturgy. The ceremonial of the old worship—the use of bells, lamps, and vestments—was largely revived, and the canonical hours as well as memorial masses for the dead were reestablished. Certain Marian festivals and Corpus Christi celebrations were reinstituted, along with compulsory fasting on Fridays and Saturdays (for reasons of public health, it was claimed). Although patronage of local churches was to remain with the nobility or municipal governments, the Roman bishops were to ordain all pastors.

The Reactions to the Leipzig Proposal

Some scholars have blurred the distinctions between the Augsburg Interim and the so-called Leipzig "Interim," but contemporaries did not. The two were seen as quite different documents, and those who supported the Leipzig Proposal all rejected the Augsburg Interim. Their opponents also differentiated the "Interimists" who supported the Augsburg Interim from the "Adiaphorists" who supported the Leipzig Proposal.[20] To be sure, the "Leipzig Proposal" also fostered a climate of controversy within the Wittenberg circle. From the exchanges over its content, and especially its purpose and method of approaching the critical situation of the time, bitterness and rancor grew on both sides. One dispute led to another, as those within the Wittenberg circle waged civil war in the effort to define what the Wittenberg Reformation meant.[21] In part, the liturgical regulations of the Leipzig Proposal represented little innovation for some areas in the territory of Meissen, the heartland of Moritz's domains, where the Reformation instituted by his father Heinrich hardly a decade earlier had been quite conservative in ecclesiastical practice. In the areas Moritz had received as war booty from John Frederick, however, the new agenda published on the basis of the Leipzig Proposal represented significant changes in church usage and church life. In fact, it was only selectively enforced. In Torgau its introduction met with stiff opposition. The elderly Gabriel Zwilling, one of Luther's first students, who had participated in the tumult surrounding the abolition of the mass in Wittenberg in 1521, lost his pastorate for his refusal to readjust his practice according to the new order. It reminded him too much of that against which he had battled thirty years earlier.

Reactions came not only from within Moritz's realm.[22] Melanchthon had taught many, and his students revered and respected him. Many of them found his attempt to save the Evangelical church through concessions much worse than ill-advised. They were sorely disappointed and felt betrayed by their Preceptor. They knew that he had stood fast against papal tyranny and false teaching in Augsburg in 1530; they had expected the same from him in 1548. His old friend Amsdorf could not keep his criticism private any longer. Fleeing from his position as first (and only) Evangelical bishop of Naumburg-Zeitz—and replaced by the papalist Julius Pflug—he had returned to Magdeburg where he had served the cause of the Reformation for eighteen years before Luther consecrated him as bishop of Naumburg in 1542. There he rallied the municipal government and assembled a group of younger theologians around him for the cause of preserving the gospel according to Luther, in the rather radical way in which he understood it.[23]

Among those who arrived in the city during the course of the months following the promulgation of the Augsburg Interim were two close friends, Matthias Flacius Illyricus[24] and Nikolaus Gallus. Both of them had studied under Luther and Melanchthon at the beginning of the decade. Charles's occupation forces had imposed the Augsburg Interim on the city of Regensburg, where Gallus had served as superintendent for several years. On the lam from Charles's troops, Gallus assumed formal leadership of the church in Magdeburg, as pastor of Saint Ulrich's congregation and thus, in practice, ecclesiastical superintendent. His friend, Flacius, came to Magdeburg from Wittenberg, where he gave up a position as Hebrew instructor because the apostasy of his theological hero and father, Melanchthon, had so deeply shaken his faith in the man from whom he had gained so much.

Born into a Croatian family of an Italian mother in the hinterlands of Trieste, Flacius absorbed influences from his older relative, Baldo Lupetino, who was executed for adherence to the Lutheran heresy by the inquisition in Venice. Flacius came to Germany in search of consolation and certainty for his troubled soul. After a brief sojourn in Basel and some time with the new Lutheran theological faculty in Tübingen, he came to Wittenberg, where Luther set his heart at rest. Arguably the most intelligent among all the students who had learned their theology from Luther and Melanchthon, he quickly won a post as Hebrew instructor at the university. The young Croatian had begun to publish on exegetical issues before his world fell apart in 1549. At that time it was becoming clear that, from his perspective, his Preceptor was acting in bad faith and was willing to surrender the gospel that had revived Flacius's spiritual life. Although he appears in the story of the controversies that led to the Formula of Concord as a stubborn, unyielding defender of the truth, he was also an intellect of great stature whose personal experiences with Luther deeply shaped his life and his interpretation of the Wittenberg legacy.[25] He cast his shadow across biblical hermeneutics for more than two centuries with the pioneering Protestant effort in that realm, his *Key to the Sacred Scriptures*,[26] and although he did not assist his colleagues in the actual writing of the first Protestant church history, the *Magdeburg Centuries*, he played a key role in planning and researching the project.[27]

Flacius, Gallus, and others supported Amsdorf in his critique of the Leipzig Proposal and amplified it. Private admonitions in correspondence soon gave way to printed rejoinders. Two pastors in Hamburg, Joachim Westphal and Johannes Aepinus, added their sharply critical analysis, along with that of their ministerium, to the public discussion of the new electoral Saxon religious policy.[28] This opposition rested on a number of concerns. Amsdorf, for instance, sadly concluded that his comrades in Wittenberg had fallen into the company of the Antichrist, as he reacted against their angry repudiation of the admonition to faithfulness which he and others had privately conveyed to them. Amsdorf regarded the Leipzig Proposal's failure to state specifically that salvation comes through faith *alone* as a surrender of the gospel to the papal party and medieval works-righteousness. He rejected the submission to papal bishops, exhibited in the policy of seeking ordination only from them, as a fatal concession. He found the reintroduction of so much of the medieval liturgical practice to be nothing more than the restoration of the blasphemous mass of sacrifice for the sins of the participants. He repeated the long-standing Evangelical judgment that compulsory fasting is the devil's doctrine (1 Tim. 4:1-3), and he believed that reinstating vestments that had been laid aside in order to demonstrate that the Reformation had rejected the old order could only lead lay people to believe that the Reformation had been a mistake.

Precisely this reinstating of long-discarded vestments elicited from Gallus and Flacius a stinging rebuke.[29] Vestments are indeed adiaphora, they observed: it is a neutral matter whether the pastor wears an academic robe or surplice or chasuble. The effect of such vestments on the congregation is not, however, a neutral matter, Flacius and Gallus argued. They formulated the principle that nothing remains neutral in a situation in which the clear confession of the faith is at stake.

Melanchthon could not understand. He believed that he had clearly separated liturgical usages and other matters of mere practice from doctrine. He suspected that his students were turning on him in bad faith. They in turn could not understand how he could be ignorant of the fact that liturgical expressions of the faith and other matters of practice were in reality inseparable from the teaching with which they were associated. Lay people were insightful enough to sense that, even if they could not always articulate such feelings. Johann Pfeffinger understood what Flacius and Gallus were saying and accused them of letting the common people become judge over the exercise of church leadership, which belonged to the clergy.

The controversy did not end when the official reasons for it ceased to exist. The Augsburg Interim became moribund with the Truce of Passau in 1552 and truly a dead letter in 1555 with the Religious Peace of Augsburg. The two sides continued to trade salvoes over adiaphora, however, for several reasons.[30] There was no one person and no way to end the dispute. As long as Luther lived, he had served as the secondary authority that, as a replacement for pope and council in the medieval church, adjudicated questions over the interpretation of Scripture in the life of the church. When Luther died, his logical successor, Melanchthon, fell almost immediately into an impossible situation, as the military outcome of the Smalcald War thrust him into the hands of the "Judas of Meissen," Duke Moritz. The Preceptor's concern to save his university, which now belonged to the duke, and his belief that God had given him Moritz as his temporal overlord, had compelled him to become a fellow traveler of this prince, whom many now viewed as a traitor to the Evangelical cause. Melanchthon's attempts to save Saxon Lutheranism from imperial eradication through the compromises of the Leipzig Proposal branded him a double betrayer, in the theological sphere as well as in the political. Melanchthon had lost the right to serve as leader and authority for Lutherans in the eyes of Flacius and his company. No one, in fact, commanded such respect that he could speak authoritatively to resolve the disputes among the Lutherans.

Furthermore, personal recriminations of the controversies had made reconciliation difficult. Suspicions reigned on both sides. For Flacius and his comrades, the issue of adiaphora was inseparably linked to their sense of betrayal: they never got over being bitterly indignant and resentful that (from their perspective) Melanchthon and his colleagues in Wittenberg had been prepared to betray the gospel and compromise away their Lutheran heritage. On the other side, Melanchthon became increasingly embittered by what he saw as bad faith and purposeful misunderstanding of his efforts to save the church and Lutheran teaching. He had taken the most prudent course and had indeed staved off the persecution of the Saxon church. For him that had been the paramount issue which drove the efforts around the "Leipzig Interim."

The concern of those in Magdeburg and Hamburg over adiaphora was grounded in their commitment to good pastoral care and to the truth of the biblical message; for the future of the church the principles of good pastoral care and proper confession of the truth had to be clearly understood and affirmed. For them, the proper conduct of the ministers of the Word when the faith is under threat of official persecution was what was most important; for them, it was an issue of the relationship of church and state. They also viewed it as a liturgical issue and a doctrinal issue. The Interims pointedly posed a critical question for the Lutherans: what did Luther's concept of Christian freedom mean for the life of the church when practical decisions had to be made regarding things which are in themselves matters of free choice, particularly when what is free to be done or left undone is not so neutral in the perceptions of opponents or parishioners.

Both parties represented the best of the Wittenberg academic tradition, and both were driven by pastoral concerns. Both desired a clear confession of the faith, but they did disagree on whether that was best effected in the present situation by compromise or by confrontation. Melanchthon and his colleagues strove to preserve the university that had been the birthplace of their confession. They operated under a kind of political pressure that their opponents did not feel as directly. Their opponents were angry with Duke Moritz for his betrayal of the Evangelical cause, and particularly of Elector John Frederick, who became a martyr in their eyes.[31] It is an exaggeration to suggest that Philip and his colleagues lived in a world of theory; their opponents in a world of practice. Nonetheless, the former tended to define the issues within the parameters of scholarly analysis; the latter wanted them defined in the midst of the thought world of their people. Those who remained in Wittenberg focused first on what words meant in themselves; those in Magdeburg pondered first how they affected their hearers. Such waters ran fast and deep. It is little wonder that the dispute over "neutral" matters lingered in the air; for confession of the faith, preserving the integrity of the church in relation to the secular government, the practice of sacred worship, and the definition of Christian freedom are not matters of indifference.

The Solution of the Formula of Concord

The Interims and the resulting controversy over adiaphora had raised three distinct issues for Lutheran theologians: (1) the relationship between Christian freedom and ceremonies or usages in the church; (2) the nature of public confession of the truth; and (3) the relationship between the church and the society in which it lives, more specifically, the secular government of that society.

All sides in the adiaphoristic controversy had recognized that liturgy and ecclesiastical usages were vital and important parts of the life of the church and the individual believer. The followers of Amsdorf and Flacius had recognized that parishioners often associated the fundamentals of their faith with outward signs and expressions of the faith. They believed that compromise in such matters could compromise the heart of the faith if the "receptors," the parishioners, perceived the connection between the faith and its expressions so intimately as they usually do. The electoral Saxon colleagues of Melanchthon insisted that such practices are inherently neutral and believed that they could be subject to adjustment in order to win advantage for the faith—and especially to preserve it in times of crisis. The Formula of Concord, in its tenth article, insisted that ceremonies and ecclesiastical usages may be changed in different places and times in such a way that is most profitable and edifying to the church (SD X,1–9). But in time of persecution, there can be no yielding to the enemies of the faith when such compromise in externals actually subverts the confession of the faith as well (SD X,10–25).[32] Thus, the Formula taught that the clear expression of the faith in the public arena is of paramount importance, and it dare not be sold for the pottage of external safety and security.

Among the Concordists there were varying positions in regard to the relationship of the prince or the municipal council and the church, and therefore the Formula does not address the issues of church and state or society as clearly as the debates leading to the Formula had addressed these issues. Not only the "Philippists" around Melanchthon but also Jacob Andreae's Swabian party had not objected to a strong role for the prince in churchly matters, and so the "Gnesio-Lutheran" concern for the integrity of the church in relationship to the state was muted in the Formula.

Gnesio-Lutherans and Philippists: The Parties of the Wittenberg Late Reformation

To think of the divisions that tore apart the friendships and collaboration of those who had studied with Luther and Melanchthon as formally organized "parties" is false. Indeed, common purposes were often combined with long-standing friendships among those who stood together on one side of a controversy or the other. On the other hand, some who made common cause together knew each other only slightly and were not always on the best of terms as they fought together for their cause. All in the Wittenberg circle shared much in common, for they had learned in the atmosphere generated by the team that had been shaped by Luther and Melanchthon. It is also true that the vast majority of former Wittenberg students and their colleagues from other universities in the ministeria of the German Lutheran churches of the Late Reformation were not involved in the "party" strife which led to the more precise definition of Lutheran theology.

It is important to note that there were other "parties" among the Lutherans. Two contemporaries of Melanchthon, men slightly younger than Luther, who had joined his call for reformation early, also gathered distinct groups around them. Andreas Osiander had very few followers; his party consisted largely of his prince, Duke Albrecht of Prussia.[33] Although he had some supporters in Nuremberg, where he had worked for more than two decades before imperial occupation forces drove him into exile in 1548, his view of justification offended nearly all others who counted themselves Evangelical in the period. Nonetheless, it continued to be, at least marginally, an issue until laid to rest by the Formula of Concord.[34]

The "Swabian" followers of the Württemberg court theologian Johannes Brenz encountered some suspicion because of their use of Christology in defense of Luther's view of the Lord's Supper, but they were far more influential and played a critical role in the public life of the Lutheran churches throughout the Late Reformation. But most important in the controversies were two loosely grouped associations, consisting largely of those who had studied in Wittenberg, dubbed "Philippists" and "Gnesio-Lutherans" since the end of the eighteenth century.[35]

In fact, the scholarly identification of "Gnesio-Lutheran" and "Philippist" groups among those who claimed to be Lutheran in the third quarter of the sixteenth century rests upon perceptions of that age itself. For those who remained faithful to Melanchthon tagged their critics with the label "Flacians." It designated them as partisans of a Slavic foreigner whose reputation grew steadily worse as he fought all the harder for his radical interpretation of Luther's message. Those who shared his view called their opponents "adiaphorists." The constellations formed slowly in the 1550s, and in a few instances their members moved to the other side. The two groups suffered from internal tensions as well, and Gnesio-Lutherans quarreled openly with other Gnesio-Lutherans on several occasions. Some Philippists shifted dramatically from the group's earlier focus on conservative liturgical practices and concern for life of new obedience to a focus on the Lord's Supper and Christology after the late 1560s. Neither group issued membership cards, nor were they able to compel conformity on those who adhered to its principles and shared its concerns. Nonetheless, a series of characteristics shared by members of the two groups and contrasting characteristics in the other group justify the analysis of the much of the discussion that gave form to Lutheran "confessionalization" in terms of the clash between these two parties. Parallels between them and those in Dutch Calvinism and English Protestantism who represent a more "radical" break with the medieval past (Dutch Calvinists and English Puritans) or a more "conservative" approach to ecclesiastical life (Arminians and mainline Anglicans) suggest a rough form for the transition from "Reformation" to "Orthodoxy" across confessional lines.

The differences between these two parties should not obscure fundamental similarities. All involved in these controversies regarded Martin Luther as a special agent of God, whose message and work had opened a new—the final—chapter in the history of the church. All had a sense that the world could not last much longer and that the confession of the truth was important. All taught justification of the sinner in God's sight by grace through faith in Christ. Indeed, all were disciples of Luther, whether they had studied in Wittenberg or not, and nearly all were students of Melanchthon (the exceptions were older by 1548: Amsdorf had shared Melanchthon's first days in Wittenberg as a colleague, for instance, but was influenced theologically relatively little by him). Indeed, Melanchthon's influence can be traced even among those who disagreed fiercely with the Preceptor over any number of issues regarding teaching and practice in the church. He had shaped some of their doctrinal instincts and much of their theological method. Nevertheless, the differences between Philippists and Gnesio-Lutherans provide most of the framework within which Lutherans struggled to define who they were between 1548 and 1577.

In four spheres of church life, the Gnesio-Lutherans represented a more radical adherence to or extension of Luther's views while the Philippists took a more conservative approach, departing less from the settled ways of the medieval church. These contrasting characteristics began to emerge already in the first years of the adiaphoristic controversy. First, the two groups had a different orientation toward the public propagation of the truth of God's Word, linked with differing senses of what the church is. Both insisted on the public confession of the gospel, but Gnesio-Lutherans were radical in confessing the faith with abandon, with little or no concern for offending those whom they believed were denying the truth. Both parties taught a view of church history as the battleground on which satanic forces had persecuted the truth and the people of God, and both took responsibility for the faithful administration of the visible church and its institutions. Philippists were more cautious, less insistent on confessing the truth recklessly and boldly, however. Their eschatological expectations were more muted than those of the Gnesio-Lutherans, and they operated with a stronger sense of the importance of the institutional concerns of the church, in their own principalities and in Western Christendom. They were willing to sacrifice some freedom of expression of the truth for the sake of preserving institutional integrity and harmony. The Gnesio-Lutherans perceived of the church as a persecuted remnant, a tiny flock, totally dependent on God's Word, and institutional concerns were secondary to the clear proclamation of that Word in their view.[36]

Consequently, they suffered division among themselves. As noted below, the group gathered originally around Flacius suffered a fierce and tragic dispute within its own ranks over the proper definition of original sin, and its members also argued, largely in private, over the use of the law in the Christian life. Although all four had stood steadfastly against a series of Philippist errors, Amsdorf and Gallus condemned Wigand and Tileman Hesshus when the latter fell into dispute over the city council's administration of the church in Magdeburg, where the former still had friends in power. Hesshus and Wigand themselves ended a long-standing friendship with a bitter dispute over Christological questions in the 1570s; Hesshus was forced to leave his post as bishop of Samland as a result. Within Gnesio-Lutheran ranks in Erfurt, questions regarding the proper relationship of Evangelical university professors to the Roman Catholic administration of the university brought friends and colleagues into sharp public disagreement, leading to the exile of Andreas Poach.

In contrast, the Philippist Georg Major so despised public controversy that he claimed never to have taught the proposition, "good works are necessary for salvation," which he had indeed promoted in his defense of the Leipzig Proposal.[37] Alexander Alesius repressed his objections to Johann Pfeffinger's doctrine of the will.[38] Philippist differences regarding the Lord's Supper were suppressed and withheld from public view; the wing of that party which promoted a spiritualizing understanding of the presence of Christ in Lord's Supper preferred to foster its view secretly and subtly, thus earning the epithets "subtle sacramentarians" and "crypto-Calvinists" (although their view of the Lord's Supper in fact had its roots in Melanchthon's, not Calvin's, teaching).[39] Indeed, they abandoned their policy of avoiding public conflicts over doctrine briefly in the late 1550s and then again a decade later, when they boldly attacked the errors they perceived in their Gnesio-Lutheran and Swabian opponents. Nonetheless, their efforts at remaining "cryptic"—hidden—failed both because they began to present more openly their views on the Lord's Supper and because others unveiled their program for advancing their views secretly. Open confession of their position would have brought ruinous controversy to the church, they believed, and for them it was far better to further their doctrine subtly and secretly.

The developments around the Leipzig Proposal also reveal differing attitudes toward the relationship of church and state. As was clear already in their contrasting approaches to the bigamy of Philip of Hesse, Amsdorf and Melanchthon reacted differently to the needs of the church and the demands upon it by the government of Moritz in 1548. This difference rested upon more than their respective situations although Melanchthon was hard-pressed to take an independent stance over against the new elector of Saxony, given his position as leader of the University of Wittenberg. Amsdorf, on the run as "exiled" bishop of Naumburg, had much less to lose.[40] But as was clear some eight years earlier, in his comments on the bigamy of Philip of Hesse, Amsdorf believed that the integrity of the church demanded a more "prophetic" stance in its relationship with society and state, whereas Melanchthon believed in principle that church leaders were obligated to work with their secular governments and to compromise with them for the general welfare when necessary.

The Gnesio-Lutherans, under Gallus' leadership, formulated a justification of armed resistance against the emperor in Magdeburg in 1550. In 1552 Joachim Mörlin distinguished the obedience he owed Duke Albrecht of Prussia as his ruler from his obligation as pastor to criticize the duke's interference in church affairs—the duke defended his favorite, Andreas Osiander, whom Mörlin regarded as heretical. Mörlin was forced from his position in Prussia because he stood stubbornly opposed to Albrecht. Hesshus lost positions in Rostock and Goslar for open opposition to the moral dereliction of patrician families, and he was sent into exile for confessing his Gnesio-Lutheran views of biblical teaching several times as well. Simon Musaeus was sent on his way eight times for opposing the moral standards or the doctrinal inclinations of the powers that were. Most of the Gnesio-Lutheran leadership experienced the hard hand of governmental authorities as these authorities ushered these pastors to the city gate and sent them into exile.

On the other hand, the Philippists supported Moritz and the composition of the Leipzig Proposal, albeit reluctantly, and in general supported the governing authorities loyally. The Gnesio-Lutherans firmly believed, as did the Philippists, that the secular authorities had God-given responsibilities to support the church. But much more than the Philippists, they maintained Luther's distinction between the realms of responsibility exercised by princes and pastors. This explains their more radical stance in insisting on the integrity of the church as it made decisions for its own sphere and their radical criticism of interference in the church's life by prince or municipal council.

The third area of difference between Philippists and Gnesio-Lutherans lies in their attitudes toward the medieval church, particularly its ceremonies or practices and its polity under bishops and popes. Although two decades later many younger Philippists sharply rejected anything that slightly smacked of "papism," the Leipzig Proposal's conservative prescription of rites and customs which had marked the practice of the medieval church fit in well with the conservative reformation introduced by Prince Georg of Anhalt and Johann Pfeffinger in the domains of Heinrich of Saxony and his son, Moritz, in the decade before the Interims.

Gnesio-Lutherans, on the other hand, tended to believe that rites and ceremonies should be simplified to avoid cultivating superstitious beliefs. Amsdorf, for instance, called for moving altars away from the wall of the church so that the words of institution could be experienced as proclamation of the gospel rather than the recital of some secret formula, which he believed was implicit in the practice of the pastor's consecrating the sacramental elements with back to the congregation. Although his attitude shifted evermore, too, Melanchthon's hopefulness to find some peaceful middle ground between Lutherans and Roman Catholics—exemplified by the Leipzig Proposal's prescription of ordination by papally appointed bishops—reflected earlier openness in relationship to Rome. (To be sure, this openness was often balanced by strong stands against, and sharp criticism of, the papal party throughout his career; after his disappointment with the Roman Catholic negotiators at the Colloquy of Worms in 1557 he expressed that criticism more harshly). In contrast, Amsdorf regarded it as hopeless to pray for good results from the Council of Trent, and Flacius and Gallus sharply criticized its decisions in its third period, 1563–1564. In general, Philippists were more open to accommodating medieval usage and practice, at least for a decade after the Leipzig Proposal, whereas the Gnesio-Lutherans were more radical in their rejection of much of the medieval heritage.

The disputes that grew out of the Adiaphoristic controversy themselves focused largely on doctrinal issues, specifically over the role of good works in salvation, the role of the law in the Christian life, and the role of the human will in conversion. In them the Philippists positions were more conservative, that is, closer to the medieval focus on human activity and contribution to salvation. The Gnesio-Lutherans were more radical in following Luther's anthropology and soteriology. Some Philippists insisted on preserving the integrity of the human creature by emphasizing good works with the proposition that they are "necessary for salvation"; the Gnesio-Lutherans insisted that they were necessary for Christian living but not for salvation. Amsdorf chose some of Luther's most radical language, that "good works are harmful to salvation" (if one trusts them as the basis of salvation), to counteract the Philippist defense of the Leipzig Proposal's phrase, "good works are necessary for salvation."

Melanchthon's concern that God not be seen as the author of evil and his interest in explaining the psychological side of conversion in order to maintain the law's insistence on human responsibility led him and colleagues such as Pfeffinger and Viktorin Strigel to emphasize the necessity of the human will's commitment to God in repentance. Gnesio-Lutherans understood that when children of God come to faith and remain in faith, that is as much a gift of God as is the gift of life and identity when a human child is born and kept in a family. In reaction to the use of an Aristotelian analysis of sin and conversion advanced by Strigel, Flacius claimed that original sin is the formal essence of the fallen human creature, thus alienating many Gnesio-Lutheran friends as well as the Philippists. This radical use of Luther's insights into sin and grace marked the Gnesio-Lutherans. The Philippists were more conservative in relationship to medieval doctrines of sin and salvation.

By the 1570s a spectrum had developed which embraced most leading theologians in the Wittenberg sphere of influence. This spectrum extended from the followers of Flacius on the doctrine of original sin, at one end, through the main body of Gnesio-Lutherans, over somewhat moderate Philippists to those who secretly were promoting their own spiritualized view of the Lord's Supper, with its Christological implications. Osiandrists were very, very few in number. The Swabian party of Brenz and Andreae stood somewhat to the side of the north German debates.

Political factors—not a desire for equal representation of everyone involved—determined the composition of the committee that created the Formula of Concord in 1576 and 1577. Jakob Andreae represented Elector August of Saxony as well as the Württemberg court; he was a leading voice in the Swabian party after Brenz's death in 1570. Martin Chemnitz's close association with Joachim Mörlin and friendships with a number of Flacius' comrades, his opposition to a number of Philippist theological positions, and his own understanding of Luther placed him roughly in the Gnesio-Lutheran camp. However, he had differed sharply with Flacius regarding original sin; he had been able to maintain a somewhat cordial relationship with Melanchthon; and he had continued to demonstrate the strong influence of the Preceptor in his writings.[41] David Chytraeus and Nikolaus Selnecker had longstanding and even closer associations with Melanchthon, but they had both begun to drift away from his followers during the later 1560s and early 1570s. Andreas Musculus had few personal associations with other Gnesio-Lutherans, but his writings had strongly represented their positions and his churchmanship had reproduced their attitudes and habits. Only Musculus' colleague from Brandenburg, Christoph Körner, stood sufficiently apart from the controversies of the day to make it difficult to place him on the party spectrum of the period.

All these theologians and their contemporaries sought the truth and believed that God's truth in Scripture described and determined reality throughout the world as they experienced it. Their search for the truth took place in specific social and political contexts, within the intellectual milieu that was transforming the medieval heritage into early modern European thought, in all its multifaceted splendor. They had personal attachments to friends, to institutions, particularly their universities, to their political superiors, as well as to their church and God. All these elements played a role in their formulation of a definition of what it meant to be Luther's heir.

9

The Majoristic and "Antinomian" Controversies

In one of his several critiques of the Leipzig Proposal, Nikolaus von Amsdorf attacked its use of the phrase "good works are necessary for salvation." Precisely that phrase had been used two decades earlier by the Roman Catholic party in Magdeburg in the attempt to have Amsdorf and his colleague, the school rector, Georg Major, burned for heresy and to end the Evangelical reform they were leading in the city.

Georg Major and the Necessity of Good Works for Salvation

The first to defend that concept as it was expressed in the Leipzig Proposal was Major. He had returned from Magdeburg to Wittenberg in 1537 as preacher in the castle church and since 1545 had served as professor of theology there. Particularly painful to Amsdorf was the fact that that his objection to the necessity of good works for salvation was rejected and belittled by this friend,[1] who had served at his side as rector of Saint John's school in Magdeburg 1529–1537 and had experienced the same harassment from the Roman party because of this phrase. His sense of betrayal and his concern for the gospel flared. For he could understand the phrase only in the sense that it had been taught in the medieval church, as an affirmation of the necessity of human contribution and merit in the salvation of sinners.

In fact, the two old friends fell into bitter dispute with each other because they were operating with different definitions of words. Amsdorf was certain that "good works" would be understood by the common people as the works of external performance, not the entire new obedience which flows from faith, Major's understanding of the term. Amsdorf defined as "necessary" that which causes or is responsible for something; Major understood the word as specifying something which accompanies or is present with another thing, without the sense in every case that it causes the first thing to exist. Amsdorf believed that "salvation" and "justification" are synonyms whereas Major defined the German word *Seligkeit* as the result of justification, the whole experience of being saved. In part, the two and those who took their respective sides talked past each other. On the other hand, their encounter took place upon the field of Luther's understanding of righteousness and of the Christian life. The tensions inherent in his viewing the righteousness of the forgiven sinner before God as fundamentally different from that person's righteousness in relationship to other people continued to call forth new formulations and redefinitions of the life of discipleship.[2] In addition, Major may have believed, as Amsdorf certainly suspected, that the phrase was sufficiently ambiguous to pacify papal critique of the Lutheran position. And yet it was not "merely" a battle of words, as Major often asserted, since the words did have impact of profound implications on hearers and readers. The Wittenberg thinkers did not regard words as "mere" but as tools of the Holy Spirit when they conveyed God's Word to his people.

Amsdorf's initial objections to Major's position on good works appeared at the time the Wittenberg professor had accepted a call to be superintendent of the churches in Mansfeld county. The ministerium there reacted immediately and with suspicion. Major had to defend his theological integrity to retain his new position. In replying to Amsdorf's attack on the Proposal, himself, and his colleague Johannes Bugenhagen, Major affirmed that he had always taught that good works are necessary to salvation, that no one will be saved through evil works, and that no one will be saved without good works. Amsdorf recognized a familiar theme, not only from the papal party in Magdeburg in the 1520s but also from the disagreement between Cruciger and Cordatus in the 1530s. He repeated his conviction that this language abandoned the Reformation teaching of salvation through faith alone. His view won immediate support from Flacius, Gallus, the ministeria of the north German cities of Magdeburg, Lüneburg, Hamburg, and Lübeck, and the ministerium of Mansfeld County.

Melanchthon expressed great reservations about Major's proposition, but Major felt compelled, in the context of the atmosphere of controversy at the time, to defend himself, insisting that he had always held that faith alone justifies. He wrote that the mercy seat of Christ is the only basis of and cause for salvation, that Christ's merit alone wins forgiveness of sin, imputes righteousness to believers, and bestows upon them the Holy Spirit and the godly life. He counted faith as the first and best of human works. He did insist as well that good works are necessary for the reception of the rewards of heavenly blessedness even though they are not necessary as a cause for salvation. He also believed that good works are necessary for the retention of salvation. They have no merit but are exercised as an obligation (*debitum*) of godly believers.[3]

The controversy stewed and boiled in the early 1550s. Melanchthon explicitly rejected the idea that good works are necessary for salvation in the years following 1555 while at the same time misrepresenting the concern of Amsdorf, Flacius, and their comrades as simple antinomianism—a desire to eliminate the law and good works from the Christian life. In fact, the Gnesio-Lutherans made crystal clear their insistence that good works are a necessary part of the Christian life. With ferocity they had attacked the open sin that Melanchthon implied they permitted. But his concern to preserve Luther's doctrine of justification led Amsdorf to publish a short tract in 1557 in which he resurrected Luther's oft-repeated phrase that "good works are detrimental to salvation"—when they become the object of trust and are regarded as contributing to salvation. In the preface to the first printed edition of Luther's sermons on John 18-20, Amsdorf recalled that Luther had written that "teaching and emphasizing works as necessary for salvation does more and greater harm that human reason can ever grasp or understand. For not only is the recognition of grace obscured through it, but Christ with all his benefits is thereby taken away and the whole gospel...is perverted." A Philippist colleague in ducal Saxony, Andreas Hügel, raised objections with Duke John Frederick the Middler, and Amsdorf felt compelled to defend himself in print, claiming that this expression of the detrimental nature of trust in works had been taught by Paul and Luther. This tract aroused very little objection, even from the Philippists, who apparently recognized the origins of the expression in Luther's writings (although they raised occasional criticism of the phrase, especially in private correspondence and memoranda to government officials, to discredit the entire "Flacian" party). The authors of the Formula of Concord recognized that the phrase could be misunderstood and therefore rejected it, but they also affirmed its intention.[4]

Major himself had only reluctantly participated in the composition of the Leipzig Proposal. He recoiled from controversy. In 1555 he protested to King Christian of Denmark that he had never taught that good works are necessary to salvation, nor did he at that time, nor would he ever in the future. For more than a decade he reaffirmed his commitment to a Lutheran doctrine of justification in print, but he never expressed himself clearly enough to permit reconciliation between him and his foes. He did visit the aged Amsdorf in 1563, and they chatted about old times in Magdeburg, but not about good works.[5]

The Formula of Concord on Good Works

By 1568, at the Colloquy of Altenburg, some of Major's followers defended his suggestion that human performance of good works can help preserve salvation and merit more reward in heaven as a way of salvaging his position. They did not recognize the implications of this position for Luther's distinction of the two kinds of righteousness. The Concordists rejected this position (SD IV, 30–36). However, for the most part, the controversy over good works was not difficult to solve when the terminological divergences and the problems of personality and politics could be set aside. Like the Gnesio-Lutheran critics of Georg Major's argument in behalf of the necessity good works for salvation, the Concordists embraced the necessity of good works for the living of the Christian life. At the same time most of the students of Luther and Melanchthon were driven by a burning concern for public order and morality that drove them to take measures against every form of antinomianism which might result in moral laxity. The fourth article of the Formula tries to walk the narrow line between this concern and that of one of its authors, Andreas Musculus. He strove to avoid every impression that might give reason to believe that good works cause salvation or that believers by necessity remain children of God only on the basis of a certain quantity or quality of good works.

Therefore, the fourth article of the Formula makes it clear that good works follow from a true, living faith (SD IV,6–13, 21–29).[6] While it must be emphasized that good works play absolutely no role in determining human righteousness in God's sight or in acquiring rewards from God apart from salvation, there is a natural obligation, based upon the nature of the human creature (as created and as reborn through the power of the Holy Spirit) to do good works. Therefore, the Formula rejected the condemnation of the "necessity" of good works advanced by Musculus (SD IV,14–20). It did note, however, that necessity properly understood is not a compelling or coercive necessity but a necessity that takes place naturally or spontaneously in the reborn, a concession to Musculus's concern. The text of article IV tries to make it clear that the motivation for doing good works is not fear of punishment but love of righteousness. Christians do good works as loving children, not as fearful slaves.

The Concordists followed Andreae's lead in his *Six Christian Sermons* and ignored the origin of the phrase "good works are detrimental to salvation" in Luther's own writings. They acknowledged that it could be rightly understood if it meant that the offering of works to God for the sake of one's own salvation was detrimental, but their fear of antinomianism made it necessary to reject the phrase and thus to avoid any mention of Luther's use of it. "People can be damned by an Epicurean delusion about faith just as much as by the papistic, pharisaic trust in their own works and merit" (Ep IV:19; cf. SD IV, 37–40).

The fourth article of the Formula demonstrates its authors' recognition of the validity of concern for proper Christian living and the dangers of focusing on good works for the troubled conscience. Its position echoed that of most Gnesio-Lutherans throughout the controversy over good works, but it also met the fundamental concerns of Georg Major and his colleagues.

The Eisenach Synod and the Abstract or Theoretical Necessity of Good Works for Salvation

Within the ministerium of ducal Saxony there always remained a spectrum of allegiances. One of the leaders in the churches of that area, alongside Amsdorf, was Justus Menius, who had studied in Wittenberg before assuming a pastorate in Erfurt in 1525. He became superintendent of the churches in Eisenach in 1529 and superintendent in Gotha in 1546. He never broke his close ties to his Preceptor; he joined with both Melanchthon and his own colleagues in ducal Saxony in sharply rejecting the Augsburg Interim. He and Amsdorf served together on a team that inspected the churches of the dukedom in 1554, at the height of the Majoristic controversy. The bishop wanted to make certain that pastors did not represent Major's view of good works and salvation in their pulpits, and so he insisted that Menius condemn Major's position. Menius demurred, claiming that he had not read Major's works, a claim that, if true, would suggest neglect of office in the highly charged situation of the day. Menius prepared 110 theses on good works, in which he rejected their necessity for salvation but suggested that the expression "good works are necessary for salvation" could be properly understood. Flacius joined Amsdorf in criticizing Menius, and their disagreement raged in print,[7] both before and after a special synod that Duke John Frederick the Middler called in Eisenach in August 1556.[8]

Flacius and his ally Johannes Wigand did not attend this synod, chaired by Viktorin Strigel, but they did approve its conclusions. It adopted seven theses that affirmed the necessity of good works for the Christian life and rejected their necessity for salvation. All participants, including Menius, pledged themselves to the theses. However, Amsdorf quickly had second thoughts on one of them: "good works are necessary for salvation abstractly in the doctrine of the law." Flacius and Wigand had no trouble with that proposition, for they followed Melanchthon's teaching that God's law, comprehended in the Decalogue, is an eternal, unchangeable rule or guiding principle, which demands perfect obedience from all reasoning creatures. The law promises blessings to all who obey it perfectly, and therefore, Strigel, Menius, Flacius, and Wigand all believed that "abstractly" or "theoretically" human creatures could attain salvation through their own performance of the law's demands, through their keeping it perfectly. Since this proposition would confuse common people, the Eisenach synod warned against using it publicly.

Amsdorf's concern went deeper. He believed that the proposition obscured Luther's understanding of righteousness. Luther had taught that human righteousness before God is passive: it consists in no way—abstractly, theoretically, or practically—in human performance. It consists alone in the favor of God. Human performance in works that reflect God's design for human life as found in his law constitute a totally different kind of righteousness, an active righteousness.[9] The ducal government was fearful that Amsdorf's objections to the Eisenach synod's conclusions would disrupt the hard-won peace in their church that the synod had produced. They implored Flacius to convince the old bishop to stay in line.

Flacius and Wigand believed that the teaching of the abstract necessity of good works corresponded to biblical teaching. It revealed the creator's will and his unchangeable order; it explained the origin of conscience. It was necessary to maintain the proper distinction of law and gospel. It made clear the necessity of the saving work of Christ. Flacius and Wigand did not notice that they were departing from Luther's distinction of the two kinds of righteousness and implying a medieval view which believed that the actions involved in the performance of the law constitute what is truly righteous and that grace only supplies what is lacking in human performance. To be sure, they did not follow their own assertions to their logical conclusions because they were focusing on a different aspect of the question. They certainly recognized that grace must now supply all righteousness because of the seriousness of sin, but they missed Luther's key point that defined righteousness before God as pure gift, totally apart from all human performance.

Gnesio-Lutheran Disputes over the Law in the Christian Life

Several other Gnesio-Lutherans became involved in private battles over this issue with fellow Gnesio-Lutherans.[10] Anton Otto, pastor in Nordhausen,[11] and Andreas Poach of Erfurt[12] represented a small group which insisted that Melanchthon's understanding of the third use of the law opened the way for Christians to become dependent on their own keeping of the law for the completion of the Christian life.[13] They taught that faith begins and completes the Christian life and that it inevitably and naturally produces the good works of everyday life in doing so. Poach and Joachim Mörlin fell into dispute because Poach's concern that no human merit be understood as sufficient to save clashed with Mörlin's concern that the law serve as a basis for judging sin. Poach and Otto rejected any discussion of the law on a theoretical level; concretely it always accuses and condemns. Furthermore, they believed that the law was never designed to be a way of salvation but rather to order the life of the creatures upon whom God had already bestowed righteousness. No human performance of the law could ever obligate God to save. His gift of righteousness and life is always pure gift, passively received, as Luther had defined it, never the product of any kind of human action or activity. Mörlin and Flacius feared that Poach's rejection of the law as the way of salvation on a theoretical level would undercut the practice of repentance.[14]

Otto and his colleague in Nordhausen, the pastor Andreas Fabricius, along with the famous humanist school rector from nearby Ilfeld, Michael Neander, became embroiled in dispute with Mörlin over the third use of the law as well between 1563 and 1571.[15] Otto rejected the expression that the life of repentance embraces new obedience, for he believed that this idea would mean that new obedience indeed contributes to righteousness in God's sight, rather than simply being the righteousness practiced in relationship to other human beings. The bride of Christ, the Christian, and the bridegroom, Christ, do not need a third partner, the law, to complete their union, he argued. The law must be preached to keep public order and to drive people to repentance, according to Otto, but it does no more: it does not produce the good works of the Christian life. It functions only in regard to the fleshly desires of believers, not in regard to their life in the Spirit. Melanchthon and other Philippists attributed to him the statement "the highest art of the Christian is not to know the law," as a slogan with which they could dismiss him without engaging his concerns.

The exchange between Otto, Fabricius, and Neander on the one side and Flacius and Mörlin flared only briefly in public, as the latter two defended the third use of the law, its application of the law in forming and shaping the good works of new obedience. The criticism of the (falsely labeled) "antinomianism" of Otto, Poach, and their colleagues continued to be a favorite theme in the writings of Philippists as well as a thorn in the side of many of their Gnesio-Lutheran compatriots.

Necessity versus Spontaneity in the Christian Life

A similar attempt to define the role of the law in the Christian life brought two faculty members of the University of Frankfurt an der Oder in electoral Brandenburg into conflict. Andreas Musculus shared the characteristics of the Gnesio-Lutherans although he never had close personal contact with Flacius or his comrades.[16] Abdias Praetorius, who became Musculus's colleague as Hebrew instructor in the Frankfurt arts faculty, did have such contact, as a coworker on the Magdeburg *Centuries*, although theologically he represented a Philippist position and personally maintained close contacts with Melanchthon. Musculus came to Frankfurt from his study at Wittenberg in 1541, the year after his brother-in-law, Johannes Agricola, arrived at Elector Joachim's court in Berlin.

Musculus' view of the law stood in marked contrast with that of his wife's sister's husband even though they were both labeled "antinomian" by some contemporaries and later scholars. Musculus in fact preached and wrote against sin in the lives of members of his congregation in Frankfurt with a strong sense of the accusing force of the law. But he believed that Luther's insights into the gospel compelled his students to reject a "third use" of the law, which he understood as the use of the law to motivate good works in believers. He rejected the word "necessity" completely when speaking of good works in the Christian life, finding instead that good works occur "naturally"—not "under coercion"—in the life of the reborn children of God. He taught that the proper office of the law is to kill so that life may come forth. The law humbles and terrifies those whom God justifies so that they may flee to Christ. The law is preached so that believers know how the Holy Spirit crucifies the flesh and gives direction against fleshly desires. Believers love God's law, he believed, and conform to it with a free and willing spirit, spontaneously, not out of necessity or coercion.

Praetorius objected to Musculus's position. With Melanchthon's encouragement he defended the necessity of the law in the Christian life so that ethical standards within the church might be maintained. The children of God are obligated to do God's will, Praetorius taught, for God had instituted it as the most absolute norm and rule for life. He rejected Musculus's contention that necessity had to be a matter of coercion or force. Instead, he held that the spontaneity and freedom which produced the Christian's works sprang from the foundation of necessity, planted by God in the human creature. He held that both continued condemnation of sinfulness and the guidance of the pedagogical use of the law are required for Christian living.

Controversy over Melanchthon's Definition of Repentance and of the Gospel

As Melanchthon continued to render biblical expressions into useable theology for the church of his day, his mind was continually opened to new ways of framing biblical thought. He recognized the importance of distinguishing law and gospel sharply, but certain biblical expressions also led him to define the term "gospel" both narrowly and broadly. The narrow definition equates the gospel with putting the burden of human sinfulness on Christ alone; the gospel is the forgiveness of sins through faith in Christ Jesus. It is God's work alone. At the same time, Melanchthon also argued that at times in Scripture "gospel" embraces the broader message for sinners, both the call for repentance and the forgiveness of sins.

In the 1550s Flacius raised concerns about the confusion this broader definition of the gospel might bring if people understood that the gospel could include human effort or preparation in repentance as well as God's gift of forgiveness and new life in Christ. Students in Wittenberg defended their Preceptor with an attack on Flacius, and in the 1570s Christoph Pezel at Wittenberg and Johannes Wigand from the Gnesio-Lutheran side continued the public discussion even though this dispute never grew large.

The Formula of Concord on Law and Gospel and the Third Use of the Law

All of the heirs of the Wittenberg reformers believed that the proper distinction between law and gospel lay at the heart of the theological enterprise. Neither preaching nor pastoral care would be possible apart from the practice of this distinction. Thus, all sides insisted that the gospel and the law be given the proper interpretation in the public theology of the church.[17] The fifth article of the Formula repeats the Gnesio-Lutheran position that while Scripture indeed employs wider and narrower definitions of the word "gospel," the preservation of the proper distinction between law and gospel depends on clear and precise definition of both these terms. Law, strictly speaking, refers to God's plan or design for human living that defines what is right and God-pleasing and rejects everything contrary to his will. Gospel, strictly speaking, is "a proclamation of comfort and a joyous message which does not rebuke nor terrify but comforts consciences against the terror of the law, directs them solely to Christ's merit, and lifts them up again through the delightful proclamation of the grace and favor of God, won through Christ's merits" (Ep V,7). The Concordists also recognized that the content of a statement alone does not determine whether it is being used as law or gospel, but rather the combination of content and impact. The functioning of the statement in actual use is determinative of its theological nature. That which condemns and terrifies functions as law, even if it describes God's love in Christ's death and resurrection. All that comforts and consoles on the basis of that love in Christ's work functions as gospel and works forgiveness of sins, life, and salvation (SD V,1–27).

The treatment of Melanchthon's concept of the third use of the law provided a special challenge for those gathered at Torgau in May 1576 to hammer out a text that could offer the basis for concord. Most Lutherans of the 1570s agreed that the law had three uses, as Melanchthon had described them. One of the few who had voiced vociferous rejection of that position sat at the table in Torgau: Andreas Musculus of Brandenburg. The sixth article carefully crafts a position that embraces his reservations while affirming a third use of the law. Musculus's concern centered upon his distinction between the Christian motivation for good works—which sprang "spontaneously" "from a free and joyous spirit"—and works motivated, compelled or coerced, by divine demand (cf. SD VI, 1, 17–19). Andreae and Chemnitz, Selnecker and Chytraeus all shared the conviction that the law does offer instruction for Christian minds that need aid in sorting out moral dilemmas (SD VI, 4–16, 20–25). Their finely woven joint statement can provoke some puzzlement if the historical situation of its authors is not recognized.

The third use of the law, according to the Formula, embraces all its functions in the Christian life. It continues the first use by disciplining unruly and disobedient believers as they fall into sin. It accuses the "fleshly inclinations" of believers and brings them back to repentance. Believers must hear the law in order to battle against their sinful desires. In addition, the Formula teaches, the fruits of the Spirit are expressions of the believers' obedience to the unchangeable will of God, performed without coercion, from a willing spirit, apart from the motivating threat of the law but in accord with its design for human life (SD VI,1–3).[18] The Philippist charges against those whom they called "antinomians" (including Musculus) had been taken into account, as had Musculus's own position, and the dominant Melanchthonian view shared by many Gnesio-Lutherans and all Philippists, had found a pastorally sensitive expression.

10

The Synergistic Controversy, the Controversy over Original Sin, and the Doctrine of Election in the Late Reformation

Luther had thanked Erasmus for putting his finger on the very heartbeat of his theology: his understanding that the sinful human will is bound and cannot choose to trust God and obey him by its own power and strength.[1] His *On Bound Choice* [*De servo arbitrio*] argued his case for God's unconditional mercy and other aspects of his theology of the cross. It may be said that this work remained to too great an extent on Erasmus's turf and thus failed to capture the pastoral dynamic of the issues under discussion as sharply as others of his writings. Readers do have to recognize, however, that in *On Bound Choice* Luther was responding to Erasmus's attack on him in the *Diatribe on the Free Will*, a work composed as a formal academic disputation. Luther followed Erasmus's style and genre in replying.

Melanchthon, too, insisted on the unconditional nature of God's grace as strongly as Luther, and he opposed Erasmus in the battle between his humanist friend and his Wittenberg colleague.[2] However, several other theological concerns led him to place Luther's stance on the bondage of the will in a larger context that also took seriously human integrity and responsibility. He had his own label for the issue, entitling it "freedom of the will," and his later discussion of this topic reflected his concern that God not be held responsible for evil and that human creatures be held responsible for their actions. His doctrine of creation also demanded that the psychological factors, implanted by God in human nature, be considered when conversion and repentance were treated.[3] As noted above, Melanchthon's views had led to tensions on the issue of necessity and contingency between him and Nikolaus von Amsdorf in the mid 1530s.

The Outbreak of Controversy: The Role of the Will in Conversion

Thus, it is no surprise that when one of Melanchthon's students who had helped formulate the Leipzig Proposal, Johann Pfeffinger, advanced his own version of Melanchthon's doctrine of the free will, he raised Amsdorf's ire, especially since Pfeffinger had been a close associate of Duke Moritz even before the Smalcald War broke out. He had left his parish in Passau to come to the University of Wittenberg in 1523. He accepted a position as superintendent in charge of introducing the Reformation in Leipzig in 1540, having served in the visitation of Albertine Saxon churches the previous year, as Duke Heinrich brought the Lutheran message officially to his newly-inherited lands. From 1544 Pfeffinger held a chair in theology at the University of Leipzig.

In 1555 Pfeffinger offered theses on the role of the human will in conversion for discussion within the university. His colleague Alexander Alesius found them objectionable,[4] and the discussion spread beyond Leipzig. When Amsdorf included a sharp critique of Pfeffinger's position in his *Public Confession of the Pure Teaching of the Gospel and Confutation of Present Day Ravers* in 1558,[5] the public debate over the freedom of the will and human cooperation with the Holy Spirit—synergism— began. Most of Pfeffinger's teaching raised no objections from other Lutherans. His theses considered five fundamental issues. First, he affirmed that, weakened by sin though it is, the human will under sin has the freedom to maintain external discipline and perform moral works; this is the righteousness of the flesh (Rom. 2:14, 9:31). Second, sinners do not have the freedom or power to overcome their inborn depravity or their mortality. Third, the Holy Spirit must aid in the performance of spiritual deeds by the believer. Fourth, the human will is not like a stone but rather functions normally in the process of conversion. It experiences psychological struggles in the gaining and retaining of faith. Finally, God cannot be the cause of sin. He wants all to be saved (1 Tim. 2:4).[6] All in the Wittenberg circle held each of these positions. But Pfeffinger elaborated this final thesis in a manner which Amsdorf and others viewed as a threat to the confession that God alone is responsible for the sinner's salvation. All people have received God's promise of forgiveness and offer of salvation through it. God is no respecter of persons. The difference between the elect and the damned must lie in themselves.[7]

This last point posed a problem. Pfeffinger strained to resolve the tensions between his desire not to compromise God's grace and his desire to protect God's honor against charges of being the cause of evil and to take God-given human psychological characteristics seriously. He strove to insist on human responsibility and yet to maintain the "grace alone, faith alone" foundation of Lutheran theology firm and unshakable. What Luther had done with the careful pastoral distinction of law and gospel, maintaining the tension between God's grace and the Spirit-wrought response to grace, Pfeffinger attempted to do with a scholarly analysis. He wanted to reconcile the contradictions between the demands of the law and promises of the gospel. Luther had more often been content to direct law to those whom he called to repentance, gospel to the repentant, and to avoid resolving tensions between his insistence on human responsibility in the former case, and on God's responsibility in the latter. Pfeffinger insisted that the mercy and merit of Christ are the only cause of God's choice of the saved, who are drawn by God through the Holy Spirit and his Word to faith. Assent must be given to the promise of the free remission of sin. We must attribute some cooperation to our will, but this assent detracts nothing from the Holy Spirit, who always initiates conversion through the preaching of the gospel. But then the Leipzig professor pushed for a fuller explanation that would admonish Christians to do what they could even though he had granted that they can do nothing: "it is necessary to assent to the extent that lies in us and not to resist the Holy Spirit as he moves." For the Holy Spirit is received by those who seek him, that is, those who do not spurn or reject him. Saul reacted differently to the Holy Spirit than did David, Peter in a different way than did Judas. By going beyond Luther's tension between the law that demands human trust, human commitment, and the gospel that bestows God's unconditional grace, Pfeffinger strayed into the mine field of having to choose between placing either divine or human responsibility in the shade. Pfeffinger's argument made human assent, as small and weak as it might be, the key to reconciliation between the sinner and God.

Amsdorf viewed this position as a return to the worst of medieval theology. He insisted that the Holy Spirit must convert the will of sinners before they can grasp God's promise. It is the Holy Spirit who moves and directs the lives of believers. The psychological factors of humanity did not interest Amsdorf; he took them for granted. He felt no need to explain his assertion that God is not the author of evil. God may choose to love Jacob and hate Esau (Mal. 1:2-3; Rom. 9:13) for no other reason than the mercy involved in that choice. First Timothy 2:4 refers to "all believers"—not all sinners—as the objects of God's desire to save. For Amsdorf the supreme issue was the comfort and certainty of salvation that believers can have through the biblical teaching on election.

His position was supported by one of John Frederick's court preachers, Johann Stolz, and Flacius. Their critiques of Pfeffinger's position, published together, echoed the old bishop's. Flacius attacked Pfeffinger's teaching both in the public forum and on the field of university disputation in Jena. He cited Luther in order to assert that fallen human creatures are "completely passive"—that is, they make no contribution of their own—in conversion from sin to faith in Christ. They are as unable to do anything to help themselves as are blocks of wood. In fact, they are worse than blocks of wood, for their wills resist God and remain hostile to God's working in them until God transforms the will. Having fallen from the image of God into the image of Satan, sinners cannot return to God under their own power. The Holy Spirit must bring them back to trust in God.

The second round of the dispute began before the appearance of these critiques. Pfeffinger defended himself in both Latin (*Exposition of the Obvious Lie with Which the Scurrilous, Sycophant Booklet of Nikolaus von Amsdorf Tries to Defame Dr. Johann Pfeffinger*) and German (*Answer of Dr. Johann Pfeffinger to the Public Confession of Nikolaus von Amsdorf*).[8] Pfeffinger protested that Amsdorf had misquoted and misinterpreted him, and he tried to say as little as possible about the freedom of the will. He affirmed his belief that the sinful will is corrupt and depraved, unable to restore itself to faith in God. Nonetheless, it still functions and must assent to the gospel when it hears this promise from God. He compared grace and human response in conversion to receiving warmth from the sun. The human creature does not earn or merit the warmth of the sun; sunlight warms without human effort. But it does not warm those who flee its light and hide themselves. It warms those who walk into its light. So it is with human creatures, who are not made of clay, stone, or wood, whose wills function as God made them to function, even when sin is in control. Such an analogy only heightened the suspicion that Pfeffinger wanted to teach that some human contribution is necessary to complete the transition from unfaith to faith. Amsdorf repeated his charges in *That Dr. Pfeffinger Maliciously and Falsely Denies His Misdeeds*,[9] and he angrily rejected the charge that he was equating fallen sinners with clay, stone, or wood. He agreed that the sinful will is active, but it is captive to Satan. God calls all people through the gospel, but he draws only those whom he has chosen as his children to himself.

Nikolaus Gallus's Criticism of Melanchthon

Amsdorf's former associate in Magdeburg, Nikolaus Gallus, who had returned to his former position as superintendent of the church in Regensburg once the Truce of Passau made that possible, picked up the lance and pointed it at the heart of the problem: Melanchthon's own "apostasy." Gallus republished the German translation of Luther's *On Bound Choice* in 1559 after unsuccessful attempts to admonish his Preceptor by letter. His preface to the work placed Melanchthon's treatment of the will's cooperation with the Holy Spirit in one basket with Erasmus's rejection of Luther's teaching on the bondage of the will and with the medieval semi-pelagian emphasis on the need and the ability of human cooperation with God in attaining grace.[10]

Gallus continued to criticize his Preceptor for teaching that "the free will in human creatures is a power through which they can turn themselves toward grace." He could only interpret that as a revival of medieval views teaching that grace is given to those who do their best and thus prepare themselves for the reception of that grace.[11] Melanchthon dismissed Gallus's objections to his position as stoic madness; Philip conceded that Luther had erred in the same direction as Gallus. The Preceptor believed that he himself had cast away what he could only understood as a determinism that deprived God of his honor and human creatures of their responsibility.[12]

The Human Modus Agendi

The focus of the debate soon shifted from the published tract to the university lecture hall. Flacius's criticism of Pfeffinger's doctrine of the freedom of the will encountered objections from his colleague at the University of Jena, Viktorin Strigel. Four years Flacius's junior, Strigel had helped organize the theological faculty in Jena when John Frederick the Middler founded the university in 1548. Both theologians had been *Wunderkinder* of sorts, both devoted disciples of Melanchthon. However, Strigel had not broken with Melanchthon over the Interims. In fact, he maintained cordial personal relationships with the Preceptor. He followed his mentor's theological direction devotedly as well even though his representation of John Frederick's policy of insisting on condemnations of Melanchthon's position on adiaphora at the Colloquy of Worms in 1557 cannot have pleased the Preceptor. When the two became colleagues at Jena in the spring of that year Strigel rebuffed Flacius's efforts at working together, trying instead to create distance between them.[13] He expressed reservations regarding Flacius's understanding of the freedom of the will and of other issues under discussion between Gnesio-Lutherans and Philippists.

The brewing contention between the two colleagues got caught up in the larger ferment of the late 1550s in Lutheran Germany. Their disagreements were played out on the field of attempts to end dissension among contemporary Lutherans and within the pressures caused by the desire of their prince, like all others in this period, to centralize power within their lands—and certainly over their churches— in their own courts, in their own hands. In late 1558, when several other efforts at reaching a proper adjudication of the raging controversies over adiaphora, the justification of the sinner before God, good works, and the Lord's Supper had failed, John Frederick the Middler embarked on a project of his own to forge Lutheran reconciliation and unity of teaching.[14] Flacius and Amsdorf proposed a confession of faith that would resolve issues primarily through demarcation of the truth from heresy; the positions that were to be rejected formed the articles of this confession, or *Book of Confutation*, as it would be called. The duke commissioned his senior theologian, Erhard Schnepf, Strigel, and a comrade of theirs, pastor in Jena, Andreas Hügel, to draft the work. The three agreed on one condition: that Amsdorf and Flacius would not have anything to say about the project.

Once the commission had completed its draft, the duke turned immediately to a group of Gnesio-Lutherans, Joachim Mörlin from Braunschweig, Erasmus Sarcerius from Mansfeld, his court preacher Johann Aurifaber, as well as two of his professors, Simon Musaeus, who had just arrived in Jena as the recently deceased Schnepf's replacement, and Flacius for revisions. The final product condemned any concession to the Philippist understanding of the role of the will in conversion and condemned both Major's view of good works and the electoral Saxon concessions on adiaphora.[15]

The *Book of Confutation* was published in February 1559. Strigel and Hügel refused to accept it. The duke insisted that it would be the standard of teaching for his lands. To bring the two recalcitrant church leaders to their senses, John Frederick sent one hundred foot soldiers and more than fifty horsemen to interdict the road between Weimar and Jena on Good Friday 1559. On Easter eve, March 25, the troops battered down Strigel's door with axes, hauled him out of bed, and took him to jail in one of the ducal castles nearby. He there met with Amsdorf, who unsuccessfully tried to persuade him to join with his colleagues in affirming the final version of the *Book of Confutation*.[16] Strigel refused and appealed to a general synod of all German Evangelicals. Flacius suggested instead a public disputation between the two of them. It was held at the ducal castle in Weimar in early August 1560.

Musaeus and Bartholomaeus Winter, a sympathetic pastor in Jena, helped Flacius set the agenda: freedom of the will, the proper distinction of law and gospel, good works, adiaphora, and academic freedom stood on the list of topics. The disputation collapsed before the discussion of the first topic was completed. Flacius fell into Strigel's trap and began to walk down the dead-end street of using Aristotelian concepts to express the biblical teaching regarding sin. He thereby alienated the duke and many of his Gnesio-Lutheran friends as well.[17]

Flacius's fundamental theological activity took form in exegesis, as his great hermeneutical work, the *Key to the Sacred Scriptures*, and his *Gloss on the New Testament* demonstrate. He tried to think in biblical categories and made less (though indeed some) use of Aristotelian categories than some of his Gnesio-Lutheran colleagues, such as Wigand and Hesshus. Strigel, on the other hand, followed Melanchthon more completely also in regard to method: he was dependent upon Aristotelian tools for his own analysis of biblical material. As the two tried to formulate a common understanding of the fallenness of sinners, Strigel introduced the categories of Aristotelian physics—substance and accidence—into the debate. A substance is that which defines and constitutes a thing and makes it a part of its species. An accident is any characteristic that is a part of the identity of the individual instance of that species. A thing loses its fundamental identity as the thing that it is if the substance is no longer present. It loses only incidental characteristics in the loss of an accident. Fatally, Flacius followed his colleague into the swamp of joining biblical concepts and Aristotelian categories; he tried to express the biblical understanding of sin within this alien paradigm. Neither of the two theologians was sophisticated enough to recognize the linguistic and logical complexities and contradictions involved in their attempt to clarify Scripture with the aid of the Stagirite.

Strigel began by arguing for Melanchthon's position that there are three concurring "causes" (the Latin *causa* is better translated in this case "factors") in conversion: the human will, the Holy Spirit, and God's Word. God draws the will, and so it is subordinate to the Holy Spirit, but it cooperates with the Spirit once he has initiated conversion. Strigel defined the fallen human will as a neutral, unbound, active force. Its powers had been damaged by the fall into sin, but they continued to act, he maintained. This mode of action—*modus agendi*—is part of the human substance, which sin could not change. Sin, Strigel insisted, is only an accident in Aristotelian terms. Human creatures do not remain the same person if their wills are removed; they do remain the same person when their sin is removed. Thus, salvation is comparable to the healing of a sick person, not to the resurrection of the dead. Strigel used an illustration from the popular physics of his day: when garlic juice is spread on a magnet, it loses its power. When the garlic juice is wiped away, its power is restored.

Flacius's entire approach to the question was different. He began with the presupposition that what defines humanity is its being created in the image of God. This image was lost in the fall and replaced by the image of Satan, which directs life into false faith and evil deeds. In relationship to God, the sinner is totally in rebellion and capable only of rejecting the author of life. In the fallen human creature sin is no Aristotelian accident: the absence or presence of trust determines what kind of being this sinner is. The absence of trust transforms and permeates the beings of unbelievers. Conversion is not merely healing; it is resurrection. Therefore, original sin may be defined as the substance of the fallen human creature. Flacius did distinguish between two aspects of substance, in good Melanchthonian-Aristotelian fashion. The material being (in Aristotelian language, the *substantia materialis*) of the fallen sinner is still human, with those physical and emotional characteristics with which God equipped all human creatures. The will indeed functions in the sinner. But the formal substance (*substantia formalis* or *forma substantialis*), that which defines human creatures at heart and core, has been changed essentially from God's child into an enemy of God.[18]

The death of John Frederick's eight-month-old son brought the disputation abruptly to an end on August 8. Though often said that the duke reacted to Flacius's position on original sin with repulsion, the evidence points to this death as the cause for ending the disputation. Flacius slowly did lose the duke's confidence over the next year, and factors of ecclesiastical policy and politcs led to his being forced into exile in December 1561, with Wigand, following Musaeus, Matthaeus Judex, and other colleagues. The steadfast Gnesio-Lutherans had been removed from the duke's inner and administrative circles.

Strigel had triumphed, but many parish pastors remained faithful to Flacius's position, even if not to his use of Aristotelian language to uphold it. John Frederick turned to Duke Christoph of Württemberg for help in settling the controversy over the freedom of the will. Christoph sent two of his theologians, Jakob Andreae and Christoph Binder, to Weimar in May 1562. They negotiated and composed the so-called "Declaration of Viktorin," a new confessional document for ducal Saxony.[19] It taught that God alone effects the salvation of sinners; the fallen human creatures are so weak that they cannot restore themselves to the kingdom of God. The original sin was not just a weakness of wisdom in Adam and Eve but a lack of righteousness and holiness in will and heart. Original sin is a corrupt inclination to doubt and to disobey God. God created human creatures with a *modus agendi* that differentiates human beings from all creatures that do not have intellect or will. This makes human creatures capable of hearing and understanding and trusting the Word of the gospel. The Holy Spirit must restore to this *modus agendi* the ability to make free decisions and thus to accept the gospel.

The venerable Bishop Amsdorf took exception. Perhaps because of the close relationship he had with John Frederick the Elder, or perhaps because he was indeed venerable, Amsdorf was untouchable. John Frederick the Middler could not send him into exile with Flacius and Wigand. Amsdorf did not rail against Strigel for playing politics in the ouster of Flacius and all Amsdorf's other comrades who had disappeared from the ducal Saxon ecclesiastical establishment in the preceding months. He did, however, attack the "Declaration of Viktorin" because of the concept of the *modus agendi*. He was suspicious of Andreae because he believed the Württemberger was soft on the doctrine of the Lord's Supper, probably because of Andreae's contacts with Theodore Beza and others from Geneva.[20] He therefore was prepared to suspect anything that proceeded from Andreae's hand.

Focusing on the theological cause for conversion, not on its psychological mechanics, the bishop insisted simply that God has the human creature totally and completely in his hands: no *modus agendi* need be discussed. Two former allies of Flacius and Wigand, Johann Stössel and Maximilian Mörlin, had remained faithful to the duke when the theologians and the government had parted ways in 1561, and they headed a visitation team that set out to enforce the "Declaration of Viktorin" upon all pastors in ducal Saxony. Resistance was so stiff that Stössel wrote a "Superdeclaration" emphasizing that the corrupted human will has no power to cooperate in conversion. It defined the term *modus agendi* as only an external factor, a passive potential or aptitude for hearing, rather than any internal ability or faculty in the sinner. Some thirty pastors still rejected the settlement and were forced to follow the Jena professors into exile. Amsdorf was given the right to compose his own subscription to the document, which rejected any use of the term.

The Substance of the Fallen Human Creature

Flacius himself seems to have found the "Declaration of Viktorin" acceptable. However, he had been forced from the ducal Saxon scene and found his way to Regensburg and a safe haven with his old friend, Nikolaus Gallus. There and later in Antwerp and Strasbourg he worked on a number of scholarly projects, including his *Key to the Sacred Scriptures*. It appeared in print in 1567 and contained a section entitled "On the essence of and terms for original sin or the old Adam." It presented the same teaching that Flacius had defended in the Weimar Disputation in 1560, that original sin is the substance of the sinful human creature, who has taken on the image of Satan through the fall into sin. Flacius continued to distinguish the material substance of the human creature, which remains after the fall, from the "formal factor," which determines the core identity of the sinner and has turned this creature of God into the image of Satan, shaped by original sin in heart and soul—and thus "substantially" sin.

In 1560 Flacius's colleagues, Simon Musaeus and Johannes Wigand, had approved this kind of language, which used citations from Luther as well as a well-woven biblical argument for its support. Indeed, Musaeus and Tileman Hesshus had approved a draft of the article for the *Key to the Sacred Scriptures*. However, when Martin Chemnitz, Joachim Mörlin, and their Gnesio-Lutheran comrades from Braunschweig raised objections to Flacius's definition of original sin as the substance or essence of the fallen human creature (and to Flacius's tendency toward controversy), Musaeus, Hesshus, and Wigand turned sharply against the Croatian. Melanchthon's unremitting, bitter attacks against the "Illyrian"—as the Preceptor preferred to designate his former student and colleague by whom he felt betrayed—finally took effect. Flacius was isolated from a majority of his former friends.[21]

However, a group of his followers did indeed continue to represent his views. Chief among them was Cyriacus Spangenberg, whose father Johann had introduced the Reformation in Nordhausen and led the church in the County of Mansfeld.

There his son also ministered until troops from Brandenburg drove him and his pregnant wife into exile in the middle of the night because of his insistence that original sin is the substance of the fallen human creature. Spangenberg's parishioners held to his teaching in defiance of Mansfeld authorities for a generation. Into the early seventeenth century, they met in homes for services and were arrested from time to time for this breaking of the public peace.[22] Perhaps Flacius's most vocal and persistent defender was Christoph Irenaeus, whose opponents forced him finally into language that went beyond Flacius and actually contradicted him.[23]

The Solution of the Formula of Concord on Original Sin and Freedom of the Will

As the committee charged with the composition of the Formula of Concord met, it contained theologians with a spectrum of views on freedom and bondage of the will, but none of its members had supported Flacius's approach to the solution to the problem by defining original sin as the substance of the fallen human creature. Andreas Musculus had represented a Gnesio-Lutheran position on the bondage of the will; David Chytraeus and Nikolaus Selnecker had used Melanchthon's concept of the three "causes" in conversion.[24] Chytraeus worked hard at revising Andreae's original suggestions for the treatment of the role of the will in conversion, and Chemnitz revised the draft extensively. The final version takes seriously the psychological factors in conversion but also decisively rejects every hint of autonomous human cooperation or contribution in the sinner's coming to faith.

The Concordists were sensitive not only to what Flacius had taught but also to potential directions with which his language identifying original sin as the substance of the fallen human creature might take.[25] They shared Flacius's determination to distinguish between the "material" of humanity, such as reason and will, which remain what God made them (even if damaged or depraved after the fall), and the central, formative trust or faith which constitutes the human creature's relationship to God and thus basic human identity. However, they believed that a consistent, logical application of the language of substance to original sin would cause serious perversions of biblical teaching regarding the integrity of the human creature as God's creation.[26] Therefore, they carefully defined the nature of sin's impact on humanity in a manner that reflected the concerns Melanchthon had often voiced in regard to an oversimplified rejection of the actions of the will. The Formula insists that the sinner remains God's creature, a product of God's creative activity, not a creation of Satan. God continues to fashion human bodies and souls even after the Fall. The Concordists argued that Flacius's view of original sin would twist and pervert the doctrines of creation, redemption, sanctification, and the resurrection of the flesh, for in each case it would ascribe false characteristics to the actions of God and to the created nature of his human creature. The Concordists were deeply concerned that the people of God could get the impression that God was responsible in any way for sin. They insisted that Christ had assumed human flesh without assuming human sinfulness. Sin is not sanctified when the human being is sanctified. Original sin will not be raised when the dead are raised. Each of these points illustrated the impossibility of equating the essence or substance of the human creature with original sin (SD I, 33–62).

At the same time the Formula insisted that original sin is not merely a slight corruption of human nature. It is not a guilt that results from Adam's sin without any actual effect on the person of the individual sinner. Certainly, this original sin is not an inevitable or natural characteristic of human nature. Everything in the fallen human creature has been perverted by original sin. The Pelagian error that the nature of the sinners has suffered no real corruption is false, according to the Formula. Original sin is far more than an insignificant smudge or superficial stain. It is more than some external obstacle which hinders the spiritual powers God has given his human creatures. Original sin permeates the whole of fallen humanity. Although not to be equated with the sinner's nature, substance, or essence, it is nonetheless deeply and inextricably embedded in every person's humanness. It has driven out every aptitude and ability to please God and at its root instills deep and abiding enmity toward God in the sinner. Only through the power of God's Word and the Holy Spirit can this perversion be recognized. Only God can free sinners from this corruption. That he will do through death and resurrection (SD I, 5–32).

The historical root of the problem came through attempts to use Aristotelian physics, with its concepts of "substance" and "accidents," to describe biblical anthropology, which operated with an entirely different metaphysical framework. The Concordists warned that these terms would not be used among the simple folk. They might, however, be used among scholars. Their use can demonstrate that the devil cannot create a substance but can only corrupt the substances God creates. The Formula insisted on the totality of this corruption of human creatures through sin but also insisted that the fallen sinner remains truly a creation of God, a creature whom God redeems, sanctifies, and raises from the dead as his own human child.

The Concordists made it clear that the second article of their document would not treat the human will as it had existed before the fall, after new birth, or after the resurrection of the flesh, but only its powers after the fall into sin (an oft-used analytical device since Augustine).[27] The fallen human will and reason understand nothing in spiritual matters on the basis of their own powers. For the will has become God's enemy, turned away from him, dead in its ability to trust in him and worship him (SD II, 1–47). Yet the will is not dead in its ability to function. It requires turning, but it functions in its willing as the Holy Spirit turns it. He does so through the Word of God, which is God's power to save. Faith comes from hearing the Word. Thus, the Concordists acknowledged the psychological functioning of the fallen will as well as its complete dependence on the power of the Spirit, working through the Word of God, for its rescue and restoration from its corrupted state (SD II, 48–60). Although they viewed formulations such as "God draws, but he draws those who are willing," and "the human will is not idle in conversion but also is doing something," as dangerous because of their usage in recent times, the Concordists believed that it was also important to recognize that those who are converted experienced in their reasoning and willing the movement which the Holy Spirit was causing through the Word. They cautioned against understanding Luther's description of the will in conversion as "purely passive" in such a way that would deny that psychological functioning (SD II, 61–90).

On the one side, the Concordists joined Melanchthon in rejecting a "stoic" or "Manichaean" concept of necessity that would destroy human responsibility. On the other side, they rejected every suggestion that the will or reason contributes in any way to conversion from sin and the restoration of true life. The crass Pelagianism of those who believed that sinners could effect their own conversion was quickly dismissed, as was the error of the semi-Pelagians who thought that sinners might initiate conversion on their own but would then need the assistance of the Holy Spirit to complete their turning back to God. The Formula also addressed the various forms of synergism that had arisen within the Wittenberg circle. The human will, it stated, cannot respond to the initiation of conversion by the Holy Spirit and complete the turning for him. It cannot dispose or prepare itself for grace and cannot accept grace apart from the power of the Holy Spirit. Therefore, the Concordists found it confusing to speak of three "causes" of conversion: they omitted Melanchthon's inclusion of the will as a "cause" or factor and left only God's Word and the Holy Spirit on their list (SD II,74–90). Thus, the Formula grants the Philippist insistence that the will is not totally inactive in conversion, as a stone or block of wood is, but it affirms the Gnesio-Lutheran position that its activity resists God apart from the power of the Holy Spirit and up to that point at which the Spirit has converted it to godliness.

God's Election of His Own

At the beginning of its treatment of the biblical teaching of God's choosing those whom he would make his children, the eleventh article of the Formula of Concord observes that the topic had caused no public offense and no interminable strife among the adherents of the Augsburg Confession. That was true. However, the topic had arisen between Lutherans and representatives of Calvin's doctrine of double predestination in Strasbourg, and it had provoked small though indeed sharp exchanges among former Wittenberg students in north Germany. It was a topic worth discussing, if for no other reason than to avoid future divisions (which it actually did not accomplish[28]).

Luther had generally avoided discussions of predestination in his writings, seeking assurance for troubled consciences in the promise of the gospel, delivered through the means of grace, even in his *On Bound Choice*.[29] Many of his disciples followed this lead in trying to steer clear of the subject. Nonetheless, Luther had found great comfort in his belief that God had chosen his own and resolved to make them believers in his Son and his own children before the foundation of the world. He fashioned his formulation of this biblical teaching within the dynamic tension between law and gospel, and thus implicit in his discussion of the means of grace rests what has been labeled a "broken" doctrine of predestination.[30] God chose his own; those who are alienated from him have only themselves to blame. Both God's sovereign grace and human responsibility remained fully integral in themselves according to Luther's view, which was pastoral if not fully logical. John Calvin opted for the logical in his attempt to remain faithful to Luther's theology and posited a belief in double predestination, a conclusion Luther's friend Nikolaus von Amsdorf and others among his followers had also drawn from Luther's writings. Most of Luther's students heard enough from Melanchthon to want to take human responsibility seriously while preserving the total responsibility of God for salvation. It was precisely this concern, anchored in the desire to preserve the preaching of repentance for the sinful side of those who remain sinners while being God's saints, that moved Johann Marbach to disagree with Calvin's theological supporter, Jerome Zanchi, in the early 1560s.

Strasbourg had experienced a "second Reformation"[31] of its own after Martin Bucer, its leading reformer in the 1520s, 1530s, and 1540s, had been forced to flee to England ahead of imperial troops bent on enforcing the Interim in 1548. A Wittenberg student, Johann Marbach, who had left the university for a pastorate in Strasbourg in 1545, was Bucer's hand-picked successor as superintendent of the city's churches. He introduced a program of "lutheranizing" the city's doctrinal stance, which had followed Bucer's mediating positions between the Swiss reformed communities and Wittenberg. The Italian exile, Jerome Zanchi, trained in the revival of the thought of Thomas Aquinas before fleeing his homeland ahead of the inquisition, arrived in Strasbourg in 1553 to teach in its famous Academy. In his inaugural address he expressed his wish to be known not as a Lutheran, Zwinglian, or Calvinist but only as a Christian. However, it was clear that the third epithet fit. In 1557 at the Colloquy of Worms, some of Marbach's university friends in the company of Flacius insisted that Strasbourg's church no longer adhered to the Augsburg Confession because of Zanchi's public statements on the Lord's Supper.

Zanchi joined the head of the Academy, Johann Sturm, in efforts to undercut Marbach's propagation of his own Lutheran theology. Their differences led to public charges against Zanchi regarding the doctrine of the Lord's Supper and regarding election and the perseverance of the saints who are the elect of God.[32] Zanchi maintained that the elect could not fall from grace. He charged that Marbach's contrary position opened the door to belief in the powers of the free will to bring a person to faith. Zanchi held, against Marbach's position, that believers can place their faith in the a priori decision of God to save them. He believed that true faith is given at one specific time during the believer's life to those who are chosen. This gift of being transplanted into Christ through the Holy Spirit can never be completely abandoned. Believers cannot totally reject the Holy Spirit and thus be totally lost to Christ. Adults can recognize this gift in themselves. Those who are truly among the elect will practice sincere repentance and avoid wanton living because they have the gift of perseverance. Even when the outer person sins, the inner person remains faithful to God.

For Marbach, Zanchi's position included too much speculation. The former Wittenberg student anchored the believers' comfort in the Scriptural promise of God, delivered through the means of grace. This promise assures believers that they have been chosen by God before the creation of the world. God's chosen children know of their election a posteriori—through Word and sacrament, through the ministry of gospel proclamation. Marbach strove to preserve the law/gospel dynamic of Luther's understanding of election, and thus he avoided the issue of the perseverance of the saints. He kept the law ready for application with its fullest condemnations for Christians who needed its terror applied to their sinfulness, just as he kept the gospel ready for those who in despair of their own righteousness and over their own sin were turned to look to Christ. This focus on God's Word rather than his hidden will reflected Luther's theology of the cross as Marbach had learned it in Wittenberg.

Personal tensions mounted, building on the rivalry between Johann Sturm, who represented the old Bucerian order in his Academy, and Marbach, pastor of the church and Lutheran theologian. Zanchi apparently told students not to attend Marbach's lectures. Marbach complained that students were becoming anxious about their salvation because they could only speculate what God's hidden will for them might be. Claiming academic freedom, Zanchi tried to avoid discussion of the issues. By the spring of 1561, the infighting over turf between faculty and ministerium and over the theological issues at hand reached a point of crisis. The maneuverings on both sides invited intervention from the municipal government. Arbitrators were to be called from outside the city to resolve the dispute. Marbach, whose service to the city had won him some favor and advantage in such a situation, was able to suggest who might serve: a Wittenberg friend Cunmann Flinsbach of Zweibrücken, Simon Sulzer of Basel, and Jakob Andreae from Württemberg.

The three came to the city in 1563 and formulated a "Concordia" on two issues: the Lord's Supper and the election of the children of God. The first article pledged the city to remain faithful to the doctrine of the Supper formulated by Melanchthon in the Wittenberg Concord of 1536 for the common agreement of Bucer's delegation from south Germany and Luther. Marbach and Bucer's followers in Strasbourg could find common ground there. The second article was more difficult. Andreae and Flinsbach followed Marbach's lead in presenting a "broken" doctrine of predestination, along the law/gospel lines Luther had taught. The statement was governed by two prime concerns: that the teaching of the church not conflict with the doctrine of repentance and the need for daily repentance in the life of the Christian, and that afflicted consciences not be deprived of consolation and hope through the teaching of election. Pastoral use of the doctrine was presupposed.

The text of the settlement based its teaching on Romans 8:28-39 and 9:6-24, as well as Ephesians 1:3-4. God is angered by sin and threatens all those who transgress his law with his wrath, under which they have fallen by their own fault. God has prepared no one for destruction, but he has fashioned vessels pleasing to himself without any preconditions required from those whom he claims as his children. God chose his own before the foundations of the world, in Christ. There can be no consideration of election apart from Christ. The gospel reveals this eternal plan of God to those who hear it. God's promise of salvation, his desire to save, extends over all sinners. Saving faith is a gift of God, given because of his mercy, according to his plan of election, not because of any human work or effort or merit. The document expressed concern that the doctrine of double predestination can lead to a false sense of security and thus to sin, and that it can condemn those who fall into sin to despair in thinking that God has given them no possibility of repentance.

Zanchi labeled the disagreement a misunderstanding; Marbach saw in it a deep, fundamental theological difference. Indeed, the two had a different orientation toward the application of the gospel, which caused and resulted from their differing views of the proper distinction of law and gospel. Zanchi left the city in November 1563. His challenge to the Lutheran teaching had forced Andreae to come to terms formally with a significant element of Luther's teaching and thus prepared him for processing it for the eleventh article of the Formula.

However, it may be that the actual occasion for inclusion of this topic came from a limited encounter in north Germany, with which Chemnitz was tangentially involved in the late 1560s. Flacius's disciple Cyriacus Spangenberg published a series of seven sermons on predestination in 1567.[33] In them he presented much of Luther's position in *On Bound Choice*. He avoided a doctrine of double predestination but sharply excluded any possibility of synergism. He emphasized that God's unconditional choice of individual believers rested upon his decision made before time began and was founded and grounded alone in his mercy. Spangenberg's views caused offense in electoral Saxony, not only among the theologians but also in the mind of the elector himself. August brought pressure to bear. Spangenberg defended his views in a very brief apology. The electoral Saxon theologians continued to criticize his views, also in the documents they used to reset the agenda of public controversy within Lutheranism.[34] They believed that this strong doctrine of election would be unacceptable to most Lutherans.

The Solution of the Formula of Concord on Election

In following the argumentation that Chemnitz had used in his *Handbook on the Chief Parts of Christian Teaching*,[35] the eleventh article of the Formula approached the subject of God's choosing of his own on the basis of the distinction of law and gospel—a "broken" doctrine of predestination.[36] The Concordists took cognizance of Philippist concerns that a "stoic necessity" not be taught in regard to God's election of his chosen people, but they affirmed that salvation depends ultimately alone on God's gracious will, a will which he had formulated in eternity, before the creation of the world. Chemnitz's reflections in the midst of discussions unleashed by the Wittenberg criticism of Spangenberg's sermons on predestination formed the basis for the Formula's presentation of the doctrine of election. The predestination of God's chosen people is to function only as gospel, that is, as comfort and assurance for believers. God's election of his own faithful must be understood as God's good news and his good gift, or it is falsely understood, the Concordists insisted. If it functions in such a way that it fosters either despair or presumption, it is being misused. This teaching of election presumes that the mystery of why some are saved and not others cannot be explained or even addressed apart from the distinction of law and gospel. For God wants all to be saved (1 Tim. 2:4, Ezek. 18:23, 33:11), and yet those who do not believe in him are responsible for their own rejection of him, while those whom he saved have only his gracious will to thank for their salvation (SD XI, 1–50).

Based upon the distinction between God's foreknowledge and his predestining election, the Formula's position affirmed unconditional election to salvation, rejected double predestination, and anchored the believer's understanding of election in the means of grace. "The Word of God leads believers to Christ, who is the Book of Life, in whom are inscribed and chosen all who shall be eternally saved" (Ep. XI,13, cf. SD XI, 51–93). Those who resist the Word have only themselves to blame. Knowing that God has chosen them to be his children moves believers to live according to God's will.

11

The Osiandrian Controversy over the Righteousness
That Avails before God

Among the early and ardent supporters of Luther's Reformation was Andreas Osiander, preacher in the city of Nuremberg, where Luther's ideas found acceptance in the early 1520s. Osiander had studied at the University of Ingolstadt 1515–1520, and there he had been exposed to the biblical humanism of Melanchthon's mentor, Johannes Reuchlin. Reuchlin had pioneered Hebrew studies in Germany. Osiander absorbed not only his insights into the Hebrew text of the Old Testament but also elements of the neoplatonic literature of medieval Jewish philosophy and theology, as found in the system of thought known as the Kabala. Its mystical metaphysic embedded itself in Osiander's mind, and as his conceptual framework it shaped the way in which he assimilated Luther's thought.

That process took place as Osiander lectured in Hebrew at the Augustinian monastery in Nuremberg, where he published the text of the Old Testament with marginal notations in 1522. In that year he also became preacher at the church of Saint Lorenz and enthusiastically helped promote the Reformation. In 1524 his preaching converted Albrecht of Hohenzollern, the grand master of the crusading order, the Teutonic Knights, which controlled much of the Baltic lands between Danzig and Tallinn. Osiander participated in the Colloquy at Marburg in 1529 and was present in Augsburg in 1530 and in Smalcald in 1537. With Johannes Brenz he composed a constitution for the evangelical churches in Nuremberg and the neighboring principality of Brandenburg-Ansbach in 1533. He fiercely opposed all papalist errors and criticized sacramentarian deviations from Luther's doctrine of the Lord's Supper. No one had really noticed that all the while the neoplatonic presuppositions of his kabalistic studies had led him to understand the righteousness that avails before God in a different way than did Luther.

Osiander in Königsberg: The Spark for Controversy

Imperial pressure drove Osiander out of Nuremberg at the end of 1548 as the Habsburg government temporarily imposed the Augsburg Interim on the city. He fled to the court of his convert, Albrecht of Brandenburg, who had secularized his lands in Prussia in 1525 and claimed the title "Duke of Prussia." Albrecht had founded a university in Königsberg in 1542. The duke invited Osiander to assume a pastorate in the city and a theological lectureship at the university, even though he had no advanced theological degree. The faculty he joined had squabbled throughout the brief history of the university, and Osiander's introductory academic disputation placed him in the middle of controversy. Matthias Lauterwald, an arts instructor trained in Wittenberg, criticized Osiander's view of repentance. Lauterwald understood his new colleague as prescribing a mere intellectual recognition of sin, whereas he held that repentance had to include painful regret and simultaneous resolution to live a better life. This critique was not fair. Formal hearings before the Evangelical bishop, Paul Speratus, exonerated Osiander. In those hearings the question of whether God dwells in eternal light did reveal that the Nuremberger's neoplatonic doctrine of God provided a different orientation to fundamental theological questions than that of those who had studied in Wittenberg.

While Osiander strengthened his personal influence in the ducal court at Königsberg during 1549 and 1550, he fell into dispute with Philippist theologians in Leipzig and Wittenberg. The Hebraist Bernhard Ziegler of Leipzig attacked his interpretation of the eternality of the "heaven of heavens," an interpretation that diminished the power of the Creator in the Wittenberg view. Osiander's denunciation of the "the new-born idol" of the Leipzig Interim, which he viewed as a first step toward a restoration of the papal Antichrist in electoral Saxony, won him no friends in Melanchthon's inner circle. His colleague Friedrich Staphylus, who soon would apostatize and return to the Roman obedience, reported privately to Melanchthon that Osiander held another view of justification than the Wittenbergers.

Public controversy over Osiander's doctrine of justification began with the publication of his *Whether the Son of God Would Have Had to Become Incarnate If Sin Had Not Invaded the World, and On the Image of God*.[1] On the basis of a differentiation of the likeness of God from the image of God (Gen. 1:27)—the former being Adam's likeness to the form of the eternal Son of God, the latter the image of the incarnate Christ which embraced his divine substance as well as his divine form—Osiander taught that Christ would have come into human flesh in order to fulfill the perfect but incomplete humanity of Adam and Eve even if they had not fallen into sin. He did not notice that he was imposing upon the biblical, "Hebraic" way of thinking a model of reality determined by the neoplatonic models and presuppositions that had developed quite apart from a conception of a personal creator-creator. More important for him than the Word made flesh or the Word conveyed through preaching was the eternally righteous substance of the Word as Christ's divine person. This divine substance delivered the very substance of divine righteousness to sinners' hearts. This definition of the image of God and of righteousness reflected a neoplatonic diminution of the created order inherent in kabalistic thinking.

Osiander's presuppositions were shaping his assimilation of Luther's thought. Fundamental to his theology was his scholastic definition of God as the divine person in whom there can be no "accident," that is, God is a single, perfect, inseparable essence. That meant for Osiander that God is totally present with his real essence wherever his characteristics, influence, or activities are perceived. Thus, everything about God had to involve his ontological essence or substance. Osiander failed to grasp Luther's biblical way of defining reality in terms of relationships, based on the creative Word of God that establishes this reality. Osiander's education had trained him to think in the categories of substance and of spirit that his neoplatonic roots used to define reality. He failed to understand that for Luther the basis of reality rested on creative speaking (Gen. 1), on the Word of God.[2]

Previous to the appearance of *Whether the Son of God Would Have Had to Become Incarnate*, Osiander had defended and then published theses on justification. As always, he used Luther's vocabulary: works-righteousness was rejected, faith emphasized. However, Osiander rejected the concept that the righteousness of the forgiven sinner is attained when God through his re-creative Word of absolution bestows Christ's righteousness as faith grasps or receives it. He held to justification through faith but taught that faith serves as the channel by which the divine Son of God comes to dwell in believers, placing in them the essential divine righteousness of his divine person.

Key to his explanation of salvation was his distinction between the historical act of redemption in Christ's crucifixion, death, and resurrection and the substantial change in believers wrought through reconciliation. This reconciliation or justification occurs in the marriage of Christ and the believer, the unifying of the believer's soul with the indwelling divine righteousness. The human nature of Christ and his blood shed on the cross fifteen hundred years earlier did not make a decisive contribution to restoring human righteousness.

Although also an Old Testament scholar, Osiander had learned to strain biblical concepts through his kabalistic grid. He never clarified the connection between redemption in Christ and reconciliation through his indwelling. He did little with the central Lutheran concept of the forgiveness of sins since in his view humanity is completed through this indwelling divine righteousness—in contrast to Luther's concept of the restoration of the proper relationship between God and human creatures through the remission of the sin that separates sinners from God. Justification for Osiander consisted in having the divinely righteous Christ dwelling in one's heart.

Criticism greeted this disputation on justification almost immediately. Melchior Isinder, a professor of theology in Königsberg, won support for his rejection of Osiander's views from the young ducal librarian, Martin Chemnitz. His interest in theology, implanted by Melanchthon in Wittenberg, now grew as he searched the ancient fathers for ammunition against Osiander. Chemnitz recognized that Osiander's views decisively differed from those he had learned from his Preceptor in Wittenberg. Joachim Mörlin, pastor of the Dom in Königsberg, initially stood by Osiander, believing his colleague's protestations that he adhered to Luther's concept of justification. Mörlin had recently arrived in Königsberg on the run from Göttingen, where Duke Erich von Braunschweig-Calenberg had ended his pastorate as part of his imposition of the Augsburg Interim on his domains. Mörlin felt a natural sympathy for Osiander, a fellow exile. But Mörlin also had learned to read Scripture through the eyes of Luther and Melanchthon. Alienation over the definition of justification ended his cordial relationship with Osiander and aborted Mörlin's mediation attempts as well, bringing him into strident theological conflict with his colleague and into political skirmishes with Duke Albrecht. The prince's interference in ecclesiastical affairs on the side of his favorite, Osiander, offended the Gnesio-Lutheran Mörlin.

After several months of seeking reconciliation between Osiander and his local critics, Mörlin joined Chemnitz in labeling Osiander's views heretical in April 1551, chiefly because Osiander mentioned Christ's suffering and death so seldom and denied that Christ's obedience to God the Father's plan for atoning for sin is a part of his righteousness which is imputed to the sinner in forgiveness. The friendship between Mörlin and Chemnitz formed here lasted a lifetime. The two worked closely together, and they influenced the development of each other's theology. Albrecht's prohibition of polemic against Osiander had no effect on Mörlin, who believed that no governmental authority could forbid the preaching of God's Word. He thundered against his colleague from his pulpit. Voices outside Prussia quickly came to Mörlin's, Isinder's, and Chemnitz's support. Within Prussia one opponent did what theological foes often do, in good faith: Francesco Stancaro countered Osiander's denial that the human nature contributes to salvation by going too far in the opposite direction.

The Stancaran Intermezzo

The Mantuan-born Stancaro had also arrived in Königsberg as an exile in 1551. He had left his native Italy for safer havens in the mid 1540s. Albrecht called him from Cracow to the duke's university in 1551 to replace a Hebrew instructor whom the duke had fired because of his opposition to Osiander. Appointed as a new mediator in the Osiandrian affair, Stancaro soon attacked Osiander on the basis of his own Christology, which he had developed out of his study of scholastic theology. He held, on the basis of his reading of Peter Lombard, that the three persons of the Trinity are identical in their essence and activity. Therefore, Christ's divine nature took part in sending the Logos into the flesh and could not assume the role of mediator between God and fallen sinners. As a result, Stancaro opposed Osiander with the argument that Christ saves sinners only through his human nature. This view was objectionable to Mörlin and Chemnitz because it offended the catholic understanding of the relationship of the two natures in Christ, a theme which continued to command Chemnitz's attention throughout his life and came to expression in the eighth article of the Formula of Concord (on Christology in the context of the discussion of the Lord's Supper) as well as the third (on Osiander and justification).

Exiled from Königsberg for his opposition to Osiander, Stancaro accepted a position in Frankfurt an der Oder, where he fell immediately into a dispute with his colleague there, Andreas Musculus, over the relationship of the two natures in

Christ. Musculus taught that Christ had suffered for sinners both as God and as a human creature, not just in his human nature. Melanchthon also issued a rejection of Stancaro's views of the communication of attributes and the mediatorship of Christ in 1553.[3] As Stancaro wandered through Poland and the Magyar lands in the succeeding decades before his death in 1574, he alienated almost all other theologians and was accused of being a Nestorian, a Judaizer, and a Muslim.[4]

Osiander's Doctrine of Justification

Only a few pastors in the Prussian countryside found Osiander's doctrine attractive, probably after it had been explained to them by ducal counselors. Apart from his own congregation in the old city of Königsberg and a few counselors at the ducal court, he won little support. The laity of Königsberg took to the streets in protest against Duke Albrecht's plan to exile the recalcitrant Mörlin for his incessant assaults on Osiander's doctrine. Also from outside Prussia came voices of concern, above all from Philip Melanchthon, first in correspondence, then in printed critiques. Without consciously focusing on questions relating to the atonement itself,[5] Melanchthon maintained that the whole of Scripture, particularly Saint Paul, teaches that the wrath of the Father is set aside through the blood, death, and obedience of the Son of God. Christ's merit in obeying the law and in being sacrificed for its demands is attributed or imputed to sinners, and therein consists their righteousness, not in some ontological indwelling of God. Sanctification flows from faith; it does not occur because of the righteousness of God is found within the sinner.[6]

Melanchthon was particularly concerned that believers' comfort in the gospel would be taken away since they would think that any sin they might commit would indicate that the essential righteousness of God was not in them because it could not coexist with sin. (In fact, Osiander intended his ontological argument regarding human righteousness to preserve the comfort of the gospel.) Melanchthon believed that Osiander's placement of saving righteousness within the sinner destroyed Luther's position that salvation comes from *extra nos* ("outside and apart from ourselves"), the dependence of faith upon God's external Word of promise, and its saving, life-restoring action in the forgiveness of sins. Osiander's theology was no more than a return to the medieval uncertainty regarding God's forgiving Word, a return to view of salvation that had to be turned inward rather than directed toward God.

Albrecht felt compelled to protect his favorite. He asked Osiander to prepare a defense, which appeared in July 1551 under the title, *On the One Mediator, Jesus Christ, and Justification by Faith, a Confession.*[7] The court also decided to submit the matter to the judgment of other Evangelical churches. Almost all replied with condemnations of Osiander's doctrine of justification. Melanchthon's official statement for the electoral Saxon church reiterated his view that the righteousness of the sinner that avails before God consists in the grace and gift of God. His grace is expressed in the word of forgiveness that imputes the merit of Christ to the sinner;

his gift is the presence of Christ through the Holy Spirit in the believer. Both the grace and the gift were won by the obedience of the whole Christ, God and human creature, and they are delivered to the forgiven sinner through faith.

Osiander's reply minimized their differences, stating that the Wittenberg theologians and he differed merely in their description of the mode of God's presence in believers. According to Osiander, he himself spoke of the *reality* of God's presence (that is, in Platonic ontological terms) whereas Melanchthon limited his description to God's way of working among sinners. Without knowing that God's presence is real, that is, without being able to recognize that the ontological righteousness of Christ unites them with the Father, believers can have no real comfort, Osiander believed. Melanchthon's reply to "Osiander's calumnies" ranged broadly, going to the root of the differences in Osiander's trinitarian speculation as well as his conception of justification.

Albrecht hoped that their common opposition to the Interim might win Osiander friends among the circle around Flacius, but Flacius had learned his understanding of the doctrine of justification from Luther and Melanchthon, as had Mörlin. Flacius issued a dozen published criticisms of Osiander, reflecting in part lines laid out in Melanchthon's critiques. The churches of Braunschweig, Brandenburg and Brandenburg-Küstrin, Pomerania, Henneberg, Hamburg, Lüneburg, and ducal Saxony also registered their objections. Even Osiander's former colleagues in Nuremberg distanced themselves from his views. The list of those who individually published criticisms of Osiander reads like the honor roll of both the Philippist and the Gnesio-Lutheran schools: from the former group Georg von Anhalt and Alexander Alesius, from the latter (in addition to Flacius), Amsdorf, Gallus, Otto, Musculus, Stolz, und Aurifaber. The former Wittenberg professor Justus Jonas and the Genevan John Calvin joined in the criticism. These critical voices expressed a variety of concerns and objections to Osiander's teaching.[8]

Only the church of Württemberg, led by Johannes Brenz, fell short of complete rejection of Osiander's views. Brenz and Osiander had worked together in south Germany to spread Luther's message. Brenz had not studied at Wittenberg and had not imbibed Luther's thought so directly as those who had. Thus, the initial response from Württemberg to Albrecht's request for evaluations of Osiander's teaching, in December 1551, noted that Osiander correctly held to the two natures in Christ and had emphasized faith. Brenz and his colleagues believed that Osiander's foes were correct in insisting that human righteousness in God's sight includes more than the indwelling righteousness of Christ: it must be taught that sinners are righteous for the sake of Christ's obedience, blood, suffering, and the forgiveness of sins which rest upon his work. They expressed the pious observation that the matter was a war of words.[9]

Such a judgment won Brenz no friends. Melanchthon attacked Brenz for not mentioning the imputation of Christ's righteousness and for obscuring the difference between his essential righteousness and the righteousness of his obedience and death. In June 1552 the Württemberg theologians tried again to mediate through a declaration which confessed that the sinner's comfort rests only upon Christ's suffering and death and the forgiveness which proceeds from his work of obedience that led him to the cross. Brenz wrote that if only others had known Osiander's spirit and his piety, there would have been no dispute. That failure to take seriously the theological concerns of the Wittenberg disciples again led to tensions between Brenz and north German Lutheran theologians of all party affiliations. It pleased Duke Albrecht, however, and fortified him in his determination to defend the man who had converted him to the Lutheran faith.

During late 1551 the internal dispute simmered in the pulpits and streets of Königsberg. His Königsberg colleagues Georg von Venediger and Peter Hegemon joined Mörlin in composing a confutation of Osiander's *On the One Mediator*. Their *On Justification through Faith: A Fundamental, Reliable Report...against the New, Seductive, and Antichristian Doctrine of Andreas Osiander*[10] was issued as a confession of the Königsberg church, not in their own names. It insisted that justification and redemption cannot be separated, that the human nature of Christ and his incarnation cannot be disregarded in the doctrine of justification. Christ's blood is our righteousness, they wrote, and the believer's faith is based upon the blood of the mediator. Justification has two sides: the forgiveness of sins and the rebirth of the child of God, which includes Christ's indwelling in believers through the Holy Spirit. The indwelling Christ is the whole Christ, God and human creature.

Osiander's justification of his own position, *Against the Fabrications, Mischief, and Defamation in the Title of Dr. Joachim Mörlin's Book on Justification by Faith, to Which He Was Afraid to Set His Name Because of a Bad Conscience*,[11] took issue with the personal criticisms of his foes as well as their theological charges. Again, he denied that he had ever taught that Christ's suffering and death were not a part of the sinner's righteousness, and he again minimized the substantial theological differences between him and his opponents. Osiander assembled excerpts from the critiques of his theology and entitled it *A Taste of the Beer from the Book of Dr. Joachim Mörlin*[12] (and other works). The excerpts were designed to demonstrate the impious spirit from which these criticisms sprang.

Albrecht stood firmly behind Osiander to his theologian's dying day in spite of mounting pressure from other princes. Osiander's death came rather soon, in the midst of the unresolved controversy, on October 17, 1552. On January 24, 1553, Albrecht published a mandate, establishing Osiander's doctrine as the law of the land, and the duke forbade all public criticism. Mörlin was sent into exile in mid-February in spite of a procession of women from his church who begged the duke for more time for their pastor. The duke later refused Mörlin's request for permission to return to the city to visit his ailing wife.

Osiander's son-in-law, the court physician Andreas Aurifaber, was a continuing source of support for the few pastors who took Osiander's views seriously. Their leader was the court preacher Johannes Funck, who had oscillated between opposition and advocacy. Other Evangelical courts continued to express concern, and resistance continued within Prussia. In April 1553 a ducal Saxon delegation headed by Justus Menius and Johann Stolz came for conversations with Osiandrians in Königsberg. Their first effort failed and then was revived before they could leave town at the request of a visitor in the city, Graf Poppo von Henneberg. In May 1554 a synod of pastors was held at Saalfeld to strengthen compliance with the ducal mandate of 1553. To win some minimal conformity the duke's people had to accept a resolution condemning both the diminution of Christ's work of redemption through his blood and the overemphasis on Christ's divine essential righteousness and on the inner Word. This practically amounted to a rejection of Osiander's theology.

Less than a month later a delegation arrived from Württemberg to bring peace to the troubled duchy. Its theologians, Jakob Beurlin and Rupert Dürr, composed a confession that essentially rejected Osiander's position. The new chief clergyman of the principality, Andreas Aurifaber's brother Johann, accepted it. Funck claimed he had always held the position enunciated in the Württemberg confession, arousing more indignation among the pastors. Dürr remained in Königsberg as professor. Amnesty was proclaimed on August 11, 1555, for those who continued to agitate against Osiandrism within the duchy. The next January Albrecht's son-in-law, Johann Albrecht of Mecklenburg, personally came to mediate. At a synod at Riesenburg, Funck, who initially excused himself from attending because of illness, was forced to recant and to pledge to teach according to the Augsburg Confession and Melanchthon's *Loci communes*. Another theologian, Matthias Vogel, attempted to end the matter finally by authoring a new constitution for the church in 1558. Both sides found it compromising and wanting. Mörlin felt compelled to attack Vogel for introducing Osiandrism in a new form.

Never a strong force theologically—except in the minds of its opponents—Osiandrism disappeared politically after it came to rest in an intellectual con artist, Paul Scalich. Trained by the Jesuits, he had become an Evangelical at the court of Maximilian of Habsburg, King Ferdinand's son, in 1555. With the appearance of broadly-ranged learning in history, philosophy, and theology, shaped in part by kabalistic thinking, his thinking compelled Lynn Thorndike to conclude that either "much study had made Paul stark mad, or that, in the words of Pope, 'a little learning' had intoxicated his brain."[13] It does appear that he sincerely affiliated with Osiandrian thought. With the use of a magic ring and a magic coin based on the Tetragramm he also impressed Albrecht, whose staff he joined in 1561. The Prussian nobility rose in protest against the goings-on at court perpetrated by Scalich. The king of Poland, Albrecht's liege lord, sent an investigating commission to Königsberg in the fall of 1565. Scalich fled; Funck was executed after he once more renounced Osiander's teaching. Albrecht was sick and unable to marshal power any longer. He recalled Mörlin and Chemnitz to restore the church of his land and died on March 20, 1568.[14]

The Solution of the Formula of Concord on Justification

Three positions came under the analysis of the Formula in its third article. The first was that of Andreas Osiander; the second, that of his opponent, the renegade Evangelical émigré Francesco Stancaro. In addition, the Concordists also took the occasion to address the doctrine of justification propagated by the Council of Trent.[15]

Osiander's doctrine of justification aroused the opposition of almost all other Lutherans and found support among none outside a very small circle in Prussia and a few old friends in Nuremberg. Based upon a different metaphysical system, its neoplatonic undergirdings separated it decisively from the Old Testament-based Ockhamist presuppositions Luther brought to the theological task. Osiander failed to see what Luther saw in the Old Testament texts they both loved: that God works through his Word, and that that Word is not some ontological category but rather a speaking that creates reality in relationships. Because Osiander sought reality in eternal ontological substances, he failed to see reality where Luther saw it, in God's creative action through his Word and in his use of elements from his created order, such as the human flesh and blood of his own incarnation and in human language that exercises God's power in pronouncing the gospel.

Thus, Luther's students rallied against Osiander, whatever other differences they may have had with one another.[16] Righteousness is bestowed by the pronouncement of God, which creates the reality of the forgiven and righteous believer out of the old sinful self. This pronouncement is possible because the whole person of Christ, God and human creature, has been obedient to his Father. In this obedience he has taken sin into his own death and restored life through his resurrection. Righteousness rests in the relationship of the loving Father and his reconciled children, not in anything "ontological" in either a Platonic or Aristotelian sense. Reality is established by the Word of the Lord.

Taking this into account, the Concordists rejected Osiander's definition of justification for several reasons. It operated from a false metaphysical base that denied that God changes reality through his Word of forgiveness. It viewed the gift of God's grace as something quasi-substantial, within the human creature, rather than as the restoration of humanity to sinners through the transformation of the relationship between them and God. The Concordists recognized that Osiander had tried to use Luther's language of grace and faith to redefine the justification of the sinner on a neoplatonic metaphysical foundation. They therefore affirmed that it is not Christ's divine nature that comes to dwell in sinners that justifies. It is instead the substitutionary, sacrificial obedience Christ rendered to the Father that atones for human sinfulness through his death and restores human creatures to their humanity as God created it through his resurrection. Christ's work accomplishes that by restoring the relationship of love and trust between God and human being. Thus, the Formula teaches clearly that to justify means to change the reality of the sinner's situation by a new word of creation that makes those who had been dead in sin alive in Christ. This was not taken to mean that the indwelling of Christ in believers could be ignored.

But both Andreae and his north German colleagues who had learned of Christ's indwelling in believers from Melanchthon clearly distinguished between this gift of Christ's indwelling and the bestowal of righteousness through his death and resurrection (SD III, 54, 63, 65).

Interestingly, the chief theological voice in the composition of the Formula of Concord, Martin Chemnitz, had gotten his start as a controversial theologian in the Osiandrian controversy, but it was Brenz's associate, Jakob Andreae, who wrote the rejection of Osiander which appears in article III of the Formula. Chemnitz was responsible for much of the article as well, but his sections were directed against the doctrine of justification decreed as dogma by the Council of Trent. Chemnitz had criticized Trent's formulation of the doctrine in his *Examination of the Council of Trent*, and he summarized that critique, especially in paragraphs 30–43 of Solid Declaration article III.[17] The justification of the sinner through the righteousness of the God-man Jesus Christ and his obedience, suffering, death, and resurrection, as his work is appropriated through the Holy Spirit's working of faith in the sinner's heart, remained the central message of Lutheran theology. "Alone" echoed through Chemnitz's treatment of justification as he emphasized that the righteousness of the sinner before God is a gift, that the righteousness of the forgiven sinner is a passive righteousness, the gift of new life in and through Christ (SD III,6–9).

At the same time, according to the Formula, the justified believer does good works. Always sensitive to charges that their view of salvation by grace through faith discouraged a moral life, Lutheran theologians throughout the sixteenth century had insisted that the forgiveness of sins produces the true and living faith which expresses itself in love and hope. This faith cannot exist in the person who does not repent, who fails to demonstrate love, who perseveres in sin against conscience (SD III, 41–43).

The Formula also rejected the view of Stancaro that Christ saves sinners only through the work of his human nature (SD III, 61). It insisted that the obedience of the whole person of Christ, in the inseparable divine and human natures, atoned for sin and restored sinners to the kingdom of God. God justifies sinners through the work of Jesus Christ, fully God and fully human.

12

The Controversies over the Lord's Supper and Christology

Osiander's theology was not the only avenue by which questions regarding Christology were raised in sixteenth-century Lutheran circles. The discussion of the presence of Christ's body and blood in the Lord's Supper also raised difficult and divisive issues regarding the person of Jesus among the students of Luther and Melanchthon. These questions arose in part because of the theologies of other Christian groups outside the Wittenberg circle and in part because of nuanced differences of emphasis in Luther's and Melanchthon's own approaches to the Lord's Supper.[1]

The Background in the First Decades of the Reformation

The mass had formed the centerpiece of medieval religion. The magic moment in the medieval village had come each week as the priest celebrated the mass. It could not help but be a key issue in the call for reform. Sectarian groups that had appeared at the edge of Christendom for a half millennium before the Reformation had often opposed the mass as a focal point of the magical practices and hierarchical oppression. Their biblicistic, moralistic, anticlerical, antisacramental, millennarian programs for renewal of the church and society aimed to abolish both superstition and priestly tyranny. The sixteenth-century representatives of this tradition and others, influenced by the revival of a spiritualizing view of reality shaped by elements of Plato's or Aristotle's ways of thinking, rejected Luther's idea that God could work his saving will and deliver his grace through the sacramental Word with the elements of bread and wine that bear Christ's body and blood.

Luther's senior colleague in Wittenberg, Andreas Bodenstein von Karlstadt, embraced such a position in the earliest days of the Reformation. He provoked Luther to refine his understanding of the Lord's Supper. Based upon Ockhamist presuppositions he had learned as a student in Erfurt, his reading of Scripture, and his deep concern for pastoral care, Luther's critique of medieval doctrines regarding the Lord's Supper included four critical points. First, he rejected the concept of the sacrifice of the mass as blasphemy against the once-for-all atoning sacrifice of Christ. Second, he affirmed that Christ intended the Lord's Supper for the community of believers, not for use in a private rite for the benefit of the priest's income and a dead soul's release from purgatory. Third, he repudiated communion in one kind—the distribution to the laity of only Christ's body—as tyranny over God's Word and the conscience of the believer. Fourth, he renounced the medieval explanation of the presence of Christ's body and blood in the elements with the Aristotelian theory of transubstantiation as an attempt to explain more than can humanly be explained.

However, Luther held fast to his belief in the true presence of Christ's body and blood in the sacramental elements. He did so because he believed that Christ had placed his body and blood there through his almighty Word and that this presence provided deep comfort and assurance for fragile souls. His Ockhamist training had prepared him to recognize that God's power is not bound by definitions that limit God's ways of accomplishing his will within his creation: God can do with his creation what he wants. Luther believed that the creator can place his power and his incarnate presence where and in whatever form he wishes. This same school of thought had also prepared Luther to think that God is comfortable in using specific particulars of the material world, since he is its sovereign creator and Lord.

Not only Karlstadt but also the Swiss reformer Ulrich Zwingli had opposed Luther's interpretation of the words of institution of the Lord's Supper. Zwingli saw in the Supper a memorial meal in which bread and wine were used as symbols of the Lord's presence. With differing explanations, Karlstadt, Zwingli, and the reformer of Basel, Johannes Oecolampadius, criticized Luther's position because they believed it remained caught in medieval magical superstition.[2] The latter two reflected the influences of biblical humanism; in Zwingli's case the influence of the Scotist understanding of the radical separation between the creator and the created order also helped produce a spiritualizing view of reality that expressed itself later in the maxim, "the finite cannot bear the infinite."[3] Luther returned their criticism because he believed that the authority of the Word of God and the consolation of Christian consciences were at stake. Furthermore, he accepted no such limits on the presence and power of God, such as Zwingli and Oecolampadius thought were philosophically necessary.[4]

In addition, even before his disagreements with the Swiss broke out, Luther had come to the conviction that the ancient Christological doctrine formulated at and in the wake of the Council of Chalcedon in the fifth century lay at the basis of the Christian faith. He consistently maintained that the presence of Christ's body and blood is based upon the words of Christ. But he also argued that Christ's presence in the Lord's Supper could be understood on the basis of the presupposition that it is possible for his body and blood to be present in bread and wine because the divine and human natures share their characteristics. This understanding of the hypostatic union that united the two natures in the person of Jesus was labeled the *communicatio idiomatum* (communication of attributes). Differing interpretations of its precise meaning existed throughout the early church, the medieval period, and even within the Wittenberg circle. Luther believed in a unique joining of the divine and human concretely in Christ's person, which was so intimate that each nature shared the characteristics of the other even though these characteristics never actually became the property of the other nature.[5]

Melanchthon shared Luther's concerns and convictions as the two began their reform efforts, but as in other areas of his thought Melanchthon continued to reconsider his formulations of how Christ is present and what he does in the Lord's Supper. In this case Luther's utterances remained rather consistent over the last quarter century of his life, whereas his colleague Philip went through what has been identified as a three-stage development in his teaching on the Lord's Supper. Even before 1533 Melanchthon paid less attention to explaining the presence of Christ and the relationship of the elements of bread and wine to his body and blood than he did to its function as a sign that delivered God's grace to recipients. Luther gradually laid aside the Augustinian usage of "sign" for the elements and closely connected the sacraments to the Word as a means by which God delivers forgiveness, life, and salvation, whereas Melanchthon emphasized the nature of the sacraments as "signs," placing the Word parallel to the elements rather than connecting them closely. He focused on the sacrament's function of assuring believers of the forgiveness of sins. He did not, as Luther did, speak of the "oral partaking" of Christ's body and blood even at this initial stage of his comment on the sacrament, although he shared Luther's insistence on the inseparability of the two natures in Christ's person. He also rejected Zwingli's assertion that Christ's human body was necessarily fixed in heaven after his Ascension. He based his understanding of Christ's sacramental presence on his general presence in his church, not, as Luther did, in the world.[6]

For more than two decades after 1533, he continued to teach along these lines. By 1533 he was grounding his understanding of Christ's presence on his ability to be where he wishes when he wishes in whatever mode he wishes according to his will. Melanchthon also became more concerned about the trinitarian implications of his Christology with the appearance of the anti-trinitarian writings of Michael Servetus, which he was countering in the early 1530s. His *Loci communes* of 1535 contained no discussion of the *communicatio idiomatum*. When he did mention that concept, he labeled it a verbal expression, avoiding the assertion so important to Luther, that the characteristics of the two natures were in actuality shared with the other nature while each retained its own integrity, exercising those characteristics without possessing them. Melanchthon focused on the concrete person of Christ. Therefore, he attributed characteristics that abstractly could only belong to one nature or the other, only to the whole person and not to the other nature within the person. Like Luther, he steadfastly maintained that all Christological statements must be made concretely of the unique union of God and human creature in Jesus, and not abstractly of divinity and humanity.[7] In this period Melanchthon repeatedly summarized his doctrine of the Sacrament with an insistence that "outside its instituted use the sacrament does not exist," and that Christ—but not specifically his body and blood—is present in the Lord's Supper and there effectively conveys forgiveness of sins. Peter Fraenkel describes this understanding of the Sacrament as "functional." Melanchthon wanted to avoid metaphysical speculation and instead to focus on what God does in the sacrament, Fraenkel argues.[8] He was particularly concerned to prevent people from accepting the medieval association of the material with spiritual power, such as that understood to be implied by an *ex opere operato* understanding that might promote a magical view of sacramental ritual.

Melanchthon's position reflected his continuing study, his new interpretation of some ancient fathers, and his ever-growing fear of superstitious use of the Supper in the manner of the medieval church. Against this background he altered his teaching on the sacrament somewhat in the last three years of his life, under the impact of one significant shift in his utterances on the Christological questions related to the Lord's Supper. Previously he had shared Luther's rejection of the idea that because Jesus ascended bodily from the earth "into heaven," his human body could only be in the one geographical spot above the earth called heaven. Luther mocked Zwingli's contention that heaven was a place and that "the right hand of God" should be understood as a physical locale. But in 1557 Melanchthon told his students that the human nature and human body of Jesus were located in heaven although he added the qualifier, "wherever that may be," and he avoided the specific language that excluded variations in interpretation.[9]

The precise meaning of this passage may be debated, but Melanchthon's contemporaries in Lutheran Württemberg as well as Reformed Switzerland viewed it as an abandonment of Luther's teaching.[10] The language is sufficiently convoluted that Duke Christoph with his theologians and Peucer, Pezel, and their comrades, like Strigel before them, were justified in their impression that Melanchthon was teaching that a corporal location of Christ's human nature in a physical, geographical place above the earth. Also in the last three years of his life Melanchthon argued on the basis of 1 Corinthians 10:16 that instead of the sacrament's being a "communion" of bread and body, wine and blood, it was the *koinonia* of Christ and his benefits with his people, even as they received the sacrament. Adapting certain expressions from Augustine, Melanchthon held that the earthly elements function as signs of the forgiveness of sins and implantation in the body of Christ that the gospel proclaims and that Christ is present with his people as a person but not through the presence of his body and blood in the earthly elements. He had long since avoided any use of Luther's test phrases for Christ's presence in the sacrament, that his body and blood are "orally consumed" and that the unworthy or impious also consume the body and blood, without receiving the benefits of Christ available only to faith, because the words of institution have made his body and blood present in the Supper.[11]

An important station in the development of Wittenberg public teaching had come in 1536, as Melanchthon attempted to bring together the positions of Luther and the reformer of Strasbourg, Martin Bucer. He was located geographically and theologically somewhere between Wittenberg and Zurich. With his close associate, Landgrave Philip of Hesse, Bucer ardently sought reconciliation between the

Wittenberg theologians and south German and Swiss Protestants who held differing views of the true presence of Christ in the Lord's Supper. In 1536 Bucer led a delegation of like-minded south Germans to Wittenberg and there negotiated an agreement with Luther and his colleagues. Composed by Melanchthon, the "Wittenberg Concordia" found language to bring Luther and Bucer together on the critical test phrases for the affirmation of the presence of Christ's body and blood in the Supper. Its text read:

> We have heard how Martin Bucer has explained his own position and that of the other preachers who came with him from the [south German] cities regarding the holy sacrament of the body and blood of Christ:
>
> They confess, in the words of Irenaeus,[12] that in this sacrament there are two things, one heavenly and one earthly. Therefore, they hold and teach that with the bread and wine the body and blood of Christ are truly and essentially present, are distributed and received. Although they do not believe in a transubstantiation, that is, in an essential transformation of the bread and wine into the body and blood, and they do not hold that the body and blood of Christ are *localiter*, that is, spatially enclosed in the bread or are permanently united in some other way apart from reception[13] in the sacrament, they nevertheless admit that through the sacramental union the bread is the body of Christ, etc. For apart from reception—for example, when the bread is laid aside and kept in the tabernacle or carried about and put on display in the procession, as happens in the papacy—the body of Christ is not present.
>
> Second, they hold that the institution of this sacrament, as it was performed by Christ, is effective throughout Christendom and that its power does not rest upon the worthiness or unworthiness of the minister who distributes the sacrament, nor upon the worthiness or unworthiness of the one who receives it because, as Saint Paul says, even the unworthy may receive the sacrament. Thus, they hold that the body and blood of Christ are truly distributed even to the unworthy, and that the unworthy truly receive the body and blood when the sacrament is conducted according to Christ's institution and command. But they receive it to judgment, as Saint Paul says [1 Cor. 11:27-32], for they misuse the holy sacrament because they receive it without true repentance and without faith. For it was instituted for this reason, that it might testify that the grace and benefits of Christ are applied to those who truly repent and find comfort through faith in Christ and that these are the ones incorporated into Christ and washed in Christ's blood.[14]

Although Bucer and Luther may not have understood this formulation of the doctrine of the true presence of Christ's body and blood in the same way, they were content to have come close enough, and they accepted the position of the other.[15] Lutherans, such as Johann Marbach, Nikolaus Selnecker, and the other Concordists, believed its text reflected Luther's position faithfully; Bucer's own writings in the following years do not fully confirm that interpretation. His theology of the Lord's Supper influenced the formulations of the new ecclesiastical constitution for the archbishopric of Cologne, which he and Melanchthon composed in 1544. Bucer remained a powerful voice within the German Evangelical churches.

Students who had studied under Melanchthon at different points in this development combined what they had heard from him with Luther's position in various ways. This resulted in the tensions that surfaced after Melanchthon's death within the Wittenberg circle. Three of the Preceptor's former students and (in the latter two cases, through their critiques of the Leipzig Proposal) his betes noir, Joachim Mörlin, Joachim Westphal, and Nikolaus Gallus, raised serious criticisms of Melanchthon's interpretation of the doctrine of the Lord's Supper in 1560, each issuing glossed editions of Philip's comments on the presence of Christ's body and blood in the sacramental elements from an earlier period of his life, when his expression of the doctrine of the true presence corresponded more closely to Luther's.[16] With the majority of his students forging their view of the Lord's Supper out of Luther's teaching and the middle stage of Melanchthon's formulation of the doctrine, and but a small group of his students adapting and extending his ideas from the last three years of his life, such tensions were inevitable. The struggle to define this critical part of biblical teaching, which had at first united Luther's followers against other Protestant opponents, finally invaded the Wittenberg circle itself.

The Dispute between Joachim Westphal and John Calvin

In the 1550s Melanchthon's views developed alongside a controversy between Calvin and one of Luther's and Melanchthon's students, Joachim Westphal, pastor in Hamburg. He saw in Calvin's theology of the sacrament a threat to the proper understanding and use of the Supper. In 1549 Calvin and his Genevan colleagues had reached an agreement regarding the Lord's Supper with Heinrich Bullinger and his associates from German-speaking Switzerland. Bullinger's position reflected Zwingli's concerns that the Protestant doctrine of the Lord's Supper avoid medieval superstition. The underlying presuppositions of the theologians from both Zurich and Geneva prevented them from understanding how God could actually be present in material elements and how he could effect his saving will through such elements.

The Zurichers were suspicious of Calvin because he affirmed that the person of Christ—though not his human body and blood—was indeed present in the Supper. In the "Zurich Consensus" [*Consensus Tigurinus*] of 1549 (published 1551),[17] Calvin moderated his language to accommodate the even more strongly spiritualizing definition of the Lord's Supper acceptable in Zurich. The *Consensus* rejected not only Lutheran positions but also the nuanced views of Calvin regarding the spiritual presence of Christ's person in the Supper. It rejected his earlier position that the sacraments are means of conveying salvation. It stated clearly that God does not bind himself to the sacraments and that he does not work his saving will through them.[18]

Through correspondence and through the edition of the *Zurich Consensus* issued in London by the Polish Reformed theologian Jan à Lasco, Westphal came into contact with the latest developments in Swiss theology. Concerned about its advance in the Netherlands and England, lands with which Hamburg had much commercial contact, this student of Luther and Melanchthon composed an *Assortment of Confused and Mutually Contradictory Opinions on the Lord's Supper*, which set forth the positions of several Zwinglian and Calvinist theologians with accompanying critique.[19] The next year he published an exegetical analysis of the New Testament passages on which the doctrine of the Lord's Supper rests, under the title *The True Faith concerning the Lord's Supper*.[20] The suggestion in recent scholarship that Westphal called on Calvin to return to his earlier view of the Supper, criticizing him for abandoning that position and submitting to Zurich, is not based on a careful reading of the sources. Westphal believed that Calvin had seemed to veer in Luther's direction and had now betrayed that impression. His reaction was clear and sharp, as he placed Calvin in the succession of Zwingli and Karlstadt.[21] Calvin replied with his own defense of his position as expressed in the *Zurich Consensus*; Westphal answered, marshaling patristic as well as biblical support for his view.[22] He also issued a defense of his position based upon statements from Melanchthon's earlier writings.

Melanchthon responded with venom in private letters, labeling Westphal's view "bread worship."[23] The alienation provoked by Westphal's critique of the Leipzig Proposal surfaced with a vengeance. Both Calvin and Westphal received help from supporters, and the controversy boiled and bubbled into the 1560s. Calvin appealed for endorsement of his position against Westphal among the Lutherans, hoping that the similarities between his viewpoint and what he understood Melanchthon's to be would win him advocates within the ranks of the Wittenberg professor's students. This hope proved to be not entirely in vain a decade later. In the 1550s the dispute did not broaden quite so far. Westphal and à Lasco exchanged public rejoinders, and the Hamburg pastor took aim at Bullinger as well; the Zurich theologian also engaged in sharp exchanges with the theologians in Württemberg.[24] Westphal also enlisted not only his own city's ministerium but also the theologians of more than a dozen cities and principalities in Lower Saxony, who issued their common confession on the Lord's Supper in 1557.[25]

The issue between Westphal and his opponents revolved around the definition of the true presence of Christ in the sacrament. Calvin believed that the person of Christ is truly present in the Lord's Supper even though his philosophical presuppositions regarding the relationship between spirit and matter prevented him from believing that Christ's body and blood could actually be consumed along with bread and wine. He believed that faith reaches out to receive the heavenly blessings of God's love while the mouth receives bread and wine. Westphal reproduced

Luther's argument quite faithfully, insisting on a literal interpretation of the words of Christ, "this is my body," "this is my blood."

Although it was less critical for his defense of Luther's teaching, the reformer's Christological argument also appeared in Westphal's *Confession* of 1557, in an appendix written by his Hamburg colleague, Johann Bötker. This argument contended that through the sharing of the characteristics between the two natures of Christ (*communicatio idiomatum*), the human nature's body and blood could be present in the Lord's Supper in sacramental form because the divine nature shared this ability to be present in more than one mode and place with that human nature. This unique coming together of a specific human being, Jesus Christ, and the second person of the Trinity took place only within the personal union, the person of Christ. Bötker used the ascension of Christ to the Father's right hand (that is, to the full exercise of his power) as proof of the personal union of his two natures: the human nature shares in the exercise of divine power with the divine nature. Therefore, as Luther had said, the human nature can also be present at the same time in more than one place. This meant that the two natures genuinely share attributes in this particular, concrete way.[26]

Westphal interpreted Calvin's insistence that the bread and wine present or exhibit what they represent in the light of the *Consensus Tigurinus*, specifically in light of its rejection of any kind of actual presence of the body and blood of Christ. He recognized that the spiritualizing framework of Calvin's way of thinking about the Lord's Supper did separate the Genevan from Luther on this question. Calvin accused Westphal of consubstantiation, that is, asserting that bread and body, wine and blood, coexist in some manner that could be grasped through the concepts of Aristotelian physics. His philosophical paradigm prevented him from grasping another alternative, such as that which Westphal actually held: Luther's understanding of a genuine, sacramental—that is, mysterious or unexplainable in terms of physics—presence.

The Dispute between Johann Timann and Albert Hardenberg

Hamburg and Bremen were neighboring cities. They shared commercial interests, and the development of the Reformation in each had similar roots. But in Bremen a serious dispute over the Lord's Supper broke out within the ministerium in the 1550s. At the heart of this controversy stood two Dutch-born, Wittenberg-educated pastors in the city, Albert Rizäus von Hardenberg and Johann Timann (sometimes called Amsterdam from his birthplace). The two sharply disagreed on the proper interpretation of the words of institution in defining the presence of Christ in the Supper.

Hardenberg was influenced by the "Sacramentarian" views of late medieval Dutch humanism, by long term friendship with his fellow student at the University of Mainz, Jan à Lasco, and particularly by the theology of Martin Bucer.[27] Educated by the Brethren of the Common Life in Groningen, he had absorbed Erasmian influences during his studies at Louvain and in Italy. He earned his doctorate at the

Roman Catholic theological faculty of the University of Mainz in 1539 but soon thereafter drifted into the reforming circles around Hermann von Wied in the arch-bishopric of Cologne. He returned there after a brief time studying in Wittenberg, where he became a friend of Paul Eber and of Melanchthon; Hardenberg began a long and lively correspondence with his Preceptor. In July 1547 Hardenberg assumed a position as cathedral preacher under the archbishop of Bremen, who had become Lutheran. Quickly his views of the Lord's Supper attracted criticism because of his emphasis on the spiritual nature of sacramental eating. He composed a confession in which he stressed God's gracious giving in the sacrament and con-fessed the presence of Christ with the elements. The Wittenberg faculty approved his position, and the Bremen city council was satisfied.

In 1555 Timann published his *Assortment of Positions which Agree with the True and Catholic Teaching of the Lord's Supper…In Accord with the Divine Word as Embraced in the Church of the Augsburg Confession.*[28] Timann rejected Zwingli's position regarding the absence of Christ's body and blood in the sacramental elements of the Supper, and with it the teaching of Jan à Lasco as well. À Lasco and Hardenberg were friends, and Timann and Hardenberg fell into dispute. Hardenberg expressed his position with citations from Bucer's formulation of the doctrine of the Supper in the ecclesiastical constitution for Cologne. Timann com-posed a new confession for the Bremen ministerium in order to end the contention within the city over the sacrament. He appealed to Westphal and to Paul von Eitzen, ecclesiastical superintendent in nearby Holstein, for support.

Hardenberg took aim at Timann's use of the Christological argument in defense of the true presence of Christ's body and blood in the Supper. Timann con-tended that because of the communication of attributes Christ's human body and blood shared the characteristics of the divine nature, holding that both natures, in their personal union, might be present in more than one place, in sacramental fashion, according to God's will. Hardenberg insisted that the body of Christ can-not be enclosed or localized in a physical element such as bread and cannot be in more than one place at the same time. This earned him the epithet "Zwinglian." Hardenberg compared the presence of Christ in the Supper to the presence of the sun on earth: Christ is present in the sacrament to effect the conveying of his grace. He claimed that he had learned this interpretation from the scholastic Rupert von Deutz and the late medieval reforming theologian Wessel Gansfort.

Timann received support from the citizenry, particularly the artisans, but in the upper middle class leadership of the city council a powerful figure, Daniel von Buren, who had studied under Melanchthon in Wittenberg in the early 1550s, sided with Hardenberg. This began a decade of maneuvering within the city council over the definition of the city's doctrine. The Wittenberg faculty was enlisted to medi-ate the dispute, but their memorandum of January 20, 1557, which advised settle-ment on the basis of the Augsburg Confession of 1530, did not address the precise problems of the debate. Melanchthon's suggested test phrase, "the body of Christ is received with the bread," was insufficiently clear to lay the dispute to rest; its rejection of the words "the bread and wine are the essential body and blood of Christ" reinforced a Bucerian position and favored Hardenberg.[29]

The dispute continued, with mounting pressures exerted from the ministeria of other Lower Saxon cities; from the city's new Lutheran archbishop, Duke Georg of Braunschweig-Lüneburg; and from King Christian III of Denmark, who penalized Bremen's commercial interests in his lands because of Hardenberg. The regional opposition led to the condemnation of Hardenberg's theology by a commission of the regional governments in the imperial region of Lower Saxony in 1561. Among others, Martin Chemnitz had written against his position for the ministerium of Braunschweig.[30] The demands of these neighbors finally swayed the city council, and Hardenberg left town in 1561, completing his career in Emden. Timann had died by the time the Gnesio-Lutheran Simon Musaeus was called to the city in 1561. His stay there was brief. The Philippist Marcus Mening strove to stake out place for a Melanchthonian sacramental doctrine, opposing both the strict Lutherans and the Zwinglians during the following decade. Musaeus had to go. After 1579 the former Wittenberg professor Christoph Pezel led the city determinedly in a Calvinist direction.[31]

In order to defend his friend Hardenberg, Melanchthon entered the lists, focusing his fire on "bread-worshipers" who can only talk about "the omnipresence [of Christ's body and blood]." This Christological concern became a preoccupation for him. He viewed this sharing of the characteristics of Christ's divine and human natures as only a rhetorical or logical construction (*communicatio dialectica*) rather than what he called a "physical" or "real" sharing (*communicatio realis*). He distinguished three kinds of predicates in formulating his argument against a "physical" interpretation of the communication of attributes. The predicate adjectives that describe the two natures are neither regular nor figurative predicates. They are employed in a unique way when applied to the person of Christ. Christ can be omnipresent, Melanchthon argued, but his human body cannot be. What can be said adjectivally of the whole person of Christ on the basis of the two natures cannot be applied to each nature individually, he contended.[32] In this view he opposed the position of Johann Brenz and his colleagues in Württemberg. They were expressing their view ever more clearly in the public arena about the time of Melanchthon's death. Brenz stressed that the characteristics of each of the two natures are truly and totally shared with the other nature within the personal union of the two natures.[33]

The Advance of Calvinism in the Palatinate

As the dispute over the Lord's Supper came to its climax around 1560 in Bremen, Brenz became personally involved in a similar dispute in southwest Germany. The electorate of the Palatinate experienced tensions similar to those in Bremen briefly and then quickly witnessed the triumph of a distinct doctrinal position under the leadership of Elector Frederick III, "the Pious." By the beginning of the seventeenth century, Heidelberg had become a Calvinistic fortress, but in the 1560s its theologians were blending emphases gained from Luther and Melanchthon as well as Zwingli and Calvin, Bullinger and Beza. Herman Selderhuis contends that Melanchthon held the key to the developing Heidelberg theology at this point,[34] but the Melanchthonian element was indeed that of his last views of the sacraments and Christology, as interpreted by only one wing of the spectrum of his students.

Frederick III succeeded two distant cousins on the throne in Heidelberg in 1559. Frederick II had tolerated the preaching of reform but did not become an Evangelical officially until the year before his death in 1556, after the Religious Peace of Augsburg was made the law of the empire. His nephew, Ottheinrich, a zealous and determined leader within Lutheran princely circles, ruled only three years before his death in 1559. The doctrinal orientation of the pastors he called to the Palatinate to implement the Reformation varied, and tensions were brewing among his theologians already before his death. For among the group responsible for church policy were the Philippist Michael Diller, the Calvinist Christoph Ehem, the Zwinglian physician Thomas Erastus, and Tileman Hesshus, called at Melanchthon's recommendation in 1558 to be professor of theology at the University of Heidelberg, president of the church council, and general superintendent of the churches of the Palatinate. Hesshus had studied with the Preceptor in Wittenberg, and the two had become friends. Hesshus's writings reflected a Melanchthonian approach to issues across the spectrum of theology.[35]

In leading the rejection of a Schwenkfeldian theology taught in the Palatinate by Bernhard Herxhamer, Hesshus condemned spiritualizing views of the Lord's Supper explicitly, using Luther's test phrases of "oral partaking of Christ's body and blood" and "the partaking of Christ's body and blood by the impious." Not all his colleagues were willing to accept these phrases. He composed a series of academic theses on the Lord's Supper for a student, Stephan Sylvius, to defend in a disputation at the university. Sylvius refused to take part in a disputation over the theses for reasons that led Hesshus to accuse him of Arianism. This increased tensions within the ministerium. So did Hesshus's conflict with the deacon of his congregation, Wilhelm Klebitz. Although they later abandoned this young minister, the Zwinglian party in Heidelberg used Klebitz to provoke Hesshus. Hesshus deposed Klebitz after tussling with him over the chalice in front of the altar of the Holy Spirit church in Heidelberg because he believed it impious for someone who denied Christ's real presence in the Sacrament to distribute it.[36]

The electoral government intervened, restoring Klebitz to office. Frederick III demanded a written confession of faith from both the deacon and the superintendent. Hesshus argued that the words of institution must be understood simply as they stand. He bolstered his position with the words of 1 Corinthians 10:16, that not faith, nor the Spirit, but the cup of wine is in communion with the blood of Christ, the bread communing with his body. Hesshus thereby upheld the interpretation Melanchthon had taught him, as he understood it. However, by the time he wrote to

Elector Frederick in 1559, the Preceptor did not believe that the assertion of the communion of the body could be interpreted "as Hesshus [states], the bread is the true body of Christ."[37] Because with God all things are possible, Hesshus believed that the words of institution could be understood literally. Christ can be trusted when he said that his blood actually conveys forgiveness in the Lord's Supper. Hesshus explicitly rejected transubstantiation, consubstantiation, worship of the host, and any doctrine of "local inclusion," but insisted that Christ is bodily present, not just spiritually present. He made relatively little out of Luther's Christological affirmation of Christ's ability to be present in body and blood on the basis of the communication of attributes, but he rejected the Zwinglian argument that Christ's human nature was not able to be present on earth in any form because it was at the right hand of God. In mid 1560 Frederick III removed both Klebitz and Hesshus from office, and soon thereafter he deposed other Lutherans from their offices in the Palatinate.

Melanchthon refused to support this friend, weighing in decisively on the side of the prince.[38] He associated Hesshus with the opponents of Hardenberg in Bremen. Just as he had rejected their confession that "the bread is the substantial body of Christ" so he rejected Hesshus's similar confession, that the bread is the true body of Christ. He favored defining the relationship instead as "an association of the bread with the body of Christ, which takes place in its use (reception)." Melanchthon claimed that the ancient fathers of the church had never taught what the Bremen theologians and Hesshus were teaching.[39] In taking this position he alienated his formerly devoted student and friend.

The drift toward a Calvinist position in the Palatinate picked up speed under the leadership of former Wittenberg and Genevan student Zacharias Ursinus and others in the months following Hesshus's departure. However, this brought the electoral government into difficulty with other Evangelical princes because they believed that this theology lay outside the legal limits imposed by the Religious Peace of Augsburg. In 1561 Frederick III tried to establish his own understanding of Melanchthon's revised (Variata) version of the Augsburg Confession as a legitimate interpretation of that document,[40] for the Confession was the legal standard used to determine who could qualify for toleration in the Empire. Strain and stress continued to haunt the relationships between the court in Heidelberg and its Lutheran neighbors, particularly in the dukedom of Württemberg, led by Duke Christoph, a committed Lutheran. As noted above, with their Christological argument his theologians represented a special position among the Lutherans on the doctrine of the Lord's Supper.

Led by Johannes Brenz, the Württemberg ministerium had established a clearly stated definition of the true presence of Christ's body and blood in the Lord's Supper as its official teaching in a confession of faith issued in 1559.[41] Following Brenz's formulation, the Württemberg pastors emphasized that Christ's body and blood could be present in the Lord's Supper because of the communication of attributes between his human and divine natures. According to Brenz's understanding of this ancient doctrine, the human nature shares the characteristic of omnipresence with the divine nature. Brenz had begun to express this way of defending the real presence of Christ's body and blood in the Lord's Supper in opposition to the Reformed position in 1526, in an exchange with Oecolampadius. In addition to this Christological argumentation, he used patristic evidence to support his literal interpretation of the words of institution and emphasized the miracle of the Word that takes place in consecration.

Living as neighbors of the Swiss, the Württemberg theologians were open to conversation on the subject. In 1557 Brenz's colleague and disciple, Jakob Andreae, attempted to compose a description of the Lord's Supper that would enable agreement between Zurich and Wittenberg. The same year he met with two Genevan theologians, Guillaume Farel and Theodore Beza, to formulate a basis for dialog between the Reformed and the Lutherans. The statement used the term "substance" to define the mode of Christ's presence in the Sacrament and affirmed that the impious, like the pious, receive Christ in the Supper, albeit with different results. From Zurich came a sharp denunciation of this effort by Heinrich Bullinger. The attempt at reconciliation came to nothing.[42]

In 1559 Andreae was commissioned with reviewing the sacramental teaching of Christoph Hagen, pastor in Dettingen. Hagen had argued against Brenz's understanding of the communication of attributes and denied that the impious receive Christ's body and blood in the Supper. Andreae found Hagen's teaching in error on both counts. He agreed that "outside the use there is no sacrament," but he affirmed Brenz's position, which was incorporated into the confession produced by the synod held to adjudicate the Hagen case.[43] It is important to note that for Andreae the Christological argument did not form the basis for the understanding of the real presence of Christ's body and blood in the Supper but functioned instead as a defense against false interpretations of this doctrine.[44] The church of Württemberg had committed itself to a position significantly different from that developing in the churches of the neighboring Palatinate.

As Frederick III drifted in the direction of Calvinism, the issue of the Lord's Supper loomed very large in efforts to preserve a united front among the Evangelical princes and cities. The appearance of the Heidelberg Catechism in January 1563 aroused suspicions among the Palatinate's Lutheran neighbors. Its seventy-eighth question, "Do the bread and wine become the very body and blood of Christ?" was answered, "No, for the water in baptism is not changed into the blood of Christ nor does it become the washing away of sins by itself, but is only a divine sign and confirmation of it, so also in the Lord's Supper the sacred bread does not become the body of Christ itself although, in accordance with the nature and usage of sacraments, it is called the body of Christ." The Catechism affirmed that Christ "feeds and nourishes my soul to everlasting life with his crucified body and shed blood as I receive from the hand of the minister and actually taste the bread and the cup of the Lord that are given to me as sure signs of the body and blood of Christ." In addressing

Christological questions, the Catechism observed that "Christ is true man and true God. As a man he is no longer on earth, but in his divinity, majesty, grace, and Spirit, he is never absent from us" (question 47). That means that "since divinity is incomprehensible and everywhere present, it must follow that the divinity is indeed beyond the bounds of the humanity which it has assumed" even though it is personally united to it (question 48).[45] The Catechism's appearance aroused consternation and concern in neighboring Lutheran territories.

Duke Christoph conferred with Elector Frederick in February 1564, and the two princes scheduled a colloquy of their theologians. On April 10–15 five theologians from Württemberg met with five from the Palatinate in the abbey at Maulbronn to discuss the issues that divided them. Jakob Andreae served as sole spokesman for Christoph; Johannes Brenz, the court preacher Balthasar Bidembach, Dietrich Schnepf from the theological faculty in Tübingen, and the abbot of Maulbronn, Valentin Wanner, stood at his side. From Heidelberg came professors Peter Boquin, Kaspar Olevianus, Zacharias Ursinus, and Peter Dathenus, and the court preacher Michael Diller. Both sides repeated their fundamental positions. The Palatine delegation insisted that Christ is received through faith in the Supper; his body and blood are not received orally and not by unbelievers. They thus categorically rejected the Württemberg position.

The colloquants turned to the subject of the definition of God's right hand and the "locality" of Christ's human nature after the ascension. The Heidelberg theologians insisted that the right hand is a place in physical heaven; the Lutherans argued that the biblical understanding of the term designates Christ's possession of the divine characteristics of power and majesty. They also contended that in the communication of the attributes of the two natures with each other, both natures enjoy the attributes of the divine nature in the unity of Christ's person even if they belong strictly speaking only to the divine nature. Andreae argued that God can be present in three distinct ways: according to his Godhead, in grace, and in Christ. Christ can be present in three ways: according to his normal humanity, in his glorified body, and at the right hand of God. Without in any way denying the distinctiveness of each of the two natures of Christ, Andreae insisted on their inseparability in the personal union. On this basis he taught a doctrine of the communication of attributes that posited the sharing of characteristics, including omnipresence, between the two.

The Palatine theologians labeled Brenz's and Andreae's belief that Christ's human nature could therefore be omnipresent in the unity of this person as "ubiquitistic," from the Latin word for "everywhere."[46] In their clash at Maulbronn the two sides hardly touched the underlying principle that separated them as they attempted to assess how God uses—or may not use—elements of the created order as vehicles and instruments of his power. This principle, later affirmed by the Reformed side in the phrase used by medieval scholastics, "the finite is not capable of bearing the infinite," was rejected by the Lutherans as a blasphemous diminution of God's power. To the Palatine delegation it was a self-evident and immutable truth.[47]

The protocols each side kept at the meeting appeared in print despite an agreement that they not be published. When Duke Christoph sent his theologians' reports to Elector August of Saxony, the reply was disheartening. The Wittenberg faculty objected to Andreae's understanding of the communication of attributes. Seeds were sown for discord between Wittenberg and Württemberg although for the time no open rift appeared.[48]

Closer to Andreae's position was that of Martin Chemnitz, who would formally treat Christological questions most extensively some six years later, with the publication of his *On the Two Natures in Christ*.[49] In his writings on the Lord's Supper, particularly in opposition to Hardenberg, Chemnitz had made the Christological argument in defense of Lutheran teaching secondary to an argument from the words of institution[50] but offered an extensive treatment of the biblical and patristic citations that supported his Lutheran position. It avoided the "ubiquitarian" position of Brenz and Andreae, upholding instead a definition of the sharing of the characteristic of divine presence as a "multivolipresence." This approach, based on God's will to be present in as many places as God wishes, in whatever form he wishes, whenever he wishes, reflected something of Melanchthon's teaching in the period when Chemnitz had been in Wittenberg.

The Crypto-Philippists in Saxony

Chemnitz believed he was faithfully reproducing Melanchthon's and Luther's theology of the Lord's Supper as he wrote against Hardenberg and on Christology. Others, however, developed Melanchthon's thought in different directions. Those who had remained around the Preceptor in Wittenberg and who carried on his tradition there after his death in 1560 continued his reworking of Wittenberg sacramental doctrine. These efforts have earned them the epithet "crypto-Calvinist" in scholarly literature, an epithet assigned them by their contemporary opponents within the Lutheran camp. However, this designation is deceptive.[51] This group of Melanchthon's students did indeed try to hide the spiritualistic tendencies in their sacramental and Christological doctrines, and therefore the designation "crypto" has basis in fact. However, in spite of contacts with Reformed theologians in Zurich, Geneva, and Heidelberg, their theology was not decisively influenced by this interchange of ideas. Their basic concepts had been largely formed by the Preceptor. They were working out the implications of what they had learned from him, as were their opponents within and outside of the ministerium of electoral Saxony.[52]

Soon after Melanchthon's death in 1560 his colleague Paul Eber wrote a faculty position paper on the Lord's Supper. His statement affirmed that in the Lord's Supper those who partake of bread and wine receive the true and essential body and blood of Christ. But he avoided saying, as Luther had in the Smalcald Articles, that the bread is the body of Christ. He also evaded any and all Christological arguments.[53] Nonetheless, he seems to have shifted his position in 1561/1562 from a more spiritualizing interpretation of the words of institution to a defense of the "Luther-an" expression of the teaching he had learned in the 1540s from Melanchthon and before his death warned students and colleagues against abandoning the common position of his two preceptors.[54] His position reflected the second stage of Melanchthon's development of his doctrine of the Lord's Supper.

With Eber's death came a shift in the faculty. A younger colleague, Christoph Pezel, became the de facto theological leader in Wittenberg. Viktorin Strigel had formed his way of thinking while Pezel studied with him in Jena. Strigel had left ducal Saxony in 1562 after gaining the upper hand in his feud with Flacius and taught at Leipzig until 1567. In that year his friend Johannes Pfeffinger, as dean of the theological faculty, suspended his right to teach because of suspicions over his doctrine of the Lord's Supper. Strigel departed for Heidelberg and found a haven among those more sympathetic with Calvin's views of the Lord's Supper there.[55]

While in Jena Strigel had cultivated the theology of his student Christoph Pezel, who was too young to have known Luther and who studied only briefly in Wittenberg during Melanchthon's life. Pezel began teaching in the arts faculty at Wittenberg in 1567 and succeeded Eber on the theological faculty at his death in 1569. Quickly he became the leading thinker on the theological faculty, and he formed a close friendship with Caspar Peucer, professor of medicine and Melanchthon's son-in-law. Together they began to reinforce what they saw as Melanchthon's views of the Lord's Supper and Christology at the end of his life.[56] They found support from two young colleagues, who had been added to the theological faculty in recent years: Melanchthon's successor, Caspar Cruciger the Younger, son of Luther's and Melanchthon's colleagues, sided with Pezel and Peucer, as did the Hebraist Heinrich Möller and Friedrich Widebram. Their colleagues, Georg Major, the dean of the faculty, and his son-in-law, Paul Crell, along with Johannes Bugenhagen the Younger, son of another of Luther's and Melanchthon's colleague, followed Eber's admonition shortly before his death to remain faithful to Luther. They held to an affirmation of the true presence of Christ's body and blood in the sacrament in the manner Melanchthon had taught it in the second stage of the development of his doctrine.

The Pezel and Peucer group advanced their view tentatively but ever more boldly. That propelled their faculty into conflict with most other Lutherans during the next few years. Within electoral Saxony a few pastors began to question the faculty's views. Two of the Wittenberg professors' own students raised objections to their positions and had to be expelled from the university. Theologians in other churches began to express suspicions about their Wittenberg colleagues as well.[57]

Among them were three whom Duke Julius of Braunschweig-Wolfenbüttel had called in 1569 to assist in introducing the Reformation to his lands after the death of his father, Heinrich. They were Jakob Andreae, Martin Chemnitz, and Nikolaus Selnecker. While resident in north Germany, Andreae also carried a portfolio from the government of ducal Württemberg that directed him to negotiate concord among the strife-ridden Lutherans in the North. After a stalled attempt at accord in Zerbst in May 1570, he visited Wittenberg. There he took exception to a proposition on Christology in a series of theses prepared for the doctoral promotion of six members of Melanchthon's circle, including Selnecker. This proposition condemned monophysitism, but did so in terms Andreae understood to deny the real communication of attributes, as taught by Luther and Brenz.[58]

Tensions the Wittenberg theologians had noted at the time of the Colloquy of Maulbronn then broke into the open. Duke Julius of Braunschweig-Wolfenbüttel sent Selnecker to Wittenberg to investigate. In July 1570 the faculty composed a confession on the communication of attributes and the Lord's Supper, insisting that they remained faithful to Scripture, the ancient creeds of the church, to Melanchthon and to Luther. In general terms they confessed that the divine and human natures of Christ are united in his one person. They confirmed that they believed in the true presence of the true and essential body and blood of Christ in the Lord's Supper. Although Chemnitz was disturbed by the Wittenberg theologians' imprecision, both Selnecker and Andreae were satisfied with the statement. Andreae believed that all sides among the Lutherans held a common doctrine of the Sacrament.[59] The Wittenberg theologians rejected his assessment, attributing to him a "golden dream" if he thought that they and the "Flacians" held the same position. Elector August abhorred Flacius as an inveterate trouble-maker and disturber of the peace of Christendom; he liked to hear that his theologians were distancing themselves from "the Illyrian." August undertook measures including censorship to repress Flacian teaching.[60] Selnecker, serving on loan from August's ministerium as superintendent for Braunschweig-Wolfenbüttel, tried to play mediator through publications and visits in Saxony, gradually alienating himself from his electoral Saxon colleagues.[61] By 1571 Caspar Cruciger the Younger was openly labeling him "a little Flacius and a new Judas."[62] Another betrayer, like Flacius and Chemnitz!

While defending themselves publicly with such statements, the theologians of Wittenberg and Leipzig proceeded to advance their spiritualizing understanding of the Lord's Supper, above all, in the *Wittenberg Catechism*, published January 1, 1571, for use on a level above the primary instruction given in Luther's Small Catechism.[63] Composed by Pezel, it defined the Lord's Supper as "the communication of the body and blood of our Lord Jesus Christ, as instituted in the words of the gospel: in this eating the Son of God is truly and substantially present and testifies that he applies his benefits to believers." This meant that the person of Christ is present, but only in his divine nature as Son of God, and that presence was implicitly understood to be spiritual. Furthermore it testified to, but did not directly convey, the benefits of Christ to his people. Pezel further wrote that Christ had assumed human nature "so that we might be made his members through faith." The Wittenberg Catechism taught that Christ's human nature is immovably fixed in heaven, at the Father's right hand since his ascension. It interpreted Acts 3:21, "heaven must receive Jesus," in such a way as to support the physical placement of Christ's human body and nature immovably in a geographically-fixed heaven above the earth. According to this translation, so rendered for the first time by the Genevan Theodore Beza only a few years earlier, Christ's human nature could not leave heaven until the Last Day. Pezel's formulations reflect the influence of two aspects of contemporary Aristotelian thinking. He held to a concept of "presence," specifically the presence or place of heaven and the right hand of God as locally or geographically fixed places, and he believed that Aristotle's concept of substance and accidence simply made it impossible to change the fixed nature of a substance.

Pezel's catechism attracted a storm of protest: from Sebastian Boetius, pastor in Halle; from Chemnitz; from the theologians of the University of Jena and the county of Mansfeld; and from the ministeria of the dukedom of Braunschweig-Lüneburg and the city of Braunschweig. They raised a number of issues. For example, the Jena faculty—consisting at this time of the Gnesio-Lutherans Johannes Wigand, John Frederick Cölestinus, and Timotheus Kirchner—found it suspicious that no individual claimed to be author of the Catechism: they conjectured that it was the work of the dean and the faculty at Wittenberg. They found its expressions ambiguous, its use of Luther's name deceptive since it abandoned his teaching and avoided mentioning his writings against sacramental heresy. It followed the baptismal teaching of Theodore Beza, making baptism into a mere sign, not a means of grace, they alleged. The Catechism assigned the benefit of the Lord's Supper to its use, not to the elements or Christ's words of institution, and avoided specific mention of the presence of Christ's body and blood in the Lord's Supper. It failed to focus on the words of institution and did not mention the partaking of the impious. It falsely defined the "right hand of God." It contained no warning against the writings of Calvin, Bullinger, Beza and their associates. The critique lodged further objections to the *Catechism's* definition of the gospel (which included the preaching of repentance as well as the forgiveness of sins) and to its definition of church discipline (it does not lead to Christ).[64] Selnecker also lodged his protest against the *Catechism's* innovative translation of Acts 3:21, winning for himself particularly bitter recriminations from the Wittenberg theologians as a traitor.[65]

In response to the Wittenberg *Catechism* the theologians at Jena devised seven test questions that could be used to identify their understanding of the Lutheran position on the Sacrament: (1) Is the true, essential, present, natural body of Christ distributed and received in the bread and wine according to Christ's words, with and under the bread and wine? (2) Is the body and blood of Christ only in heaven, remaining there until the Last Day and not essentially present in the Lord's Supper, but rather, as Beza and others claim, so far from the Lord's Supper as heaven is from earth? (3) Is the true, essential body of Christ received only by faith or also with the mouth? (4) Is the position that one receives the true, essential, present body of Christ in some other way than by the mouth to be rejected? (5) Are the words "this is my body" etc. to be understood literally or as symbol, figure, type, as the false glosses on the text by Karlstadt, Oecolampadius, Zwingli, Bullinger, Beza, and others argue? (6) Do the unworthy as well as the worthy receive the true, essential body of Christ (albeit to their condemnation) in the Supper? (7) Are Luther's books against the sacramentarians true, to be taken to heart, and confessed?[66]

The leadership of the electoral Saxon court faced criticism from within Elector August's domains as well as from external critics. August's court preacher Philip Wagner expressed his reservations, and a pastor in Torgau, Kaspar Heiderich, had to be disciplined because he expressed the belief that the Wittenberg Catechism could be misunderstood as antithetical to Luther's teaching.[67] An anonymous defense of its teaching appeared in May 1571, and the Wittenberg faculty also issued a defense of its teaching, but the electoral government began to notice the pressures from inside and outside August's lands. The theologians forged a reply, published in September 1571 under the title, *The True Church's Firm Foundation: On the Person and Incarnation of Our Lord Jesus Christ*.[68] This statement, composed by Christoph Pezel, rehearsed at length the reservations his circle had regarding the communication of attributes, as understood by Chemnitz or Andreae (the *Firm Foundation* lumped all the opponents of the electoral Saxon ecclesiastical leadership together under the name "Flacians"). In it Pezel treated the communication of attributes as a rhetorical tool rather than a real description of the relationship between the divine and human in Christ.

Following one element of Melanchthon's treatment of Christology, Pezel emphasized the function of the person of Christ and tried to avoid specifics regarding the nature of the union between his divine and human sides. He clearly separated the two natures when describing Christ's suffering and death. The divine nature could not suffer, so when Scripture speaks of crucifying the Lord of glory (1 Cor. 2:8), it refers to the person of Christ, within which only the human nature was able to suffer. Pezel wrote that the rule of faith, as derived from the ancient fathers, must govern the reading of Scripture, not vice versa, and this *analogia fidei* firmly supported his position, he was convinced.[69] Pezel rejected the positions of both the followers of Flacius, among whom he grouped all north German opponents, and the followers of Brenz, whom he engaged in detail, also extensively criticizing the positions of Wigand, Chemnitz, and Mörlin. The attacks on Chemnitz and others could not be left unanswered. The ministeria in Lower Saxony commissioned Chemnitz to draft a confession, which expressed the critique of the various theologians from the Lower Saxon circle.[70]

Similar positions to that of the *Firm Foundation* appeared in summary form in a *Consensus* issued at Dresden in October 1571 in the name of the Wittenberg and Leipzig theological faculties and the consistories and superintendents of electoral Saxony.[71] In four articles, on the person and incarnation of Christ, on his majesty and glory, on the term "seated at the right hand of God," and on the Holy Supper, the electoral Saxon theologians reaffirmed their positions. The *Consensus* elicited criticism as sharp as that against the *Catechism*. Selnecker interpreted it in a Lutheran manner, eliciting censure from others who opposed the electoral Saxon position, such as the Württemberg theologians, who broke a longer public silence to express their concerns.[72]

Indeed, the text of the *Consensus* attracted too much attention. Peter Dathenus, pastor of a Reformed congregation in Frankfurt am Main, appealed to it to gain legal status for his congregation within the city.[73] From the Palatinate Frederick III's son, August's son-in-law, Count Johann Kasimir, an ardent Calvinist, wrote Elector August in December 1571, rejoicing in the agreement between his theologians and the elector's.[74] August was not happy with such an appraisal of the position paper of his theologians. He demanded that they explain how indeed they differed from the "ravers" (*Schwärmer*) of the Palatinate. The consistory in Meissen, now under the leadership of the former Wittenberg professor, Paul Crell, replied that the Calvinists were simply trying to hide under the cloak of the Augsburg Confession and were actually teaching that the Sacrament was merely symbolical. In fact, Pezel was corresponding with Zacharias Ursinus in Heidelberg at the time, secretly because of his fears of the elector's disapproval. Nonetheless, the Wittenberg and Leipzig theologians assured the elector that there were great differences between their position and that of the Heidelberg theologians, without giving details. Johann Stössel composed a critique of the Heidelberg Catechism to set August's mind at rest; it worked, and the elector did in fact express confidence in his theologians once again.

In May 1572, August rebuffed the claims of Margrave Georg Friedrich of Brandenburg-Ansbach that his theologians were viewed as Calvinists throughout Evangelical lands outside Saxony. In June his government did ban the Latin version of the Wittenberg Catechism but authorized its German translation. At the same time Nikolaus Selnecker's work on the Lord's Supper had elicited a sharp critique from Theodore Beza in Geneva. While one of August's court preachers, Christian Schütz, endorsed Beza's work, the consistory in Meissen rejected it, encouraging August's trust in Saxony's ecclesiastical establishment. But the tensions within that establishment continued to rise, particularly in regard to sacramental teaching.[75]

Two years later the tensions exploded. The situation worsened for the Saxon theological establishment with the appearance of *A Clear and Quite Complete Exegesis of the Controversy concerning the Lord's Supper.*[76] It was printed in Leipzig by Ernst Vögelin on French paper with French type. Some copies bore the imprint "Geneva." Vögelin, an ally of Pezel's circle and a personal friend of Zacharias Ursinus in Heidelberg, apparently wanted above all to keep the Saxon origin of the work a secret. Suspicion fell upon the Wittenberg faculty when it became clear that it was indeed a home-grown product, but Vögelin was identified as the one responsible for its publication. He confessed that he had obtained a manuscript composed by a physician, Joachim Curaeus, who had studied at Wittenberg under Melanchthon and his son-in-law, the elector's personal physician, Caspar Peucer, in the early 1550s.[77]

More than a decade earlier, Vögelin related, Curaeus had prepared a defense of what he understood to be Melanchthon's teaching on the Lord's Supper, in opposition to Tileman Hesshus, who had studied at Wittenberg at the same time Curaeus had. Curaeus had attempted to demonstrate that Luther's true doctrine of the

Lord's Supper differed from the positions expressed in his polemical critiques of his opponents. Although Luther's polemic put him at odds with Melanchthon, the two agreed in essence if one looks at the elder reformer's more sober expressions of his teaching, Curaeus argued. He also rejected the Christological defense of the presence of Christ's body and blood in the Lord's Supper. He argued against the claim that those who receive the elements receive the Lord's body and blood orally and that the impious also receive his body and blood in the bread and wine. The *Clear Exegesis* made it clear that the position ascribed here to Melanchthon did not differ significantly from that of the Heidelberg theologians, who were perceived as adherents of Calvin's teaching.

Those who were pursuing a course aimed at "improving" the teaching of Luther with a more spiritualized understanding of the Lord's Supper continued to advance their views without openly rejecting Luther or advertising a change in theological position. But Elector August's concerns mounted. He had grown up in the court of his father, Heinrich, whose elder brother, Duke Georg, had been a fierce opponent of Luther's message. August recalled the price his father had paid for adhering to the theology of the Wittenberg reformer. His mother, too, had been fiercely devoted to Luther and his cause. So was his wife, the Danish princess, Anna. Furthermore, August knew that any diversion from the teaching of the Augsburg Confession would run afoul of the Religious Peace of Augsburg and return him to the outlaw status he had worked so hard to set aside as he had campaigned for the legal recognition of the Augsburg Confession two decades earlier.

What finally brought the Crypto-Philippist dominance in electoral Saxony to an end, however, was August's discovery that he was being hoodwinked and betrayed by some of his closest confidants. The revelation of their aim of spiritualizing Saxon teaching on the Lord's Supper had proved their critics correct, much to August's embarrassment. In early 1574 August repeatedly tried to pin down the position of his superintendent in Pirna, Johannes Stössel, on the presence of Christ in the Lord's Supper, without satisfactory progress. At the end of March one of his court preachers, Christian Schütz, held a sermon that sharply condemned the concept that the human nature of Christ could be present outside heaven and that he could make his body and blood present in the sacrament. Another court preacher Georg Listhenius openly contradicted Schütz's position. At the very same time communications between members of the ministerium and advisors at court came to August's attention. In these communications it was clear that his court physician, Melanchthon's son-in-law, Caspar Peucer, baptismal sponsor of August's youngest child, had subtly tried to win Electress Anna for the spiritualized understanding of the Lord's Supper that Peucer held[78] and that he tried to do this in such a way that she would not recognize that she was leaving Luther's doctrine behind. Peucer, Schütz, Stössel, and Georg Cracow, the elector's chancellor, were at the heart of the conspiracy, August believed. In the first week in April they were imprisoned on a variety of charges. The committee of the Saxon estates that met in May recommended punishments too mild for August. He had placed his life and his lands in the hands of Peucer, Schütz, and Cracow, and he would not take the contempt of betrayal lightly. Stössel and Cracow died in confinement within two years; Peucer and Schütz won release only after more than a decade in prison. Other theologians were briefly incarcerated and then exiled.[79]

The Philippist ministerium of Saxony had not been of one mind on the subject of the Lord's Supper throughout the period after Melanchthon's death. Across the Melanchthonian theological landscape shades of nuanced understanding of the issues at hand had created a spectrum of positions. In Meissen Crell, Georg Major's son-in-law, communicated his views to the elector soon after the power vacuum in the Saxon church became evident, on April 11. On the basis of an unpublished manuscript commentary on the Nicene Creed from Melanchthon's pen, Crell began a campaign to prove that Luther and Melanchthon had indeed shared the same view of the Lord's Supper and Christ's ascension to the right hand of God.[80] Crell's interpretation of Melanchthon's views confirmed August's own inclinations to anchor the theology of his lands in the teaching of both Wittenberg reformers—against medieval scholasticism, "Flacianism," and "sacramentarianism." Crell assisted August's court in beginning to create a new ecclesiastical order in the electorate. August imposed censorship on works regarding the Lord's Supper in his lands. The works of two authors on these subjects were permitted to be distributed: Martin Chemnitz, for whom the Elector apparently had great respect, and Hieronymus Weller, whose treatment of the Lord's Supper had also aimed at demonstrating the agreement of Luther and Melanchthon on an essentially "Luther"-an interpretation of the words of institution.[81] The court preacher Peter Glaser compiled and published documentation to show that while Melanchthon lived, there had been essentially only one theology of the Lord's Supper in Saxony, that which taught the true, essential presence of Christ's body and blood in the Sacrament, received orally and received by the impious.[82]

The critical event redirecting Saxon public theology in the direction of Luther's understanding of the Lord's Supper came at a diet of the Saxon estates held at Torgau at the end of May 1574. The electoral government issued requirements for pastors and professors: All had to agree on the Lord's Supper. Both universities were to condemn Calvin, Zanchi, Peter Martyr Vermigli, Beza, and other sacramentarians and to defend Luther and Melanchthon, who were to be the model for all preaching. Calvinist books were no longer to be published in Saxony. The theologians in attendance composed a confession of ten positive articles of teaching, to which were attached condemnations of twenty false formulations. They wove together the basic elements of the sacramental teaching of both Luther and Melanchthon. This confession taught that the words of institution and 1 Corinthians 10:16 are to be understood literally, that the true substantial body and blood of Christ are present in and sacramentally united with the bread and wine of the Lord's Supper and are received through the mouth, by which the benefits of Christ's death are conveyed to believers. Any figurative or symbolic interpretation was rejected, as was a "spiritual" reception by faith. The Confession claimed that this teaching reaffirmed that of the Augsburg Confession, the Apology, the *Corpus Doctrinae Misnicum*, which had previously set the standards for the public teaching in Saxony, and the Dresden *Consensus*.[83] Most of the theologians present subscribed this *Confession*; five professors from Wittenberg did not: Friedrich Widebram, Caspar Cruciger the Younger, Heinrich Möller, and Christoph Pezel from the theological faculty, and the humanities professor Esrom Rüdinger. Crell tried to convince them to subscribe, and they did finally when he permitted them subscription under the interpretation that indeed this *Confession* taught nothing other than the Dresden *Consensus* and the *Corpus Doctrinae Misnicum*. Crell did not inform the elector of this provision.

The five were freed from custody and left the land. They gravitated to courts or cities in which some form of Calvinist confession of faith was taught, confirming in the public mind that they had indeed been "Crypto-Calvinists." A more accurate description of their theological sojourn posits that the trajectory on which they found themselves launched by Melanchthon's theological concerns brought them finally to rest in such places. The ecclesiastical landscape of the 1570s and 1580s permitted no other definitions and categories than those set by the Augsburg Confession of 1530/1531 and the Consensus Tigurinus of 1549. There was no place for a Philippist confession of faith between Luther's and Calvin's. His followers were forced to find a home in one of those two havens.

August believed that his own newly formed ecclesiastical leadership needed outside assistance, and so he called upon one of the most important leaders of the church, Jakob Andreae, to come to Saxony for a five-year period to reestablish a firm Lutheran footing in his lands. As it had loaned Andreae to Julius of Braunschweig-Wolfenbüttel a few years earlier, the Württemberg court dispatched him once again to the North. August and Andreae decided not only to work on the reform of electoral Saxony but also to dedicate their efforts to the task of Lutheran unity.[84] Thus, the collapse of the Crypto-Philippist fortress in electoral Saxony led directly into the efforts that resulted in the Formula of Concord.

The Formula of Concord on the Lord's Supper and Christology

In his revision of Andreae's draft of a settlement to the controversies over the Lord's Supper Chemnitz took the Swabian's critique of the Crypto-Philippist positions on the Lord's Supper and Christology and wove his concerns together with those of those who took a Melanchthonian approach to the Supper among both Gnesio-Lutherans and Philippists. In so doing he staked out a position that he intended to convey Luther's sacramental theology of the mid 1520s. Some distinctive formulations from Melanchthon's later doctrine of the Lord's Supper were not incorporated into this position.[85]

The seventh article of the Formula focused first of all on the teachings of the "subtle" or "cunning" "sacramentarians," the Crypto-Philippists within the Lutheran church of Saxony, although its treatment of their teaching constituted a rejection of the sacramental theology of Reformed theologians, followers of both Zwingli and Calvin, Bullinger and Beza. Clearly stated as presupposition for the Formula's treatment of the Lord's Supper is Luther's conviction that God's Word, also in sacramental form, is a word of power, a word that bestows forgiveness of sins, life and salvation (SD VII, 1–8).

Three key elements to a Lutheran definition of the Real Presence were stated clearly: (1) Christ's body and blood are "truly and essentially present and distributed with the bread and wine," united in a "sacramental union;" (2) they are received by mouth when distributed, and (3) they are received by both the worthy and the unworthy, the godly and the ungodly, believers and unbelievers—believers for life and salvation, unbelievers to their judgment. The Formula defined the "unworthy" as "those without true remorse and sorrow for their sins, without true faith and good intentions to improve their life" (SD VII,68). The Formula's position rejected a "spiritual" understanding of the presence of Christ that limited that presence in the Sacrament to a spiritual presence, which was available on a heavenly level, only on the level of the soul. The Concordists based their position on the literal interpretation of Christ's words of institution and secondarily on the sharing of attributes between Christ's divine and human natures that enables Christ to be present in his body and blood when and where he wills it (SD VII, 9–87).

The seventh article clearly demarcated the Crypto-Philippist position from its own. Its position, however, takes into account specific concerns of Melanchthon and many of his followers that the medieval view that the Preceptor liked to label with the pejorative epithet "bread-worship" (inaccurate when applied to Westphal and others of Melanchthon's former students) not be perpetuated within Lutheran circles. The Formula rejects errors of the Roman Catholic party, including its view of the sacrifice of the mass, its prohibition of the communion of the laity with Christ's blood, and its Aristotelian explanation of Christ's presence through the concept of transubstantiation. The seventh article repudiates the charge that the Lutherans taught a "capernaitic" eating of Christ's body and blood, in the manner of other ingested substances. It also honored Melanchthon's worry that medieval superstitious use of the elements could return and therefore tied the presence of Christ's body and blood closely to the words of institution and the use of the sacrament to convey the benefits of Christ (SD VII,73–76).[86]

On the other hand, it rejected both spiritual and symbolic interpretations of Christ's presence, sweeping with broad strokes the positions of Zwingli, Calvin, and the Wittenberg theologians gathered around Pezel and Peucer together. It focused on specific phrases used in the Wittenberg defense of the Crypto-Philippist position of the early 1570s, such as the belief that in the Supper Christ is present in his divine nature by means of the communication of attributes but not in his human body and blood (SD VII,4), or that the Supper serves only as a token, external pledge, or badge for Christians (SD VII,115, 116). The Formula rejected the Crypto-Philippist interpretations of Acts 3:21, in support of the view represented by Selnecker and others in criticism of the Wittenberg theology in the period: Christ's human nature is not restricted to some physical location above the clouds, as Pezel had insisted (SD VII:119). The Formula embraced a "spiritual eating" in faith but did not equate it with God's nourishing believers with Christ's body and blood and the Word of forgiveness and life they convey in the Lord's Supper. Sacramental eating and drinking of Christ's body and blood certainly does involve this spiritual eating and drinking, however, for all who receive the sacrament in faith.

While affirming that Luther's Christological argument on behalf of the Lord's Supper indeed supports his understanding of the true presence of Christ's body and blood, the Concordists did not emphasize that element of Lutheran argumentation in this article. It followed Chemnitz's lead in moderating the interpretation of the position of Brenz and Andreae, which asserted an omnipresence of Christ's human nature that Beza and others had misinterpreted as placing human cells in every stone and rock of creation (indeed, a polemical misrepresentation of the Swabian argument).[87] Chemnitz's description of the sharing of the characteristic of divine presence with the human nature of Christ, labeled "multivolipresence," affirmed that Christ could be present in his whole person, embracing both natures, in a variety of ways not possible for other human beings, because he was also true God (SD VII, 6–87).[88]

The Formula also repeated the themes from Luther's sacramental writings and his catechisms, which emphasized the comfort for guilty consciences and the strengthening of faith that the Lord's Supper effects in believers' lives. In the final analysis, the sacrament's conveying the gospel of forgiveness and new life to God's people remained the foremost focus on Lutheran sacramental teaching even though the Formula itself, in resolving disputes, placed its emphasis on the nature of Christ's presence in the elements.

The eighth article of the Formula affirms that the divine and human natures of Christ share characteristics within the personal union of those natures without losing their own integrity because of that sharing.[89] The Concordists intended to anchor their Christology firmly in the doctrine of the early church expressed in the decisions of the Council of Chalcedon (451) regarding the "communication of attributes." Taking special care to avoid the charges of monophysitism or Eutychianism, the Concordists insisted that the divine characteristics of the second person of the Trinity never become the characteristics of the human nature—and vice versa. But the personal union, a "most complete communion" between God and this human creature, Jesus of Nazareth, enables this sharing of characteristics. Thus, the Concordists reaffirmed the conclusion of the Council of Ephesus (431), that Mary is the Mother of God, and that the Son of Man was exalted to the right hand of majesty and power because he was assumed into God the Son upon conception. The historical person of Jesus, God in human flesh, exhibits both divine and human characteristics because of this communication of attributes between the two natures. In the unity of his person the characteristics are ascribed to both natures even though they belong only to one, in principle (SD VII, 14–15, 17–19, 46–47, 59, 76).

Not only the ancient heresies of Nestorius, Eutyches, Arius, Marcion, and others were rejected by the Concordists. They specifically rejected expressions based on Melanchthon's later views as interpreted by the circle around Pezel and Peucer. They rejected the idea that the ancient doctrine of the communication of attributes could be speaking only of verbal association, a figure of speech. At the same time Chemnitz's delimitation of the concept of this communication of attributes found its place in the Formula. The human nature did not become an infinite essence; it is not present everywhere in the same way the divine nature is present. It does not extend spatially into all parts of heaven and earth. The Concordists also tried to prevent other misunderstandings they feared might arise in the course of further discussion of the sharing of the characteristics of Christ's divine and human nature (SD VII, 88–96).

To explain how Christ's human nature could share this characteristic of divine presence, the Concordists used distinctions expressed in three principles Chemnitz was developing in his treatments of the doctrine. The first principle, the principle of properties (or characteristics or attributes), later called the *genus idiomaticum*, stated that the characteristics unique to each nature are to be ascribed to Christ's person, designated by either nature alone or by both natures. The second principle, the principle of the actions of office, later labeled the *genus apotelesmaticum*, stated that each nature performed actions appropriate to itself in Jesus' ministry but the other nature, within the unity of the person, shared in that action. The third principle, the principle of majesty, later the *genus majestaticum*, stated that the second person of the Trinity shares his divine attributes with the human nature within the personal union (SD VIII, 37–55).

The Concordists understood this Christology as biblically faithful and pastorally sensitive, a formulation that accurately described how God became human and continues to be the incarnate Son of God. They also had experienced the comfort that Luther's teaching on the wonder of the incarnation could give. Although the eighth article came into the Formula by way of controversy over the Lord's Supper, it expressed the heart of the Wittenberg message: that the second person of the Godhead became Jesus "for us and for our salvation."

The Descent into Hell

Although Lutheran theologians had published varying descriptions of Christ's descent into hell—in Wittenberg Bugenhagen did not agree with Luther and Melanchthon on how to explain the descent[90]—only in the cities of Hamburg and Augsburg and in the duchy of Mecklenburg had somewhat serious controversies erupted over the subject. The teaching of the Heidelberg Catechism on Christ's descent had also aroused Lutheran criticism in the 1560s because it rejected the physical descent of the whole Christ, divine and human natures, into hell at the same time he lay in the grave. This position, according to Lutheran critics in the ministerium in Mansfeld, was based on principles of Aristotelian physics, not on the Word of God, and was compelled by the Heidelberg theologians' rejection of the Christological argument in behalf of the doctrine of the true presence of Christ's body and blood in the Lord's Supper.[91] For if Christ's body could have lain in the grave and at the same time descended into hell, it could also be at the "right hand of God" in heaven and on earth in the Supper. That the Heidelberg theologians were not willing to allow.

At the last stages of the creation of the Formula of Concord, its authors decided to add article nine on this doctrine as a sort of appendix to its treatment of Christology in reaction to the Heidelberg Catechism. The article is brief and refers the readers to a sermon preached by Luther on the descent into hell and the resurrection in 1532.[92] The Formula wanted to "cut off all unprofitable, unnecessary questions" regarding doctrine. Moving beyond the controversies over this article, the Concordists simply affirmed that Christ descended into hell in both natures as one person and destroyed hell for all believers, redeeming them from the power of death, the devil, and eternal damnation. They thus affirmed the position of Melanchthon and rejected that of Calvinists and some Lutherans (including Luther at times as well as Johannes Brenz and Jakob Andreae) who interpreted the descent into hell as merely the culmination of Christ's sufferings. The Formula commits its subscribers to avoiding speculation and to a simple confession of Christ's descent to celebrate his victory over every evil.[93]

The first six articles and article eleven of the Formula of Concord deal with problems arising from the Wittenberg reformers' understanding of who God is and what it means to be human. Articles seven through nine address issues raised by Luther's understanding that almighty God works his re-creative will through selected elements of the created order. Specifically according to the Formula of Concord, he effects his saving will through the uniting of his divine second person, the Logos, with a truly human being, Jesus of Nazareth, and through his decision to bestow forgiveness, life, and salvation through several forms of his Word, including the sacramental form that is linked to Christ's body and blood, conveyed to recipients through and in bread and wine. These three articles reflect the concern for pastoral care and faithfulness to biblical revelation that permeates the other articles.[94]

13

Efforts at Attaining Concord, 1552–1569

No Christian regards disunity in the church as good. The church is always committed to the fulfillment of Christ's prayer that his disciples might be one on the basis of a unity of confession of Christ and the battle against error and deception (John 17:11-21). Whatever factors may in fact cause disunity in the church, Christians often explain their own separation from others in terms of the others' false understanding and confession of the faith. Sometimes this explanation is correct. The disunity among the followers of the Wittenberg reform in the third quarter of the sixteenth century was largely discussed in terms of proper representation of the truth (although the Philippists also tended to blame it on the Gnesio-Lutherans' propensity for quarreling, particularly on the contentiousness of the Slavic foreigner, the "Illyrian," Matthias Flacius). In any case, both Gnesio-Lutherans and Philippists, as well as other Lutherans, yearned for harmony and peace within their confession of the faith. Particularly their princes and other political leaders longed for unity among their churches and devoted a great deal of financial support and diplomatic effort to the search for concord. Likewise, the theologians of the time sought agreement while practicing the polemic they believed would lead all sides toward the common confession of the truth.

Princes and Theologians Strive for Unity, 1553–1569

The public controversies had hardly begun in the early 1550s before the search for unity was launched, both by theologians and by princes. Slowly the feuding interpreters of Luther's legacy worked out different approaches to the reestablishment of unity of confession among the Lutherans. In general, the Gnesio-Lutherans sought a detailed statement of faith and insisted on specific condemnation of false teachings and false teachers while (at least until the late 1550s and then again until 1570) the Philippists favored a short summary of teaching on controverted topics and wanted to practice *amnistia*—"forgetting"—in regard to those who had erred in their expression of the church's teaching. Both sides appealed on suitable occasions to a general synod of Evangelical churches. But for the most part, the Gnesio-Lutherans pressed for a synod of theologians to settle the theological problems; the Philippists feared that a pack of theologians would only fall into worse quarreling with each other than had existed previously. They favored placing the attainment of unity in the hands of the Evangelical princes.

Both parties wanted to rest their doctrinal decisions upon the Scripture as summarized in the Augsburg Confession.[1] However, Melanchthon preferred to secure
his interpretation more with citations from the ancient Fathers.[2] For the Gnesio-
Lutherans, although they also used patristic materials to bolster their arguments,
the primary supplement to the Augsburg Confession as a theological orientation
point was the corpus of Luther's writings, and above all his Smalcald Articles.

As princely governments negotiated with each other and with the imperial court
after the Truce of Passau (1552) in the search for religious peace, Duke Christoph
of Württemberg took the lead in organizing the princes to establish a solution. In
May 1553 he called together the first conference of princes and theologians to hammer out a formula for concord among the Lutherans. Nothing came of the meeting, but the pressures increased as it became increasingly likely that the estates of
the Augsburg Confession might gain legal recognition. The Evangelical princes met
in Naumburg in May 1554 to define the faith they wanted to become legal in the
Empire. In that process they addressed the theological issues dividing them.[3]

Once the Religious Peace of Augsburg had been established, Christoph continued to take the lead in seeking a solution to the differences that were tearing the
Lutheran camp apart. At his side stood Landgrave Wilhelm of Hesse. Christoph
and Elector Frederick II of the Palatinate sent a delegation to Weimar in January
1556 to advance the settlement of the disputes by finding common ground with
the Gnesio-Lutheran leadership within ducal Saxony. In particular, the theologians
there (at this time including Viktorin Strigel) pressed for condemnation of false
teachings and false teachers in any settlement. During the course of 1556 Flacius
himself composed his "Gentle Proposals" for settling the disputes and sent them to
Melanchthon's colleague, Paul Eber, to use in opening the door between Preceptor
and former student. Flacius's proposals were, of course, not gentle enough.
Melanchthon had become so embittered by "the Illyrian's" attacks that he could not
believe that Flacius was willing to be genuinely reconciled with him and his compatriots in electoral Saxony. He entertained the suggestion of meeting personally with
Flacius and then rejected the idea.[4]

In anticipation of Evangelical participation in a dialogue with Roman Catholic
parties, which Emperor Ferdinand was planning for September 1557, a group of
negotiators headed by Joachim Mörlin conducted a "colloquy" by horseback in
January of that year, shuffling back and forth between the town of Coswig, where
Flacius and others from Magdeburg had assembled, and Wittenberg with documents aimed at reconciliation. Their endeavor failed.[5] So did a similar attempt at
mediation sponsored by Duke Johann Albrecht of Mecklenburg, an ally of John
Frederick the Middler, a few weeks later.[6]

On both sides, the sense of betrayal and the resulting bitterness had destroyed
the trust necessary to reconcile the foes who eight years earlier had been friends.
Melanchthon took every opportunity to defend his wounded honor against Flacius.
His resentment against this foreigner often spilled into the letters and memoranda

he wrote. His hurt at what he viewed as a malicious failure to acknowledge his honest efforts at saving the Lutheran confession through the Leipzig Proposal grew. Philip's rancorous reactions were fed by the suspicion and grief with which these former students regarded their beloved Preceptor, whom they had come to mistrust because they believed he had broken faith with them, with their other theological hero, Luther, and with God. Flacius and Gallus never ceased reflecting their frustration and sense of betrayal at the hands of the Preceptor on whom they had counted for a continuing clear confession of the faith. They found many supporters among their contemporaries from Wittenberg. In this climate of mutual distrust and antagonism serious theological discussion quickly gave way to exaggeration of the other side's weaknesses and misinterpretation of the other side's concerns. Nonetheless, the longing for unity and for a common confession of the truth, joined with political necessity, propelled all parties to the disputes to try again and again to establish concord.

Emperor Charles retired in discouragement, abdicating the imperial throne in 1556; his brother Ferdinand succeeded him and immediately sought religious reconciliation on a larger scale within his empire. He arranged for a colloquy between Evangelicals and Roman Catholics in Worms. It began on September 1, 1557. Melanchthon, Brenz, and other leading theologians represented the Lutherans; the Gnesio-Lutherans were also present. From ducal Saxony came Schnepf, Strigel, and Stössel, representing the strict position of the court in Weimar. Flacius himself had contributed to the formulation of the duke's instructions for the delegation, which insisted that the basis for presenting the Evangelical position had to be the Unaltered Augsburg Confession, the Apology of the Augsburg Confession, and the Smalcald Articles. Furthermore, the ducal theologians were to insist on Evangelical condemnation of Majorism, Adiaphorism, Osiandrism, and a number of other heresies. Flacius's and Amsdorf's point of view was also represented by Erasmus Sarcerius of Mansfeld and Joachim Mörlin of Braunschweig. (Accompanying Mörlin was his colleague Martin Chemnitz; accompanying Brenz was his colleague Jakob Andreae.) The divisions among the Evangelical negotiators became apparent quickly. The Gnesio-Lutheran theologians insisted on explicit condemnation of false teachings, including those of the Osiandrians, adiaphorists, and Majorists. Melanchthon made extensive concessions to their position, and they demonstrated a willingness to find a stance to which the others could agree. But Johannes Brenz resisted every effort to condemn false teachers, as he defended the reputation, if not the teaching, of Andreas Osiander. The Roman Catholic theologians exploited these divisions. Peter Canisius led the effort to give the Gnesio-Lutherans no choice but to withdraw from the colloquy. They did, to the deep frustration of the leading Lutheran princes as well as their theologians. Embarrassed before their Roman Catholic foes and chagrined over disunity in their own ranks, they recognized more clearly than ever the need for concord among the adherents of the Augsburg Confession in the aftermath of the collapse of the colloquy.[7]

The princes immediately began to try again. Melanchthon was commissioned to draw up a statement of consensus before the parties left Worms. Through the winter of 1557–1558, negotiations continued among the Evangelical courts. In February 1558 the Lutheran princes gathered in Frankfurt for the coronation of Emperor Ferdinand. There they issued a statement, the Frankfurt Recess, composed on the basis of drafts by Melanchthon, calling for unity on the basis of four articles: justification, new obedience, the Lord's Supper, and adiaphora. The article on justification explicitly ruled out an Osiandrian position, embracing the Wittenberg teaching that sinners become righteous in God's sight through the blood and obedience of Christ. The Recess taught that new obedience is necessary for the Christian life but not for salvation. It confessed that Christ is truly, essentially present with the bread and wine of the Lord's Supper. It emphasized that the sacrament bestows its blessings only in its use. It rejected papist abuse of the mass and transubstantiation as an explanation of the true presence. It approved of Christian freedom in regard to adiaphora.[8] Flacius led the ducal Saxon reaction with an unpublished critique entitled "Refutation of the Samaritan Interim, in which true religion is wantonly and perniciously confused with sects and corruptions of doctrine." The omission of the Smalcald Articles as part of the confessional basis for the Lutheran churches outraged him, as did what he viewed as Melanchthon's diminution of the importance of the issues at stake. The rejection of Major's teaching on good works was insufficient, and the articles on the Lord's Supper and adiaphora were ambiguous, Flacius claimed.[9]

The princes' efforts at unity had foundered again on the rock of Flacian opposition. From the Flacian side came a new approach to unity: a new document based on the principle that concord could be attained best by a clear exclusion and rejection of false doctrine. Ducal Saxon court theologians—Viktorin Strigel, Erhard Schnepf, and Andreas Hügel—accepted their prince's commission to compose a *Book of Confutation* in Latin and German.[10] Against their specific request, the duke submitted their draft for revision and improvement to Flacius, Amsdorf, and others in their circle, including the two theologians who in Worms had stood by the representatives from John Frederick's government, Mörlin and Sarcerius. In its final form the *Book* contained detailed condemnations of the anti-trinitarian Michael Servetus, the spiritualist Caspar Schwenckfeld, the antinomians, the anabaptists, the sacramentarians, Andreas Osiander, Francesco Stancarus, Georg Major, the adiaphorists, and those who erred on the doctrine of the freedom of the will, as well as a summary of the biblical teaching that countered each of these false teachings. Completed in late 1558, the *Book* did nothing to convince the Philippist side that it was wrong on the controverted questions.

Soon Flacius tried again to bring an end to the controversies, this time through a petition he authored, which appealed for a synod of theologians to adjudicate all disputed questions. It was subscribed to by fifty-one sympathetic theologians from territories throughout the Empire.[11] Duke Christoph and Elector August rejected the idea, however, with full support from Melanchthon and his followers. The synod did not come to pass.

The princes had to try again. In January 1561 the Evangelical political leaders were brought together in Naumburg by Dukes Christoph and John Frederick the Middler, who attempted to win them all for a unified commitment to the doctrine of the Augsburg Confession.[12] However, a new factor was developing in the princely collegium. Frederick III of the Palatinate stood in danger of being outlawed by the empire because he was leading his land in the direction of Calvinism, which was not a legally recognized option within the German Empire according to the Religious Peace of Augsburg. The Palatine government had to try to retain its identification with the Augsburg Confession. The Diet of Naumburg in fact made the Altered Augsburg Confession a vital issue because it was viewed both by Frederick and by his strict Lutheran opponents, such as John Frederick the Middler, as a legal cover for Calvinism. David Chytraeus, professor in Rostock and a loyal disciple of Melanchthon, was serving as theological advisor to Duke Ulrich of Mecklenburg. He strongly advocated returning to the Unaltered Augsburg Confession as the text that should have the force of law in the Empire.[13] The majority of princes pledged themselves to the Unaltered Confession but, as a concession to Elector Frederick, in a note of explanation of their position composed for the emperor, they acknowledged the Altered Confession as a proper interpretation of the original text. John Frederick and Duke Ulrich of Mecklenburg walked out of the conference because of this provision; other princes opposed it as well.

Collecting Confessional Documents: The Corpora Doctrinae

Whatever their problems on the imperial level, princes also needed to define the faith for their own lands and to have at hand an instrument for enforcing the unity of teaching among their own pastors. Two approaches to the problem of defining the faith for the general use of the church developed in the years around 1550. In some places a confession of faith according to the model of the Augsburg Confession was written for a specific situation; in almost all cases these new Lutheran confessions presumed and built upon the Augsburg Confession, the Apology, the Smalcald Articles, and Luther's catechisms.[14] These confessions contained both positive expositions of biblical teaching in summary form and condemnations of false teachings that were threatening that exposition of what Scripture taught. It was these rejected positions that usually gave occasion for confession in the specific context in which the confession was composed. The second confessional genre took form simply around the condemnation of false teaching; the Weimar *Book of Confutation* of 1559 inaugurated this confessional genre. Other examples of such confessions include those of Mansfeld County (1559, 1564).[15]

The confessions following the model of the Augsburg Confession more closely and focused on the positive exposition of biblical teaching usually were written to confront some new, special challenge: for example, those of Magdeburg (1550) and the Saxon counties of Reuss and Schönburg. The confessions prepared by the electoral Saxon theologians and those of Strasbourg and Württemberg for presentation of Lutheran teaching at the second session of the Council of Trent fall into this category as well.[16] Other confessions arose out of the need to define the Lutheran confession in "frontier" situations, where the Lutheran church had not enjoyed official support: Carinthia (1566), Lower Austria (1566), and Antwerp (1567).[17]

Other principalities created collections of already existing documents that were gathered into one volume to serve as the land's official definition of the faith, its doctrinal rule and norm. These collections were called "Bodies of Doctrine"—a *corpus doctrinae*. The term *corpus doctrinae* had been used in Wittenberg for several decades to designate the whole of biblical doctrine or teaching, an analogy of faith, as a summary—"a binding summary, basis, rule and norm, how all teaching is to be judged in accord with God's Word and the errors that have arisen are to be explained and decided in Christian fashion," to use the language of the Formula of Concord, as it explained to its readers how it was to be used as just such a *corpus doctrinae*. This usage can be seen in the title of the first Protestant biblical theology, the *Syntagma or corpus doctrinae [the summary or body of doctrine] of Christ, drawn from the New Testament*, composed by Johann Wigand and Matthaeus Judex in the late 1550s.[18] At the same time the term *corpus doctrinae* was employed to refer to a list of documents that were being used for the purpose of establishing such a summary of biblical teaching. Finally, the title "Body of Doctrine" was given to a formal, published collection of such documents.[19]

The first of these collections was edited by Melanchthon near the end of his life, as a formal counterweight to the appearance of the *Book of Confutation*. It contained the authoritative writings that the Wittenberg faculty had been using in the 1550s for adjudicating theological disputes.[20] All came from Melanchthon's own pen. His *Corpus doctrinae Philippicum* or *Misnicum* (Meissen was the home territory of the Albertine Saxon family) included the ecumenical creeds, the Unaltered as well as the Altered Augsburg Confession (editions of 1533 [German] and 1542 [Latin]), the Apology, the Saxon Confession of 1551, the final revision of the *Loci communes theologici*, the *Examination for Candidates for Ordination*, which Melanchthon composed for the duchy of Mecklenberg on the basis of electoral Saxon usage in 1552; the Preceptor's *Response to the Impious Articles of the Bavarian Inquisition* (1558), which he regarded as a kind of theological last will and testament, and which was supplemented by his earlier *Response to the Controversies around Stancaro* (1553) and his *Refutation of the Error of Servetus and the Anabaptists*, composed shortly before his death.[21] Originally published without governmental support, the *Corpus doctrinae Misnicum* was officially accepted as the standard for teaching by electoral Saxony in 1566. The Pomeranian church accepted and expanded it in its *Corpus doctrinae* in 1565; the Pomeranian standard also included Luther's catechisms, the Smalcald Articles, his *Confession on the Lord's Supper* of 1528, and two other memoranda from his hand.[22] Similar was the *Norm for Teaching* issued by the city of

Nuremberg in 1573, with the documents of the Melanchthonian *Corpus doctrinae* plus several from Luther's pen.

Other *Corpora doctrinae* were less dependent on Melanchthon's contributions (although the Augustana and its Apology were always included). The ministerium in Lübeck issued its collection, with the ancient creeds, the Augsburg Confession and its Apology, the Smalcald Articles, and Luther's Catechisms, in 1560.[23] Martin Chemnitz had worked on the preparation of four separate *Corpora doctrinae* in the dozen years before he began work on the Formula of Concord. He had assisted his predecessor as superintendent of the churches in the city of Braunschweig, Joachim Mörlin, in bringing together five documents to guide teaching there: the Augsburg Confession, the Apology, the Smalcald Articles, the city's 1528 ecclesiastical constitution prepared by Johannes Bugenhagen, and the Lüneburg Declaration of 1561, which Mörlin had composed with help from Chemnitz.[24] These two men wrote a new standard for Prussian teaching when Mörlin was recalled to Königsberg to clean up the Osiandrian situation there in 1567. They attached the Augsburg Confession, the Apology, and the Smalcald Articles to their own newly formulated "Repetition of the Summary and Content of the True, General Christian Teaching of the Church."[25] Two dukes of Braunschweig also commissioned Chemnitz to prepare similar *Corpora doctrinae* in 1576. Duke Wilhelm of Braunschweig-Lüneburg and Duke Julius of Braunschweig-Wolfenbüttel issued almost identical collections,[26] containing the ecumenical creeds, the Augsburg Confession, the Apology, the Smalcald Articles, the catechisms of Luther, and the *Formulas for Speaking Carefully* of Urbanus Rhegius,[27] who had been serving as superintendent of the churches in Braunschweig-Lüneburg when he wrote that piece in 1535; an appendix on current controversies and the proper language for addressing their questions, composed by Chemnitz, was attached. Duke Julius added a "Declaration" on the fundamental articles of Christian teaching to his *Corpus doctrinae*.

Before these two Braunschweig books had been issued, before the road toward concord rose up before the German Lutherans, two other principalities and one city had published their own official guides to teaching in the form of the *Corpus doctrinae*. Göttingen included its own church order from 1530, Luther's catechisms with other catechetical writings from his hand, the Smalcald Articles, the Augsburg Confession, and the Apology in its constitution of 1568.[28] Duke John William of ducal Saxony had his theologians collect ten confessions for his lands in 1570. They included the three ecumenical creeds, Luther's catechisms, the Augsburg Confession, the Apology, the Smalcald Articles, the Thuringian confession against the Interim of 1548, the *Book of Confutation*, and—as a separate document— Luther's admonition to confession and absolution from the Large Catechism.[29] Two years later Elector Joachim II of Brandenburg had his theologians assemble a similar volume containing the Augsburg Confession, the Small Catechism, and a summary of Luther's teachings in selected citations from his works on nine topics organized by his leading theologian, Andreas Musculus.[30]

These collections gave witness to a common core of Lutheran confession of the faith even if very few of them commanded much acceptance as authoritative collections outside their respective lands. However, because they demonstrated this common core of public teaching in the several documents that were widely accepted as confessions of the faith, they helped prepare the way for the acceptance of the *Book of Concord*. Its development, however, could only be completed after more controversy and more attempts at formulating harmony. One of these, the last attempt to resolve theological differences on the basis of the framework set by the controversies around the Leipzig Proposal, took place in 1568 and 1569 in Altenburg.

The Altenburg Colloquy

In 1567 John Frederick the Middler supported a renegade knight named Wilhelm von Grumbach in his feud with the imperial government; Grumbach and the duke lost. Grumbach was executed, and the duke went to jail for life. His brother John William assumed rule of his lands, and he immediately began to seek concord with a project of his own. Sympathetic to the Gnesio-Lutherans, he brought back Wigand to the University of Jena and placed other like-mind theologians at his side on the faculty. Two of them, Timotheus Kirchner and John Frederick Cölestinus, joined Wigand in executing John William's proposal to end the disputes between the theologians of the two Saxon governments through a colloquy. John William assumed the presiding chair of the colloquy himself as it began in the Electoral Saxon town of Altenburg on October 21, 1568. The electoral Saxon delegation was headed by Paul Eber and Caspar Cruciger the Younger. In a series of meetings during the winter of 1568–1569, the two sides deliberated on the proper definition of justification in relationship to good works. The agenda included freedom of the will and adiaphora as well, and the Jena delegation had prepared documents to guide the discussion of these topics. But in the session held in early March the electoral Saxon delegation felt that progress toward reconciliation was beyond reach; without informing even their own political advisors from the court of Elector August, they left town March 9. The colloquy died.[31]

On some issues the Philippists in Altenburg began to justify the criticism of the Gnesio-Lutherans by expressing their position in terms the Gnesio-Lutherans had long attributed to them. They tried to salvage something of Major's concern for morality and order by insisting that good works do earn a reward in heaven even though they do not earn the reward of heaven, an idea that Major had tentatively advanced earlier. This seemed to violate Luther's distinction of active and passive righteousness, permitting active righteousness to play a role in the believer's relationship with God. They defined justification as consisting of both imputed righteousness and the sanctified righteousness of human performance that resulted from the imputation of Christ's righteousness to the sinner. This, too, seemed to blur edges designed to protect a clear enunciation of God's gracious deliverance from sin solely through the merits of Christ. By taking such positions as these Eber and his colleagues only enflamed the suspicion and contempt of Wigand and his colleagues.[32]

The collapse of the colloquy of Altenburg signaled the hopelessness of the situation. The two sides had solidified the walls between them, based as they were on different concerns and points of view, different fears, resentments, and suspicions. If Lutheran concord was to be attained at all, a new start would have to be made, a new paradigm would have to be found.

14

Jakob Andreae's Drive for Lutheran Unity and the Composition of the Formula of Concord and the Book of Concord

The court of Christoph of Württemberg had played a leading role in attempting to create concord among the strife-ridden churches of the Augsburg Confession since 1552. Jakob Andreae had often found himself in the middle of such efforts, at the duke's right hand as both ecclesiastical diplomat and theological advisor. (He was better suited, despite a rather difficult personality, for the former than the latter.) Early on in his career, Andreae had striven to reach understanding, albeit on his own terms, with representatives of the Calvinist theological school.[1] His prince had used him throughout the 1550s and early 1560s for a number of ecclesiastical diplomatic missions, in various parts of Germany and even in France, at the Colloquy of Poissy, in 1561. Andreae was driven by a concern for the spiritual damage done to the consciences of the laity through theological controversy and by his desire to meet Roman Catholic reproaches against the Evangelicals for their disunity. However, at the beginning of his career as agent of reconciliation, he damaged his credibility by trying too often to minimize or marginalize the controverted issues dividing Luther's followers.

Earlier the Gnesio-Lutherans had emphasized the need for a synod of theologians to restore Lutheran unity of confession. Melanchthon and his circle had despaired of achieving peace through a synod of theologians. They were convinced that only the guiding hand of the princes could get beyond the madness of theologians to attain harmony among Luther's, Melanchthon's, and Brenz's followers. Duke Christoph had long shared Melanchthon's orientation toward these efforts. What he initiated, however, in 1568, was a combination of both approaches to concord. Andreae traveled at the behest of his own and other princes, but he went on his way functioning as a theologian, seeking agreement among fellow theologians. The combination of princely support and hard theological work on the problems at hand survived Andreae's first attempt at creating unity—he again made the mistake of trying to solve the disputes at the simplest level possible. Others, however, came to his aid. By 1574 other theologians had been enlisted to sharpen the focus of the theological analysis that proved necessary to achieve a wide degree of ecclesiastical harmony among the German Lutherans. Christoph's last attempt to promote Lutheran unity, launched shortly before his death, crowned his efforts by bringing Lutheran governments and Lutheran theologians together in a campaign that used diplomacy to support and protect the careful and strenuous theological efforts of his confidant, Andreae, and Andreae's new partners from the North.

Andreae's First Attempt at Concord, 1568–1570

In 1568 Christoph's cousin, Duke Julius of Braunschweig-Wolfenbüttel, assumed the rule of his duchy after the death of his father, Heinrich, an ardent defender of the old faith. Julius needed help in introducing the Reformation. The young duke called upon Martin Chemnitz from the city of Braunschweig, within his own domains, and he borrowed Nikolaus Selnecker from electoral Saxony and Andreae from Württemberg to institute religious change in his lands. Although their relationships, personal and theological, proved stormy at many points, this common experience helped form the core of the team that would compose the Formula of Concord less than a decade later.

Shortly before his death Christoph sent Andreae north with a twofold mission: not only to assist Julius but also to launch a new attempt at reconciling contentious factions among the north German Lutherans.[2] Julius and Landgrave Wilhelm of Hesse supported Andreae's effort. Already in 1567 Andreae had been at work forging an instrument for uniting the factions within the Lutheran churches; his correspondence with David Chytraeus and others reflects his attempts to float trial balloons in behalf of Lutheran concord. He cast his proposal for unity into "Five Articles," and he kept revising and improving them as he traveled from one Evangelical court or city to another in summer and fall 1569.[3] He sought to unify quarreling Lutheran parties on the topics of justification through faith, good works, freedom of the will, adiaphora, and the Lord's Supper (with an appendix on Christology for most versions of the text).

This was the agenda of controversy set in the 1550s, largely by the Gnesio-Lutherans, addressing the concerns raised by the Leipzig Proposal, Osiander, and Calvin's doctrine of the Lord's Supper. Without condemnations and cumbersome detail, the "Five Articles" corresponded roughly to the strategy that Philippists had tended to follow in promoting an end to strife. Andreae initially hoped to accomplish unity as an agent of the princes, and he wanted at all costs to avoid a synod of theologians, the preferred Gnesio-Lutheran instrument for reaching harmony. His program set forth simple statements of belief on each of the controverted issues. For the most part it used language on which all sides could agree but that stopped short of addressing the controversial issues that had given rise to disputes. The Articles treated the differences plaguing German Lutheranism as issues not significant enough to divide the churches if only the proper very simple formulations for them could be found.

Thus, it is little wonder that the inexactitude of Andreae's document and the indifference of his approach aroused harsh criticism from the Gnesio-Lutherans in ducal Saxony and Mansfeld. Andreae did not trust them, and they certainly did not trust him. Nonetheless, he believed that he commanded widespread support throughout northern Germany and therefore had his princely supporters arrange for a synod of Evangelical theologians at Zerbst on May 9–10, 1570. Representatives of some fifteen churches gathered and agreed to pledge themselves to the ancient creeds, the Augsburg Confession, its Apology, the Smalcald Articles, and Luther's catechisms as the standard for interpreting all other writings, including those of Luther, Melanchthon, and Brenz, which were widely used among the Evangelical churches. Andreae believed he had achieved success.

However, in the aftermath of a visit to Wittenberg soon after the synod Andreae slowly became convinced that the theologians of electoral Saxony opposed the Württemberg theologians' doctrine of the Lord's Supper, particularly its Christological defense. Andreae turned bitterly against them as he returned to south Germany in mid 1570. In turn, he lost the support of Landgrave Wilhelm of Hesse. However, he did not give up his efforts at fostering unity. He remained in contact with Martin Chemnitz, with whom he now shared a growing suspicion of and concern over the drift of the Wittenberg theologians away from Luther's teaching on the Lord's Supper as Chemnitz and Andreae understood it.[4]

The theologians of Wittenberg and Leipzig with whom Andreae was experiencing these new tensions had assiduously tried to avoid public controversy most of the time during the previous two decades. However, after the collapse of the Altenburg Colloquy and the failure at Zerbst to resolve differences, they abandoned this strategy. In 1570 they emerged from their polemical reticence with their *Final Report and Explanation of the Theologians of the Two Universities of Leipzig and Wittenberg and the Superintendents of the Churches in Electoral Saxony Concerning Doctrine.*[5] This *Report* reviewed the history of the Wittenberg Reformation, emphasizing the close relationship between Luther and Melanchthon, justifying the improvements in the Augsburg Confession incorporated by the latter in his *Variata* version and condemning Flacius for a series of deceptions and dishonest financial maneuvering. Then the document leveled charges of heresy against the "Flacian" opponents. It treated the errors of Flacius and his rabble on justification, good works, and the freedom of the will, the traditional points of conflict between the two parties. Then, like the *Corpus Doctrinae Prutenicum*, which Mörlin and Chemnitz had composed three years earlier, the *Report* added new topics to the questions that had to be settled: Flacius's own errors on original sin, the antinomianism of the pastors at Nordhausen, and the doctrine of predestination advanced by Cyriakus Spangenberg. These errors placed the foes of electoral Saxon theology outside the pale of the Lutheran tradition. Noteworthy is the Wittenberg theologians' omission of any mention of the Lord's Supper and related Christological issues, which Andreae and many others outside electoral Saxony increasingly viewed as the chief problem with the Philippist theology there.

The Wittenberg theologians issued a tentative overview of their own public confession in early 1571, through the publication of a series of disputations and addresses conducted or delivered at the university during 1570.[6] In this volume Christology was extensively treated, as were the doctrines of justification, good works, freedom of the will, and the proper definition of the terms law and gospel. Laments over the persecution of the theological faculty in Wittenberg through the public criticism of its enemies were also registered in the book.

The storm of critique that swept over the electoral Saxon church with the appearance of the *Wittenberg Catechism* in January 1571 necessitated further defense of the integrity of the electoral Saxon theology. The best defense in this case was a good offense. By September of that year *The True Church's Firm Foundation: On the Person and Incarnation of Our Lord Jesus Christ* had appeared as a doctrinal critique of all the opponents of the Philippists and a defense of Wittenberg Christology. The document insisted that the Lord's Supper was not an issue at all—despite the critique of their opponents—since they taught what Luther had taught on the sacrament of the altar.[7]

The *Firm Foundation* grouped Andreae, Brenz, and their Swabian critics with the Gnesio-Lutherans of all stripes under the epithet "Flacian," accused them all of various heresies, and insisted that the chief problem besetting the Lutheran churches was the false teaching of Brenz, Westphal, and those who agreed with them regarding the communication of attributes between the two natures of Christ. The position of these foes of the Wittenberger on the doctrine of Christ threatened even the legal standing of the Lutherans under the Religious Peace of Augsburg because it so deviated from the catholic tradition. The *Firm Foundation* found the Christology of Brenz, Andreae, Chemnitz, Mörlin, and Wigand similar to that of ancient heretics, such as the "Marcionites, Samosatenes, Sabellians, Arians, Nestorians, Eutychians, and Monothelites," and of contemporary false teachers, above all Caspar von Schwenckfeld.

The gauntlet had been thrown. The Wittenberg theologians refused to be pushed around any longer. Although the exposition of their position on the person of Christ claimed 384 of the treatise's 400 pages, the work also expanded the agenda of public controversy, embracing all the errors to be attributed to the "Flacians." In addition to Christology their false teachings affected the interpretation of the term "Word" in John 1 and 1 John 1 (a false reading of Flacius's interpretation of these verses led to the charge), and they also included Flacius's teaching on original sin, his denial of any freedom of the will, his narrow definition of the term "gospel," his limitation of justification to the single act of forgiveness, Amsdorf's teaching that good works are detrimental for salvation, the antinomianism of the pastors at Nordhausen, and Spangenberg's doctrine of election. A new agenda had been set for the discussion of differences among the heirs of Melanchthon and Luther (though antinomianism, original sin, and election had already appeared on Chemnitz's and Mörlin's list of concerns in 1567[8]).

Andreae's Second Attempt at Concord

This new agenda did not go unnoticed by the Wittenbergers' critics. In February 1573 Andreae published *Six Christian Sermons on the Divisions among the Theologians of the Augsburg Confession, How a Simple Pastor and a Common Christian Layperson*

Should Deal with Them on the Basis of the Catechism,[9] a continuation of *Thirty-Three Sermons against Papists, Zwinglians, Schwenkfelder, and Anabaptists*, which had appeared from his pen in 1568. These six sermons treated justification through faith, good works, original sin and the freedom of the will, adiaphora, the distinction of law and gospel and the third use of the law, and Christology, with particular focus on the communication of attributes. This reflected the Philippists' expansion of the agenda of controversy from that which Andreae had treated in his earlier "Brief Confession"—through the addition of original sin, the definition of law and gospel, the third use of the law, and Christology. The Wittenberg theologians earned Andreae's special attention in the *Sermons*: he specifically singled out their positions and identified them by name, above all in his treatment of Christology but also of the definition of the gospel.

The *Six Christian Sermons*, Andreae's new proposal for unity among the Lutherans, also exhibited a new approach to the task of unifying his quarreling brothers. First, he left no doubts among his readers where he believed the truth lay in regard to the disputes. He rejected the doctrine of original sin advanced by the Flacian wing of the Gnesio-Lutheran party, and he dismissed Amsdorf's proposition "good works are detrimental to salvation." On these and all other issues he sided with the main body of Gnesio-Lutherans, who had also rejected Flacius's formulation of the doctrine of original sin. Second, his method for seeking unity had abandoned the style and program the Philippists had followed. He treated the issues in detail, confronting them directly, albeit on a simple level that could provide clarity for the laity with arguments from the Catechism. He condemned false teachings explicitly and clearly in the text, and in marginal notes he identified the false teachers who had been guilty of advancing false doctrine. Although dedicated to Duke Julius, the *Six Christian Sermons* were an appeal from a theologian to the whole church for unity on the basis of theological deliberation.

These sermons reflect the conversations with Chemnitz and the reading of his works, which had helped Andreae grow theologically in the half decade since the two had worked together in Braunschweig-Wolfenbüttel. Andreae had changed tactics and was employing a new strategy for gaining Lutheran concord. Without specifically embracing the Gnesio-Lutherans, he had clearly come down on their side. Yet like the Gnesio-Lutheran Chemnitz, he sought to honor and take seriously Philippist concerns when possible.[10] He sent copies of the *Sermons* to Chemnitz, Chytraeus, and two leading Gnesio-Lutheran leaders, Johannes Wigand and Joachim Westphal, to elicit their support.[11]

Westphal died before he could become actively involved in carrying the process further, and Wigand's suspicions of Andreae remained too great. However, Chemnitz and Chytraeus greeted the appearance of the *Six Christian Sermons*; the sermons addressed their concerns, and did so in a manner they found congenial. Nonetheless, Andreae's reputation was so badly damaged in all camps that his north German colleagues believed that his name could not carry any program for concord to a successful completion. They also found the catechetical argument and the homiletical genre unsuitable for an official closure of theological controversy. Therefore, they proposed that the ministerium of the church in Württemberg recast Andreae's proposal in a theologically respectable form.

Andreae took the task upon himself and issued his "Swabian Concord," as it was later labeled, in the name of the faculty of the University of Tübingen, of which he was chancellor, in March 1574. This "Swabian Concord" continued to seek unity among the Evangelicals for the sake of defending the faith against Roman Catholic reproaches, but Andreae also made clear that he was seeking the best way of delivering the truth to the people of God as he composed this "Concord." The document was intended to clarify disputed points in the Augsburg Confession and thus to serve as a kind of commentary on that document.[12] Andreae's text reflected accents in Chemnitz's theology and also added an introductory chapter on the "body" or "form" of teaching, which included a description of the entire purpose and effort of the document while placing it under biblical authority, in the line of the confessional documents Lutherans had taken as their secondary source of defining theology in the previous decades. The Philippist critique of Spangenberg's doctrine of predestination necessitated adding this topic to the agenda of controversy as well.[13]

And Also the Schwärmer

In constructing Lutheran agreement, Andreae also intended to differentiate the faith of the Augsburg Confession from other sects and factions of Western Christendom. Two of the Lutheran confessions that had taken form as confutations—those composed in 1559 by theologians in Saxony and in Mansfeld—had condemned various forms of *Schwärmerei*, including anti-trinitarian views, spiritualizing theologies, and Anabaptist positions.[14] Anti-trinitarian critiques of the dogma of the medieval church had rarely reached public view during the centuries preceding the Reformation, but protest groups with a biblicistic, moralistic, anti-clerical, anti-sacramental, millenarian basis had often arisen—and disappeared—during the course of previous centuries. Such groups arose again in the 1520s and following decades. Roman Catholic polemic had often associated Lutherans with them. In 1568 Andreae himself had asserted Lutheran identity over against other groups within Western Christendom in the series of sermons he preached in Esslingen while the Tübingen faculty was holding lectures there during an outbreak of the plague at home. In addition to Roman Catholics and Zwinglians, Andreae examined and rejected doctrines of the spiritualist Schwenkfelder and the Anabaptists.[15] His Swabian Concord introduced this kind of demarcation of Lutheran theology from that of such groups, and the concluding article of the Formula of Concord treated them as well.

In repudiating Anabaptist theologies, especially that of the Hutterite, Peter Riedemann, the Concordists used the framework of medieval social theory, criticizing "intolerable teachings" in regard to the church, public affairs, and domestic life. Anabaptist teaching regarding the "celestial flesh" of Christ—that his flesh came from heaven and was thus different from the flesh of all other human beings—was rejected along with views that denied his divinity and salvation by grace—views not held by all Anabaptists but by some. The general disavowal of sacramental efficacy, particularly in infant baptism, was also condemned, as was Anabaptist ecclesiology. The Formula affirmed that service in government is a God-pleasing calling for Christians and that Christians may take oaths in court. It also rejected the Anabaptist denunciation of capital punishment. It repudiated those Anabaptists who proscribed possession of private property as well as the callings of innkeeper, merchant, or arms-maker for Christians. The Formula also found the idea that married people may divorce for the sake of the faith in order to marry another who shares the same faith intolerable.[16]

The followers of Caspar Schwenkfeld, the Silesian nobleman who dismissed the efficacy of the external Word of God[17] as well the significance of the incarnation of Christ, earned the denunciation of the Formula for rejecting the incarnation and upholding a doctrine of Christ's celestial flesh. The Schwenkfelder ecclesiology, especially with its rejection of the means of grace and its Donatist view of church and ministry, were also condemned by the Formula's twelfth article.[18] So were all forms of denial of the Trinity.[19]

Andreae's inclusion of these "other sects" found approval in those who worked further on the task of defining Lutheran doctrinal identity.

The Swabian-Saxon Concord and the Maulbronn Formula

Chemnitz and Chytraeus had been deeply involved in efforts to settle doctrinal disputes throughout their careers. Chemnitz had even drafted a formula for addressing the controversies of the 1550s in a document that remained in manuscript until after his death, his "Judgment on Certain Controversies around Certain Articles of the Augsburg Confession," composed in 1561.[20] Perhaps drafted as a critique of positions affirmed in the *Corpus Doctrinae Misnicum*, this document began with a treatment of the form of teaching, under the title, *Corpus doctrinae*. The discussions of controversial issues in this manuscript as well as Chemnitz's work on the *corpora doctrinae* for Prussia, Braunschweig-Wolfenbüttel, and Braunschweig-Lüneburg served as basis and pattern for Chemnitz's treatment of these topics fifteen years later. For more than a year in late 1574 and 1575 Chemnitz and Chytraeus worked on revising Andreae's document with help from their colleagues, particularly in the ministeria of Hamburg, Lüneburg, and Lübeck. In September 1575 the combination of their efforts had produced materials that were put to use in drafting the settlement that led to the Formula of Concord. Scholars have usually dubbed the proposal that Chytraeus and Chemnitz put together the "Swabian-Saxon Concord."

In November 1575 Elector August of Saxony, faced with the rebuilding of his church after the collapse of its "crypto-Philippist" leadership the previous year, initiated another effort toward Lutheran concord. His appeal to Count Georg Ernst of Henneberg for aid in the resolution of doctrinal disputes moved the count to enlist Duke Ludwig of Württemberg and Margrave Karl of Baden in an attempt at formulating Lutheran unity while the three were together at Ludwig's wedding. This effort brought together Ludwig's court preacher, Lukas Osiander; the chief pastor in Stuttgart, Balthasar Bidembach; two pastors from Henneberg, Abel Scherdinger and Petrus Streck; and a pastor from Baden, Rupert Dürr. In January 1576 they met at Maulbronn monastery in Württemberg and composed the "Maulbronn Formula," a document closer to Andreae's proposals than to the formulations of his north German editors. Their introductory treatment of the form of Christian doctrine was taken with little revision into the Formula of Concord; their articles on original sin, the person of Christ, justification through faith, law and gospel, good works, the Lord's Supper, ecclesiastical usages, freedom of the will, and the third use of the law contributed to the Formula's text on occasion.

The New Electoral Saxon Impulse toward Lutheran Concord

After soliciting advice from a number of princes, including those who stood behind the Maulbronn effort, Landgrave Wilhelm of Hesse, and Elector Johann Georg of Brandenburg, August assembled a dozen of his theologians at Lichtenberg in mid-February 1576. They deliberated on measures to regularize teaching in the electoral domains. Among other measures, particularly at Selnecker's suggestion, they urged the elector to borrow Andreae from Württemberg for a five-year period to aid in the reconstruction of the electoral Saxon church.[21] Two-thirds of the team that had aided Julius in the reformation of Braunschweig-Wolfenbüttel now joined forces as this pair of theologians again became partners in another kind of reform effort. Soon Chemnitz, the third partner in the reformation of Braunschweig-Wolfenbüttel, joined them.

Andreae arrived in Saxony in early April and arranged for a meeting in Torgau of the Lichtenberg group with Chemnitz, Chytraeus, and two representatives from electoral Brandenburg, Andreas Musculus and Christoph Körner. Andreae had condemned Musculus's rejection of the third use of the law in his *Six Christian Sermons*. When this enlarged committee assembled in Torgau at the end of May 1576, Musculus stoutly defended his views against the others, winning at least some concession in the language of the treatment of the law in the Christian life in the new document that was produced in Torgau. That document was hammered out on the basis of the "Swabian-Saxon Concord" and the "Maulbronn Formula," with some additions and corrections formulated during the sessions in Torgau. Andreae had hoped to make the "Maulbronn Formula" the basis of the formula for concord; in fact, sections of it were integrated into the "Swabian Saxon Concord," which Chemnitz and Chytraeus had produced on the basis of Andreae's earlier work.[22] The Formula of Concord was designed to be an authoritative interpretation of, or commentary on, the Augsburg Confession, as its preface made clear. It was, as well, an interpretation of Luther's teaching and of Melanchthon's, from the standpoint of theologians devoted to both. The wide range of interpretations of the theological legacies of each had made some such synthesis necessary, and under the leadership of Martin Chemnitz the Concordists composed theirs.

The theological labor invested in the document becomes clear in a number of ways. Following Andreae's lead in the *Six Christian Sermons* and the Swabian Concord, Chemnitz, Chytraeus, and the others who contributed to the text in general favored the positions held by the main body of Gnesio-Lutherans, rejecting Flacius's view of original sin and the positions of the Crypto-Philippists on the Lord's Supper, Christology, and a variety of other issues. However, the Concordists understood and honored many concerns that had shaped Philippist thought, voiced often initially by Melanchthon. Thus, particularly Chemnitz skillfully wove into the text of the Formula those concerns while at the same time affirming positions he and the other Concordists, and those like Wigand and Hesshus, who had shared most of Flacius's points of view, believed. He fashioned them into a consensus that represented what these disciples of the Wittenberg reformers believed to be the heart of Luther's—and Melanchthon's—teaching. They proceeded carefully with positive expositions of teaching and with explicit rejections of doctrines to be avoided. They struggled with theological vocabulary, not infrequently reduced to recourse to Latin phrases because no, or no common, German expression lay readily at hand. They strove for brevity and conciseness but at the same time insisted on clear and complete analysis of controverted points and the doctrinal setting in which they lay within the analogy of faith, the body of biblical teaching.[23]

Their draft was not brief enough to please their princes. Therefore, Andreae composed a summary of this "Torgau Book"—the "Epitome"—to introduce its conclusions particularly to interested princes, and the entire text was submitted to ministeria of Evangelical churches throughout Germany for their criticism and suggestions.[24] Such critiques were sent to the Saxon court from more than twenty groups of pastors and theologians representing some thirty different churches. Particularly incisive criticism came from Gnesio-Lutheran leaders such as Wigand and Hesshus. The intensive and widespread effort to gather reactions and glean constructive criticism of their draft has earned the Concordists praise from Ernst Koch, who finds their willingness to subject their attempt at concord to such appraisal by so many churches the mark of "an ecumenical undertaking which is unique in the sixteenth century."[25] In March 1577 Andreae met with Selnecker and Chemnitz at the monastery in Bergen near Magdeburg to review the criticisms and begin reworking the document. They were joined there at the end of May by Chytraeus, Musculus, and Körner, and these six refined and revised the "Torgau Book" into the "Bergen Book," which was later called the "Solid Declaration" of the Formula of Concord.[26]

On the Body of Doctrine

Although the Concordists avoided calling their work a *corpus doctrinae*—a summary of biblical teaching—they intended their document to function as such, as a guide to proper public teaching, a rule of faith (*analogia fidei*), as the ancient church had called it. The Formula of Concord thus began with an explanation of how its authors viewed its function as a "binding summary, rule, and norm, according to which all teaching is to be judged and errors...are to be explained and decided in Christian fashion."

Whereas Melanchthon's presentation of the whole body of biblical teaching, in his second and third edition of his *Theological Topics* (*Loci communes theologici*), had begun with the doctrine of God, his disciples, in the course of the late 1550s and thereafter, decided that the topic "Word of God" stood epistemologically and pedagogically as a presupposition to any Christian speaking about God.[27] That conformed to the Wittenberg understanding of God as a Creator who has created and re-creates through his Word. Because Luther and Melanchthon had held that God is present in the Scriptures and effects his power for salvation through them,[28] and because they believed that the Holy Spirit works through the message of Scripture in oral, written, and sacramental forms of that Word of God, they recognized that the church had always used secondary authorities, for example, the ancient creeds of the church, to aid and govern the formulation of public teaching. The Concordists perceived that their contemporaries also needed such an orientation for their proclamation of the gospel.[29]

That orientation prefaced Andreae's Swabian Concord and the revisions that followed. Therefore, the Formula of Concord, which advertises itself as "the binding summary, basis, rule, and guiding principles of how all teaching is to be judged in accord with God's Word and how the errors that have arisen are to be explained and decided in Christian fashion,"[30] lays out its sources and operating principle at the beginning of the document. The prophetic and apostolic writings of the Old and New Testament were to serve as the only rule and norm for teaching and teachers; all other writings were subject to Scripture. Nonetheless, the Concordists knew that the early church had adopted summaries of the biblical message that also served as hermeneutical guides for guiding the church in adjudicating disputes over the meaning of Scripture. They accepted the traditional standards of the Western church, the Apostles, Nicene, and Athanasian Creeds, as secondary authorities for public teaching. In addition, the Formula recognized that the unaltered Augsburg Confession, the Apology of that Confession, and Luther's Smalcald Articles, as well as his catechisms, had served the Lutheran churches well as the same kind of hermeneutical guide and summary of the faith. All these documents the Concordists defined as not judges of Scripture but witnesses and explanations of its content.

Subscribing to the Formula

Efforts to win subscription to this document and to the "Epitome" of the teaching Andreae had composed began almost immediately, with Andreae taking the lead in meeting with ministeria in many principalities and with some leading individuals, such as Cyriakus Spangenberg, to overcome objections and concerns about the new Formula of Concord.[31] One of the most important diplomatic efforts concerned attempts to win the new elector of the Palatinate, Ludwig, the eldest son of Frederick III, who had died on October 26, 1576. Andreae was commissioned to formulate a preface for the Formula that would explain the historical developments leading to its composition and the setting in which it was to be understood as a commentary on the Augsburg Confession. Revised a number of times during 1578 and 1579, this preface was to serve as an instrument that would ease fears and build confidence in the document as the solution to the controversies of the past quarter century.[32] The preface did in fact succeed, in part. Ludwig joined the other two secular electors, Saxony and Brandenburg, in supporting the Formula and accepting the Book of Concord, of which it became apart. The electors enlisted six other princes— Ludwig of Württemberg, Julius of Braunschweig-Wolfenbüttel, Georg Friedrich of Brandenburg-Ansbach, Wolfgang of Braunschweig-Lüneburg, Philip of Palatinate-Neuburg, and Carl of Baden—to assist in gathering subscriptions from other princes and lords as well as from Evangelical cities.[33] August's court sent copies of the preface of the Book of Concord to princely and municipal governments, and they returned their subscriptions to the Saxon government. Pastors and teachers set their signatures to the text of the Solid Declaration and Epitome.[34] The efforts to bring all Evangelical churches into doctrinal agreement through acceptance of the Book of Concord were quite successful, but a few princes and cities stood apart, for a variety of reasons.

The most critical question still under debate among the Evangelical theologians of Germany was the Christological argument used in behalf of the doctrine of the presence of Christ's body and blood in the Lord's Supper, focusing upon the communication of attributes between Christ's divine and human natures. To demonstrate the catholicity of the solution to the debates over this issue proposed by Article VIII of the Formula, Andreae and Chemnitz, with help from Selnecker, composed a "Catalog of Testimonies" comprised of citations from the ancient church that supported the doctrine of that article. This "Catalog" was prepared at the end of February 1580 and published with some early editions of the Book of Concord.[35]

The Concordists in Torgau and Bergen purposely avoided the term *corpus doctrinae*, in order to escape the appearance of direct opposition to the *Corpus doctrinae Misnicum* (*Philippicum*) and thus to allay fears of Melanchthon's most ardent supporters that he was being brushed aside. Nonetheless, Andreae, Chemnitz, and their colleagues intended that the Formula of Concord be used as a substitute for the legal definitions of public teaching found in the various *Corpora doctrinae* of the Lutheran estates. Therefore, they assembled a collection of documents, beginning with the ancient creeds and the Augsburg Confession, which were to serve all Lutheran estates as the basis of church life. In addition to these documents, the Concordists included the Apology of the Augsburg Confession, the Smalcald Articles and the Treatise on the Power and Primacy of the Pope, and Luther's Catechisms. The work, entitled *Concordia* (the Book of Concord), was officially published on June 25, 1580, the fiftieth anniversary of the presentation of the Augsburg Confession.

Its publication was only to be the beginning of its usefulness. It was to provide active guidance for preaching and teaching to its readers. Following the model of Melanchthon's *Corpus doctrinae Philippicum*, the electoral Saxon team that had worked to compose the Formula of Concord provided the Book with an index of topics on the model of Melanchthon's *Loci communes* to guide pastors and teachers in their use of the volume. Peter Glaser, its compiler, made certain that readers could easily find the relevant passages to help them answer questions that had grown out of the controversies as well as other queries of pastoral care.[36] Nikolaus Selnecker prepared a study edition of the Formula to make the full text available to students in both German and Latin.[37] The authors and sponsors intended the Book of Concord to be well-used tool for the life of the church.

15

Reactions to the Formula of Concord in the 1580s

The Formula of Concord fulfilled the dreams of a quarter century. Its authors had pursued the goals of theologians and princes in seeking to establish concord among the Lutheran churches of Germany. Jakob Andreae had changed tactics at the beginning of the 1570s. His *Six Christian Sermons* had abandoned the attempt at establishing some neutral central point squarely in the middle of the warring parties among his comrades in the faith. Andreae had rejected the positions of the electoral Saxon theologians of "crypto-Philippist" convictions on the Lord's Supper and related Christological issues, and he had condemned Flacius's doctrine of original sin as well as the teaching of Poach, Otto, and their associates on the law (positions rejected by most of their former comrades). The *Six Christian Sermons* called for a settlement that agreed with the principal concerns of the majority of Gnesio-Lutherans and which was so expressed that the moderate Philippists and Andreae's own Swabian colleagues could accept it. As Chemnitz and Chytraeus revised and refined Andreae's program for Lutheran harmony in the Swabian Concord, they carefully reworked and extended the document's formulations to meet the concerns of the Philippists, particularly in the range of questions relating to original sin, the freedom of the will, and election and to good works as well as to the Lord's Supper and Christology.

And yet, such an effort never satisfies everyone. David Chytraeus and Andreas Musculus expressed their own reservations about the finished product[1] although neither opposed its acceptance in their own principalities. Those followers of Flacius who found that his understanding of original sin had indeed represented the doctrine of Luther most faithfully criticized the Formula sharply and worked against its adoption in the few places where they had influence—largely without success apart from Lutheran enclaves in Austria where they served as pastors.[2] Nonetheless, the tireless efforts of Andreae and others brought a large measure of success to the efforts of the authors of the Formula. More than two-thirds of German Evangelical governments and pastors accepted this work as their standard for teaching and ecclesiastical life.[3]

However, resistance and criticism kept the Formula and the Book of Concord in the forefront of ecclesiastical concerns for a time. Roman Catholic criticisms of the specific approaches of the Formula were very limited. They criticized the Book of Concord as a patchwork of contradictory positions—proof, they maintained, that such apostates from papal obedience had lost the gift of divine authority in their midst. The Roman theologians also rejected the understanding of the communication of attributes in Formula Article VIII. In general, such attacks blended with the continuing general polemic against Lutheran theology.[4]

Calvinist theologians within Germany and abroad criticized both the content of the Formula and the method by which it won acceptance by Lutheran churches across the Empire. Their concerns about the political consequences of the Formula, particularly in regard to the ability of Calvinist churches to win protection under the provisions of the Religious Peace of Augsburg, were shared by the English government of Queen Elizabeth, who wanted to preserve the broadest possible consensus among the opponents of the papacy in princely courts throughout Europe. They believed that the Lutherans were playing into the hands of the papal foes with what they considered too narrow and restrictive definitions of doctrine as well as outright false teaching in the Formula.[5]

Particularly under the leadership of the Count Palatine Johann Kasimir, second son of Frederick the Pious, brother of the Lutheran elector of the Palatinate, Ludwig, efforts were made to block acceptance and recognition of the Formula. From his court and its circle of theologians in Neustadt an der Hardt, and from the presses of his printer, Matthaeus Harnisch, there streamed a series of critiques that sought to disprove particularly the doctrine of the Lord's Supper in the Formula and the Christological argument that undergirded it. In addition, Johann Kasimir launched a diplomatic effort, which climaxed in the Frankfurt assembly of Reformed theologians and governmental representatives in September 1577. Its attempts at creating a united political front that could stop the Concordianist movement failed.[6]

More successful was Johann Kasimir's encouragement of theological critique, represented, for example, by the works of his court theologian and former Heidelberg professor, Zacharias Ursinus, another of Melanchthon's former students. His *Christian Admonition on the Book of Concord* (1581) addressed the critical theological and ecclesiastical issues raised by the Concordianist effort in great detail.[7] Colleagues in the Palatinate as well as Genevan, French, and Dutch theologians anticipated and echoed his objections.[8] Not only Calvinist theologians but also a municipal official from Nuremberg, a lawyer who had studied under Melanchthon in Wittenberg, Christoph Herdesianus, attacked the Formula and the entire concordianist effort from several directions. Among the most sophisticated Calvinist theological critiques in the period must be counted his pseudonymously published attacks against Lutheran teaching, as represented in the theology of contemporaries such as Andreae and Chemnitz, as well as their Formula, and against the Concordianist understanding of the Augsburg Confession and the authority of both the Confession and Luther. He argued that Melanchthon's *Variata* represented the proper development of the teaching of the Augsburg Confession and that the Formula of Concord's interpretation of the Confession was wrong. Especially his use of the ancient fathers of the church in the service of his critique demanded reply.[9]

In northern Germany the city of Bremen had experienced two decades of debate over the Lord's Supper within its ministerium. In the late 1570s, under the leadership of the former Crypto-Philippist Wittenberg professor, now pastor in Bremen, Christoph Pezel, the city tried to avoid controversy over the Formula itself. In formulating a solution to internal controversy over the Lord's Supper and in defense against accusations from outside the city, Pezel and his colleagues had prepared a *Reliable and Christian Account on the Articles and Points at Issue* in mid 1581, with chapters on the person of Christ, baptism, the Lord's Supper, election, and ceremonies. Even though this document did not address the text of the Formula directly, it also demanded reply from the Concordianist side. Under the leadership of another Philippist sympathizer, Tileman Hesshus's former student, Wolfgang Amling, the church of Anhalt rejected the Formula although its theologians held to the document's doctrine of the Lord's Supper. They found it impossible, however, to accept its Christology.[10]

The criticism of the Formula called into question not only its teaching but also the method by which it presented its doctrine and its adoption without a general synod of churches from throughout the Protestant world. Particularly critical—and thus open to criticism—was its condemnation of false doctrine since that rejection of Crypto-Philippist (and thus of Calvinist) teaching on the Lord's Supper threatened the political situation of the adherents of these theological positions under the Religious Peace of Augsburg. In the city of Strasbourg, where Johann Marbach had pursued a Lutheran "second Reformation" since Martin Bucer had left the city a quarter of a century earlier, the Concordianist efforts provoked a controversy over the propriety of the condemnation of false teaching. Johann Sturm, the grand old master of the Bucerian tradition, rector of the city's famous academy, long sympathetic with the French Calvinist church, objected to the Formula's condemnations of positions his Calvinist friends held. Sturm feared the implications of the Concordian settlement for the program of his academy, which served an international princely and upper middle class clientele of various confessional commitments. He was also concerned about what the Formula might mean for the policies that permitted French religious refugees to find haven in his city. Johann Pappus, Marbach's successor as leader of the Lutheranizing movement within the city, came to the defense of the Formula, and the city became involved in complicated diplomatic maneuvering among the political forces of southwest Germany, led by the Palatinate Calvinists and the Lutherans of Württemberg. Although the city did not accept the Formula as a doctrinal standard until 1598, Sturm had to concede to the forces gathered around Pappus.[11]

The Crypto-Philippists had attempted to win adherents through publications on the popular level.[12] Thus, those in the Concordianist camp felt compelled to come to the defense of their cause among lay readers as well. On the popular level, efforts were made in several literary forms—poetic and catechetical, for example— to explain to the common people what the Formula of Concord taught and why it had been prepared and endorsed in the way in which it had been.[13]

The theological response took form first in tracts from the Württemberg theologians and then in the Apology of the Book of Concord.[14] Representatives of the Lutheran electors gathered in Erfurt at the end of 1580 to draw up a defense of the Formula and Book of Concord against specific attacks upon them. Martin Chemnitz was there at the request of the elector of Brandenburg; Nikolaus Selnecker represented Saxony and Timotheus Kirchner the government of Ludwig of the Palatinate. The Apology of the Book of Concord did not follow the model of the Apology of the Augsburg Confession of fifty years earlier, for it did not systematically meet specific arguments against its specific articles. Instead, it addressed four published critiques, that of the Flacianist Christoph Irenaeus on original sin, those of the Bremen theologians and of Zacharias Ursinus on the Lord's Supper and related issues, and those of Christoph Herdesianus and others on the use of Luther and of the Augsburg Confession as authorities for public teaching.[15]

The Apology of the Book of Concord provided the occasion for further tensions and negotiations between the promoters of the Concordianist settlement and the government of Duke Julius of Braunschweig-Wolfenbüttel. His funding and active diplomatic support had helped launch the final, successful efforts at concord, but he distanced himself from those efforts because Martin Chemnitz had sharply criticized the duke's having his sons tonsured according to Roman Catholic rites so that they might assume ecclesiastical territories in his region (1578).[16] Led by Tileman Hesshus, then professor at Julius's infant university at Helmstedt, the ducal theologians expressed reservations about formulations regarding the communication of attributes that tended toward Andreae's "ubiquitarian" position, which Hesshus rejected. They also objected to certain developments connected with the publication of the Book of Concord. A colloquy at Quedlinburg between representatives of the Braunschweig court and the leaders of the Concordianist effort in January 1583 failed to reconcile Julius to the Formula even though his theologians accepted its theology.[17]

In two-thirds of Evangelical Germany, the Book of Concord became the official definition of what it meant to be Lutheran. The observation that the book was cited relatively seldom in the period of Lutheran "Orthodoxy"[18] may be true for the grand dogmatic tomes of the Orthodox theologians, but it is also true that it served as an important basis for the instruction of theological candidates, in lectures and occasionally in the disputations on which the students sharpened their thinking skills throughout the seventeenth century.[19] It served as guidepost and hermeneutic for further developments in Lutheran confession of the faith as Lutheran theology continued to develop and reformulate itself in the so-called "age of orthodoxy."

Postscript

Ernst Koch has called attention to the ecumenical significance of the efforts to reach concord among disputing parties within the Evangelical churches of sixteenth-century Germany.[1] Although these efforts excluded some who wanted to find a political umbrella in the Augsburg Confession, they did bring agreement to many churches and theologians who had been at odds for a quarter century. This search for concord did so not by finding some blurred middle ground between contending factions but by honoring the concerns of these groups in so far as its authors believed that to be biblically faithful and ecclesially responsible.[2] The attitude of those who composed the Formula was formed by the Wittenberg way of understanding how God works in the world to reconcile sinners to himself. He works, Luther and Melanchthon taught their students, through his Word. It is a reliable Word as it is found in Scripture, for God is present and is speaking when his message is conveyed from the pages of Scripture to the people of God. It is a Word, therefore, that through his presence in it conveys his power to condemn in his law, above all the power to save sinners from their condemnation. That power is effective through the promise of God in Jesus Christ—God incarnate—whose death and resurrection bring comfort and hope to those who trust in him.

This concern for conveying God's Word faithfully to hearers and readers for their consolation and assurance informed the efforts of the authors of the Formula of Concord. They shared Luther's conviction that God and his truth are continually under attack from Satan, who is the author of the lie that is always trying to pervert the understanding of God's people for his Word. Therefore, they took very seriously the task their churches had given them, to formulate a presentation of God's Word on the controverted issues of their time. They did so within the context of their own time, with reference to the specific attacks on God's message for his people as they understood the attacks and the Word.

To make use of the Book of Concord in the twenty-first century, it is necessary to understand the documents in their historical context. Scholarship in the past quarter century has opened up new windows into the world in which the documents contained in the Book of Concord were shaped. This volume, it is hoped, will help readers look into that world with much greater precision than was possible a century ago. If so, that will serve not only adherents of the Book of Concord but also all who seek to proclaim God's Word in the twenty-first century as they assess their own contexts and bring the message of the salvation in Jesus Christ to their generation.

Notes

Preface

1. *The Book of Concord*, ed. Robert Kolb and Timothy J. Wengert (Minneapolis: Fortress, 2000).

2. *Sources and Contexts of the Book of Concord*, ed. Robert Kolb and James A. Nestingen (Minneapolis: Fortress, 2001).

Introduction. The Book of Concord, a Confessing of the Faith

1. Ninian Smart, *Worldviews: Cross Cultural Explorations of Human Beliefs* (New York: Scribner's, 1983), 62–158.

2. "Evangelical" was used as a synonym in this period to designate those later called "Lutheran" and "Reformed," and specifically it was the term employed by adherents of the Wittenberg Reformation for themselves. When capitalized in this volume, it refers to the Evangelical political leaders or theologians who openly advocated Luther's path to reform. When it is not capitalized, it refers to the theological position held by Luther and his colleagues and adherents.

3. See pages 99–101 of this volume. Much of what follows is taken from Robert Kolb, "Confessing the Faith, the Wittenberg Way of Life," *Tidskrift for teologi og kirke* 14 (2009): 247–65.

4. *BSLK*, xvi–xvii.

5. See pages 97–98 of this volume. For the original Latin text, see Johann Eck, *Articulos 404* [Ingolstadt, 1530], in *D. Johann Ecks Vierhundertundvier Artikel zum Reichstag von Augsburg 1530*, ed. Wilhelm Gussmann (Kassel: Pillardy, 1930). For the English translation, see *Sources and Contexts of the Book of Concord*, ed. Robert Kolb and James A. Nestingen (Minneapolis: Fortress Press, 2001), 33–82.

6. *Thesavrvs Lingvae Latinae* (Leipzig: Teubner, 1906–1909), 4: 188–192, 230–233; *Mediae Latinitatis Lexicon Minus*, ed. J. F. Niermeyer, C. Van de Kieft, and J. W. J. Burgers (Darmstadt: Wissenschaftliche, 2002), 1: 318, 320.

7. See Heinrich Denzinger, *Enchiridion symbolorum definitionum et declarationum de rebus fidei et morum*, ed. Peter Hünermann, 37th ed. (Freiburg: Herder, 1991).

8. *Decrees of the Ecumenical Councils*, ed. Norman P. Tanner, S. J., vol. 2, *Trent to Vatican II* (Washington, D.C: Georgetown University Press, 1990).

9. Denzinger, *Enchiridion*, 241, 265.

10. Ibid., 260: *atque concorditer nobiscum confessa est*.

11. Examples include letters of Pope Innocent III, ibid., 353, §792 (*corde credimus et ore confitemur*) and 355, §795; the doctrinal statement of the Fourth Lateran Council,

357, §800 (*firmiter credimus et simpliciter confitemur*) and the Bull for Union with Copts and Ethiopians of 1442 (*firmiter credit, profitetur et praedicat*), 460, 463, 467, §1330, 1337, 1350, 1351.

12. Robert Kolb, *Confessing the Faith, Reformers Define the Church, 1530–1580* (Saint Louis: Concordia, 1991), 13–42.

13. Peter Fraenkel, "Revelation and Tradition, Notes on Some Aspects of Doctrinal Continuity in the Theology of Philip Melanchthon," *Studia theologica* 13 (1959): 97–133.

14. See Uwe Schell, *Die homiletische Theorie Philipp Melanchthons*, AGTL 20 (Berlin: Lutherisches, 1968), and, on Melanchthon's use of rhetoric in the Apology of the Augsburg Confession, Charles P. Arand, "Melanchthon's Rhetorical Argument for *Sola Fide* in the Apology," *LQ* 14 (2000): 281–308.

15. See pages 90–91 of this volume.

16. *Mediae Latinitatis Lexicon Minus*, 2:1129.

17. WA 3:389.

18. WATr 3:127, §2974b.

19. WA 33:341,40–342,20, 346,13–34, 405,22–406, 9, 652,16–653,14, LW 23:217, 219, 255, 400.

20. *Georgii Spalatini Annales reformationis Oder Jahr-Bücher von der Reformation Lutheri*, ed. Ernst Solomon Cyprian (Leipzig: Gleditsch and Weidmann, 1718), 134.

21. For example, Johannes Mathesius, *Historien Von des Ehrwirdigen in Gott Seligen Theuren Manns Gottes, Doctoris Martini Luthers anfang, lehr leben vnd sterben* (Nuremberg: von Berg and Neuber, 1566), 79a; Nikolaus Selnecker, *Historica Oratio Vom Leben vnd Wandel des Ehrwirdigen Herrn vnd thewren Mannes Gottes, D. Martini Lutheri* (Wittenberg: Rhambau, 1576), 59b–60a.

22. See *Die Bekenntnsischriften der reformierten Kirche*, ed. E. F. Karl Müller (1903; Zürich: Theologische Buchhandlung, 1987), *Reformierte Bekenntnisschriften*, ed. Eberhard Busch et al. (Neukirchen: Neukirchener, 2002–). On the dispute regarding the significance of confessional documents between Reformed and Lutherans in the late sixteenth century, see Irene Dingel, *Concordia controversa: Die öffentlichen Diskussionen um das lutherische Konkordienwerk am Ende des 16. Jahrhunderts*, QFRG 63 (Gütersloh: Gütersloher, 1996), 607–29; and Dingel, "Ablehnung und Aneignung, Die Bewertung der Autorität Martin Luthers in den Auseinandersetzungen um die Konkordienformel," *ZKG* 105 (1994): 35–57.

23. *Confessio Tetrapolitana und die Schriften des Jahres 1531* in *Martin Bucers Deutsche Schriften*, vol. 3, ed. Robert Stupperich (Gütersloh: Mohn, 1969), 13–185.

24. *Die Bekenntnisschriften der reformierten Kirche*, 95–100, 101–9.

25. See John C. Wengert, "The Schleitheim Confession of Faith," *Mennonite Quarterly Review* 19 (1945): 243–54.

26. On the use of the term *Konfession*, see Carl Heinz Ratschow, "Konfession/Konfessionalität," in *TRE* 19:419–26. On the development of the "Konfessionen" in the course of the sixteenth and seventeenth centuries, see Ernst Walter Zeeden, *Die Entstehung der Konfessionen: Grundlagen und Formen der Konfessionsbildung im Zeitalter der Glaubenskämpfe* (Munich: Oldenbourg, 1965); and Zeeden, "Grundlagen und Formen der Konfessionsbildung im Zeitalter der Glaubenskämpfe," in Zeeden, *Konfessionsbildung: Studien zur Reformation, Gegenreformation und katholischen Reform* (Stuttgart: Klett-Cotta, 1985), 67–112. On the development of the concept of "confessionalization" in the wake of Zeeden's work (though somewhat independent of

it), see the overviews of Thomas A. Brady Jr., "Confessionalization—The Career of a Concept," in *Confessionalization in Europe, 1555–1700, Essays in Honor and Memory of Bodo Nischan*, eds. John M. Headley et al. (Aldershot: Ashgate, 2004), 1–20; and Heinz Schilling, "Confessionalization: Historical and Scholarly Perspectives of a Comparative and Interdisciplinary Paradigm," in *Confessionalization in Europe*, 21–35. See also essays from three conferences sponsored by the Verein für Reformationsgeschichte between 1985 and 1993 to provide impulses to further study: *Die lutherische Konfessionalisierung in Deutschland*, ed. Hans-Christoph Rublack, SVRG 197 (Gütersloh: Gütersloher, 1992); *Die reformierte Konfessionalisierung in Deutschland—Das Problem der "Zweiten Reformation,"* ed. Heinz Schilling, SVRG 195 (Gütersloh: Gütersloher, 1986); *Die katholische Konfessionalisierung: Wissenschaftliches Symposion der Gesellschaft zur Herausgabe des Corpus Catholicorum und des Vereins für Reformationsgeschichte*, eds. Wolfgang Reinhard and Heinz Schilling, SVRG 198 (Gütersloh: Gütersloher, 1995).

27. Kolb, *Confessing the Faith*, 46–49.

28. *BSLK* 833, BC 526. See pages 273–74 of this volume. And see Irene Dingel, "Bekenntnis und Geschichte: Funktion und Entwicklung des reformatorischen Bekenntnisses im 16. Jahrhundert," in *Dona Melanchthoniana: Festgabe für Heinz Scheible zum 70. Geburtstag*, ed. Johanna Loehr (Stuttgart-Bad Cannstatt: Frommann-Holzboog, 2001), 61–81.

29. See pages 174–75 of this volume.

30. Dingel, "Melanchthon und die Normierung des Bekenntnisses."

31. Thomas Kaufmann, "Das Bekenntnis im Luthertum des konfessionellen Zeitalters," *Zeitschrift für Theologie und Kirche* 105 (2008), 281–314, brings together a number of elements on the topic, although his extensive footnotes fail to note several significant contributions to his topic both in German and in other languages. Thus, he fails to use certain insights under discussion already available for students of the Lutheran Confessions. His article does not explore the theological significance of confessing the faith. It does propose that the use of the confessional documents effected a self-contained *Corpus Christianum* within each territory which accepted them, but in fact, while the Augsburg Confession and other confessions of faith did foster the Lutheran identity of specific territorial churches, they also gave witness to that which bound them together, functioning as an ecumenical tie of powerful proportions.

32. See pages 125–38 of this volume.

33. See Kolb, *Confessing the Faith*, 120–30, 141–48.

34. See Dingel, "Bekenntnis und Geschichte," 75–81.

35. Irene Dingel, "Melanchthon und Westeuropa," in *Philipp Melanchthon als Politiker zwischen Reich, Reichsständen und Konfessionsparteien*, ed Günther Wartenberg and Matthias Zenter, Themata Leucoreana (Wittenberg: Drei Kastanien, 1998), 105–22. Charles P. Arand has shown that this readiness to allow a variety of practices so long as the doctrine of justification is preserved already guided the composition of Augsburg Confession and Apology article XV. See his "The Apology as a Backdrop for the Interim of 1548," in *Politik und Bekenntnis: Die Reaktionen auf das Interim von 1548*, ed. Irene Dingel and Günther Wartenberg, LStRLO 8 (Leipzig: Evangelische Verlagsanstalt, 2007), 211–27.

36. Timothy J. Wengert, *Priesthood, Pastors, Bishops: Public Ministry for the Reformation and Today* (Minneapolis: Fortress Press, 2008), 62. Wengert is commenting on Wilhelm Maurer, *Historical Commentary on the Augsburg Confession*, trans. H.

George Anderson (Philadelphia: Fortress Press, 1986), 64. He directs readers to Wenz, *Theologie*, 1:437–464.

37. WA 50: 641,35–642,21; LW 41:164–165.

38. Richard Schenk, "The Unsettled German Discussions of Justification: Abiding Differences and Ecumenical Blessings," *dialog* 44 (2005): 161–62.

39. Robert Kolb, "Jeder Christ ist in die Pflicht genommen, Zeugnis vom Glauben abzulegen: Die Verkündigung der Lutheraner in der Spätreformation zu Mission und Bekenntnis," in *Gottes Wort in der Zeit: Verstehen—Verkündigen—Verbreiten*, ed. Werner Klän and Christoph Barnbrock (Münster: LIT, 2005), 127–42; translated as "Late Reformation Lutherans on Mission and Confession," *LQ* 20 (2006), 26–43.

40. Timothy J. Wengert, *A Formula for Parish Practice* (Grand Rapids: Eerdmans, 2007). Cf. Melanchthon's statement in the Apology of the Augsburg Confession, XI, esp. §2, *BSLK*, 249–52; *BC*, 185–87. See also Robert Kolb, "Ministry in Martin Luther and the Lutheran Confessions," in *Called and Ordained: Lutheran Perspectives on the Office of the Ministry*, ed. Todd Nichol and Marc Kolden (Minneapolis: Fortress Press, 1990), 49–66.

41. See Dingel, *Concordia controversa*, 207–79, on the interpretation of the Nuremberg jurist Christoph Herdesian; and 603–85, on the Lutheran response to his and other criticisms of the Formula of Concord. See also Rudolf Keller, *Die Confessio Augustana im theologischen Wirken des Rostocker Professors David Chyträus (1530–1600)*, FKDG 60 (Göttingen: Vandenhoeck & Ruprecht, 1994).

42. Kenneth G. Appold, *Orthodoxie als Konsensbildung: Das theologische Disputationswesen an der Universität Wittenberg zwischen 1570 und 1710*, BHTh 127 (Tübingen: Mohr Siebeck, 2004), 129–33.

43. Fr. H. R. Frank, *Die Theologie der Concordienformel, historisch-dogmatisch entwickelt und beleuchtet*, vols. 1–4, (Erlangen, 1858–1865).

44. Henry Eyster Jacobs, *The Book of Concord*, 3 vols. (Philadelphia: United Lutheran Publication House, 1882–1883).

45. James W. Richards, *The Confessional History of the Lutheran Church* (Philadelphia: Lutheran Publication Society, 1909).

46. T. E. Schmauk and C. T. Benze, *The Confessional Principle and the Confessions of the Lutheran Church* (Philadelphia: General Council, 1911).

47. George J. Fritschel, *The Formula of Concord: Its Origin and Contents* (Philadelphia: Lutheran Publication Society, 1916).

48. J. L. Neve, *Introduction to Lutheran Symbolics* (Columbus: Heer, 1917).

49. Friedrich Bente, *Historical Introductions to the Symbolical Books of the Evangelical Lutheran Church* (Saint Louis: Concordia, 1921).

50. Eric W. Gritsch and Robert W. Jenson, *Lutheranism, The Theological Movement and Its Confessional Writings* (Philadelphia: Fortress Press, 1976).

51. Edmund Schlink, *Theology of the Lutheran Confessions*, trans. Paul F. Koehneke and Herbert J. A. Bouman (Philadelphia: Muhlenberg, 1961).

52. Günter Gassmann and Scott Hendrix, *Fortress Introduction to the Lutheran Confessions* (Minneapolis: Fortress Press, 1999).

53. Günter Wenz, *Theologie der Bekenntnisschriften der evangelisch-lutherischen Kirche*, 2 vols. (Berlin: de Gruyter, 1996, 1998).

1. A History of the Ancient Creedal Texts

1. This is one of the important points made by Robert F. Webber, in *Ancient-Future Faith: Rethinking Evangelicalism for a Postmodern World* (Grand Rapids: Baker, 1999), and by essays in *Nicene Christianity: The Future for a New Ecumenism* (Grand Rapids: Brazos, 2001). Similarly, the projects initiated by Thomas Oden and Intervarsity Press seek to highlight the doctrinal consensus or exegetical consensus of the early church. Even among North American Evangelicals there has been a renewed interest in creedal Christianity. See Keith A. Mathison, *The Shape of Sola Scriptura* (Moscow: Canon, 2001), who issues a call for a creedal reading of Scripture among Evangelicals.

2. Charles Arand, "Toward a Hermeneutics of the Lutheran Confessions," *Concordia Journal* 28 (2002): 9–22.

3. *BSLK* 3–4, BC 5.

4. *BSLK* 833–834, BC 526–27.

5. *BSLK* 50–51, BC 36–37.

6. *Philipp Melanchthon: Enarratio secundae tertiaeque partis Symboli Nicaeni (1550)*, ed. Hans-Peter Hasse, QFRG 64 (Gütersloh: Gütersloher, 1996), 14–15.

7. Ibid., 59–183.

8. *Die drei Symbola*, 1538, WA 50:262–83; cf. his sermons on the Creed of 1537, preached in Smalcald, first published 1563, WA 45:11–24.

9. Among many examples are David Chytraeus, *Catechesis in Academia Rostochiana ex praelectionibus Dauidis Chytraei collecta*, ed. Simon Pauli (Rostock: Dith, 1554), and Nikolaus Gallus, *Catechismvs Predigsweise gestelt* (Regensburg: Kohl, 1554).

10. Georg von Anhalt, *Kurtze Vnnd tro[e]stliche Betrachtunge vnsers heiligen Christlichen Glaubens* (Leipzig: Günther, 1550), and Hieronymus Weller, *Ein kurtze vnd tro[e]stliche außlegung des allgemeinen/ Christlichen bekentniß oder glaubens/ so man nennet Symbolum Apostolicum* (Nuremberg: Neuber and Berg, 1564).

11. Georg Major, *Auslegung des Glaubens/ welcher das Symbolum Apostolicum genandt wird* (1550; Wittenberg: Cretuzer, 1554), and Christoph Irenaeus, *Symbolvm Apostolicvm* (Eisleben: Gaubisch, 1562), with the augmentation of the third article in *Des dritten Artickels vnsers Christlichen Glaubens folgende stu[e]ck* (Eisleben: Gaubisch, 1563).

12. *Symbolicorvm, Apostolici, Niceni, et Athanasiani Exegesis* (Leipzig: Rhamba, 1575).

13. *Articulorum Symboli Apostolici de Filio Dei Domino Nostro Iesv Christo* (Wittenberg: Crato, 1584).

14. See Charles Arand, "Luther on the Creeds," *LQ* 20 (2006): 1–25.

15. A great deal of creedal scholarship in the twentieth century strove to trace the origins of the Apostles Creed and track its development. J. N. D. Kelly, *Early Christian Creeds*, 3rd ed. (London: Longman, 1972), remains the standard work on the textual history and development of the creeds. He also provides good theological analyses of the phrases employed by the creeds. This work deals with the Apostles and Nicene Creed. More recently, Liuwe H. Westra's comprehensive and thorough work, *The Apostles Creed: Origin, History, and Some Early Christian Commentaries* (Turnhout: Brepols, 2002), has reexamined the evidence and latest scholarship and confirmed most of the conclusions of Kelly. Westra, however, fills in some gaps by examining the regional variants of the Apostles Creed between the fourth and seventh centuries. Most helpful introductions to the history and theology of the creeds include Frances Young, *The Making of the Creeds* (Philadelphia: Trinity International, 1992), and Gerald Bray, *Creeds, Councils,*

and Christ: Did the Early Christians Misrepresent Jesus? (Fearn: Mentor, 1997), who expounds the creeds in light of contemporary theological developments. On recent German scholarship on the Apostles Creed, see Oskar Skarsaune, "The Most Recent Debate on the Origin of the Apostles Creed," *Tidsskrift for Teologi og Kirke* 80 (2009): 294–305. These works provide the foundation for much of the subsequent discussion.

16. Much study has been devoted in the twentieth century to these confessional statements. See Vernon H. Neufeld, *The Earliest Christian Confessions* (Grand Rapids: Eerdmans, 1963); Oscar Cullmann, *The Earliest Christian Confessions*, trans. J. K. S. Reed (London: Lutterworth, 1949); and Herman Sasse, "The Confession of Faith according to the New Testament," *Springfielder* (1964): 1–8.

17. Young, *The Making of the Creeds*, 7 (Eph. 18.2).

18. Such summaries are already provided in the New Testament as in Romans 1 and 1 Corinthians 15. But they did not always serve a polemical purpose (Westra, *The Apostles Creed*, 71).

19. Docetism was a movement that denied the incarnation of the Son of God and instead maintained that he simply adopted the appearance of a man. The apostle John deals with this view already in his first epistle.

20. Frances Young calls these rules of faith important precursors to the creeds and also provides examples from Irenaeus, Tertullian, and Origen (*The Making of the Creeds*, 8–12). Bray points out that in Roman law, a *regula* (rule) was a summary of a statute. "Regulae or canones were composed by lawyers to provide a quick guide to the statute-book for those who were too busy to read the fine print themselves. They were not arbitrary productions but carefully ordered statements of the main points of the law," Bray, *Creeds, Councils, and Christ*, 92.

21. MSG 7:855, cited in Kelly, *Early Christian Creeds*, 80. See also Paul J. Grime, "Confessional Pre-Understanding in the Interpretation of Scripture" (S.T.M. thesis, Concordia Theological Seminary, Fort Wayne, 1987). Young, *The Making of the Creeds*, 22–23, notes that Irenaeus developed two strategies for addressing the Gnostics. One was the development of a systematic theology or overarching and coherent view of the world; the second was an appeal to the authority of tradition.

22. Westra, *The Apostles Creed*, 48, 66–67. This dating stems from Pieter Smulders.

23. Ibid., 43.

24. Ibid., 60.

25. See E. C. Whitaker, *Documents of the Baptismal Liturgy* (London: SPKC, 1986), and Edward Yarnold, *The Awe Inspiring Rites of Initiation: The Origins of the R.C.I.A.* (Collegeville: Liturgical, 1994).

26. See Young, *The Making of the Creeds*, 6–7.

27. Westra, *The Apostles Creed*, 55; late fourth century date, 66.

28. Ibid., 55–56.

29. Kelly, *Early Christian Creeds*, 31–39. For samples of the sermons/lectures delivered during the season of Lent to catechumens, see *Egeria: Diary of a Pilgrimage*, Ancient Christian Writers (Mahwah: Paulist, 1970), Cyril of Jerusaelm's thirty-eight catechetical lectures, and William Harmless, *Augustine and the Catechumenate* (Collegeville: Liturgical, 1995).

30. Westra, *The Apostles Creed*, 403.

31. See the Old Roman Creed text: Kelly, *Early Christian Creeds*, 1976, 102. See Westra, *The Apostles Creed*, 27, for the Greek and Latin version. Rufinus's commentary

is "the only place in the extant patristic literature that provides explicit clues to both the existence and the outline of a form of the Apostles Creed in Rome" (Westra, *The Apostles Creed*, 28). For manuscripts of the wording, see Westra, *The Apostles Creed*, 28–29.

32. Kelly, *Early Christian Creeds*, 102.

33. Westra, *The Apostles Creed*, 69.

34. Ibid., 59.

35. Kelly, *Early Christian Creeds*, 40–49; Westra, *Creed*, 56.

36. Westra, *The Apostles Creed*, 57, 59.

37. In his *explanatio symboli*, cited in ibid., 71–72.

38. *Rufinus: A Commentary on the Apostles Creed*, trans. J. N. D. Kelly, Ancient Christian Writers (Westminster: Newman, 1955), 29–30.

39. Westra, *The Apostles Creed*, 81–84.

40. Ibid., 96ff., 73.

41. Ibid., 405–6. The study of these lies at the heart of Westra's contribution to creedal studies.

42. Ibid., 77–84, 495.

43. Kelly, *Early Christian Creeds*, 415.

44. Ibid., 398–99.

45. Hughes Oliphant Old, *The Reading and Preaching of the Scriptures in the Worship of the Christian Church* (Grand Rapids: Eerdmans, 1998), 137–40.

46. Kelly, *Early Christian Creeds*, 398, 399, 414. Kelly notes that nearly similar forms of the Apostles Creed are found in other liturgical texts of the same period, 404ff.

47. Ibid., 413–15.

48. Ibid., 423–24.

49. Ibid., 421, 424.

50. Westra, *The Apostles Creed*, 73.

51. Kelly, *Early Christian Creeds*, 424–25.

52. Kelly notes that an abbreviation of the Old Roman Creed was used in the baptismal rite itself, ibid., 427.

53. Ibid., 432–33.

54. Ibid., 433.

55. Westra, *The Apostles Creed*, 74.

56. Kelly, *Early Christian Creeds*, 434.

57. Again, Kelly's *Early Christian Creeds* remains the standard on the textual history of the Nicene Creed and most of his work is devoted to it. For the history and theology of the events surrounding the Council of Nicaea, see Colm Luibhéid, *The Council of Nicaea* (Galway: Galway University Press, 1982), who provides a brief yet enlightening and riveting account. John Behr's two volume work, *Formation of Christian Theology: The Nicene Faith, Volume 2 Part One: True God of True God* and *Part Two: One of the Holy Trinity* (Crestwood: St. Vladimir's Seminary Press, 2004), provides one the most complete treatments of Nicene Creed, both its historical context and theology. For the contemporary relevance and ecumenical appropriation of the Nicene Creed, see *Nicene Christianity: The Future for a New Ecumenism*, ed. Christopher R. Seitz (Grand Rapids: Brazos, 2001), and *Confessing the Faith: An Ecumenical Explication of the Apostolic Faith as It Is Confessed in the Nicene-Constantinopolitan Creed (381)*, Faith and Order Paper No. 153 (Geneva: WCC, 1991). For an accessible exegetical reflection on the Nicene Creed, see Luke Timothy Johnson's *The Creed: What Christians Believe and Why It*

Matters (New York: Doubleday, 2003). For a systematic reflection on the Creed's theology, see David Willis, *Clues to the Nicene Creed: A Brief Outline of the Faith* (Grand Rapids: Eerdmans, 2005).

58. Quoted in Robert L. Wilken, *Remembering the Christian Past* (Grand Rapids: Eerdmans, 1995), 66. Similarly, Celsus also charged them with not being monotheists. "If these men worshipped no other God but one, perhaps they would have a valid argument against the others. But in fact they worship to an extravagant degree this man who appeared recently, and yet think it is not inconsistent with monotheism if they also whip his servant," *Contra Celsum* VIII.12, quoted in Young, *The Making of the Creeds*, 33.

59. Luibhéid, *Council*, 40.

60. Young, *The Making of the Creeds*, 35. She discusses the Apologists from 3–37. For a thorough discussion of the views of the various Apologists, see Justo L. González, *A History of Christian Thought: Volume 1: From the Beginnings to the Council of Chalcedon* (Nashville: Abingdon, 1970), 98–122 and Wilken, *Remembering the Christian Past*, 67–68.

61. González, *History*, 256–257. Young, *The Making of the Creeds*, 44, cautions that while Paul of Samosata appears to be an adoptionist, his union of the divine power and Jesus was more "constitutive" in its uniting of the two.

62. Wilken, *Remembering the Christian Past*, 71–75.

63. See Richard Bauckham, *Jesus and the God of Israel: God Crucified and Other Studies on the New Testament's Christology of Divine Identity* (Grand Rapids: Eerdmans, 2008), for a helpful discussion of how Paul interpreted the Shema of the Old Testament in 1 Corinthians 8.

64. Quoted in Wilken, *Remembering the Christian Past*, 78; see his discussion of Hilary, 77–81. See *Saint Hilary of Poitiers: The Trinity*, trans. Stephen McKenna (Washington, DC: Catholic University of America Press, 1954).

65. Behr, *Formation of Christian Theology*, I: 62-68.

66. Leo Donald Davis, *The First Seven Ecumenical Councils (325–787): Their History and Theology* (Collegeville: Liturgical, 1990), 51.

67. See ibid., 51–59.

68. For analyses of Arius's position and concerns, see Young's discussion, *The Making of the Creeds*, 45–48. Bray provides helpful account of how Arius took into account biblical, philosophical, and spiritual concerns, *Creeds, Councils, and Christ*, 105–111. See also Catherine Mowry LaCugna, *God for Us: The Trinity and Christian Life* (San Francisco: Harper, 1973), 30–35.

69. Davis, *The First Seven Ecumenical Councils*, 53.

70. Ibid., 53–54.

71. See ibid., 54–55.

72. Kelly, *Early Christian Creeds*, 209–11.

73. Luibhéid, *The Council of Nicaea*, 73.

74. Ibid., 77.

75. Ibid., 77–79.

76. Numbers vary. Euseubius of Caesaria reports about 215. By the mid-fourth century 318 became the traditional number (perhaps a reference to Abraham's armed servants in Genesis 14:14, a number that in Greek read TIH, symbol of the cross and Jesus). See Davis, *The First Seven Ecumenical Councils*, 57–58.

77. Luibhéid provides a good summary of those three stages, *The Council of Nicaea*, 85–88.

78. Ibid., 88.

79. The completed Creed was preserved in the writings of Athanasius by the historian Socrates, Basil of Caesarea, and acts of the Council of Chalcedon of 451. See Kelly, *Early Christian Creeds*, 227–30.

80. Basil became one of those who helped to distinguish these in their definition during the second half of the fourth century (Davis, *The First Seven Ecumenical Councils*, 112).

81. Quoted in Kelly, *Early Christian Creeds*, 215–16.

82. See Davis, *The First Seven Ecumenical Councils*, 75–77 and 81–91.

83. Behr, *Formation of Christian Theology*, I:72.

84. Davis details nicely all the ebbs and flows of the debate following Nicaea (*The First Seven Ecumenical Councils*, 91–103).

85. Bray, *Creeds, Councils, and Christ*, 109. Athanasius's key work during this period is *On the Incarnation: The Treatise De Incarnatione verbi dei* (Crestwood: St. Vladimir's Orthodox Theological Seminary, 1979).

86. Davis, *The First Seven Ecumenical Councils*, 111–13. He notes that when the Arians rioted against him, Gregory wanted to flee, but his flock pleaded that he not take the Trinity from them! (118).

87. Ibid., 67, 112. See also LaCugna, *God for Us*, 66–68.

88. For a good account of these developments, see Behr, *Formation of Christian Theology*, I:370-78.

89. See Robert C. Schultz, "An Analysis of the Augsburg Confession Article VII, 2, in its Historical Context, May and June 1530," *SCJ* 11(1980): 25–35.

90. Davis, *The First Seven Ecumenical Councils*, 118–19.

91. Ibid., 119, 130, 121–24.

92. Kelly, *Early Christian Creeds*, 297–98.

93. Davis, *The First Seven Ecumenical Councils*, 126.

94. Kelly, *Early Christian Creeds*, 338.

95. Davis, *The First Seven Ecumenical Councils*, 124, 126–27. Kelly details the Council's rebuttal of Apollinarianism, 332–38. Young provides a good account of the struggle to speak of the humanity of Christ from the Arians, for whom the Logos took the place of the soul in Jesus, to Athanasius's word-flesh theology, and Athanasius's friend Apollinaris's position that "every mind is self-directing and it was impossible for two such entities to exist in one person," *The Making of the Creeds*, 65–69.

96. Douglas Macleane, *The Athanasian Creed* (London: Pitman, 1914), 174, 172.

97. Davis, *The First Seven Ecumenical Councils*, 104.

98. See Kelly, *Early Christian Creeds*, 340, and Young, *The Making of the Creeds*, 49–57, esp. 53.

99. Saint Basil, Bishop of Caesarea, *On the Holy Spirit* (Crestwood: St. Vladimir's Seminary Press, 1980).

100. See Kelly, *Early Christian Creeds*, 341, for an explanation of each phrase.

101. Young, *The Making of the Creeds*, 57.

102. See Kelly, *Early Christian Creeds*, 301–5, for a comparison of the differences, and Davis, *The First Seven Ecumenical Councils*, 123, for details.

103. Kelly, *Early Christian Creeds*, 325. The Creed probably used the framework of a previously existing baptismal creed drawn up in the 370s and used in Jerusalem or Antioch, both of which supported the Nicene faith (Davis, *The First Seven Ecumenical Councils*, 123).

104. Davis, *The First Seven Ecumenical Councils*, 123.

105. Kelly, *Early Christian Creeds*, 325.

106. Davis notes that in the West Pope Felix III (d. 492) recognized only three ecumenical councils—Nicaea, Ephesus, Chalcedon. Pope Hormisdas (d. 523) finally recognized Constantinople on a par with the other three (*The First Seven Ecumenical Councils*, 130).

107. Kelly, *Early Christian Creeds*, 322–23, 329–30. Bray notes that it was on July 22, 431, that the council decreed "that the Creed of Nicaea should never be changed, but should remain for ever as the standard of the Church's faith" (*Creeds, Councils, and Christ*, 156).

108. Kelly, *Early Christian Creeds*, 317–18, 331. It appears that the council promoted the creed of Constantinople partly to enhance the importance of Constantinople as the new Rome, ibid., 317.

109. Ibid., 296–301.

110. Bray, *Creeds, Councils, and Christ*, 117.

111. Kelly, *Early Christian Creeds*, 361. See also Bray, *Creeds, Councils, and Christ*, 185–89. Bray also notes that the last Arians were forcibly converted after this council, but an underground Arianism persisted into the eight century (107).

112. Kelly, *Early Christian Creeds*, 364.

113. Ibid., 365–66.

114. Not as much scholarly work has taken place on the Athanasian Creed. The standard remains J. N. D. Kelly, *The Athanasian Creed: The Paddock Lectures for 1962–1963* (London: Black, 1964). He examines issues of authorship, history, theology, and textual development. For an older, also insightful work, see Macleane, *The Athanasian Creed*.

115. Bray suggests that the decline began with attacks on it by influences shaped by Deism and the Enlightenment (*Creeds, Councils, and Christ*, 175).

116. Westra, *The Apostles Creed*, 5, n.1.

117. Kelly, *Athanasian Creed*, 35.

118. Westra, *The Apostles Creed*, 313. He cites P. Lejay, *Le rôle théologie de Césaire d'Arles: Etude sur l'histoire du dogme chre'tien en occident au temps des royaumes barbares* (Paris, 1906), 46–54. Lejay contends that the Athanasian Creed was the fourth and final product of that process (n.125).

119. Kelly, *Athanasian Creed*, 36.

120. Ibid., 109–10. He thus rejects the idea that its origin lies with a liturgical function or as originally a hymn.

121. Ibid., 105, 119, 123–24.

122. Ibid., 39–43.

123. Ibid., 48–51.

124. Bray, *Creeds, Councils, and Christ*, 172–73.

125. Helpful are George A. Lindbeck, *The Nature of Doctrine: Religion and Theology in a Postliberal Age* (Louisville: Westminster John Knox, 1984), and Johnson, *The Creed*.

126. Indeed, the subtitle to the Athanasian Creed reads, "which he [Athanasius] made against the heretics called Arians" (*BSLK* 28, BC 23).

127. Kelly, *Athanasian Creed*, 94–98, 105, 106.

128. Bray, *Creeds, Councils, and Christ*, 176–77, providing a good commentary on the Athanasian Creed. See also Kelly, *Athanasian Creed*, 70–104.

129. Ibid., 125.

2. The Theological Contributions of the Ancient Creeds

1. Hermann Sasse, "Church and Confession: 1941," in *We Confess Jesus Christ, Volume 1* (Saint Louis: Concordia, 1984), 71–87.

2. A great deal of work on the doctrine of the Trinity has taken place over the last several decades. Despite certain biases, LaCugna, *God for Us*, provides in the first half of her book one of the most accessible (and insightful) historical and theological treatments of the Trinity in the early church through the Middle Ages.

3. This leads to one of the questions with which scholars have wrestled over the past several decades, namely, what is the relationship between these two ways of speaking about the Trinity? Karl Rahner's famous rule that the "economic Trinity is the immanent Trinity" has provided a starting point for that discussion. See Karl Rahner, *Trinity* (London: Continuum, 2001), and Dennis W. Jowers, *The Trinitarian Axiom of Karl Rahner: The Economic Trinity Is the Immanent Trinity and Vice Versa* (Lewiston: Mellen, 2006).

4. See LaCugna on various ways the church fathers used *oikonomia*, *God for Us*, 24–30.

5. See LaCugna's discussion of prepositions used by the Arians and Cappadocians, ibid., 119–23.

6. Ibid., 2–4.

7. Ibid., 10–11.

8. See LaCugna's discussion in chapter 4, "Christian Prayer and Trinitarian Faith," ibid., 111–35, and also how these issues were dealt with in the Middle Ages as the question arose, "Does it matter which person we pray to?" After all, they are all God.

9. For example, "One God" refers to the Father in Acts 7:40; 14:11; 19:26; 1 Cor. 8:5; Gal. 4:8. "Only God" refers to the Father in John 5:44; 17:3; Rom. 16:27; 1 Tim. 1:17; Jude 1:25. "God alone" refers to the Father in Mark 2:7; 10:18; 12:29–32; Luke 18:19; Rom. 3:30; 1 Cor. 8:4,6; Gal. 3:20; Eph. 4:6; 1 Tim 2:5; James 2:19. Why assign that word to the Father preeminently? In 1 Cor. 8, the "one God" is contrasted with many gods. It is used over and against idolatry. This relates to the importance of creation as well.

10. LaCugna, *God for Us*, 22–24. See her discussion of the debates over the meaning of the Greek *vocables*, ibid., 30–33.

11. The words "begotten" and "proceed" come from John's gospel but when used for describing the immanent Trinity they are being used in a way other than what is probably their context in John. That is certainly true of the word "proceed." But what it means to speak of "only-begotten" in context is not entirely clear.

12. The insertion of the *filioque* in the ninth century upsets the nice symmetry whereby both the Son and Spirit come from the Father along the lines of Irenaeus' two hands of God. Now the Spirit comes from the Father and the Son, but could appear to be somewhat subordinate as neither Father or Son come from the Spirit. See Bray's helpful discussion and diagrams, *Creeds, Councils, and Christ*, 112–14.

13. LaCugna, *God for Us*, 54, 8.

14. For a discussion of the debates over these terms from Arius through the Cappadocians, see ibid., 53–73.

15. *BSLK* 660, BC 439–440. See Albrecht Peters's discussion of Luther's relationship to the tradition in Albrecht Peters, *Kommentar zu Luthers Katechismen Band 2: Der Glaube* (Gottingen: Vandenhoeck & Ruprecht, 1991).

16. It is important to note that these are not two "different" Trinities. They are related. LaCugna points out that the theological work has sought to relate them by grounding the economic Trinity in the immanent Trinity, Introduction to *God for Us*, 1–17.

17. *Theology Is for Proclamation* (Minneapolis: Fortress Press, 1990), 135–90.

18. Alois Grillmeier, *Christ in Christian Tradition* (New York: Sheed and Ward, 1965), remains one of the standard works in this area, but its comprehensiveness and thoroughness might intimidate those who are making their first foray into early church Christology. A more accessible work to the Christology of the church fathers from Nicaea to Chalcedon is *Christology of the Later Fathers,* ed. Edward R. Hardy, Library of Christian Classics (Louisville: Westminster John Knox, 1954).

19. The Nicene Creed has an interesting play on words here that makes the point that in order to save his human creatures he became a human creature. The Greek has "who for us *anthropous*" (human creatures/men) "*enanthropesanta*" (became a human creature/man). Interestingly, the translation of this clause in the Wisconsin Evangelical Lutheran Synod's hymnal reads, "For us and for our salvation, he came down from heaven, was incarnate of the Holy Spirit and the virgin Mary, and became *fully human*" [italics added], *Christian Worship Supplement* (Milwaukee: Northwestern, 2008). For an explanation, see Theodore Hartwig, "The Creeds in Contemporary English," *Wisconsin Lutheran Quarterly* 86 (1989), who writes, "The change in line 16 from 'was made man' to 'became fully human' may be counted as one of the finest improvements in the new translation; it catches quite satisfactorily what the original participle (*enanthropesanta*) intends to communicate. The Greek text here asserts that God's Son took on all that makes a human being a human being; that he became a genuine human being with soul, body, mind, senses, emotions and everything else that constitutes the human person in God's original creation." The hymnal of the Evangelical Lutheran Church in America reads, "For us and for our salvation he came down from heaven, was incarnate of the Holy Spirit and the virgin Mary, and became *truly human*" [italics added], *Evangelical Lutheran Worship* (Minneapolis: Augsburg Fortress, 2006). The Lutheran Church–Missouri Synod's hymnal retains, "Who for us men and for our salvation came down from heaven and was incarnate by the Holy Spirit of the virgin Mary and was made man" [italics added], *Lutheran Service Book* (St. Louis: Concordia, 2006).

20. The following summarizes Young's description of development of this debate, *The Making of the Creeds*, 65–68.

21. R. P. C. Hanson, *The Search for the Christian Doctrine of God* (Edinburgh: Clark, 1988), 488, quoted in Young, *The Making of the Creeds*, 66. One must be careful, however, in emphasizing this point too strongly, as if Athanasius might be moving in a Nestorian direction. Athanasius does strive to maintain a balance. For example, in his letter to Epictetus, Athanasius rejects both the position that "what hung upon the tree was not the body, but the very creative Essence and Wisdom" (par. 2) and the idea that "Christ Who suffered in the flesh and was crucified is not Lord, Saviour, God, and Son of the Father" (par. 2). This latter statement suggests that he does attribute human weakness and suffering to the Logos but on the basis of the incarnation: "The incorporeal Word made His own the properties of the Body, as being His own Body" (Ep. 6). This indicates that one must be a bit cautious of attributing a "spacesuit Christology." Some statements point in that direction, but judgments need to be nuanced. Thanks to David Maxwell for this insight. The Letter to Epictetus is his Ep. 59, and is found in *Nicene and Post-Nicene Fathers* (Edinburgh: T & T Clark, 1989), Second Sermon, 4:570-74.

22. Young, *The Making of the Creeds*, 67–68.

23. Ibid., 72–73.

24. Ibid., 74–75.

25. Both *mia* and *mono* would be translated as "one," but Copts—who count among the Miaphysitic churches—in particular prefer *mia* because it has a connotation of "unity" or "completeness," while mono has a connotation of "sole" or "alone."

26. Bray, *Creeds, Councils, and Christ*, 159. He gives the date on page 161 and discusses Chalcedonian Christology in connection with the Alexandrian and Antiochene schools of thought, 158–59.

27. Young, *The Making of the Creeds*, 77. She provides a helpful analysis of the consequences of the council and its success or lack there of in resolving the theological issues, ibid., 78–79. Bray suggests that it is a turning point in the history of theological thought as it welded the eastern and western traditions together, "though the price paid for this in the East was to be very high" (*Creeds, Councils, and Christ*, 163). He has a helpful discussion of the subsequent histories of the Nestorian traditions and missions in China, and the Monophysite theological developments, *Christ*, 163–66.

28. See David R. Maxwell, "Crucified in the Flesh: Christological Confession or Evasive Qualification?" *Pro Ecclesia* 13 (2004): 70–81. Maxwell borrows the term from Brian Daley's chapter, "Christology," in *Augustine Through the Ages* (Grand Rapids: Eerdmans, 1999), 165.

29. Bray, *Creeds, Councils, and Christ*, 165.

30. Young, *The Making of the Creeds*, 79.

31. See FC VIII, 21–31, citing Luther, *BSLK*, 1023–27, BC, 619–21.

32. Maxwell, "Crucified in the Flesh," 71, 74, 77–79.

33. See David R. Maxwell, "Christology and Grace in the Sixth-Century Latin West: The Theopaschite Controversy," Ph.D. dissertation, University of Notre Dame, 2003. Bray notes that though this council condemned some of the Antiochene theologians, it did not go far enough for the extreme Monophysites, who set up their own churches in Syria, *Creeds, Councils, and Christ*, 166.

34. Maxwell, "Crucified in the Flesh," 81.

35. "The Anathemas of the Second Council of Constantinople," in *Christology of the Later Fathers*, ed. Edward Rochie Hardy, Library of Christian Classics (Philadelphia: Westminster, 1954), 381.

36. Bray, *Creeds, Councils, and Christ*, 166. Bray also notes that by 680 the Monophysites had become a separate church living under Muslim rule and that, today, most Christians living in Middle East, Egypt, and Libya belong to this tradition.

37. Bray, *Creeds, Councils, and Christ*, 167–68. He contemporizes the application: "Jesus could be fully God without knowing, as a man, the secrets of nuclear physics." "His omniscience as God did not automatically carry over into his life on earth as a man."

38. See Jesus' statement in John 14:9, "Whoever has seen me has seen the Father." The portrayal of Jesus in picture form also became important for instruction (see Ap XV). But the council's decree regarding the veneration of images caused problems later. Bray notes, however, that the Latin text used the word *salutare*, which means "to greet or acknowledge the image," while the Greek used the word, *aspazein*, "to kiss." See also Christoph Schönborn, *God's Human Face: The Christ-Icon* (San Francisco: Ignatius, 1994).

39. See Lindbeck, *The Nature of Doctrine*, and Johnson, *The Creed*.

40. Ep 101.32, cited in Behr, *Formation of Christian Theology*, 76.

41. See Kathryn Green-McCreight, "He Spoke through the Prophets," in *Nicene Christianity*, 167–78.

42. Dorothy L. Sayers, *Creed or Chaos?* (Manchester: Sophia Institute Press, 1974; originally published in 1949), 3.

43. Young, *The Making of the Creeds*, 29.

44. Diogenes Allen, *Philosophy for Understanding Theology* (Louisville: Westminster John Knox, 2007), provides the best introduction for understanding of the philosophical world in which Christian theology was expounded.

45. Young notes that it is not clear how this formulation emerged but seems to have emerged in the struggle with Gnosticism. It is expressed shortly before the time of Irenaeus by Theophilus of Antioch, *The Making of the Creeds*, 25.

46. See Oswald Bayer, who develops the connection between creation and justification at length in *Martin Luther's Theology*, trans. Thomas H. Trapp (Grand Rapids: Eerdmans, 2008), 95–119. See also Johannes Schwanke, "Luther on Creation," *Harvesting Martin Luther's Reflections on Theology, Ethics, and the Church*, ed. Timothy J. Wengert (Grand Rapids: Eerdmans, 2007), 78–99.

47. Young, *The Making of the Creeds*, 28.

48. LC, Creed14, *BSLK* 648, BC 432.

49. For a development of this theme, see *Together with All Creatures: Caring for God's Living Earth* (A Report of the Commission on Theology and Church Relations of the Lutheran Church-Missouri Synod, 2010).

50. *Christus Victor* (New York: Macmillan, 1967). See Ted Peters, "Atonement in Anselm and Luther: Second Thoughts about Gustaf Aulen's *Christus Victor*," *LQ* 24 (1972), 301–14, and David R. Maxwell, "The Resurrection of Christ: Its Importance in the History of the Church," *Concordia Journal* 34 (2008): 22–37.

51. Maxwell, "The Resurrection of Christ," 27, 30. He notes that this connection is made by Irenaeus, Eusebius of Caesarea, Cyril of Jerusalem, Gregory of Nazianzus, and Augustine, among others.

52. Robert Kolb, "Resurrection and Justification: Luther's Use of Romans 4:25," LuJ 78 (2011): 41–62; Uwe Rieske-Braun, *Duellum mirabile: Studien zum Kampfmotiv in Martin Luthers Theologie* (Göttingen: Vandenhoeck & Ruprecht, 1999).

53. Ibid., 32.

54. Kelly provides a good overview of these interpretations and defense for the inclusion of the descent into hell, *Early Christian Creeds*, 378–83. See also James F. Kay, "He descended into Hell," *Word and World* 31 (2011): 17–26, and Wayne A. Grudem, "He did not descend into hell: a plea for following Scripture instead of the Apostles Creed," *Journal of the Evangelical Theological Society* 34 (1991): 103–13.

55. Thus, in icons and in churches, the scene painted depicts Christ crashing down the doors to hell and then lifting Adam and Eve out of their coffins or tombs. Also frequently depicted are the souls of the Old Testament awaiting release.

56. Kelly, *Early Christian Creeds*, 383.

57. See pages 252–53 of this volume.

58. Although the German and Latin of Augsburg Confession Article III expresses this in slightly different ways, making either the Son or the Spirit the subject of the verbs.

59. Thomas Smail provides a good discussion and makes an interesting proposal in "The Holy Spirit in the Holy Trinity," in *Nicene Christianity*, 149–66.

60. LC Creed, 43–46, *BSLK* 655, BC 436.

61. The emphasis on the hope of the resurrection has received renewed attention by theologians across the theological spectrum. N. T. Wright's *Surprised by Hope: Rethinking*

Heaven, the Resurrection, and the Mission of the Church (New York: HarperOne, 2008), is but one prominent and influential example.

62. Kelly, *Early Christian Creeds*, 387.

63. Bray, *Creeds, Councils, and Christ*, 103.

3. Luther's Small and Large Catechisms

1. Four works lay the foundation for further study of Luther's catechisms: Charles P. Arand, *That I May Be His Own: An Overview of Luther's Catechisms* (St. Louis: Concordia, 2000); Herbert Girgensohn, *Teaching Luther's Catechism*, 2 vols. (Philadelphia: Muhlenberg, 1959); Albrecht Peters, *Kommentar zu Luthers Katechismen*, ed. Gottfried Seebass, 5 vols. (Göttingen: Vandenhoeck & Ruprecht, 1990–1995); and Timothy J. Wengert, *Martin Luther's Catechisms: Forming the Faith* (Minneapolis: Fortress Press, 2009); additionally, see Wenz, *Theologie der Bekenntnisschriften*, 1:233–347. The bibliographies in each cover older bibliography. The classic studies of J. Michael Reu also deserve attention: *Dr. Martin Luther's Small Catechism: A History of its Origin, Its Distribution, and Its Use* (Chicago: Wartburg, 1929), and *Explanation of Dr. Martin Luther's Small Catechism* (Chicago: Wartburg, 1904). The standard collection of catechetical literature in the German Reformation remains J. Michael Reu, ed., *Quellen zur Geschichte des kirchlichen Unterrichts in der evangelischen Kirche Deutschlands zwischen 1530 und 1600* (Gütersloh: Bertelsmann, 1902–1924).

Also the classic analyses of Johannes Meyer, *Historischer Kommentar zu Luthers Kleinem Katechismus* (Gütersloh: Bertelsmann, 1929), and Otto Albrecht's introduction to the catechisms in WA 30, 1:499–665, and his *Luthers Katechismen* (Leipzig: Verein für Reformationsgeschichte, 1915), are helpful.

The prejudices of his times colored the nonetheless helpful study of the later use of the catechisms in the Lutheran church in Hans-Jürgen Fraas, *Katechismustradition: Luthers Kleiner Katechismus in Kirche und Schule*, APTh 5 (Göttingen: Vandenhoeck & Ruprecht, 1971). As a corrective read Gerhard Bode, "Instruction of the Christian Faith by Lutherans after Luther," in *Lutheran Ecclesiastical Culture, 1550–1675*, ed. Robert Kolb (Leiden: Brill, 2008), 159–204.

Martin E. Marty combined a devotional style with theological perspicacity in his commentary on the Large Catechism, *The Hidden Discipline* (St. Louis: Concordia, 1961). See also Karin Bornkamm, "Das Verständnis christlicher Unterweisung in den Katechismen von Erasmus und Luther," *Zeitschrift für Theologie und Kirche* 65 (1968): 204–30, and *Die Gegenwartsbedeutung der Katechismen Martin Luthers*, ed. Norbert Dennerlein et al. (Gütersloh: Gütersloher, 2005).

2. But see Robin Barnes, *Prophesy and Gnosis: Apocalypticism in the Wake of the Lutheran Reformation* (Stanford: Stanford University Press, 1988), 13–59; Ulrich Asendorf, *Eschatologie bei Luther* (Göttingen: Vandenhoeck & Ruprecht, 1967), and, for the impact of Luther's apocalyptic views on his students, Volker Leppin, *Antichrist und Jüngster Tag: Das Profil apokalyptischer Flugschriftenpublizistik im deutschen Luthertum, 1548–1618*, QFRG 69 (Gütersloh: Gütersloher, 1999), passim.

3. Heiko A. Oberman, *Forerunners of the Reformation* (New York: Holt, Rinehart and Winston, 1966). 14.

4. Though not necessarily reproductions of sermons he actually preached, the following writings of Luther reflect the kind of catechetical preaching he engaged in as a monk: "Sermo de Poenitentia," 1518, WA 1:319–24; "Sermon von der Sakrament der Buße,"

1519, WA 2:713–23, LW 35:9–22; "Sermon von der…Taufe," 1519, WA 2:727–37, LW 35:29–43; "Sermon von der…Sakrament des heiligen wahren Leichnam Christi," 1519, WA 2:742-58, WA 2:49–73. On Luther's later preaching on baptism, see Robert Kolb, "'What Benefit Does the Soul Receive from a Handful of Water?' Luther's Preaching on Baptism, 1528–1539," *Concordia Journal* 25 (1999), 346–63.

5. WA 10, 3:18, 15–16.

6. WA 7:466–537, 10,1,2:1–208.

7. Jaroslav Pelikan, *Spirit versus Structure: Luther and the Institutions of the Church* (New York: Harper and Row, 1968).

8. See Scott Hendrix, *Recultivating the Vineyard: The Reformation Agendas of Christianization* (Louisville, Westminster John Knox, 2004), 69–96.

9. James M. Estes, *Peace, Order, and the Glory of God: Secular Authority and the Church in the Thought of Luther and Melanchthon, 1518–1559* (Leiden: Brill, 2005), 42–52.

10. Eric W. Gritsch and Robert W. Jenson, *Lutheranism: The Theological Movement and Its Confessional Writings* (Philadelphia: Fortress Press, 1976). As the title indicates, Gritsch and Jenson sought to extend the concept of "movement" over the whole Lutheran reform and its Confessions, minimizing the significance of differences between traditional Roman Catholicism and the Lutheran Reformation. While this may have served the ecumenical purposes of their time, it is an essentially romantic reading of the reform that, by obviating difference, cannot do justice to the historical realities. Provisional and loosely organized as it was, in the eyes of Charles V and the Roman Catholic hierarchy Lutheranism was no longer a movement within but a separate body. Theologically, the Reformers remained within the larger Catholic tradition; ecclesiastically, unintentionally or intentionally, they broke with it, in part on the basis of differing definitions of the church: whether it is a hierarchical organization in submission to the pope or the assembly of believers gathered by and around God's Word.

11. J. Michael Reu, *Luther's Small Catechism: A Jubilee Offering* (Chicago: Wartburg, 1929).

12. WA 18:601,5–6, LW 33: 16.

13. StA 2,1: 1–163.

14. Timothy J. Wengert, *Human Freedom, Christian Righteousness: Philip Melanchthon's Exegetical Dispute with Erasmus of Rotterdam* (Oxford: Oxford University Press, 1998), 5–20, 67–109.

15. Timothy J. Wengert, "Melanchthon and Luther / Luther and Melanchthon," LuJ 66 (1999), 55–88.

16. See Robert Kolb, *Martin Luther, Confessor of the Faith* (Oxford: Oxford University Press, 2009), 42–71.

17. WA 1:353–374, LW 31:39–69. See Gerhard O. Forde, *On Being a Theologian of the Cross: Reflections on Luther's Heidelberg Disputation, 1518* (Grand Rapids: Eerdmans, 1997).

18. Robert Kolb and Charles P. Arand, *The Genius of Luther's Theology: A Wittenberg Way of Thinking for the Contemporary Church* (Grand Rapids: Baker, 2008), 53–76; and Robert Kolb, *Bound Choice, Election, and Wittenberg Theological Method from Martin Luther to the Formula of Concord* (Grand Rapids: Eerdmans, 2005), 70–102.

19. CR 26:9.

20. CR 28:10.

21. See part 3, chapter 8, of this volume.

22. On various aspects of the entire Agricolan controversy, see Timothy J. Wengert, *Law and Gospel: Philip Melanchthon's Debate with Johann Agricola of Eisleben over Poenitentia* (Grand Rapids: Baker, 1997). See also Joachim Rogge, *Johann Agricolas Lutherverständnis* (Berlin: Evangelische Verlagsanstalt, 1960); Steffan Kjellgaard-Pedersen, *Gesetz, Evangelium und Busse: Theologiegeschichtliche Studien zum Verhältnis zwischen dem jungen Johann Agricola (Eisleben) und Martin Luther* (Leiden: Brill, 1983); Ernst Koch, "Johann Agricola neben Luther: Schülerschaft und theologische Eigenart," in *Lutheriana*, ed. Gerhard Hammer and Karl-Heinz zur Mühlen (Cologne: Böhlau, 1984), 131–50; and Jeffrey G. Silcock, "Luther and the Third Use of the Law," Th.D. dissertation, Concordia Seminary, St. Louis, 1993.

23. Wengert, *Law and Gospel*, 131–38.

24. See *Sources and Contexts*, 15–30.

25. Robert Kolb, "'The Noblest Skill in the Christian Church': Luther's Sermons on the Proper Distinction of Law and Gospel," *Concordia Theological Quarterly* 71 (2007): 301–18.

26. Arand, *That I May Be His Own*, 58–67, 70; William Harmless, *Augustine and the Catechumenate* (Collegeville: Liturgical, 1995). See Dietrich Kolde's catechism of 1480, translated in Denis Janz, *Three Reformation Catechisms: Catholic, Anabaptist, Lutheran* (New York: Mellen, 1982), 29–130.

27. Gottfried Krodel, "Luther's Work on the Catechism in the Context of Late Medieval Catechetical Literature," *Concordia Journal* 25 (1999), 364–404. On the historical setting for sixteenth-century catechetical teaching, see Robert James Bast, *Honor Your Fathers: Catechisms and the Emergence of a Patriarchal Ideology in Germany, 1400–1600* (Leiden: Brill, 1997).

28. Mark U. Edwards Jr., *Printing, Propaganda, and Martin Luther* (Minneapolis: Fortress Press, 2004).

29. Two attempts at writing the catechism Luther wished to have written from the Wittenberg circle are translated in *Sources and Contexts*, "A Booklet for Laity and Children, 1525," 1–12, and Johann Agricola's "One Hundred Thirty Common Questions, 1527," 13–30.

30. Arand, *That I May Be His Own*, 199–211.

31. Ibid., 192.

32. Bode, "Instruction of the Christian Faith."

33. James M. Nestingen, "Luther's Cultural Translation of the Catechism," *LQ* 15 (2001), 440–52.

34. SC, Creed, Article 2; *BSLK* 511, BC 355.

35. WA 10, 2:376,19–377,3; LW 43:13. See Albrecht Peters, "Die Theologie der Katechismen Luthers anhand der Zuordnung ihrer Hauptstücke," LuJ 43 (1976): 7–35.

36. Karl Barth, *Evangelium und Gesetz: Theologische Existenz Heute* (Munich: Kaiser, 1956); and the critique of Gustaf Wingren, *Theology in Conflict*, trans. Eric H. Wahlstrom (Philadelphia: Muhlenberg, 1958), 23–44.

37. Gerhard O. Forde, *Theology Is for Proclamation* (Minneapolis: Fortress Press, 1990), 135–90.

38. Birgit Stolt, "Martin Luther on God as Father," *LQ* 8 (1994): 385–95.

39. James A. Nestingen, "Preaching the Catechism," *Word and World* 10 (1990): 33–42; Ulrich Asendorf, "Luthers Theologie nach seinen Katechismuspredigten," *Kerygma und Dogma* 38 (1992): 2–19.

40. Robin A. Leaver, "Luther's Catechism Hymns," (in eight parts), *LQ* 11 (1997): 397–410, 12 (1998): 79–99, 161–169, 170–180, 303–323, brought together with other related materials in Leaver, *Luther's Liturgical Music: Principles and Implications*, LQ Books 8 (Grand Rapids: Eerdmans, 2007), 107–69; Wichmann von Meding, "Luthers Katechismuslieder," *Kerygma und Dogma* 40 (1994): 250–71.

41. On Luther's proclamation of Christ and his work, see, among other works, Ian A. K. Siggins, *Martin Luther's Doctrine of Christ* (New Haven: Yale University Press, 1970); Marc Lienhard, *Luther: Witness to Jesus Christ: Stages and Themes of the Reformer's Christology*, trans. Edwin H. Robertson (Minneapolis: Augsburg Fortress, 1982); Uwe Rieske-Braun, *Duellum mirabile: Studien zum Kampfmotiv in Martin Luthers Theologie*, FKDG 73 (Göttingen: Vandenhoeck & Ruprecht, 1999).

42. WA 39,1:347,33–36.

43. Kolb and Arand, *The Genius of Luther's Theology*, 23–76.

44. *BSLK* 517, BC 360.

45. *BSLK* 566–67, BC 390. See Charles P. Arand, "Luther on the God behind the First Commandment," *LQ* 8 (1994): 42–65; Michael Beintker, "Das Schöpfercredo in Luthers Kleinem Katechismus," *Neue Zeitschrift für systematische Theologie* 31 (1989): 1–17; Timothy J. Wengert, "'Fear and Love' in the Ten Commandments," *Concordia Journal* 21 (1995): 14–27; idem, "Luther and the Ten Commandments in the Large Catechism," in *The Pastoral Luther: Essays on Martin Luther's Practical Theology*, ed. Timothy J. Wengert, LQ Books 12 (Grand Rapids: Eerdmans, 2009), 131–146; Christoph Burger, "Gottesliebe: Erstes Gebot und menschliche Autonomie bei spätmittelalterlichen Theologen und bei Martin Luther," *Zeitschrift für Theologie und Kirche* 89 (1992): 280–301; and Aarne Siirala, *Gottes Gebot bei Martin Luther: Eine Untersuchung der Theologie Luthers unter besonderer Berücksichtigung des ersten Hauptstückes im Grossen Katechismus* (Helsinki: Luther-Agricola-Gesellschaft, 1956). On the Ten Commandments in the Catechisms, see also Gunther Wenz, "Die Zehn Gebote als Grundlage christlicher Ethik: Zur Auslegung des ersten Hauptstücks in Luthers Katechismen," *Zeitschrift für Theologie und Kirche* 89 (1992): 404–39.

46. Arand, "Luther on God."

47. Charles P. Arand, "Luther on the Creed," in *The Pastoral Luther*, 147–70.

48. SC Creed, Article 1; *BSLK*, 510–11, BC, 354. See Oswald Bayer, "'I believe That God Made Me with All That Exists': An example of Catechetical-Systematics," *LQ* 8 (1994): 129–61.

49. See Elert Herms, *Luthers Auslegung des Dritten Artikels* (Tübingen: Mohr Siebeck, 1987).

50. Timothy J. Wengert, "Luther on Prayer in the Large Catechism," *LQ* 18 (2004): 249–74, reprinted in Wengert, *The Pastoral Luther*, 171–97.

51. WA 39,1: 356,15–18.

52. *BSLK*, 513; BC, 357.

53. On Luther's understanding of baptism, see Timothy J. Wengert, "Luther on Children: Baptism and the Fourth Commandment," *dialog* 37 (1998): 185–89; Jonathan Trigg, *Baptism in the Theology of Martin Luther*, SHCT 56 (Leiden: Brill, 1994). On the Lord's Supper, see Hermann Sasse, *This Is My Body: Luther's Contention for the Real Presence in the Sacrament of the Altar* (Minneapolis: Augsburg, 1959); Carl F. Wisløff, *The Gift of Communion: Luther's Controversy with Rome on Eucharistic Sacrifice*, trans.

Joseph Shaw (Minneapolis: Augsburg Fortress, 1964); Timothy J. Wengert, "Luther's Catechisms and the Lord's Supper," *Word and World* 17 (1997): 54–60.

54. WA 30,1:345,6–12, LW 53:118.

55. *BSLK*, 515–17, 519–21; BC, 359–60, 362–63.

56. *BSLK*, 517–19; BC 360–62.

57. Werner Klän, "Anleitung zu einem Gott-gelenkten Leben: Die inner Systematik der Katechismen Luthers," *Lutherische Theologie und Kirche* 29 (2005): 18–37.

58. Joachim Mörlin, *Der kleine Catechismus Doct. Martini Lutheri* (Magdeburg, 1554), B3a.

59. *BSLK*, 521–27; BC, 363–64.

60. See Kolb and Arand, *The Genius of Luther's Theology*, 106–18; Gustaf Wingren, *Luther on Vocation*, trans. Carl C. Rasmussen (Philadelphia: Muhlenberg, 1957); George W. Forell, *Faith Active in Love: An Investigation of the Principles Underlying Luther's Social Ethics* (Minneapolis: Augsburg, 1954).

61. Timothy J. Wengert, "'Per mutuum colloquium et consolationem fratrum'": Monastische Züge in Luthers ökumenischer Theologie," in Christoph Bultmann et al., eds., *Luther und das monastische Erbe*, SMHR 39 (Tübingen: Mohr Siebeck, 2007), 253–59.

62. *BSLK*, 523–27; BC, 365–67.

63. *BSLK*, 528–41; BC, 367–75.

64. *BSLK*, 517; BC, 360.

4. The Augsburg Confession

1. Lamin Sanneh, *Translating the Message: The Missionary Impact on Culture*, 2nd ed. (Maryknoll: Orbis, 2008).

2. WADB 6 and 7.

3. WA 19:72–113; LW 53: 61–90.

4. WA 12:205–20; LW 53: 19–40.

5. Hendrix, *Recultivating the Vineyard*, 1–35.

6. WA 6:497–573; LW 36:11–126.

7. Gerhard Müller, *Die römische Kurie und die Reformation, 1523–1534: Kirche und Politik während des Pontifikates Clemens' VII* (Gütersloh: Mohn, 1969).

8. WA 26: 195–240; LW 40: 269–320.

9. WA 26: 499–509; LW 37: 360–72.

10. WA 30,3:172, text 178–82: *Die bekentnus Martini Luthers auff den jezigen angestelten Reichstag zu Augspurgk eynzulegen* (printed 1530); translated in *Sources and Contexts*, 83–87.

11. On Zwingli's debt to Scotist realism, see Daniel Bolliger, *Infiniti contemplatio: Grundzüge der Scotus- und Scotismusrezeption im Werk Huldrych Zwinglis* (Leiden: Brill, 2003).

12. WA 30,3: 91–244; Sasse, *This Is My Body*.

13. WABr 12:35–45.

14. Mark U. Edwards Jr., *Luther's Last Battles: Politics and Polemics 1531–1546* (Ithaca: Cornel University Press, 1983), 20–37; W. J. D. Cargill Thompson, "Luther and the Right of Resistance to the Emperor," *Studies in Church History*, ed. Derek Baker (Oxford: Blackwell, 1975), 159–202.

15. Gottfried Krodel, "Law, Order, and the Almighty Taler: The Empire in Action at the 1530 Diet of Augsburg," *SCJ* 13,2 (1982): 75–106. On the efforts of Evangelical governments in the Reichstag in the 1520s, see Armin Kohnle, *Reichstag und Reformation: Kaiserliche und ständische Religionspolitik von den Anfängen der Causa Lutheri bis zum Nürnberger Religionsfrieden*, QFRG 72 (Gütersloh: Gütersloher, 2001).

16. Karl E. Förstemann, *Urkundenbuch zu der Geschichte des Reichtages zu Augsburg im Jahre 1530* (Halle: Waisenhauses, 1833, 1835), 1:8.

17. See Wenz, *Theologie der Bekenntnisschriften*, 1:419–429.

18. *BSLK* 61; BC 43. See Charles P. Arand, "The Apology as a Backdrop for the Interim of 1548," in *Politik und Bekenntnis: Die Reaktionen auf das Interim von 1548*, ed. Irene Dingel and Günther Wartenberg, LStRLO 8 (Leipzig: Evangelische Verlagsanstalt, 2007), 211–27.

19. WA 31,1: 65–182, 30,2: 268–356; LW 14:43–106, 34: 9–61.

20. See page 3 of this volume. For the original Latin text, see Johann Eck, *Articulos 404*. English translation in *Sources and Contexts*, 33–82. See Gerhard Müller, "Johann Eck und die Confessio Augustana," *Quellen und Forschungen aus italienischen Archiven und Bibliotheken* 38 (1958): 205–42.

21. On the context for these condemnations, see Hans Werner Gensichen, *We Condemn: How Luther and Sixteenth-Century Lutheranism Condemned False Doctrine*, trans. Herbert J. A. Bouman (St. Louis: Concordia, 1967).

22. Along with Wenz, *Theologie der Bekenntnisschriften*, 1:349–487 (with ample bibliography of earlier relevant publications), basic introductions to the Augsburg Confession include: Leif Grane, *The Augsburg Confession: A Commentary*, trans. John H. Rasmussen (Minneapolis: Augsburg, 1987), and Regin Prenter, *Das Bekenntnis von Augsburg: Eine Auslegung* (Erlangen: Martin-Luther, 1980). Old standard works are also useful: Förstemann, *Urkundenbuch*; Wilhelm Gußmann, *Die Ratschläge der evangelischen Reichsstände zum Reichstag von Augsburg 1530*, 2 vols. (Leipzig: Teubner, 1911). The four-hundred-fiftieth anniversary of the Confession elicited a number of studies, particularly volumes of essays: *Das Augsburger Bekenntnis in drei Jahrhunderten 1530–1630–1730*, ed. Horst Jesse (Stuttgart: Kaiser, 1980); *Das Augsburger Bekenntnis von 1530 damals und heute*, ed. Bernhard Lohse and Otto Hermann Pesch (Munich: Kaiser, 1980); *Confessing One Faith: A Joint Commentary on the Augsburg Confession by Lutheran and Catholic Theologians*, ed. George W. Forell and James McCue (Minneapolis: Fortress Press, 1982); *Confessio Augustana 1530–1580, Commemoration and Self-Examination*, ed. Vilmos Vajta, trans. David Lewis (Tübingen: Mohr Siebeck, 1980); *Die Confessio Augustana im ökumenischen Gespräch*, ed. Fritz Hoffmann and Ulrich Kühn (Berlin: Evangelische Verlagsanstalt, 1980); *Confessio Augustana und Confutatio: Der Augsburger Reichstag 1530 und die Einheit der Kirche*, ed. Erwin Iserloh (Münster: Aschendorff, 1980); *Bekenntnis und Geschichte: Die Confessio Augustana im historischen Zusammenhang*, ed. Wolfgang Reinhard (Munich: Vögel, 1981); *Kirche und Bekenntnis: Historische und theologische Aspekte zur Frage der gegenseitigen Anerkennung der lutherischen und der katholischen Kirche auf der Grundlage der Confessio Augustana*, ed. Peter Meinold (Wiesbaden: Steiner, 1980); *The Role of the Augsburg Confession: Catholic and Lutheran Views*, ed. Joseph A. Burgess and George Lindbeck (Philadelphia: Fortress Press, 1980). Wilhelm H. Neuser, *Bibliographie der Confessio Augustana und Apologie, 1530–1580* (Nieuwkoop: de Graaf, 1987).

See also a variety of more specifically oriented studies: Bernd Moeller, "Augustana Studien," *ARG* 57 (1966): 76–95; H. Neuhaus, "Der Augsburger Reichstag des Jahres

1530: Ein Forschungsbericht," *Zeitschrift für historische Forschung* 9 (1982): 167–211; Eugéne Honée, *Der Libell des Hieronymus Vehus zum Augsburger Reichstag 1530* (Münster: Aschendorff, 1988); *Vermittlungsversuche auf dem Augsburger Reichstag 1530. Melanchthon–Brenz–Vehus*, ed. Rolf Decot (Stuttgart: Steiner, 1989). A number of essays by Gerhard Müller on the Augsburg Confession are gathered in *Causa Reformationis: Beiträge zur Reformationsgeschichte und zur Theologie Martin Luthers*, ed. Gottfried Maron and Gottfried Seebass (Gütersloh: Mohn, 1989).

23. Wilhelm Maurer, *Historischer Kommentar zur Confessio Augustana*, 2 vols. (Gütersloh: Mohn, 1976, 1978); translated as *Historical Commentary on the Augsburg Confession*, trans. H. George Anderson (Philadelphia: Fortress Press, 1986). Maurer's work must be read in light of more recent treatments, see Wenz, *Theologie der Bekenntnisschriften*, 1:349–486.

24. WABr 5:319, §1568.

25. Maurer, *Historical Commentary on the Augsburg Confession*, 12.

26. Jacob und Wilhelm Grimm, *Deutsches Wörterbuch*, 6, ed. Moriz Heyne (Leipzig: Hirzel, 1885), 719–720.

27. WABr 5:435, §1621, 5:479–480, §1648, 5:498–499, §1659, 516–517, §1668.

28. See Volker Leppin, "Text, Kontext und Subtext: Eine Lektüre von Luthers Coburgbriefen," in *Martin Luther: Biographie und Theologie*, ed. Dietrich Korsch and Volker Leppin, SMHR 53 (Tübingen: Mohr Siebeck, 2010), 169–88; cf. Dietrich Korsch, "'Sic sum': Der Theologe Martin Luther auf der Veste Coburg 1530," ibid., 183–94.

29. WABr 5:496, §1657.

30. See Kolb, *Bound Choice*, 81–82.

31. Wengert, *Human Freedom*, 80–109 While Melanchthon's later emphasis on human responsibility led him to focus more on the exercise of the human will than he had earlier, it did not diminish his opposition to Erasmus; see Kolb, *Bound Choice*, 70–102.

32. BSLK 44–49; BC 30–35. See Wenz, *Theologie der Bekenntnisschriften*, 455–70.

33. Wenz, *Theologie der Bekenntnisschriften*, 1:389.

5. The Apology of the Augsburg Confession

1. Christian Peters, *Apologia Confessionis Augustanae: Untersuchungen zur Textgeschichte einer lutherischen Bekenntnisschrift, 1530–1584* (Stuttgart: Calwer, 1997), 390–497.

2. Peters, *Apologia Confessionis Augustana*, 485–97, argues that Luther's Galatians commentary of 1531 stands much closer to Melanchthon's argument in the Apology than earlier scholars recognized. Bengt Hägglund objected to this earlier interpretation already in 1980, "Melanchthon versus Luther: The Contemporary Struggle," *Concordia Theological Quarterly* 44 (1980): 123–33. For an overview of their relationship in general, see Wengert, "Melanchthon and Luther," and Helmar Junghans, "Das Theologieverständnis von Martin Luther und Philipp Melanchthon," in *Dona Melanchthoniana: Festgabe für Heinz Scheible*, ed. Johanna Loehr (Stuttgart-Bad Cannstatt: Fromann-Holzboog, 2001), 193–210. See also Junghans's survey of the literature prepared for the Melanchthon Jubilaeum, 1997, "Das Melanchthonjubiläum 1997," LuJ 67 (2000):95–162, and LuJ 70 (2003):175–214.

3. See Irene Dingel, "The Culture of Conflict in the Controversies Leading to the Formula of Concord (1548–1580), in *Lutheran Ecclesiastical Culture, 1550–1675*, ed. Robert Kolb (Leiden: Brill, 2008), 15–28, and Irene Dingel, "Pruning the Vines, Plowing

Up the Vineyard: The Sixteenth-Century Culture of Controversy between Disputation and Polemic" (forthcoming).

4. See Luther's account, WA 2:6–26; LW 31:259–292. Their encounter led Cajetan to write the most authoritative treatment of the church's teaching on indulgences to date, see Bernhard A. R. Felmberg, *Die Ablasstheologie Kardinal Cajetans (1469–1534)* (Leiden: Brill, 1998).

5. On Eck and the subsequent figures discussed here, see David V. N. Bagchi, *Luther's Earliest Opponents, Catholic Controversialists, 1518–1525* (Minneapolis: Fortress Press, 1991).

6. *Commentaria De Actis et Scriptis Martini Luther* (Mainz, 1549) = *Luther's Lives,* trans. E. Vandiver et al. (Manchester: Manchester University Press, 2002).

7. Heiko Augustinus Oberman, *The Harvest of Medieval Theology: Gabriel Biel and Late Medieval Nominalism* (Durham: Labyrinth, 1983).

8. For example, on Luther's mentor Johannes Staupitz, see David C. Steinmetz, *Luther and Staupitz,* (Durham: Duke University Press, 1980), 9–16, 97–108; and Bernd Hamm, *Frömmigkeitstheologie am Anfang des 16. Jahrhunderts: Studien zu Johannes von Paltz und seinem Umkreis* (Tübingen: Mohr Siebeck, 1982), 45–58. On Luther's own use of Thomas Aquinas and his followers in relation to his own Ockhamistic orientation, see Denis Janz, *Luther and Late Medieval Thomism* (Waterloo: Wilfrid Laurier University Press, 1983), and Janz, *Luther on Thomas Aquinas: The Angelic Doctor in the Thought of the Reformer* (Stuttgart: Steiner, 1989).

9. Irmgard Höss, *Georg Spalatin, 1484–1545: Ein Leben in der Zeit des Humanismus und der Reformation* (Weimar: Böhlau, 1989).

10. *Justus Jonas (1493–1555) und seine Bedeutung für die Wittenberger Reformation,* ed. Irene Dingel, LStRLO 11 (Leipzig: Evangelische Verlagsanstalt, 2009).

11. WA 31,1: 65–182; 50:440–60.

12. See the treatment of Luther's statements concerning Melanchthon's *leise treten* on page 100 of this volume.

13. On the Confessio Augustana Variata, see pages 174–75 of this volume.

14. Timothy J. Wengert, "Philip Melanchthon's 1557 Lecture on Colossians 3:1–2," in Irene Dingel, Nicole Kuropka, Timothy J. Wengert, and Robert Kolb, *Philip Melanchthon in Classroom, Confession, and Controversy* (forthcoming).

15. Johannes Hund, *Das Wort ward Fleisch: Eine systematisch-theologische Untersuchung zur Debatte um die Wittenberger Christologie und Abendmahlslehre in den Jahren 1567 bis 1574,* FSÖTH 114 (Göttingen: Vandenhoeck & Ruprecht, 2006), 66–87; Ralph W. Quere, *Christum Cognoscere: Christ's Efficacious Presence in the Eucharistic Theology of Melanchthon* (Nieuwkoop: de Graaf, 1977).

16. Kolb, *Bound Choice,* 31–102.

17. WA 7: 3–38 (German), 42–73 (Latin); LW 31: 333–37 (based on the Latin text).

18. WA 39,1: 82–126; LW 34: 151–196. This work remained unpublished during his lifetime.

19. On Luther's and Melanchthon's references to an "apology" by Luther, see Peters, *Apologia Confessionis Augustanae,* 390–421.

20. Maurer, *Historical Commentary,* 24–26.

21. On Ritschl's use and interpretation of Luther in general, see David Lotz, *Ritschl and Luther: A Fresh Perspective on Albrecht Ritschl's Theology in the Light of His Luther Study* (Nashville, Abingdon, 1974).

22. A good overview of the "Luther Renaissance" is found in James Stayer, *Martin Luther, German Saviour: German Evangelical Theological Factions and the Interpretation of Luther, 1917–1933* (Montreal: McGill-Queens University Press, 2000).

23. Grane, *Augsburg Confession*, chapter 6.

24. See, e.g., Reinhard Flogaus, "Luther versus Melanchthon? Zur Frage der Einheit der Wittenberger Reformation in der Rechtfertigungslehre," *ARG* 91 (2000): 6–46.

25. Forde, *Justification by Faith: A Matter of Death and Life* (Philadelphia: Fortress Press, 1983), 36; cf. Oswald Bayer, *Aus dem Glauben leben: Über Rechtfertigung und Heiligung* (Stuttgart: Calwer, 1984), 41; and Jörg Baur, *Salus Christiana: Die Rechtfertigungslehre in der Geschichte des christlichen Heilsverständnisses*, Band 1 (Gütersloh: Mohn, 1968), 61–63.

26. Galatians lectures, 1531, WA 40,1:45,24–27; LW 26:7.

27. Charles P. Arand, "Two Kinds of Righteousness as a Framework for Law and Gospel in the Apology," *LQ* 15 (2001): 417–39; cf. Kolb and Arand, *The Genius of Luther's Theology*, 21–128.

28. On the synergistic controversy of the 1550s and 1560s, see pages 201–11 of this volume.

29. Kolb, *Bound Choice*, 81–102.

30. Wengert, *Law and Gospel*, 177–210.

31. See Kolb, *Bound Choice*, 70–102.

32. Wengert, *Law and Gospel*, 200–4. On his negotiations with the French, see also Irene Dingel, "Melanchthon und Westeuropa," in *Philipp Melanchthon als Politiker zwischen Reich, Reichsständen und Konfessionsparteien*, ed Günther Wartenberg and Matthias Zenter (Wittenberg: Drei Kastanien, 1998), 107–15.

33. Forde, *Law and Gospel*, 189.

34. Wengert, *Law and Gospel*, 178. Cf. Robert Kolb's presentation of how the difference of opinions of the 1530s and 1540s between Nikolaus von Amsdorf and Melanchthon foreshadowed those within the Wittenberg circle in the 1550s and 1560s: *Nikolaus von Amsdorf (1483–1565), Popular Polemics in the Preservation of Luther's Legacy* (Nieuwkoop: de Graaf, 1978), 49–59.

35. WA 7:463–537.

36. Peter Fraenkel, "Revelation and Tradition, Notes on Some Aspects of Doctrinal Continuity in the Theology of Philip Melanchthon," *Studia theologica* 13·(1959): 97–133.

37. For a modern application of Luther's and Melanchthon's concept of confession as proclamation "for you," see Forde, *Theology Is for Proclamation*.

38. Estes, *Peace, Order*.

39. WABr 5: 496,7–9.

40. WABr 5: 458–59.

41. On the work to prepare the Confutation, see Peters, *Apologia*, 118–33; Wenz, *Theologie der Bekenntnisschriften*, 1:399–409.

42. *Die Confutatio der Confessio Augustana vom 3. August 1530*, ed. Herbert Immenkötter (Münster: Aschendorff, 1979). See also CR, 27:82–184; translated in *Sources and Contexts*, 106–39.

43. Bagchi, *Luther's Earliest Opponents*, 176.

44. On Melanchthon's understanding of the relationship between ritual and doctrine, particularly the doctrine of justification by faith in Christ, see Arand, "Apology as a Backdrop," 211–27.

45. WABr 5:598,20–22; CR, 2:328.

46. Wenz, *Theologie der Bekenntnisschriften*, 1:412–14.

47. Gottfried Seebass, *Das reformatorische Werk des Andreas Osiander* (Nuremberg: Verein für Bayerische Kirchengeschichte, 1967), 141–43. See pages 217–26 of this volume.

48. Frederick Bente, *Historical Introduction to the Book of Concord* (St. Louis: Concordia, 1965), 41–42. Bente cites Christian August Salig, *Vollständige Historie der Augspurgischen Confession und derselben Apologie*, I (Halle: Renger, 1730), 377.

49. WATr 2:541,8–9, §2606b.

50. Peters, *Apologia Confessionis Augustanae*, 390–497.

51. Jonas's text is given in the German column of the *BSLK* edition of the Apology, *BSLK* 145–404. Jonas used the first edition for the first two articles and then began to use the second edition when it appeared.

52. Letters to Joachim Camerarius, January 1, 1531, CR, 2:470, MBWR, 2:15, §1111; Johannes Brenz, ca. February 1531, CR, 2:484, MBWR, 2:24, §1132; to Martin Bucer, May 1531, CR, 2:498, MBWR §1154.

53. Charles P. Arand, "The Apology as Polemical Commentary," in *Philip Melanchthon (1497-1560) and the Commentary*, ed. Timothy J. Wengert and M. Patrick Graham (Sheffield: Sheffield Academic, 1997), 174–91; see Arand, "Melanchthon's Rhetorical Composition of the Apology," in *Hermeneutica Sacra: Studien zur Auslegung der Heiligen Schrift im 16.- und 17. Jahrhundert*, ed. Torbjörn Johansson, Robert Kolb, and Johann Anselm Steiger (Berlin: de Gruyter, 2010), 165–88.

54. Melanchthon, *Elementa Rhetorices*, CR, 13:429.

55. *BSLK*, 56; BC, 38/40.

56. Charles P. Arand, "Melanchthon's Rhetorical Argument for the Sola Fide in the Apology," *LQ* 14 (2000): 281–308.

57. Arand, "Polemical Commentary," 178.

58. CA Part I, conclusion 1; *BSLK*, 83c; BC 58/59.

59. Ap II, 2, 15, 50; VII, 7: *BSLK*, 146, 150, 157; BC, 112, 114, 120.

60. Ap IV, 357; XII,22, 119; XV, 15, 18; XVI, 8; XXI, 13, 43; XXIII, 23, 25, 67; XXIV, 41, 63; XXVII, 29

61. Peter Fraenkel, *Testimonia Patrum: The Function of the Patristic Argument in the Theology of Philip Melanchthon* (Geneva: Droz, 1961), 22–23; Timothy J. Wengert, "Philip Melanchthon and Augustine of Hippo" *LQ* 22 (2008): 249–67.

62. Scott H. Hendrix, "Deparentifying the Fathers: The Reformers and Patristic Authority," in *Auctoritas Patrum. Zur Rezeption der Kirchenväter im 15. und 16. Jahrundert*, ed. Leif Grane et al., VIEG Religionsgeschichte 37 (Mainz: Zabert, 1993), 55-68.

63. Bente, *Historical Introduction*, 45, citing Salig, *Vollständige Historie*, 1:377.

64. CR, 2:494, MBWR, 2:28, §1143.

65. Arand, "Polemical Commentary," 173.

66. See Arand, "Apology as a Polemical Commentary," 171–91.

67. Charles P. Arand, "Melanchthon's Rhetorical Argument," 281–308.

68. Charles P. Arand, "Two Kinds," 417–39; Kolb and Arand, *The Genius of Luther's Theology*, 29–128.

69. Robert Kolb, "God Calling, 'Take Care of My People': Luther's Concept of Vocation in the Augsburg Confession and Its Apology," *Concordia Journal* 8 (1982): 4–11.

70. *BSLK*, 560–63; BC, 386–388.

71. Forde, *Justification by Faith*, 36.

72. See the translation in BC, 129, at §58.

73. Arand, "The Apology as a Backdrop."

74. *BSLK*, 516–17; BC, 360.

75. *BSLK*, 438–49; BC, 313–19, and "The Antinomian Disputations," WA 39,1: 342–584.

76. See page 201 of this volume.

6. The Smalcald Articles and the Treatise on the Power and Primacy of the Pope

1. See Eike Wolgast, *Die Wittenberger Theologie und die Politik der evangelischen Stände: Studien zu Luthers Gutachten in politischen Fragen*, QFRG 47 (Gütersloh: Mohn, 1977).

2. Dingel, "Melanchthon und Westeuropa."

3. On current debate over the degree to which Calvin shared Luther's perceptions of natural law and civil society, see David van Drunen, *Natural Law and the Two Kingdoms: A Study in the Development of Reformed Social Thought* (Grand Rapids: Eerdmans, 2010).

4. Estes, *Peace, Order*, 7–52.

5. *BSLK*, 61; BC 42–43. See Robert Kolb, "The Sheep and the Voice of the Shepherd: The Ecclesiology of the Lutheran Confessions" *Concordia Journal* 36 (2010):324–41.

6. W. J. D. Cargill Thompson, *The Political Thought of Martin Luther* (Sussex: Harvester, 1984), 155–62.

7. Hubert Jedin, *A History of the Council of Trent*, trans. Ernest Graf, 1 (St. Louis: Herder, 1957): 160–354.

8. H. G. Haile, *Luther: An Experiment in Biography* (New York: Doubleday, 1980), 7–29. Cf. Ernst Bizer, "Die Wittenberger Theologen und das Konzil 1537," *ARG* 47 (1956): 77–101; Eike Wolgast, "Das Konzil in der Erwartung der kursächsischen Theologen und Politiker 1533–1537," *ARG* 73 (1982): 122–52.

9. Jedin, *History of Trent*, 1:310–312; cf. *Concilium Tridentinum, Diariorum, Actorum, Epistolarum, Tractatuum Nova Collectio* 4 (Freiburg: Herder, 1964), 4–6.

10. Haile, *Luther*, 208–221.

11. The Smalcald Articles have been a sort of neglected child in confessional studies. See Wenz, *Theologie der Bekenntnisschriften*, 1:499–549; the introduction to the text of the Smalcald Articles in WA 50:160–91, by O. Reichert and O. Brenner. See the larger studies of Werner Führer, *Die Schmalkaldischen Artickel* (Tübingen: Mohr Siebeck, 2009), and of William R. Russell, *The Schmalkald Articles: Luther's Theological Testament* (Minneapolis: Fortress Press, 1994), reflecting his articles: "The Smalcald Articles, Luther's Theological Testament," *LQ* 5 (1981): 277–96, "A Theological Guide to the Smalcald Articles," *LQ* 5 (1981): 469–92, and "A Neglected Key to the Theology of Martin Luther: The Smalcald Articles," *Word and World* 16 (1996): 84–90. Other studies include Franz Lau, "Luthers Schmalkaldische Artikel als seine Einführung in seine Theologie," *Zeitschrift für Theologie und* Kirche 18 (1937): 289–307; Carl Stange, "Die Schmalkaldischen Artikel Luthers," *Zeitschrift für systematische Theologie* 14 (1937): 416–64; Johannes Stier, *Luthers Glaube und Theologie in den Schmalkaldischen Artikeln* (Gütersloh: Bertelsmann, 1937); Hans Volz, *Luthers Schmalkaldische Artikel und Melanchthons Tractatus de potestate papae, Ihre Geschichte von der Entstehung bis zum Ende des 16. Jahrhunderts* (Gotha: Klotz, 1931), which was subject to the critique of Ernst Bizer, in "Zum geschichtlichen Verständnis von

Luthers Schmalkaldischen Artikeln," *ZKG 67* (1955–56):61–92, to which Volz replied in "Luthers Schmalkaldische Artikel," *ZKG 68* (1957): 259–86, to which Bizer in turn replied, "Nocheinmal: Die Schmalkaldischen Artikel," *ZKG 68* (1957): 287–94; cf. also his "Zur Entstehungsgeschichte von Luthers Schmalkaldischen Artikel," *ZKG 74* (1963): 316–20; Robert Kolb, "Luther's Smalcald Articles: Agenda for Testimony and Confession," *Concordia Journal* 14 (1988): 115–37. Volz also compiled relevant primary source material in *Urkunden und Aktenstücke zur Geschichte von Martin Luthers Schmalkaldischen Artikeln, 1536–1574* (Berlin: de Gruyter, 1957). On the Roman Catholic response to the Smalcald Articles, see Hans Volz, *Drei Schriften gegen Luthers Schmalkaldische Artikel von Cochlaus, Witzel und Hoffmeister, 1538–1539,* CCath 18 (Münster: Aschendorff, 1932).

12. WA 26:261–509; LW 37:161–372. The third part, Luther's personal confession, is found in WA 26:499–509; LW 37:360–72.

13. In his work William Russell has emphasized this explanation of the motives for composing the Smalcald Articles.

14. *BSLK,* 409–10; BC, 297–98.

15. Führer reviews the case for both points of view effectively, *Die Schmalkaldischen Artikel,* 7–25.

16. *BSLK,* 438; BC, 313.

17. Führer, *Die Schmalkaldischen Artikel,* 73–87.

18. Ibid., 88–177.

19. Ibid., 178–401.

20. Ibid., 73–401.

21. The most recent study of Karlstadt that provides bibliography and a good introduction is Amy Nelson Burnett, *Karlstadt and the Origins of the Eucharistic Controversy: A Study in the Circulation of Ideas* (Oxford: Oxford University Press, 2011). See also English translations of relevant sources in *The Eucharistic Pamphlets of Andreas Bodenstein von Karlstadt,* trans. and ed. Amy Nelson Burnett (Kirksville: Truman State University Press, 2011).

22. George Hunston Williams, *The Radical Reformation,* 3rd ed. (Kirksville: Sixteenth Century Journal, 1992). Cf. pages 270–71 of this volume.

23. Ronald A. Knox, *Enthusiasm: A Chapter in the History of Religion, with Special Reference to the Seventeenth and Eighteenth Centuries* (Oxford: Clarendon, 1950).

24. *BSLK,* 453–54; BC, 322.

25. *BSLK,* 454; BC, 322.

26. Führer, *Die Schmalkaldischen Artikel,* 51–59.

27. Ibid., 402–16.

28. Scott H. Hendrix, *Luther and the Papacy: Stages in a Reformation Conflict* (Philadelphia: Fortress Press, 1981).

29. Hans Preuss, *Die Vorstellungen vom Antichrist im späteren Mittelalter, bei Luther und in der konfessionellen Polemik* (Leipzig, 1906).

30. These additions are placed in italics in BC.

31. *BSLK,* 408; BC, 297.

32. *BSLK,* 411; BC, 298–99.

33. *Open Letter to the German Nobility,* WA 6:415,19–469,17; LW 44:139–217. Cf. similar admonitions to governments in *On Good Works,* WA 6:242,20–245,18; LW 44:95–97.

34. *BSLK,* 412; BC, 299.

35. Führer, *Die Schmalkaldischen Artikel,* 432.

7. Theological Tensions among Luther's Followers before His Death

1. See, for example, Mark U. Edwards Jr., *Printing, Propaganda, and Martin Luther* (Berkeley, Los Angeles, London: University of California Press, 1994).

2. For example, in the title of Helmut Gollwitzer's *Coena Domini: Die altlutherische Abendmahlslehre in ihrer Auseinandersetzung mit dem Calvinismus dargestellt an der lutherischen Frühorthodoxie* (Munich: Kaiser, 1937).

3. Peter Barton, *Um Luthers Erbe, Studien und Texte zur Spätreformation, Tilemann Heshusius, 1527–1559* (Witten: Luther, 1972), 7–18. The suggestion that the Reformation came to an end in the struggle of the Magdeburg city council and ministerium against the imperial enforcement of the Augsburg Interim and the electoral Saxon religious policy labeled the Leipzig Interim by its foes—see Thomas Kaufmann, *Das Ende der Reformation: Magdeburgs "Herrgotts Kanzlei," 1548–1551/2,* BHTh 123 (Tübingen: Mohr Siebeck, 2003)—cannot be sustained in view either of the stance of the Magdeburg ministerium on which Kaufmann focuses or of the views of the wider spectrum of the Wittenberg circle, which he does not treat (for example, the parallel and somewhat coordinated campaign of the Lower Saxon cities of Hamburg, Lüneburg, and Lübeck, against the Leipzig "Interim").

4. Much of the discussion of this topic and wider bibliography on it can be found in the titles listed in the Introduction, note 26, pages 284–285, of this volume.

5. "Die Konfessionalisierung im Reich, Religiöser und gesellschaftlicher Wandel in Deutschland zwischen 1555 und 1620," *Historische Zeitschrift* 246 (1988): 6, 1–45, esp. 6 and 30; in English translation, "Confessionalization in the Empire, Religious and Societal Change in Germany between 1555 and 1620," in Heinz Schilling, *Religion, Political Culture, and the Emergence of Early Modern Society* (Leiden: Brill, 1992), 205–45.

6. On the use of the term *Konfession,* see Introduction, note 25 above.

7. Here I am particularly indebted to Irene Dingel, "The Culture of Conflict in the Controversies Leading to the Formula of Concord, 1548–1580," in *Lutheran Ecclesistical Culture, 1550–1675,* ed. Robert Kolb (Leiden: Brill, 2008), 16–18.

8. Hans Werner Gensichen, *We Condemn: How Luther and Sixteenth-Century Lutheranism Condemned False Doctrine,* trans. Herbert J. A. Bouman (St. Louis: Concordia, 1967).

9. On "pure doctrine" among Lutheran reformers, see Theodore Mahlmann, "*Doctrina* im Verständnis nachreformatorischer lutherischer Theologen," in *Vera Doctrina: Zur Begriffsgeschichte der Lehre von Augustin bis Descartes,* ed. Philippe Büttgen et al. (Wiesbaden: Harrasowitz, 2009), 199–264.

10. Irene Dingel, "Bekenntnis und Geschichte: Funktion und Entwicklung des reformatorischen Bekenntnisses im 16. Jahrhundert," in *Dona Melanchthoniana: Festgabe für Heinz Scheible zum 70. Geburtstag,* ed. Johanna Loehr (Stuttgart: Frommann-Holzboog, 2001), 61–81.

11. While lecturing at Concordia Seminary, St. Louis, March 30, 1973.

12. Volker Leppin, *Antichrist und Jüngster Tag: Das Profil apokalyptischer Flugschriftenpublizistik im deutschen Luthertum 1548–1618,* QFRG 69 (Gütersloh: Gütersloher, 1999).

13. With the dawning of new historical interests and standards in the eighteenth century, a number of historical studies appeared in print. Their attention to documentary evidence makes them helpful sources for work on the period of the Late Reformation to this day. The earliest attempts at historical coverage of the period leading to the Formula of Concord include Christian August Salig, *Vollständige Historie der Augspurgischen Confession und derselben Apologie*, vols. I–III (Halle: Renger, 1730–1733); Johann Georg Walch, *Historische und Theologische Einleitung in die Religions-Streitigkeiten der Evangelisch-Lutherischen Kirche von der Reformation an bis auf letzige Zeiten*, vols. I–IV (Jena: Mezer, 1733–1739); and Gottlieb Jacob Planck, *Geschichte der Entstehung, der Veränderungen und der Bildung unseres protestantischen Lehrbegriffs vom Anfang der Reformation bis zur Einführung der Konkordienformel* vols. IV–VI (Leipzig: Crusius, 1796–1800). Gunther Wenz offers a good introduction to these works and others, Wenz, *Theologie der Bekenntnisschriften*.

Nineteenth- and twentieth-century scholars have produced a variety of general treatments of the period as well as specific treatments of the historical background of the Formula of Concord, and/or the wider context of the period. Among others, they include the masterful work of the Lutheran theologian Fr. H. R. Frank, *Die Theologie der Concordienformel, historisch-dogmatisch entwickelt und beleuchtet*, vols. I–IV, (Erlangen 1858–1865); as well as volumes by Heinrich Heppe, Reformed defender of his own interpretation of the course of Calvinism in the German lands, *Geschichte der deutschen Protestantismus in den Jahren 1555–1581*, vols. I–IV (Marburg, 1852–1859); Wilhelm Preger, *Matthias Flacius Illyricus* (Erlangen: Blaesing, 1859–1861); Otto Ritschl, *Dogmengeschichte des Protestantismus: Grundlage und Grundzüge der theologischen Gedanken- und Lehrbildung in den protestantischen Kirchen*, vols. I–IV, (Leipzig: Hinrichs, 1908–1927); Paul Tschackert, *Die Entstehung der lutherischen und der reformierten Kirchenlehre samt ihren innterprotestantischen Gegensätzen*, 1919 (Göttingen: Vandenhoeck & Ruprecht, 1979); Hans Leube, *Kalvinismus und Luthertum im Zeitalter der Orthodoxie* (Aalen: Scientia, 1966); and Leube, *Orthodoxie und Pietismus: Gesammelte Studien* (Bielefeld: Luther, 1975); Hans Emil Weber, *Reformation, Orthodoxie und Rationalismus*, Part I–II, (Gütersloh: Mohn, 1937–1951); and Ernst W. Zeeden, *Die Entstehung der Konfessionen: Grundlagen und Formen der Konfessionsbildung im Zeitalter der Glaubenskämpfe* (Munich: Oldenbourg, 1964). This scholarship has culminated in Gunther Wenz's *Theologie der Bekenntnisschriften*.

In English the overviews of the period include studies by George J. Fritschel, *The Formula of Concord: Its Origin and Contents* (Philadelphia: Lutheran Publication Society, 1916); F. Bente, *Historical Introductions to the Symbolical Books of the Evangelical Lutheran Church* (St. Louis: Concordia, 1921); and Eric W. Gritsch and Robert W. Jenson, *Lutheranism: The Theological Movement and Its Confessional Writings* (Philadelphia: Fortress Press, 1976).

The anniversaries of the Formula of Concord and the Book of Concord in 1977 and 1980 produced a number of volumes of collected essays. They include *Bekenntnis und Einheit der Kirche: Studien zum Konkordienbuch*, ed. Martin Brecht and Reinhard Schwarz (Stuttgart: Calwer, 1980); *Bekenntnis zur Wahrheit: Aufsätze über die Konkordienformel*, ed. Jobst Schöne (Erlangen: Martin-Luther, 1978); *Discord, Dialogue and Concord: Studies in the Lutheran Reformation's Formula of Concord*, ed. by Lewis W. Spitz and Wenzel Lohff, (Philadelphia: Fortress Press, 1977); *The Formula of Concord, Quadricentennial Essays*, SCJ VIII,4 (1977); *Vom Dissensus zum Konsensus: Die*

Formula Concordiae von 1577 (Hamburg: Lutherisches, 1980); *Widerspruch, Dialog und Einigung: Studien zur Konkordienformel der Lutherischen Reformation*, ed. Wenzel Lohff and Lewis W. Spitz (Stuttgart: Calwer, 1977).

A brief overview of the topic of this section that has appeared recently is Irene Dingel, "Culture of Conflict," 15–64. In addition, though it is dangerous to pick out a few from several excellent monograph studies or collections of essays, the following are commended to readers: Harry Oelke, *Die Konfessionsbildung des 16. Jahrhunderts im Spiegel illustrierter Flugblätter* (Berlin: de Gruyter, 1992); and *Melanchthon in seinen Schülern*, ed. Heinz Scheible (Wiesbaden: Harrassowitz, 1997). See also Robert Kolb, *Luther's Heirs Define His Legacy: Studies on Lutheran Confessionalization* (Aldershot: Variorum, 1996). For a specifically practice-oriented assessment of the Formula of Concord, see Timothy J. Wengert, *A Formula for Parish Practice* (Grand Rapids: Eerdmans, 2006).

Of special significance is a research project that has constructed an online bibliographical and biographical resource for primary sources for the study of this period and is also editing selected documents that played key roles in the controversies leading to the Formula of Concord. The project and series of volumes, which contain well-edited documents that played a prominent role in the controversies, is called *Controversia et Confessio: Theologische Kontroversen 1548–1577/80, Kritische Auswahledition* and is being conducted under the direction of Irene Dingel, a member of the Academy of Sciences and Literature of Mainz, professor of church history and the history of dogma on the faculty of evangelical theology at the Johannes-Gutenberg University, and director of the Institute for European History (Department for Western Church History), under the auspices of the Academy, in cooperation with the Johannes Gutenberg University and the Institute of European History. The first three of eight volumes of texts from the period have appeared.

14. See Dingel, "Bekenntnis und Geschichte." Cf. Robert Kolb, *Martin Luther as Prophet, Teacher, and Hero: Images of the Reformer, 1520–1620* (Grand Rapids: Baker, 1999), 39–65.

15. *BSLK*, 4; BC, 5–6.

16. Studies of the relationship between the two Wittenberg reformers abound. See Timothy J. Wengert, "Melanchthon and Luther/Luther and Melanchthon" *LuJ* 66 (1999): 55–88; Lowell C. Green, *How Melanchthon Helped Luther Discover the Gospel* (Fallbrook: Verdict, 1980); and Martin Greschat, *Melanchthon neben Luther: Studien zur Gestalt der Rechtfertigungslehre zwischen 1528 und 1537* (Witten: Luther, 1965).

17. Robert Kolb, *Martin Luther: Confessor of the Faith* (Oxford: Oxford University Press, 2009), 42–71; Robert Kolb and Charles P. Arand, *The Genius of Luther's Theology: A Wittenberg Way of Thinking for the Contemporary Church* (Grand Rapids: Baker, 2008), 21–128, 148–59, 175–79.

18. On various aspects of the entire Agricolan controversy, see Timothy J. Wengert, *Law and Gospel: Philip Melanchthon's Debate with Johann Agricola of Eisleben over Poenitentia* (Grand Rapids: Baker, 1997); and also Joachim Rogge, *Johann Agricolas Lutherverständnis* (Berlin: Evangelische Verlagsanstalt, 1960), Steffan Kjellgaard-Pedersen, *Gesetz, Evangelium und Busse: Theologiegeschichtliche Studien zum Verhältnis zwischen dem jungen Johann Agricola (Eisleben) und Martin Luther* (Leiden: Brill, 1983); Ernst Koch, "Johann Agricola neben Luther: Schülerschaft und theologische Eigenart," in *Lutheriana*, ed. Gerhard Hammer and Karl-Heinz zur Mühlen (Cologne: Böhlau, 1984), 131–50; Jeffrey G. Silcock, "Luther and the Third Use of the Law,"

Th.D. dissertation, Concordia Seminary, St. Louis, 1993. Most helpful is the theological analysis of Walter Sparn, "'Lex iam adest', Luthers Rede vom Gesetz in den Antinomerdisputationen," in *Martin Luther: Biographie und Theologie*, ed. Dietrich Korsch and Volker Leppin (Tübingen: Mohr Siebeck, 2010), 211–49. See also Martin Brecht, "Luthers Antinomerdisputationen: Lebenswirklichkeit des Gesetzes," in Korsch and Leppin, *Martin Luther*, 195–210.

19. Wengert, *Law and Gospel*, 23–102, 154–69.

20. Ibid., 102–38.

21. WA 39,1:334–584. See Silcock, "Luther," 113–620.

22. WA 50:468–477.

23. See Luther's sermon on the topic from September 30, 1537, published as *Ein schone Predigt von dem Gesetz vnd Euangelio. Matth. 22.* (Wittenberg: Hans Lufft, 1537), WA 45:145–56.

24. Timothy J. Wengert, "Caspar Cruciger (1504–1548): The Case of the Disappearing Reformer," *SCJ* 20 (1989): 431–37; Greschat, *Melanchthon neben Luther*, 217–30.

25. WA, 10,3:18,15–19,3.

26. Robert Kolb, *Nikolaus von Amsdorf (1483–1565): Popular Polemics in the Preservation of Luther's Legacy* (Nieuwkoop: De Graaf, 1978), 49–59.

27. WABr 7:539–540.

28. Robert Kolb, *Bound Choice, Election, and Wittenberg Theological Method from Martin Luther to the Formula of Concord*, LQ Books 6 (Grand Rapids: Eerdmans, 2005), 11–66.

29. Timothy J. Wengert, *Human Freedom*.

30. Kolb, *On Bound Choice*, 67–97. Cf. Kolb, "Nikolaus von Amsdorf on Vessels of Wrath and Vessels of Mercy: A Lutheran's Doctrine of Double Predestination," *Harvard Theological Review* 69 (1976): 325–43; *Luther's Heirs*, essay II.

31. William W. Rockwell, *Die Doppelehe des Landgrafen Philipp von Hessen* (Marburg: Elwert, 1904), 323–25.

32. CR, 4:446–69.

33. CR, 5:459, 461, 462; WABr 10:614–18.

34. Kolb, *Amsdorf*, 49–59.

8. The "Culture of Controversy"

1. Günther Wartenberg, "Moritz von Sachsen," *TRE* 23:302–11; and Wartenberg, "Philipp Melanchthon und die sächsisch-albertinische Interimspolitik," *LuJ* 55 (1988): 60–82.

2. The text, edited by Wilhelm Neuser, is found in *Reformierte Bekenntnisschriften* 1/2 (Neukirchen: Neukirchener, 2006): 153–221. See Gottfried Seebass, "Der Abendmahlsartikel der Confessio Augustana Variata von 1540," in *Dona Melanchthonia*, 411–24, for a clarification of the significance of the article over against earlier work by Maurer, "Confessio Augustana Variata," *ARG* (1962): 97–151, which was already the occasion of some expansion by Peter Fraenkel, "Die Augustana und das Gespräch mit Rom, 1540–1541," in *Bekenntnis und Einheit*, 89–103.

3. Walter Hollweg, *Der Augsburger Reichstag von 1566 und seine Bedeutung für die Entstehung der Reformierten Kirche und ihres Bekenntnisses* (Neukirchen-Vluyn: Neukirchener, 1964).

4. *BSLK*, 65,45–46.

5. *Ausführliche Lateinisch-Deutsch Handwörterbuch*, ed. Karl Ernst Georges (Leipzig: Hahn, 1879), 1:2375–76, defines the verb *exhibere* (among other definitions, including verbs indicating the meaning "exhibit" or "show") as *darbieten* ("offer"), *darbringen* ("bring to"), *darreichen* ("hand over to"), and *liefern* ("deliver").

6. The text of the Interim is found in *Das Augsburger Interim von 1548, deutsch und lateinisch*, ed. Joachim Mehlhausen, (Neukirchen-Vluyn: Neukirchener, 1970). The controversy over the Augsburg Interim is documented in *Controversia et Confessio. Theologische Kontroversen 1548–1577/80, Kritische Auswahedition*, ed. Irene Dingel, *Band 1* (Göttingen: Vandenhoeck & Ruprecht, 2010). On the Augsburg Interim, see Dingel, "Culture of Conflict," 18–34; Joachim Mehlhausen, "Der Streit um die Adiaphora," in *Bekenntnis und Einheit*, 105–28; Horst Rabe, *Reichsbund und Interim: Die Verfassungs- und Religionspolitik Karls V. und der Reichstag von Augsburg 1547/1548* (Cologne: Böhlau, 1971); and Gustav Wolf, "Das Augsburger Interim," *Deutsche Zeitschrift für Geschichtswissenschaft* NF 2 (1897–1898): 39–88.

7. Armin Kohnle, "Die Folgen des Interims am Beispiel Württembergs," in *Politik und Bekenntnis: Die Reaktionen auf das Interim von 1548*, ed. Irene Dingel and Günther Wartenberg, LStRLO 8 (Leipzig: Evangelische Verlagsanstalt, 2006), 83–96.

8. A series of essays on the impact of the Augsburg Interim may be found in *Das Interim 1548/50: Herrschaftskrise und Glaubenskonflikt*, ed. Luise Schorn-Schütte, SVRG 203 (Gütersloh: Gütersloher, 2005).

9. See Roxane Berwinkel, *Weltliche Macht und geistlicher Anspruch: Die Hansestadt Stralsund im Konflikt um das Augsburger Interim* (Berlin: Akademie, 2008), and Rainer Postel, "Die Hansestädte und das Interim," in *Herrschaftskrise und Glaubenskonflikt*, 192–204.

10. Thomas Töpfer, *Die Leucorea am Scheideweg: Der Übergang von Universität und Stadt Wittenberg an das albertinische Kursachsen 1547/48, Eine Studie zur Entstehung der mitteldeutschen Bildungslandschaft*, BLUWiG B3 (Leipzig: Evangelische Verlagsanstalt, 2004), 77–90.

11. Irene Dingel, "'Der rechten lehr zuwider': Die Beurteilung des Interims in ausgewählten theologischen Reaktionen," in *Das Interim 1548/50*, 292–311. See also Günther Wartenberg, "Philipp Melanchthon und die sächsisch-albertinische Interimspolitik"; Luther D. Peterson, "The Philippist Theologians and the Interims of 1548: Soteriological, Ecclesiastical, and Liturgical Compromises and Controversies within German Lutheranism" (Ph.D. dissertation, University of Wisconsin-Madison, 1974), 113–214, 312–446; and Emil Sehling, *Die Kirchengesetzgebung unter Moritz von Sachsen 1544–1549 und von Georg von Anhalt* (Leipzig: Deichert, 1899).

12. Daniel Gehrt, *Ernestinische Konfessionspolitik: Bekenntnisbildung, Herrschaftskonsolidierung und dynastische Identitätsstiftung vom Augsburger Interim 1548 bis zur Konkordienformel 1577*, AKThG 34 (Leipzig: Evangelische Verlagsanstalt, 2011), 41–84.

13. See Anja Moritz, *Interim und Apokalypse: Die religiösen Vereinheitlichungsversuche Karls V. im Spiegel der magdeburgischen Publizistik 1548–1551/52*, SMHR 47 (Tübingen: Mohr Siebeck, 2009).

14. See several essays in *Das Interim 1548/50*, including Dingel, "Der rechten lehr zuwider"; Joachim Bauer, "Der Kampf um das 'wahre' Luthertum: Jena und Wittenberg 1548," 277–91; Ernst Koch, "Theologische Aspekte der ernestinischen Reaktionen auf das Interim," 312–30; Inge Mager, "Antonius Corvins Kampagne gegen das Augsburger Interim im welfischen Fürstentum Calenberg-Göttingen," 331–41; Günther Wartenberg,

"Zwischen Kaiser, Konfession und Landesherrschaft: Das Interim in Mitteldeutschland," 233–54; and Bodo Nischan, "Die Interimskrise in Brandenburg," 255–73. See also Armin Kohnle, "Nikolaus von Amsdorf und das Interim," in *Nikolaus von Amsdorf (1483–1565) zwischen Reformation und Politik*, ed. Irene Dingel, LStRLO 9 (Leipzig: Evangelische Verlagsanstalt, 2008), 135–51.

15. Irene Dingel, "Die Kultivierung des Exulantentums im Luthertum am Beispiel des Nikolaus von Amsdorf," in *Amsdorf zwischen Reformation und Politik*, 153–75.

16. Charles P. Arand, "The Apology as a Backdrop for the Interim of 1548," in *Politik und Bekenntnis*, 211–27.

17. Irene Dingel, "Melanchthon und Westeuropa," in *Philipp Melanchthon als Politiker zwischen Reich, Reichsständen und Konfessionsparteien*, ed Günther Wartenberg and Matthias Zenter (Wittenberg: Drei Kastanien, 1998), 105–22.

18. Dingel, "Culture of Conflict," 34–39.

19. The text is found in *Politische Korrespondenz des Herzogs und Kurfürsten Moritz von Sachsen*, ed. Johannes Herrmann and Günther Wartenberg (Berlin: Akademie, 1992): 254–60.

20. Irene Dingel, "The Culture of Conflict in the Controversies Leading to the Formula of Concord (1548–1580), in *Lutheran Ecclesiastical Culture*, 30–39. The controversy over the Leipzig Proposal is documented in *Controversia et Confessio: Theologische Kontroversen 1548–1577/80, Kritische Auswahledition*, ed. Irene Dingel, Band 2 (Göttingen: Vandenhoek & Ruprecht).

21. Dingel, "Culture of Conflict," 15–64.

22. On the "adiaphoristic controversy," see Joachim Mehlhausen, "Der Streit um die Adiaphora," in *Bekenntnis und Einheit*, 105–28; Preger *Flacius*, 1:108–204; and Hans Christoph von Hase, *Die Gestalt der Kirche Luthers: Der casus confessionis im Kampf des Matthias Flacius gegen das Interim von 1548* (Göttingen: Vandenhoeck & Ruprecht, 1940); Robert Kolb, *Confessing the Faith: Reformers Define the Church, 1530–1580* (St. Louis: Concordia, 1991), 63–91; and Oliver K. Olson, "Politics, Liturgics, and *Integritas Sacramenti*," in *Discord, Dialog, and Politics*, 74–85. As mentioned above, it is important to distinguish the criticism of the Augsburg Interim from the controversy over adiaphora and the Leipzig Proposal, see Dingel, "Culture of Controversy," 28–39.

23. In *Das Ende der Reformation*, Thomas Kaufmann has updated and expanded the bibliography of Magdeburg's struggles created by Friedrich Hülsse in 1880, with extensive commentary on the aspects of the critical period in the 1550s that took place in Magdeburg or were related to the city. See also Moritz, *Interim und Apokalypse*.

24. Oliver K. Olson, *Matthias Flacius and the Survival of Luther's Reform* (Wiesbaden: Harrassowitz, 2002).

25. See Jörg Baur, "Flacius—Radikale Theologie," *Zeitschrift für Theologie und Kirche* 72 (1975): 365–80; Irene Dingel, "Flacius als Schüler Luthers und Melanchthons," in *Vestigia pietatis: Studien zur Geschichte der Frömmigkeit in Thüringen und Sachsen*, ed. Gerhard Graf, Hans-Peter Hasse, et al. (Leipzig, 2000), 77–93.

26. Rudolf Keller, *Der Schlüssel zur Schrift: Die Lehre vom Wort Gottes bei Matthias Flacius Illyricus* (Hannover: Lutherisches, 1984).

27. Ronald E. Diener, "The Magdeburg Centuries: A Bibliothecal and Historiographical Analysis" (Th.D. dissertation, Harvard Divinity School, 1978).

28. Irene Dingel, "Strukturen der Lutherrezeption am Beispiel einer Luther-zitatensammlung von Joachim Westphal," in *Kommunikationsstrukturen im*

europäischen Luthertum der Frühen Neuzeit, ed. Wolfgang Sommer (Gütersloh: Gütersloher, 2005), 32–50.

29. *Antwort M. Nicolai Galli vnd M. Fla. Illyrici auff den brieff etlicher Prediger in Meissen von der frage Ob sie lieber weichen denn den Chorrock anzihen sollen* (Magdeburg, 1550).

30. Robert Kolb, "Controversia perpetua: Die Fortsetzung des adiaphoristischen Streits nach dem Augsburger Religionsfrieden," in *Politik und Bekenntnis,* 191–209.

31. Gehrt, *Ernstinische Konfessionspolitik,* 74–81; Robert Kolb, "The Legal Case for Martyrdom, Basilius Monner on John Frederick the Elder and the Smalcald War," in *Reformation und Recht,* ed. Irene Dingel et al. (Gütersloh: Gütersloher, 2002), 145–60.

32. See Wenz, *Theologie der Bekenntnisschriften,* 2:734–45.

33. Jörg Rainer Fligge, "Herzog Albrecht von Preussen und der Osiandrismus, 1522–1568" (Th.D. dissertation, University of Bonn, 1972).

34. See Timothy J. Wengert, *Defending Faith: Lutheran Responses to Andreas Osiander's Doctrine of Justification, 1551-1559* (Tübingen: Mohr Siebeck, 2012).

35. Robert Kolb, "Dynamics of Party Conflict in the Saxon Late Reformation: Gnesio-Lutherans vs. Philippists," *The Journal of Modern History* 49 (1977): D1289–1305; *Luther's Heirs,* essay I. The rest of this chapter summarizes this article. Cf. also Ernst Koch, "Der kursächsische Philippismus und seine Krise in den 1560er und 1570er Jahren," in *Die reformierte Konfessionalisierung,* 60–77.

36. Leppin, *Antichrist,* 220–43.

37. Robert Kolb, "Georg Major as Controversialist: Polemics in the Late Reformation," *Church History* 45 (1976): 455–68.

38. CR, 7:625, n.2.

39. On the origins of the term "Crypto-Calvinism," see Theodor Mahlmann, "Melanchthon als Vorläufer des Wittenberger Kryptocalvinismus," in *Melanchthon und der Calvinismus,* ed. Günter Frank and Herman J. Selderhuis (Stuttgart-Bad Cannstatt: Frommann-Holzboog, 2005), 173–230; Irene Dingel, ed., Concordia et Controversia, Band 8., *Die Debatte um die Wittenberger Abendmahlslehre und Christologie, 1570-1574* (Göttingen: Vandenhoeck & Ruprecht, 2008), and Johannes Hund, *Das Wort ward Fleisch: Eine systematisch-theologische Untersuchung zur Debatte um die Wittenberger Christologie und Abendmahlslehre in den Jahren 1567 bis 1574,* FSÖTH 114 (Göttingen: Vandenhoeck & Ruprecht, 2006).

40. Dingel, "Die Kultivierung des Exulantentums im Luthertum."

41. See Robert Kolb, "The Braunschweig Resolution: The *Corpus Doctrinae Prutenicum* of Joachim Mörlin and Martin Chemnitz as an Interpretation of Wittenberg Theology," in *Confessionalization in Europe,* 67–89.

9. The Majoristic and "Antinomian" Controversies

1. Timothy J. Wengert, "Georg Major (1502–1574), Defender of Wittenberg's Faith and Melanchthonian Exegete," in *Melanchthon in seinen Schülern,* 129–56.

2. The Majoristic controversy will be documented in *Controversia et Confessio: Theologische Kontroversen 1548–1577/80, Kritische Auswahledition,* Bd. 3, ed. Irene Dingel, (forthcoming). See Dingel, "Culture of Conflict," 39–43; Wengert, "Georg Major;" Robert Kolb, "Georg Major as Controversialist: Polemics in the Late Reformation," *Church History* 45 (1976): 455–68; Kolb, *Luther's Heirs,* essay IV; and Peterson, "Philippist Theologians," 215–79.

3. See, for example, Major's *Sermon von S. Pauli und aller gottfürchtigen Menschen Bekehrung zu Gott* (1553).

4. Amsdorf's defense of the expression and reactions to it are discussed in Robert Kolb, "Good Works are Detrimental to Salvation: Amsdorf's Use of Luther's Words in Controversy," *Renaissance and Reformation/Renaissance et Réforme* 4 (1980): 136–51; *Luther's Heirs*, essay III.

5. Major's letter of October 8, 1563, to Amsdorf, in Walter Friedensburg, "Ein Brief Georg Majors an Nikolaus von Amsdorff, 1563," *ARG* 21 (1924): 254–55; and a report on their conversation in a letter of Cyriakus Spangenberg to Hartmann Beier, August 22, 1564, in *Der Briefwechsel des M. Cyriacus Spangenberg* 1 (Dresden: Naumann, 1887): 8.

6. Wenz, *Theologie der Bekenntnisschriften*, 2:612–22.

7. Gehrt, *Ernstinische Konfessionspolitik*, 89–92, 99–109.

8. On the Eisenach Synod and its aftermath, see Matthias Richter, *Gesetz und Heil: Eine Untersuchung zur Vorgeschichte und zum Verlauf des sogenannten Zweiten Antinomistischen Streits* (Göttingen: Vandenhoeck & Ruprecht, 1996), 132–69.

9. Kolb and Arand, *The Genius of Luther's Theology*, 21–128.

10. The "antinomian" controversies of this period will be documented in *Controversia et Confessio: Theologische Kontroversen 1548–1577/80, Kritische Auswahledition*, Bd. 4 (forthcoming). Cf. Dingel, "Culture of Conflict," 43–45.

11. Richter, *Gesetz und Heil*, 251–73; Ernst Koch, "Anton Otho: Weg und Werk eines Lutherschülers," *Herberge des Christentums* 13 (1981/82): 67–92.

12. Richter, *Gesetz und Heil*, 170–207; Matthias Richter, "Andreas Poach und sein Anteil am 2. Antinomistischen Streit," *ARG* 85 (1994): 119–37.

13. On the development of Melanchthon's concept of the third use of the law, see Wengert, *Law and Gospel*, 177–210.

14. Richter, *Gesetz und Heil*, 319–29.

15. Ibid., 273–329.

16. On Musculus, see Ernst Koch, "Andreas Musculus und die Konfessionalisierung im Lutherum," in *Lutherische Konfessionalisierung in Deutschland*, 250–70. The most extensive biographical study of his life remains Christian Wilhelm Spiecker, *Lebensgeschichte des Andreas Musculus: General-Superintendent der Mark Brandenburg* (Frankfurt/O, 1858; reprint: Nieuwkoop: de Graaf, 1964). On the dispute between Musculus and Praetorius, see Richter, *Gesetz und Heil*, 208–50.

17. Wenz, *Theologie der Bekenntnisschriften*, 2:622–44.

18. See Oswald Bayer, "Gesetz und Evangelium," in *Bekenntnis und Einheit*, 155–73.

10. The Synergistic Controversy, the Controversy over Original Sin, and the Doctrine of Election in the Late Reformation

1. *De servo arbitrio*, WA 18: 614,3–6, and 786,26–35, LW 33: 35, 294. The controversy over the freedom of the will will be documented in *Controversia et Confessio: Theologische Kontroversen 1548–1577/80, Kritische Auswahledition*, Bd. 5, ed. Irene Dingel (forthcoming). On the controversies treated in this chapter, see Irene Dingel, "Culture of Conflict," 45–54.

2. See Wengert, *Human Freedom*, 21–64; Kolb, *On Bound Choice*, 70–102.

3. The text of the topic on freedom of the will in Melanchthon's 1559 *Loci communes theologici* is found in StA II,1:236–52.

4. CR, 7:625, n.2.

5. *Offentliche Bekentnis der reinen lere des Euangelij Vnd Confutatio der jtzigen Schwermer* (Jena: Thomas Rewart, 1558). See Robert Kolb, "'Bekentnnis der reinen lere des Euangelij Vnd Confutatio der jtzigen Schwermer, Nikolaus von Amsdorf und die Entfaltung einer neuen Bekenntnisform," in *Nikolaus von Amsdorf (1483–1565) zwischen Reformation und Politik*, 307–24.

6. On treatments of this passage in the period, see Lowell C. Green, "The Problem of the 'Universal Will of God unto Salvation' of 1 Timothy 2:4 in Sixteenth-Century Thought," *LQ* 9 (1995): 281–300.

7. *In hoc Libello continentur utiles disputationes de praecipuis capitibus doctrinae Christianae* (Frankfurt am Main, 1558).

8. *Demonstratio Manifesti Mendacii, Qvo Infamare Conatvr Doctorem Iohannem Pfeff* (Wittenberg, 1558), and *Nochmals gründlicher, klarer warhaffftiger Bericht vnd Bekentnis der bittern lautern Warheit reiner Lere* (n.p., 1559).

9. *Das D. Pfeffinger seine missethat bößlich vnd felschlich leugnet* (Magdeburg, 1559).

10. *Das der freye Wille nichts sey. Antwort/ D. Martini Lutheri/ an Erasmum Roterodamum* (Regensburg: Heinrich Geissler, 1559). Cf. Kolb, *On Bound Choice*, 113–17.

11. For example, Gallus's *Qvaestio libero arbitrio, qvatenvs illa qvibvsdam nunc disceptatur in Ecclesijs Augustanae Confessionis* (Regensburg: Heinrich Geissler, 1559); and *Erklerung vnd Consens vieler Christlichen Kirchen/ der Augspurgischen Confession* (Regensburg: Heinrich Geissler, 1559). See Kolb, *On Bound Choice*, 113–17.

12. Kolb, *On Bound Choice*, 70–102.

13. Gehrt, *Ernstinische Konfessionspolitik*, 109–14; Preger, *Flacius*, 2:181–227. See Ernst Koch, "Victorin Strigel (1524–1569), Von Jena nach Heidelberg," in *Melanchthon und seinen Schülern*, 391–404, and Kolb, *On Bound Choice*, 118–20.

14. On the details of the origin of the Weimar Confutations-Book, see page 258 of this volume.

15. Robert Kolb, "'Bekenntnis der reinen lere,'" 307–24.

16. Gehrt, *Ernstinische Konfessionspolitik*, 144–78.

17. Ibid., 184–86.

18. Hans Kropatscheck, "Das Problem theologischer Anthropologie auf dem Weimarer Gespräch von 1560 zwischen Matthias Flacius Illyricus und Victorin Strigel," Dissertation, University of Göttingen, 1940; Albert Pommerien, *Viktorin Strigels Lehre von dem Peccatum Originis* (Hannover: Stephanusstift, 1917).

19. The text is edited and analyzed in Daniel Gehrt, "Strategien zur Konsensbildung im innerlutherischen Streit um die Willensfreiheit: Edition der Declaratio Victorini und der ernestinischen Visitationsinstruction von 1562," *Zeitschrift für Thüringische Geschichte* 63 (2009): 143–90. Cf. Gehrt, *Ernstinische Konfessionspolitik*, 216–46.

20. Kolb, *Amsdorf*, 214–24. On Andreae's contacts with the Swiss, see Robert M. Kingdon, "Barriers to Protestant Ecumenism in the Career of Theodore Beza," in *Probing the Reformed Tradition: Historical Studies in Honor of Edward A. Dowey Jr.*, ed. Elsie Anne McKee and Brian G. Armstrong (Louisville: Westminster John Knox, 1989), 237–43.

21. The controversy over original sin will be documented in *Controversia et Confessio: Theologische Kontroversen 1548–1577/80, Kritische Auswahledition*, Bd. 6 (forthcoming).

22. Robert Christman, "Heretics in Luther's Homeland: The Controversy over Original Sin in Late Sixteenth-Century Mansfeld" (Ph.D. disseration, University of Arizona, 2004).

23. On Irenaeus's theological position, see Irene Dingel, *Concordia controversa: Die öffentlichen Diskussionen um das lutherische Konkordienwerk am Ende des 16. Jahrhunderts*, QFRG 63 (Gütersloh: Gütersloher, 1996), 499–514.

24. Lowell C. Green, "The three causes of Conversion in Philipp Melanchthon, Martin Chemnitz, David Chytraeus, and 'the Formula of Concord,'" LuJ 47 (1980): 89–114.

25. Wenz, *Theologie der Bekenntnisschriften*, 2:542–59.

26. Dingel, *Concordia controversa*, 526–40; Robert C. Schultz, "Original Sin: Accident or Substance—The Paradoxical Significance of FC I, 53–62, in Historical Context," in *Discord, Dialog, and Concord*, 38–57; Walter Sparn, "Substanz oder Subjekt? Die Kontroverse um die anthropologischen Allgemeinbegriffe im Artikel von der Erbsünde," in *Widerspruch, Dialog und Einigung*, 107–35; and Sparn, "Begründung und Verwirklichung: Zur anthropologischen Thematik der lutherischen Bekenntnisse," in *Bekenntnis und Einheit*, 129–53.

27. Wenz, *Theologie der Bekenntnisschriften*, 2:559–80.

28. On the debate within the Wittenberg faculty in the 1590s, see Rune Söderlund, *Ex praevisa fide, Zum Verständnis der Prädestinationslehre in der lutherischen Orthodoxie*, AGTL, Neue Folge 3 (Hamburg: Lutherisches, 1983), 49–151; Gottfried Adam, *Der Streit um die Prädestination im ausgehenden 16. Jahrhundert: Eine Untersuchung zu den Entwürfen von Samuel Huber und Aegidius Hunnius* (Neukirchen: Neukirchener, 1970).

29. Kolb, *On Bound Choice*, 38–43.

30. By Söderlund, *Ex praevisa fide*, 15–28.

31. Although the term "second Reformation" was used originally in the sixteenth and seventeenth centuries by Reformed theologians who wanted to "complete" Luther's Reformation by "going further," to Calvin's allegedly higher stage of Reformation, the term may be aptly applied to cities like Strasbourg and Ulm, which experienced a move from a mediating "Bucerian" theology or a mild form of Reformed thought to Lutheran positions in the middle decades of the sixteenth century.

32. Kolb, *On Bound Choice*, 173–79. Cf. Klaus Schwarzwäller, "Vom Lehren der Prädestination zur Lehre von der Prädestination: FC 11 im Lichte der Prädestinationsaussage Luthers," in *Widerspruch, Dialog und Einigung*, 249–73.

33. *De praedestinatione: Von der Ewigen Vorsehung und Göttlicher Gnadenwahl: Sieben Predigten* (Erfurt: Georg Baumann, 1567). Kolb, *On Bound Choice*, 205–20.

34. On the entire controversy, see Kolb, *Bound Choice*, 198–226.

35. *Die fürnemsten heuptstück der christlichen Lehre* (Wolfenbüttel: Conrad Horn, 1569); translated as *Ministry, Word, and Sacraments: An Enchiridion*, trans. Luther Poellot (St. Louis: Concordia, 1981), 85–96. See Kolb, *On Bound Choice*, 226–36.

36. Wenz, *Theologie der Bekenntnisschriften*, 2:715–33.

11. The Osiandrian Controversy over the Righteousness That Avails before God

1. Osiander's works on justification are found in *Andreas Osiander der Ältere, Gesamtausgabe*, ed. Gerhard Müller and Gottfried Seebass (Gütersloh: Gütersloher, 1975–1997), 9 and 10. On the entire controversy, see Theodor Mahlmann, *Das neue Dogma der lutherischen Christologie: Problem und Geschichte seiner Begründung* (Gütersloh: Gütersloher, 1969), 93–124; Martin Stupperich, *Osiander in Preussen, 1549–1552* (Berlin: de Gruyter, 1973); Stupperich, "Lehrentscheidung und theologische

Schematisierung; Die Sonderrolle Württembergs im Osiandrischen Streit und ihre Konsequenzen für die Formulierung des dritten Artikels der Solida Declaratio," *Widerspruch, Dialog, und Einigung*, 171–95; and Stupperich, "Zur Vorgeschichte des Rechtfertigungsartikels in der Konkordienformel," in *Bekenntnis und Einheit*, 175–94. On Osiander's earlier career, see Gottfried Seebass, *Das reformatorische Werk des Andreas Osiander* (Nuremberg: Verein für Bayerische Kirchengeschichte, 1967); Ronald K. Rittgers, *The Reformation of the Keys: Confession, Conscience, and Authority in Sixteenth-Century Germany* (Cambridge: Harvard University Press, 2004).

2. Though anachronistic, Wenz's description of Osiander's doctrine of reconciliation as one which "effects 'theosis'" rightly associates his position with the Platonically grounded doctrine of some Eastern Orthodox thinkers. Cf. the view of Simo Peura, "Gott und Mensch in der Unio: Die Unterschiede im Rechtfertigungsverständnis bei Osiander und Luther," in *Unio: Gott und Mensch in der nachreformatorischen Theologie*, ed. Matti Repo and Rainer Vinke (Helsinki: Luther-Agricola-Gesellschaft, 1996), 33–61.

3. Stupperich, *Osiander in Preussen*, 166–71; and Ernst Koch, "'Das Geheimnis unserer Erlösung': Die Christologie des Andreas Musculus als Beitrag zur Formulierung verbindlicher christlicher Lehre im späten 16. Jahrhundert," in *Veritas et Communicatio: Ökumenische Theologie auf der Suche nach einem verbindlichen Zeugnis*, ed. Heiko Franke et al. (Göttingen: Vandenhoeck & Ruprecht, 1992), 143–56.

4. George Huntston Williams, *The Radical Reformation*, (3rd ed., Kirksville: Sixteenth Century Journal, 1992), 854–55, 883–85, 1025–27.

5. A topic not discussed as such in the Reformation era. Because it was not a polemical issue in itself, the description of the atonement was taken for granted. On the differences between Luther and his followers on the atonement, see Robert Kolb, "'Not without the Satisfaction of God's Righteousness': The Atonement and the Generation Gap between Luther and His Students," in *ARG Sonderband: Die Reformation in Deutschland und Europa: Interpretation und Debatten*, ed. Hans R. Guggisberg und Gottfried G. Krodel (Gütersloh: Gütersloher, 1993), 136–56; *Luther's Heirs*, essay VIII.

6. Timothy J. Wengert, *Defending Faith: Lutheran Responses to Andreas Osiander's Doctrine of Justification, 1551–1559* (Tübingen: Mohr Siebeck, 2012), ch. 5.

7. *De unico mediatore Jesu Christo et justificatione fidei* (Königsberg: Hans Lufft, 1551); *Gesamtausgabe* 10:49–300.

8. On the political and theological disputes over Osiander, see Jörg Rainer Fligge, "Herzog Albrecht und der Osiandrismus," and Wengert, *Defending Faith*, ch. 4.

9. Wengert, *Defending Faith*, chap. 5. The treatises written against Osiander will be edited in *Controversia et Confessio: Theologische Kontroversen 1548–1577/80, Kritische Auswahledition*, Bd. 7 (forthcoming).

10. *Von der Rechtfertigung des glaubens* (Königsberg, 1552).

11. *Wider den Erlognen Schelmischen Ehrndiebischen Titel auff D. Joachim Mörleins Buch* (Königsberg: Hans Weinreich, 1552); *Gesamtausgabe*, 10:698–710.

12. *Schmeckbier: Aus D. Joachim Mörleins Buch* (Königsberg: Hans Weinreich, 1552); *Gesamtausgabe*, 10: 742–96. Another importance defense of his position is found in his *Widerlegung: Der vngegrundten vndienstlichen Antwort Philipi Melanthonis* (Königsberg, 1552), *Gesamtausgabe* 10:561–670.

13. *A History of Magic and Experimental Science* (New York: Columbia University Press, 1941), 456–57.

14. Kolb, "The Braunschweig Resolution."

15. Wenz, *Theologie der Bekenntnisschriften*, 2:581–611; Robert Kolb, "Human Performance and the Righteousness of Faith: Martin Chemnitz's Anti-Roman Polemic in Formula of Concord III," in *By Faith Alone: Essays on Justification in Honor of Gerhard O. Forde*, ed. Joseph A. Burgess and Marc Kolden (Grand Rapids: Eerdmans, 2004), 125–39.

16. Wengert, *Defending Faith*, analyzes the full spectrum of the opposition.

17. *Examinis concilii Tridentini* (Frankfurt/M, 1574; original edition, 1566–1573), I:160–63, 193–94; *Examination of the Council of Trent*, 4. vols., trans. Fred Kramer (St. Louis: Concordia, 1971–1986), I:505–13, 601–4.

12. The Controversies over the Lord's Supper and Christology

1. Hund, *Wort ward Fleisch*, 45–96.

2. Walter Köhler, *Zwingli und Luther: Ihr Streit über das Abendmahl nach seiner politischen und religiösen Beziehungen* 2 vols. (Leipzig: Heinsius, 1924, Gütersloh: Bertelsmann, 1953); Hermann Sasse, *This Is My Body: Luther's Contention for the Real Presence in the Sacrament of the Altar* (Minneapolis: Augsburg, 1959).

3. Daniel Bolliger, *Infiniti Contemplatio: Grundzüge der Scotus- und Scotismusrezeption im Werk Hundrych Zwinglis* (Brill: Leiden, 2003).

4. Hund, *Wort ward Fleisch*, 45–65.

5. Ibid., 45–65.

6. Ibid., 66–76.

7. Ibid., 76–87.

8. Peter Fraenkel, "Ten Questions concerning Melanchthon, the Fathers, and the Eucharist," in *Luther and Melanchthon in the History and Theology of the Reformation*, ed. Vilmos Vajta (Philadelphia: Muhlenberg, 1961), 146–64. Cf. Ralph W. Quere, *Christum Cognescere: Christ's Efficacious Presence in the Eucharistic Theology of Melanchthon* (Nieuwkoop: de Graaf, 1977).

9. CR, 15: 1270–71. See Timothy J. Wengert, "Philip Melanchthon's 1557 Lecture on Colossians 3:1-2," in Irene Dingel, Nicole Kuropka, Timothy J. Wengert, and Robert Kolb, *Philip Melanchthon in Classroom, Confession, and Controversy*.

10. A letter from Duke Christoph of Württemberg to Melanchthon, November 3, 1559, in Heinrich Bindseil, *Epistolae, iudicia, consilia… quae in Corpore Reformatorum desiderantur* (1874, Hildesheim: Olms, 1975), 457–58, §463, MBWR 8:409, and Melanchthon's reply, Bindseil, 459–60, §465, MBWR 8:417, §9147. Calvin mentioned his citation of Melanchthon in his own defence in his *Ultima admonitio ad Joachimum Westphalum*, CR, 37/*Calvini Opera* 9 (Braunschweig: Schwetske, 1870): 137–252, in a letter of August 3, 1557, MBWR 8:97, §8293, Bindseil, 417–19, §431. Cf. Calvin's letters to Melanchthon of November 19, 1558, MBWR 8:287, §8782, Bindseil, 435–38, §448. Cf. also Bullinger's letter of October 27, 1557, MBWR 8:148, §8408, Bindseil, 423–25, §435.

11. Hund, *Wort ward Fleisch*, 87–96, Irene Dingel, "The Creation of Theological Profiles: The Understanding of the Lord's Supper in Melanchthon and the Formula of Concord," in *Melanchthon in Classroom, Confession, and Controversy*.

12. *Adversus Haeresios*, IV, 18,5, MSG 7:1028–29.

13. The German translation of the Wittenberg Concord used here employs the word *Niessung* ("reception"), although the Latin translation of the Formula of 1584 employs *usum* ("use"), reflecting the rule set forth in paragraph 85, *nihil habet rationem sacramenti extra usum a Christo institutum*, which postulates the existence of the sacrament based upon the entire use as instituted by Christ.

14. Cited in the Solid Declaration of the Formula of Concord, VII, §13–16. See *Martin Bucers Deutsche Schriften, Bd. 6,1, Wittenberger Konkordie (1536), Schriften zur Wittenberger Konkordie (1534–1537)*, ed. Robert Stupperich et al. (Gütersloh: Mohn, 1988), 120–26.

15. Ernst Bizer, *Studien zur Geschichte des Abendmahlsstreits im 16. Jahrhundert* (1940; Darmstadt: Wissenschaftliche, 1962), 11–130.

16. Westphal, *Clarissimi Viri Philippi Melanchthonis sententia de coena Domini ex scriptis ejus collecta* (Hamburg: Johannes Wickradt, 1557); Gallus, *Iudicium Phillippi Melanthonis de controversia coenae Domini* (Regensburg: Heinrich Geisler, 1560); and *Bericht vnd Rathschlag Philippi Melanthonis, Vom streit des heiligen Nachtmals* (Regensburg: Heinrich Geisler, 1560). See Robert Kolb, "The Critique of Melanchthon's Doctrine of the Lord's Supper by his 'Gnesio-Lutheran' Students," in *Melanchthon in Classroom, Confession, and Controversy*.

17. *Consensus Tigurinus: Heinrich Bullinger und Johannes Calvin über das Abendmahl* (Zurich: TVZ, 2009).

18. Bizer, *Studien zur Geschichte des Abendmahlsstreits*, 243–74; Paul Rorem, "Calvin and Bullinger on the Lord's Supper," *LQ* 2 (1988): 155–84, 357–89.

19. *Farrago confusanearum et inter se dissidentium Opinionum de coena Dominia* (Magdeburg: Christian Rhode, 1552). Cf. also Bizer, *Studien zur Geschichte des Abendmahlsstreits*, 275–84; Joseph N. Tylenda, "The Calvin-Westphal Exchange: The Genesis of Calvin's Treatises against Westphal," *Calvin Theological Journal* 9 (1974): 182–209.

20. *Recta fides de coena Domini* (Magdeburg: Michael Lotther, 1553).

21. Against Wim Jansse, "Joachim Westphal's Sacramentology," *LQ* 22 (2008): 137–60, see the accurate reading of the treatise by Irene Dingel, "Calvin in the Context of Lutheran Consolidation" *Reformation and Renaissance Review* 12 (2010): 155-87.

22. *Collectanea sententiarum D. Aurelii Augustini de Coena Dominae* (Regensburg, 1555) and *Fides Cyrilli Episcopi Alex* (Frankfurt/M: Peter Brubach, 1555). See Esther Chung-Kim, *Inventing Authority: The Use of the Church Fathers in Reformation Debates over the Eucharist* (Waco: Baylor University Press, 2011).

23. For example, in letters to Albert Hardenberg, June 17, 1556, CR, 8:782, MBWR, 7:446, or to Christoph Leib, March 6, 1557, CR, 9:113, MBWR, 8:45. See Kolb, "Gnesio-Lutheran Critique."

24. Irene Dingel, "Bullinger und das Luthertum im Deutschen Reich," in: *Heinrich Bullinger. Life–Thought–Influence, International Congress Heinrich Bullinger (1504–1575)* (Zurich: TVZ, 2007), 2:755–77. Cf. the similar polemic between Lutherans and Theodore Beza on these issues, Reinhard Bodenmann, "Le manifeste retrouvé de Théodore de Bèze et de ses collègues contre la Formule de concorde (1578)," *Bulletin de la Société de l'Histoire du Protestantisme Français* 142 (1996): 345–87, trans. "Die wiederaufgefundene Kampfschrift Theodor Bezas und seiner Kollegen gegen die Konkordienformel (1578)," *Lutherische Theologie und Kirche* 21 (1997): 59–98. On Beza's larger role in the campaign against the Formula of Concord, see Dingel, *Concordia controversa*, esp. 134–40, 215–33.

25. *Confessio fidei de eucharistiae sacramento, in qua ministeri ecclesiarum Saxoniae … astruunt corporis et sanguinis D. n. J. Christi praesentiam in coena sancta, et de libro Calvini ipsis dedicato respondent* (Magdeburg, 1557).

26. Mahlmann, *Christologie*, esp. 40–44, 82–93.

27. Wim Jansse, *Albert Hardenberg als Theologe: Profil eines Bucer-Schülers* (Leiden: Brill, 1994).

28. *Farrago sententiarum consentientium in vera et catholica doctrina, de Coena Domini...*(Frankfurt am Main: Peter Brubach, 1555). On this controversy, see Mahlmann, *Christologie*, 44–61.

29. CR, 9:15–19.

30. *Repetitio sanae doctrinae de vera praesentiae corporis et sanguinis Domini in coena* (Leipzig: Ernst Vögelin, 1561), translated as *The Lord's Supper*, trans. J. A. O. Preus (St. Louis: Concordia, 1979).

31. Dingel, *Concordia Controversa*, 352–412.

32. *Die Abgo[e]ttische Artickel: Gestellet von einem Mo[e]nch in Bayern* (Wittenberg, 1558). StA 6:298–300, and in his appendix refuting Servetus, StA 6:374–77. See Robert Kolb, "Melanchthon's Doctrinal Last Will and Testament: The *Responsiones ad articulos Bavaricae inquisitionis* as His Final Confession of Faith," *SCJ* 36 (2005): 97–114.

33. Otto Fricke, *Die Christologie des Johann Brenz* (Munich: Kaiser, 1927); Hans Christian Brandy, *Die späte Christologie des Johannes Brenz*, BHTh 80 (Tübingen: Mohr, 1991). On the development of Melanchthon's understanding of the communication of attributes and his discussion with students over this issue, see Hund, *Wort ward Fleisch*, 66–96; Mahlmann, *Christologie*, 62–92; on Brenz's position, Mahlmann, 125–204.

34. Herman J. Selderhuis, "Eine attractive Universität: Die Heidelberger Theologische Fakultät, 1583–1622," in *Bildung und Konfession*, ed. Selderhuis and Markus Wriedt, SuRNR 27 (Tübingen: Mohr Siebeck, 2006), 4.

35. Barton, *Um Luthers Erbe*, 196–225.

36. See Wim Jansse, "Die Melanchthonrezeption des Nonkonformisten Wilhelm Klebitz (ca. 1533–1568)," in *Melanchthon und der Calvinismus*, 257–89.

37. CR, 9:962; MBWR, 8:408.

38. See Melanchthon's letter of support to Frederick III, November 1, 1559, CR, 9:960–966, MBWR, 8:408. Cf. Hund, *Wort ward Fleisch*, 93–95. Cf. Kolb, "Gnesio-Lutheran Critique."

39. In a letter to Johann Aurifaber, November 1, 1559, CR, 9:959–960, MBWR, 8:407–8.

40. CR, 9:962; MBWR, 8:408.

41. *Confessio Virtembergica, 1552: Das württembergisches Bekenntnis*, ed. Martin Brecht (Holzgerlingen: Hänssler, 1999).

42. See Robert M. Kingdon, "Barriers to Protestant Ecumenism in the Career of Theodore Beza."

43. Brandy, *Die späte Christologie*, 51–54.

44. Wenz, *Theologie der Bekenntnisschriften*, 2:653.

45. *The Heidelberg Catechism with Commentary* (Philadelphia: United Church Press, 1963), 132, 128, 91. See Lyle D. Bierma, ed., *An Introduction to the Heidelberg Catechism: Sources, History, and Theology* (Grand Rapids: Baker, 2005).

46. Jörg Bauer, "Ubiquität," in *TRE* 24 (2002): 224–41.

47. The most extensive analysis of the Maulbronn Colloquy is found in Bizer, *Studien zur Geschichte des Abendmahlsstreits*, 335–52. Cf. Dingel, "Religionsgespräche IV," 655–56, and Marion Hollerbach, *Das Religionsgespräch als Mittel der konfessionellen und politischen Auseinandersetzung im Deutschland des 16. Jahrhunderts* (Frankfurt/M: Peter Lang, 1982), 230–36.

48. Brandy, *Die späte Christologie*, 61–67; on the relationship between the Württemberg theologians and those of electoral Saxony. See Hund, *Wort ward Fleisch*, 97–136.

49. *De duabus naturis in Christo* (Jena, 1570; extensively revised and expanded in response to the developing Wittenberg Christiology in a second edition, Leipzig, 1578); in translation, *The Two Natures in Christ*, trans. J. A. O. Preus (St. Louis: Concordia, 1971). See Mahlmann, *Christologie*, 205–49; and Bengt Hägglund, "'Majestas hominis Christi': Wie hat Martin Chemnitz die Christologie Luthers gedeutet?" LuJ 47 (1980): 71–88. Cf. on the development of the Christology of Chemnitz's partners in the Concordianist efforts, Koch, "'Das Geheimnis unserer Erlösung': Die Christologie des Andreas Musculus als Beitrag zur Formulierung verbindlicher christlicher Lehre im späten 16. Jahrhundert;" and Kolb, "The Doctrine of Christ in Nikolaus Selnecker's Interpretation of Psalms 8, 22, and 110," *Biblical Interpretation in the Era of the Reformation*, ed. Richard A. Muller and John L. Thompson (Grand Rapids: Eerdmans, 1996), 313–32.

50. *Repetitio sanae doctrinae de vera praesentia corporis et sanguinis in Coena.*

51. On the origin of the term in the midst of the mutual accusations of the two sides, see Mahlmann, "Melanchthon als Vorläufer." The epithet is apt for those who tried to reformulate the teaching of electoral Saxony two decades later under the brief reign of Elector Christian I, son of Elector August, 1586–1592. See Thomas Klein, *Der Kampf um die zweite Reformation in Kursachsen, 1586–1591* (Cologne: Böhlau, 1962). Although Irene Crusius, "'Nicht calvinisch, nicht lutherisch': Zu Humanismus, Philippismus und Kryptocalvinismus in Sachsen am Ende des 16. Jahrhunderts," *ARG* 99 (2008): 139–74, correctly asserts that the ascription of Calvinism to some of Melanchthon's disciples is not apt, this article fails to offer any theological or philosophical analysis of the ideas of the figures whose biographical details are presented, and it blurs the distinctions between the Crypto-Philippism of 1567–1574 and the Crypto-Calvinism of Christian I's reign, thereby confusing rather than clarifying the nature of each of these two movements.

52. The most thorough coverage of these developments in Wittenberg are found in Irene Dingel, ed., *Controversia et Confessio. Theologische Kontroversen 1548-1577/80. Kritische Auswhaledition. Bd 8: Die Debatte um die Wittenberger Abendmahlslehre und Christologie, 1570-1574* (Göttingen: Vandenhoeck & Ruprecht, 2008). See particularly her introduction to these disputes, 3–15, and Hund, *Wort ward Fleisch*, passim. See also Robert Calinich, *Kampf und Untergang des Melanchthonismus in Kursachsen in den Jahren 1570 bis 1574 und die Schicksale seiner vornehmsten Häupter* (Leipzig, 1866); Ernst Koch, "Auseinandersetzungen um die Autorität von Philipp Melanchthon und Martin Luther in Kursachsen im Vorfeld der Konkordienformel von 1577," LuJ 59 (1992): 128–59; and Koch, "Der kursächsische Philippismus und seine Krise in den 1560er und 1570er Jahren," in *Die reformierte Konfessionalisierung in Deutschland*, 60–77. The range of positions developed by Melanchthon's students is shown in the analysis of the critiques of the Formula of Concord by Irene Dingel in *Concordia Controversa*, 101–60, 207–466.

53. Paul Eber, *Vom heiligen Sacrament des Leibs und Bluts unsers Herren Iesv Christi: Unterricht und Bekentnis* (Wittenberg: Rhau, 1562).

54. Johannes Hund, "Vom Philippisten zum Melanchthonianer. Die Entwicklungen in Paul Ebers Abendmahlslehre im Kontext des Zweiten Abendmahlsstreits" (forthcoming).

55. Ernst Koch, "Victorin Strigel (1524–1569). Von Jena nach Heidelberg," in *Melanchthon in seinen Schülern*, 391–404; and Robert Kolb, "Die theologische Pilgerschaft

von Viktorin Strigel: Vom 'gnesiolutherischen' Hoftheologe zum 'calvinistischen' Professor" in *Anti-Calvinismus und Krypto-Calvinismus im 16. Jahrhundert* (Göttingen: Vandenhoeck & Ruprecht, 2011). Arguments against labeling the Heidelberg faculty "Calvinist" at this time point to strong Melanchthonian elements and even elements of Luther's thought represented there, but the Heidelberg Catechism demonstrates that on critical issues regarding the Lord's Supper and Christology, Strigel's formulation of Melanchthon's later views on these subjects would have fit in with those on that faculty who had studied in Geneva.

56. Hund, *Wort ward Fleisch*, 113–36; and Richard Wetzel, "Christoph Pezel (1539– 1604), Die Vorreden zu seinen Melanchthon-Edition als Propagandatexte der 'Zweiten Reformation,'" in *Melanchthon in seinen Schülern*, 465–568. On Peucer, see *Caspar Peucer (1525-1602): Wissenschaft, Glaube und Politik im konfessionellen Zeitalter*, ed. Günther Wartenberg and Hans-Peter Hasse (Leipzig: Evangelische Verlagsanstalt, 2004), esp. Robert Kolb, "Caspar Peucers Abendmahlsverständnis," 111–34. The attribution of Peucer's position to platonic or neoplatonic influences rather than to Aristotelian concepts of substance and presence in this essay is false.

57. Hund, *Wort ward Fleisch*, 113–36.

58. The theses prepared for the doctoral promotion of several faculty members and other Saxon pastors are edited in *Debatte um die Wittenberger Abendmahlslehre*, 16–74; Hund, *Wort ward Fleisch*, 137–57.

59. Hund, *Wort ward Fleisch*, 157–207. The Wittenbergers did not publish their confession. See the reports of Selnecker, *Exegema collationis...cum theologis Wittenbergensibus 28. Julii Anno 1570 Wittebergae institutae* (Wolfenbüttel, 1570); and Andreae, *Gründlicher, warhafftiger und bestendiger Bericht: Von christlicher Einigkeit der Theologen und Predicanten* (Wolfenbüttel, 1570), L4–O3.

60. Hund, *Wort ward Fleisch*, 157–62; Hans-Peter Hasse, *Zensur theologischer Bücher in Kursachsen im konfessionellen Zeitalter: Studien zur kursächsischen Literatur- und Religionspolitik in den Jahren 1569 bis 1575*, AKThG 5 (Leipzig: Evangelische Verlagsanstalt, 2000), 71–83.

61. Hund, *Wort ward Fleisch*, 162–207.

62. Ibid., 264.

63. *Catechesis continens explicationem simplicem et breuem, Decalogi* (Wittenberg, 1571), introduced and edited in *Debatte um die Wittenberger Abendmahlslehre*, 76–289. See Hund, *Wort ward Fleisch*, 209–21, and Harm Klueting, "'Wittenberger Katechismus' (1571) und 'Wittenberger Fragestücke' (1571), Christoph Pezel (1539-1604) und die Wittenberger Theologie," ZKG 112 (2001): 1–43.

64. *Debatte um die Wittenberger Abendmahlslehre*, 290–355; Hund, *Wort ward Fleisch*, 223–97.

65. Hund, *Wort ward Fleisch*, 209–20, 238–67. On Selnecker's continuing admonitions, see 393–405.

66. *Warnung Vor dem vnreinen/ vnd Sacramentirischen catechism etlicher zu Wittenberg* (Jena, 1571), 318–355. Cf. *Bedencken Der Theologen zu Braunschweigk/ von dem newen Wittenbergischen Catechismo gestellet/ Der gantzen Christenheit zur Warnung ausgangen* (Jena: Donatus Richtzenhain, 1571).

67. Hund, *Wort ward Fleisch*, 299–310.

68. *Von der Person vnd Menschwerdung vnsers HERRN Jhesu Christi, Der waren Christlichen Kirchen Grundfest* (Wittenberg, 1571), *Debatte um die Wittenberger*

Abendmahlslehre, 382–673; Hund, *Wort ward Fleisch*, 311–92; Robert Kolb, "Altering the Agenda, Shifting the Strategy: The *Grundfest* of 1571 as Philippist Program for Lutheran Concord," *SCJ* 30 (1999): 705–26.

69. Hund, *Wort ward Fleisch*, 329–330.

70. Ibid., 406–22, 454–62.

71. *Kurtze Christliche vnd Einfeltige widerholung der Bekentnis der Kirchen Gottes In des Churfürsten zu Sachsen Landen Von dem Heiligen Nachtmal* (Dresden, 1571), *Debatte um die Wittenberger Abendmahlslehre*, 794–822; Hund, *Wort ward Fleisch*, 432–54; Hasse, *Zensur*, 111–19.

72. Hund, *Wort ward Fleisch*, 462–69, 485–540

73. Ibid., 469–82.

74. Ibid., 541–57.

75. Hasse, *Zensur*, 120–35.

76. *Exegesis perspicua et ferme integra controversiae de sacra Coena* (Leipzig, 1574); *Debatte um die Wittenberger Abendmahlslehre*, 1014–89; Hund, *Wort ward Fleisch*, 565–94.

77. Hund, *Wort ward Fleisch*, 541–64; Hasse, *Zensur*, 140–52; Gustav Wustman, "Geschichte der heimlichen Calvinisten (Kryptocalvinisten) in Leipzig 1574 bis 1593," *Neujahrsblätter der Bibliothek aus dem Archiv der Stadt Leipzig* 1 (1905): 1–94.

78. Kolb, "Caspar Peucers Abendmahlverständnis."

79. Hund, *Wort ward Fleisch*, 595–668.

80. *Philipp Melanchthon: Enarratio secundae tertiaeque partis Symboli Nicaeni (1550)*, ed. Hans-Peter Hasse, QFRG 64 (Gütersloh: Gütersloher, 1996). On Crell, see Hans-Peter Hasse, "Paul Krell (1531–1579): Melanchthon's 'Enarratio Symboli Nicaeni' (1550) und der Sturz des Philippismus in Kursachsen im Jahre 1574," in *Melanchthon und seinen Schülern*, 427–63.

81. *Ein kurzer Bericht/ warumb man offt vnnd gern zum…Sakrament gehen soll* (Nuremberg, 1566).

82. Hasse, *Zensur*, 183–211.

83. *Kurtz Bekentnis vnd Artickel vom heiligen Abendmal des Leibs vnd Bluts Christi* (Wittenberg, 1574); *Debatte um die Wittenberger Abendmahlslehre*, 1090–1151. See Hund, *Wort ward Fleisch*, 630–44; Hasse, *Zensur*, 172–79; Irene Dingel, "Die Torgauer Artikel (1574) als Vermittlungsversuch zwischen der Theologie Luthers und der Melanchthons," in *Praxis Pietatis: Beiträge zu Theologie und Frömmigkeit in der Frühen Neuzeit: Festschrift Wolfgang Sommer* (Stuttgart: Kohlhammer, 1999), 44–59.

84. Ulrike Ludwig, *Philippismus und Orthodoxes Luthertum an der Universität Wittenberg: Die Rolle Jakob Andreäs im lutherischen Konfessionalisierungsprozeß Kursachsens, 1576–1580*, RST 153 (Münster: Aschendorff, 2009); Kenneth G. Appold, *Orthodoxie als Konsensbildung: Das theologische Disputationswesen an der Universität Wittenberg zwischen 1570 und 1710*, BHTh 127 (Tübingen: Mohr Siebeck, 2004), 15–39.

85. Wenz, *Theologie der Bekenntnisschriften*, 2:645–81.

86. On the controversy in Mecklenburg, in which Chytraeus played a role, over the contention of Johann Saliger that the elements remain body and blood outside their sacramental use, see Jürgen Diestelmann, *Actio sacramentalis: Die Verwaltung des Heiligen Abendmahles nach den Prinzipien Martin Luthers in der Zeit bis zur Konkordienformel* (Gross Oesingen: Harms, 1996), 267–304.

87. Jörg Baur, "Ubiquität," *TRE* 34: 224–41.

88. Wenz, *Theologie der Bekenntnisschriften*, 2:685, points out that the difference between Chemnitz and Andreae on the omnipresence of Christ's human nature was a difference in accent, not in substance. The significance of this difference should not be minimized even though it was not substantial. See Hund, *Wort ward Fleisch*, 694–702.

89. Wenz, *Theologie der Bekenntnisschriften*, 2:682–711.

90. CR, 2:490, MBWR, 2:26.

91. *Confessio de sententia ministrorum verbi in comitatu Mansfeldensi, de dogmatis quorundam proximo triennio publice editis* (Eisleben: Gaubisch, 1565), 47a–58b. The confession was composed in 1564. Cf. Robert Kolb, "Christ's Descent into Hell as Christological Locus: Luther's 'Torgau Sermon' as Confessional Instrument in the Late Reformation," LuJ 69 (2002):101–18.

92. Translated in *Sources and Contexts*, 246–55. The sermon was not preached in Torgau in 1533 but in Wittenberg in 1532. Cf. WA 37:21–22, 62–72 (the printed version of the sermon). The third part of this work, which is the text referred to in FC IX, is clearly the same sermon as that in the notes of Georg Rörer, in WA 36:159–64, dated March 31, 1532. See Erich Vogelsang, "Luthers Torgauer Predigt von Jesu Christo vom Jahre 1532," LuJ 13 (1931): 114–30.

93. See David G. Truemper, "The *Descensus ad Inferos* from Luther to the Formula of Concord," S.T.D. thesis, the Joint Project for Theological Education and the Lutheran School of Theology at Chicago, 1974; and Wenz, *Theologie der Bekenntnisschriften*, 2:712–15.

94. Wengert, *Formula for Parish Practice*, 103–64.

13. Efforts at Attaining Concord, 1552–1569

1. Dingel, "Bekenntnis und Geschichte," 75–81.

2. Peter Fraenkel, *Testimonia Patrum: The Function of the Patristic Argument in the Theology of Philip Melanchthon* (Geneva: Droz, 1961).

3. The analysis of Karl Müller, *Kirchengeschichte 2/2* (Tübingen: Mohr Siebeck, 1919), 80–81, repeated by Wenz, *Theologie der Bekenntnisschriften*, 2:497, is both imprecise and false in dividing the steps toward concord under princely leadership into three periods: (1) early attempts to attain unity by ignoring theological differences, (2) attempts at consolidation of the churches and doctrinal positions their own lands, and (3) the largely successful attempt which resulted in the Formula of Concord. Most early attempts did not diminish, to say nothing of ignore, doctrinal differences, and such attempts continued while individual governments assembled *Corpora doctrinae* for their own lands.

4. Preger, *Flacius*, 2:8–32; Olson, *Survival*, 309–17.

5. Preger, *Flacius*, 32–59.

6. Ibid., 59–62.

7. Gehrt, *Ernstinische Konfessionspolitik*, 114–22; Irene Dingel, "Religionsgespräche IV," *TRE* 28:661–62; Benno von Bundschuh, *Das Wormser Religionsgespräch von 1557, unter besonderer Berücksichtigung der kaiserlichen Religionspolitik*, RST 124 (Münster: Aschendorff, 1988), esp. 399, 411–12, 421, 453, 459; and Bjorn Slenczka, *Das Wormser Schisma der Augsburger Konfessionsverwandten von 1557: Protestantische Konfessionspolitik und Theologie im Zusammenhang des zweiten Wormser Religionsgesprächs*, BHTh 155 (Tübingen: Mohr Siebeck, 2010). This well-executed study falsely labels the result of the colloquy in Worms a "schism" within the Wittenberg circle, following the mistaken judgment of Kaufmann, *Ende der Reformation*, 280, who labels the divide after Worms "the

second schism" in the Wittenberg movement, following the first, that between Luther and Karlstadt, an erroneous comparison. Both in public teaching and in the course of the relationships the two simply cannot be compared. Slenczka bases his case upon two uses of the term "schism," by the Pomeranian Jakob Runge and an anonymous report from a Prussian representative, ignoring the much milder estimates of both Melanchthon and the Gnesio-Lutheran participants. In view of the facts that both sides continued to strive for agreement and a common confession of the faith, and that Andreae, Brenz's right-hand man at the colloquy, and Chemnitz, Mörlin's right-hand man at the colloquy, led the efforts which brought their sides together with most of Melanchthon's followers twenty years later, suggests that the label "schism" is exaggerated and misleading.

8. Irene Dingel, "Melanchthons Einigungsbemühen zwischen den Fronten: Der Frankfurter Rezess," in *Philipp Melanchthon: Ein Wegbereiter für die Ökumene*, ed. Jörg Haustein, 2nd ed. (Göttingen: Vandenhoeck & Ruprecht, 1997), 121–43. The document's text is found in CR, 9: 489–507.

9. Gehrt, *Ernstinische Konfessionspolitik*, 122–29; Preger, *Flacius*, 2:69–77.

10. *Des Durchleuchtigen…Herrn Johans Friderichen des Mittlern* (Jena: Thomas Rebart, 1559). See Gehrt, *Ernstinische Konfessionspolitik*, 129–37; and Robert Kolb, "'Bekentnis der reinen lere des Euangelij Vnd Confutatio der jtzigen Schwermer,' Nikolaus von Amsdorf und die Entfaltung einer neuen Bekenntnisform," in *Nikolaus von Amsdorf (1483–1565) zwischen Reformation und Politik*, 307–24.

11. It was printed with other documents in *Supplicatorii libelli quorundam Christi ministrorum de Synodo propter controversias gravissimas congreganda* (Ursel, 1561).

12. Gehrt, *Ernstinische Konfessionspolitik*, 178–84; Ernst Koch, "Striving for the Union of Lutheran Churches, the Church-Historical Background of the Work Done of the Formula of Concord at Magdeburg," *SCJ* 8,4 (1977): 106–12; Robert Calinich, *Der Naumburger Fürstentag 1561: Ein Beitrag zur Geschichte des Luthertums und des Melanchthonismus aus den Quellen des Königlichen Hauptstaatsarchivs zu Dresden* (Gotha: Perthes, 1870).

13. On Chytraeus's later defense of the text of the "Invariata," see Rudolf Keller, *Die Confessio Augustana im theologischen Wirken des Rostocker Professors David Chyträus, 1530–1600* (Göttingen: Vandenhoeck & Ruprecht, 1994).

14. Dingel, "Bekenntnis und Geschichte," 75–81; Kolb, *Confessing the Faith*, 99–131. Thomas Kaufmann, "Das Bekenntnis im Luthertum des konfessionellen Zeitalters," *Zeitschrift für Theologie und Kirche* 105 (2008), 281–314, proposes that the use of the confessional documents effected a self-contained *Corpus Christianum* within each territory which accepted them. In a limited sense this is true, but in fact, while the Augsburg Confession and other confessions of faith did foster the Lutheran identity of specific territorial churches, they also gave witness to that which bound them together across territorial borders, functioning as an ecumenical tie of powerful proportions.

15. Robert Kolb, "Bekentnis der reinen lere," 307–24.

16. The text of the Saxon Confession is found in StA 6:81–167; CR, 28:369–478; that of the Württemberg Confession in *Confessio Virtembergica*, ed. Martin Brecht.

17. Kolb, *Confessing the Faith*, 120–30

18. Σύνταγμα, *seu corpus doctrinae Christi, ex novo Testamento tantum, Methodica ratione, singulari fide et diligentia congestum* (Basel: Johannes Oporinus, 1558). Cf. Robert Kolb, "The First Protestant 'Biblical Theology': The *Syntagma* of Johannes Wigand and Matthaeus Judex," in *Hermeneutica Sacra*, 189–206.

19. A helpful overview of this process of establishing the secondary authority of the Augsburg Confession is found in Dingel, "Bekenntnis und Geschichte," 61–81. In 1561, in Martin Chemnitz's manuscript summary of the controversies which beset the German Evangelical churches at the time, Chemnitz reflected the Wittenberg understanding of how the teaching of the church functions when he argued that the churches needed a guiding set of hermenutical principles—a "correct form and organized summary"—for the adjudication of disputes over the proper interpretation of Scripture and that such principles should be given legal force within churches through the adoption of documents collected in a "Corpus doctrinae" (translation in *Sources and Contexts*, 200–203). To avoid the impression that the Formula of Concord was being written in opposition to the Melanchthonian collection, the concordists decided at Torgau to avoid the term *corpus doctrinae*. The entire Formula of Concord, however, may be seen as the binding summary, basis, rule, and guiding principle by which, like a *corpus doctrinae*, the public teaching of churches was to be set. See Irene Dingel, "Melanchthon und die Normierung des Bekenntnisses," in *Der Theologe Melanchthon*, Günter Frank, ed., MSSB 5 (Stuttgart: Thorbecke, 2000), 195–211, translated as "Philip Melanchthon and the Establishment of Confessional Norms," *LQ* 20 (2006): 146–69.

20. See Dingel, "Melanchthon und die Normierung."

21. *Corpus Doctrinae Christianae, das ist, gantze Summa der rechten wahren Christlichen Lehre des heiligen Evangelii* (Leipzig: Ernst Vögelin, 1560); the Latin version followed shortly thereafter. Some texts of these documents are found in StA 6. See Dingel, "Melanchthon und die Normierung."

22. *Corpus doctrinae Christianum* (Wittenberg, 1565).

23. *Formula consensus de doctrina evangelii* (Lübeck, 1560).

24. *Corpus doctrinae Christianum* (Braunschweig, 1563).

25. *Repetitio Corporis Doctrinae Ecclesiasticae* (Königsberg, 1567). Cf. Kolb, "The Braunschweig Resolution," 67–89.

26. *Corpus doctrinae, das ist, die Summe, Form und Vorbilde der reinen Christlichen Lere* (Ülzen, 1576), the so-called "Corpus Wilhelmanum," and the similarly entitled "Corpus Julianum" (Heinrichstadt, 1576).

27. In English translation, *Preaching the Reformation: The Homiletical Handbook of Urbanus Rhegius*, trans. Scott Hendrix (Milwaukee: Marquette University Press, 2003).

28. *Christliche und in Gottes Wort ... gegründete Kirchenordnung* (Frankfurt, 1568).

29. *Corpus Doctrinae Christianum: Das ist Summa der Christlichen Lere* (Jena, 1570).

30. *Die Augsburgische Confession* (Frankfurt, 1572).

31. Dingel, "Religionsgespräche IV," 667–68; Gehrt, *Ernstinische Konfessionspolitik*, 288–91, 328–34.

32. The theologians in Jena began the publication of the protocols of the meeting and then separate addresses to issues involved: *Colloquium zu Altenburgk in Meissen Vom Artikel der Rechtfertigung vor Gott: Zwischen Der Churfürstlichen vnd Fürstlichen zu Sachsen etc.* (Jena, 1569). The Philippists published their own version of the proceedings: *Gantze vnd Vnuerfelschete Acta vnd Handlung des Colloquij zwischen den Churfürstlichen vnd Fürstlichen zu Sachsen etc.* (Wittenberg: Hans Lufft, 1570).

14. Jakob Andreae's Drive for Lutheran Unity and the Composition of the Formula of Concord and the Book of Concord

1. See page 239, on his meeting with Beza and Farel, 1557, Kingdon, "Barriers to Protestant Ecumenism," 237–243. On Andreae, see Theodor Mahlmann, "Jakob Andreä im Lichte neuerer Forschung," *Lutherische Theologie und Kirche* 14 (1990): 139–53.

2. On Andreae's efforts at Concord, see Jobst Ebel, "Jacob Andreae (1528–1590) als Verfasser der Konkordienformel," *ZKG* 89 (1978): 78–119; Inge Mager, *Die Konkordienformel im Fürstentum Braunschweig-Wolfenbüttel: Entstehungsbeitrag— Rezeption—Geltung* (Göttingen: Vandenhoeck & Ruprecht, 1993), 33–125, 175–259; Wenz, *Theologie der Bekenntnisschriften*, 2:502–13; and Robert Kolb, *Andreae and the Formula of Concord: Six Sermons on the Way to Lutheran Unity* (St. Louis: Concordia, 1977). On the background of his efforts, see Rosemarie Müller-Streisand, "Theologie und Kirchenpolitik bei Jacob Andreä bis zum Jahr 1568," *Blätter für württembergische Kirchengeschichte* 60/61 (1960/61): 224–395.

3. Inge Mager, "Jakob Andreaes lateinische Unionsartikel von 1568," *ZKG* 98 (1987): 70–86; and Hans Christian Brandy, "Jacob Andreaes Fünf Artikel von 1568/69," *ZKG* 98 (1987): 338–51. The text of the Five Articles is given in *Die Bekenntnisschriften der evangelisch-lutherischen Kirche. Band II/2. Quellen zur Entstehung der Konkordienformel*, ed. Irene Dingel, with assistance of Marion Bechtold-Meyer and Hans Christian Brandy (Göttingen: Vandenhoeck & Ruprecht, 2013). Brandy demonstrates in his preface to the Five Articles in this volume that Andreae's adjustments in the text were in fact minimal.

4. Dingel, "Religionsgespräche IV," 668. Andreae's report of the matter is found in *Gründtlicher, warhafftiger vnd bestendiger bericht: Von Christlicher Einigkeit der Theologen vnd Predicanten* (Wolfenbüttel: Conradt Horn, 1570). Cf. Hund, *Wort ward Fleisch*, 137–47.

5. *Endlicher Bericht vnd Erklerung der Theologen beider Vniuersiteten/ Leipzig vnd Wittemberg Auch der Superintendenten der Kirchen in des Churfu[e]rsten zu Sachsen Landen* (Wittenberg: Hans Lufft, 1570).

6. *De praecipvis horvm temporvm controversiis propositiones, orationes et qvaestiones, continentes svmmam confessionis ac Academiae Vvitebergensis* (Wittenberg: Johannes Schwertel, 1571); *Debatte um die Wittenberger Abendmahlslehre*, 17–74.

7. *Von der Person vnd Menschwerdung*, 2a–8b, *Debatte um die Wittenberger Abendmahlslehre*, 392–403.

8. Kolb, "The Braunschweig Resolution," 78–89.

9. *Sechs Christlicher Predig Von den Spaltungen so sich zwischen den Theologen Augspurgischer Confession von Anno 1548. biss auff diss 1573* (Tübingen: Gruppenbach, 1573). The text is edited in the forthcoming *Die Bekenntnisschriften der evangelisch-lutherischen Kirche. Band II/2*. For commentary and translation, see Kolb, *Andreae and the Formula of Concord*. Cf. *Drey vnd dreissig Predigten von den fu[e]rnembsten Spaltungen in der christlichen Religion* (Tübingen: Morhart, 1568). Cf. Robert Kolb, "The Formula of Concord and Contemporary Anabaptists, Spiritualists, and Anti-Trinitarians," *LQ* 15 (2001): 453–82.

10. Robert Kolb, "The Formula of Concord as a Model for Discourse in the Church," *Concordia Journal* 32 (2006): 189–210.

11. On the process of reaching Concord, see the essays by Ernst Koch gathered in *Aufbruch und Weg: Studien zur lutherischen Bekenntnisbildung im 16. Jahrhundert*

(Berlin: Evangelische Verlagsanstalt, 1983); and his "Der Weg zur Konkordienformel," in *Vom Dissensus zum Konsensus: Die Formula Concordiae von 1577* (Hamburg 1980) 10–46. Cf. Ernst Koch, "Striving for the Union of Lutheran Churches: The Church-Historical Background of the Work Done on the Formula of Concord at Magdeburg," *SCJ* 8,4 (1977): 105–21.

12. Dingel, "Bekenntnis und Geschichte," 75–81. The text of the "Swabian Concord," the "Swabian-Saxon Concord," the "Maulbronn Formula," and other related layers of editing will be published in *Die Bekenntnisschriften der evangelisch-lutherischen Kirche. Band II/2.*

13. Following the introduction on the nature of the *corpus doctrinae,* the Swabian Concord treated original sin, freedom of the will, the righteousness of faith, good works, the necessity and spontaneity of good works, law and gospel, the third use of God's law, ecclesiastical usages, or adiaphora, the Lord's Supper, the Person of Christ, predestination, other factions and sects.

14. *Schwärmerei* comes from the root *schwärmen,* which means "to swarm." It conveyed the sense of "raving," of a madness that rejected reason and revelation. It was applied by Lutheran theologians to those designated by Williams, *Radical Reformation,* as "radicals." Cf. the Saxon *Confutation* and the Mansfeld *Confessio de sententia ministrorum verbi in comitatu Mansfeldensi, de dogmatis* (Eisleben: Gaubisch, 1565).

15. *Drey und dreissig Predigten*; and Wenz, *Theologie der Bekenntnisschriften,* 2:745–49.

16. On Riedemann, see Andrea Chudaska, *Peter Riedemann: Konfessionsbildendes Täufertum im 16. Jahrhundert,* QFRG 76 (Gütersloh: Gütersloher, 2003); Robert C. Holland, "The Hermeneutics of Peter Riedemann (1506–1556)" (Th.D. dissertation, University of Basel, 1970); Williams: *Radical Reformation,* 281–82, 646–50.

17. Whether his own suffering from deafness contributed to this view is unclear.

18. See Williams, *Radical Reformaton,* 201–11, 383–87, 1213–14, 1255–56, 1275–77; Selina Gerhard Schulz, *Caspar Schwenkfeld von Ossig (1489–1561), Spiritual Interpretation of Christianity* (Norristown: Board of Publication of the Schwenkfelder Church, 1946); and Paul L. Maier, *Caspar Schwenkfeld on the Person and Work of Christ* (Assen: Van Gorcum, 1959).

19. Williams, *Radical Reformation,* 459–77, 1135–75.

20. A translation of some parts of the document is found in *Sources and Contexts,* 200–19. See Jobst Ebel, "Die Herkunft des Konzeptes der Konkordienformel: Die Funktionen der fünf Verfasser neben Andreae beim Zustandekommen der Formel," *ZKG* 91 (1980): 245–47.

21. See Ludwig, *Philippismus und orthodoxes Luthertum.*

22. Kolb, "Formula of Concord," 195–200. On four of the members of the committee, see Theodore R. Jungkuntz, *Concordists of the Formula of Concord: Four Architects of the Lutheran Unity* (St. Louis: Concordia, 1977). On Chytraeus, see Rudolf Keller, "David Chytraeus (1530–1600), Melanchthons Geist im Luthertum," in *Melanchthon und seinen Schülern,* 361–72. On Selnecker, see Werner Klän, "Der 'vierte Mann': Auf den Spuren von Nikolaus Selneckers (1530–1592)—Beitrag zu Entstehung und Verbreitung der Konkordienformel," *Lutherische Theologie und Kirche* 17 (1993): 145–74. On the theological orientation of the committee, see Jobst Christian Ebel, *Wort und Geist bei den Verfassern der Konkordienformel: Eine historisch-systematische Untersuchung* (Munich: Kaiser, 1981).

23. Kolb, "Formula of Concord," 200–10.

24. Wenz, *Theologie der Bekenntnisschriften,* 2:513–19.

25. Ernst Koch, "Ökumenische Aspekte im Entstehungsprozeß der Konkordienformel," in Koch, *Aufbruch und Weg*, 47, cf. 34–47.

26. Ernst Koch, "Striving for the Union of Lutheran Churches," 103–21.

27. Robert Kolb, "The Ordering of the *Loci Communes Theologici*: The Structuring of the Melanchthonian Dogmatic Tradition," *Concordia Journal* 23 (1997): 317–37.

28. Kolb and Arand, *The Genius of Luther's Theology*, 131–159.

29. Cf. Robert Kolb: "Confessing the Faith, the Wittenberg Way of Life," *Tidskrift for Teologi og Kirke* 80 (2009): 247–65.

30. Solid Declaration, Preface, in *BSLK*, 833; BC, 526.

31. Wenz, *Theologie der Bekenntnisschriften*, 2:520–30.

32. Irene Dingel, "The Preface of the Book of Concord as a Reflection of Sixteenth-Century Confessional Development," *LQ* 15 (2001): 373–95. See texts of the several drafts of the preface as well as the theologians' preface that was not included in the Book of Concord in *Die Bekenntnisschriften der evangelisch-lutherischen Kirche. Band II/2*.

33. Sächsisches Hauptstaatsarchiv, Geheimrat (Geheimes Archiv) Locat. 10304–6 contain some of the subscription documents gathered in the course of this effort.

34. *BSLK*, 762–66, provides a partial list of princely and municipal subscribers, based on one document, the "Heidelberger Abschied" of July 31, 1579. Twenty-five princes, twenty-six counts, and thirty-five city governments, as well as an estimated nearly eight thousand pastors subscribed to the Formula.

35. *BSLK*, 1103–35; translation in *Sources and Contexts*, 220–44. See Thomas A. von Hagel, "The 'Genus Maiestaticum'—Christology of the Catalog of Testimonies" (Ph.D. dissertation, Saint Louis University, 1997).

36. Robert Kolb, "Melanchthonian Method as a Guide to Reading Confessions of Faith: The Index of the Book of Concord and Late Reformation Learning," *Church History* 72 (2003): 504–24.

37. *Aus der Christlichen Concordia, erklerung etlicher streitigen Artickel*, ed. Nikolaus Selnecker (Leipzig: Georg Defner for Henning Gross, 1582).

15. Reactions to the Formula of Concord in the 1580s

1. Ebel, "Herkunft des Konzeptes," 263–64, 273. Cf. Inge Mager, "Der Beitrag des David Chytraeus zur Entstehung und Rezeption der Konkordienformel," *Berliner Theologische Zeitschrift* 18 (2001): 207–21.

2. Dingel, *Concordia controversa*, 467–541; Dingel's analysis expands and deepens all previous assessments of the various opponents to the Concordian settlement. Cf. Robert Kolb, "The Flacian Rejection of the Concordia: Prophetic Style and Action in the German Late Reformation," *ARG* 73 (1982): 196–216; *Luther's Heirs*, VI.

3. On efforts to introduce the Formula and Book of Concord, see, e.g., Inge Mager, "Aufnahme und Ablehnung des Konkordienbuches in Nord-, Mittel- und Ostdeutschland," in *Bekenntnis und Einheit*, 271–302; Werner-Ulrich Deetjen, "Concordia Concors—Concordia Discors: Zum Ringen um das Konkordienwerk im Süden und mittleren Westen Deutschlands," in *Bekenntnis und Einheit*, 303–49.

4. Dingel, *Concordia Controversa*, 542–600. For a brief overview, see James J. Megivern, "The Catholic Rejoinder," in *Discord, Dialogue, and Concord*, 191–207.

5. Dingel, *Concordia Controversa*, 113–82. For a brief overview of English reactions, see W. Brown Patterson, "The Anglican Reaction," in *Discord, Dialogue, and Concord*, 150–65.

6. Dingel, *Concordia Controversa*, 101–29. See also Henry J. Cohn, "The Territorial Princes in Germany's Second Reformation, 1559–1622," in *International Calvinism 1541–1715*, ed. Menna Prestwich (Oxford: Clarendon, 1985), 135–65; Jill Raitt, "Elizabeth of England, John Casimir, and the Protestant League," in *Controversy and Conciliation: The Reformation and the Palatinate, 1559–1583*, ed. Derk Visser (Allison Park: Pickwick, 1986), 117–45.

7. Dingel, *Concordia Controversa*, 132–48.

8. Ibid., 161–206.

9. Ibid., 207–79. See also Irene Dingel, "Das Streben nach einem 'Consensus Orthodoxus' mit den Vätern in der Abendmahlsdiskussion des späten 16. Jahrhunderts," in *Die Patristik in der Bibelexegese des 16. Jahrhunderts*, ed. David Steinmetz (Wiesbaden: Harrassowitz, 1999), 181–204.

10. Dingel, *Concordia Controversa*, 280–351.

11. Ibid., 39–100; and Gensichen, *We Condemn*, 175–87.

12. Hund, *Wort ward Fleisch*, 393–98, 423–32.

13. Irene Dingel, "The Echo of Controversy: Caspar Fuger's Attempt to Propagate the Formula of Concord among the Common People," *SCJ* 26 (1995): 515–31.

14. Dingel, *Concordia Controversa*, 352–412.

15. Irene Dingel, "Ablehnung und Aneignung: Die Bewertung der Autorität Martin Luthers in den Auseinandersetzungen um die Konkordienformel," *ZKG* 105 (1994): 35–57; und Dingel, *Concordia Controversa*, 607–29. For a summary of the early historiography of the Augsburg Confession among Lutherans, see Kolb, *Confessing the Faith*, 43–62. On David Chytraeus's interpretation of the Augsburg Confession and its history, see Keller, *Confessio Augustana*.

16. Mager, *Konkordienformel*, 325–66.

17. Dingel, *Concordia controversa*, 425–48; Dingel, "Religionsgespräche IV," 668–69.

18. Johannes Wallmann, "Die Rolle der Bekenntnisschriften im älteren Luthertum," in *Bekenntnis und Einheit*, 381–92; Robert D. Preus, "The Influence of the Formula of Concord on the Later Lutheran Orthodoxy," in *Discord, Dialog, and Politics*, 86–101.

19. Kenneth G. Appold, *Orthodoxie als Konsensbildung: Das theologische Disputationswesen an der Universität Wittenberg zwischen 1570 und 1710* (Tübingen: Mohr Siebeck, 2004), 127–30. See, e.g., Peter Piscator, *Commentarius in Formulam Concordiae: Librum Symbolon omnium ecclesiarum Augustanam Confessionem invariatam amplectentur Disputationibus XIV* (Jena: Steinmann, 1610).

Postscript

1. Koch, "Ökumenische Aspekte im Entstehungsproceß der Konkordienformel," in *Aufbruch und Weg*, 34–47, and Koch, "Striving for the Union of Lutheran Churches: The Church-Historical Background of the Work Done on the Formula of Concord at Magdeburg," *SCJ* 8, no. 4 (1977): 105–21.

2. Robert Kolb, "The Formula of Concord as a Model."

Index of Scriptural Citations

Index of Names and Subjects

baptism, 17, 19–24, 32–34, 43, 58, 62,
74–75, 82–84, 121, 136, 138, 146,
150, 179, 239, 244, 271, 279
Basil of Caesarea, 30–31
Beurlin, Jakob, 224
Beyer, Christian, 3–4, 105, 107
Beza, Theodore, 207, 237, 239, 244, 246,
248, 250–51
Bidembach, Balthasar, 240, 272
Biel, Gabriel, 109–10, 129, 137
Binder, Christoph, 207
Boetius, Sebastian, 244
Bötker, Johann, 234
Boquin, Peter, 240
both kinds, communion in, 99, 176, 227–28
Brenz, Johannes, 95, 125, 129, 177, 184,
188–89, 217, 222–23, 236, 238–41,
243, 251, 253, 257, 265, 267–68
Brück, Gregor, 95, 99, 110, 118, 124–25,
144, 146
Bucer, Martin, 94, 112, 125, 147, 152,
169–70, 212–13, 230–32, 234–36, 279
Bugenhagen, Johannes, Jr., 242
Bugenhagen, Johannes, Sr., 118, 145, 147,
192, 252, 261
Bullinger, Heinrich, 232–33, 237, 239,
244, 250
Buren, Daniel von, 235

Caesarius of Arles, 23, 36, 56
Cajetan, Thomas de Vio, cardinal, 108
callings in daily life, 74, 78, 83–85, 132–33,
271
Calvin, John, 63–64, 141, 211–12, 222, 232–
34, 236–37, 242, 244, 247–50, 266
Campeggio, Lorenzo, 97, 104, 110, 119–21
Canisius, Peter, 257
Cappadocians, the, 30, 38, 44
Carl, count of Baden. See Karl, count of
Baden
Catalog of Testimonies, 275
celibacy, clerical, 67, 123, 127, 176
Chalcedon, Council of, 31, 34, 38, 48–49,
51, 228, 251
Charlemagne, Emperor, 23–24, 34–36, 75,
87, 171

Charles V, Emperor, 2–4, , 63, 65, 73,
89–92, 95–96, 98–100, 104–05, 107,
110, 118–24, 129, 139–44, 152, 161,
170–76, 178, 257
Chemnitz, Martin, 189, 199, 208–9, 214–
15, 219–20, 224, 226, 236, 241–45,
248–49, 251–52, 257, 261, 266–73,
275, 277–78, 280
Christ, Christology, 17–19, 25–35, 38–39,
41–51, 54–57, 69, 80–81, 130–32,
146, 218–26, 228–30, 234–36, 238–
41, 243–52, 267–69, 275
Christian III, king of Denmark, 236
Christoph, Duke of Württemberg, 174,
207, 230, 238, 240–41, 256, 258–59,
265–66
Chrysostom, John, 128
church and state, 141, 162, 182–83, 186–87
church, doctrine of the, 58, 142, 185
Chytraeus, David, 189, 17, 199, 209, 259,
266, 269, 271–73, 277
Clement VII, pope, 91, 95, 110, 120,
143–44, 153
Cochlaeus, Johannes, 109, 119–20, 124, 128
Cölestinus, Johann Friedrich, 244, 262
Cologne, Ecclesiastical Constitution of,
169–70, 232, 235
communicatio idomatum, communication
of attributes, 221, 228–29, 234–36,
238–41, 243–46, 250–52, 268–69,
275, 278, 280
communion in both kinds. See both kinds,
communion in
Concord, Book of, 2, 7–9, 16, 37, 54, 77,
157, 262, 275, 278, 280–82
condemnation of false teaching. See rejection
of false teaching
Confessio Tetrapolitana, 5
confession of the faith, 1–11, 77, 117–18,
183, 185,
confessionalization, 162, 184–85, 284–85n26
Confutation, papal (1530), 118–30,
135–38
Confutation, Weimar Book of, 205,
258–61, 270
Consensus Tigurinus, 232–34, 249